The Barley Hole Chronicles

From Hell to Hamburg
23/47

Harry Leslie Smith

With J.M. Smith

Happy Leslie Smith

The Barley Hole Chronicles: From Hell to Hamburg 23/47

Copyright @ 2011 Harry Leslie Smith

Barley Hole Press
Sydney Street
Belleville, Ontario, Canada
K8P 4Y1
www.1923thebook.ca

ISBN: 978-0-9878425-2-7 (sc)

ISBN: 978-0-9878425-3-4 (e-book)

Printed in the United States of America

Contents

From Hell to Hamburg 23/47

Hamburg 1947:   A Place for the Heart to Kip

Author's Introduction

Gentle Reader:

Barley Hole was for my great grandfather Canaan, the land
of milk and honey. For my father, it was paradise lost and for my
mother, Barley Hole was a curse. It was a place that haunted her
spirit and her soul throughout her life. To me, Barley Hole is a name
forever etched on the map of my family's heart; it is where betrayal
and injustice nearly thrust us into oblivion.

The Barley Hole Chronicles are an odyssey of the human
spirit that stretch across time and geography to incorporate, diverse
personalities, personal hardships, World Wars and the struggle
for peace and love, in a society fallen from grace. The Chronicles
document one Yorkshire family's decent into the wilderness of
poverty and hunger in a forsaken coal pit community. It is a personal
record of one young man's struggle to survive the great depression,
the Second World War and the hazards and wonders of life in post
war Germany. The Barley Hole Chronicles is the summation of my
two memoirs 1923 and *Hamburg 1947*. The Barley Hole Chronicles
are a true account of a time and place when life, full of raw emotion,

was never so real. It is also a social history of the 20th century at its bloodiest and deadliest time.

To you dear reader, I leave this book as a tribute to my tribe because I am the last of my kind and no one else is left alive to tell this tale. I am the first and last son who can recall our passing across this specter, this enchanting world we all leave too soon.

Acknowledgements

This book would not have been possible without my wonderful, kind cousin and friend, Mary Mallison. Her historical work on the Smith/Dean family tree has greatly assisted me in writing this book. 1923 would also have suffered greatly without the historical insights of my dear friend and relation, Gail Woodhead. The wonderful memories from the ever-smiling and thoughtful Pat Sherwood, my cousin, were also of great assistance to me. Lastly, the memories, funny stories, and great love for me by my younger brother, Matt Smith, greatly influenced my writing this book. I would also like to extend my love to my three sons. Their support and love for me throughout the years and during the writing and researching of this book was a blessing. I also owe a great deal of thanks to the 1911 Census. Finally, I owe a debt of gratitude to the Bradford, Barnsley, Wakefield, and Rotherham archivists for your research on my behalf. Everyone always displayed great professionalism and deep humanity concerning my request. They are truly wonderful resources that are a national treasure for Great Britain.

Book One:
1923: A Memoir

"Lies and Testaments"

Harry Leslie Smith

With J.M. Smith

"For My Sister, Mary: Who Held My Hand Through The Storms of Childhood."

Prologue

My sister and I were children of the one true Church, which took its orders from the Vatican. We were commanded by God's Earthly representatives to arise early each Sunday and dress in clean, presentable clothes. On Sundays, Mam stayed in bed late while Dad always escaped our ritual with an early morning walk. After a breakfast of a shared piece of stale toast, my sister would clean my face and hands with an old soapy dishrag. Until the age of six, I had been excluded and shielded from religious penance and paying homage to Jesus, snug in his heaven. So I was mystified and frustrated by this weekly occurrence of stomping across city streets with stores shuttered and bolted. I was envious of our town's well-fed but less-devout brethren, who were still wrapped up warm in their beds, while my sister and I traversed two or three miles to the parish cathedral.

In front of St. Joseph's, we lined up with the other hungry children from our school and from other parochial establishments in the parish. We formed neat lines and rows designated by age and classroom. Nuns from the *Sisters of the Cross and Passion* barked up and down the street like sergeant majors at inspection. They pulled and dragged sleepy-eyed worshippers into their correct drill formation. Nuns in wimples wearing long black gowns, impenetrable to human emotions and suffering, demanded silence from us. Nuns commanded, while pulling ears or twisting arms, that there was to be order and no shuffling of feet. They ordered us to demonstrate reverence for the Holy Father and for the Church. The street was a parade ground of regimented child soldiers for Christ. We were twisted in military boxed squares, divided and codified by our school and by our level of education. All of us waited impatiently to be marched into Sunday Mass and confession. "Father, forgive me, it has been seven days since my last confession and I have had impure thoughts about my pudding for tea." I was seven then when I shivered before the entrance to God's Holy House, in Bradford.

Now I am twenty-two and I am sitting in the back of a truck that is part of a long convoy of vehicles. We are moving like an enormous centipede up a dual carriage way. There are fifteen men in each lorry. Woodbine cigarettes and Capstans dangle from our mouths. The straps to our tin helmets hang loosely around our chins. We are cocksure and unafraid. We are survivors and conquerors pushing our way through Northern Germany. Opposite our convoy, there is an endless procession of refugees. They are pushing their scant possessions in handcarts, or dragging along worn luggage with ropes wrapped around it. The procession contains men and women, the young and the old. Thin, cadaverous horses follow the throng, dragging their hooves in the thin soil beside the road. The jetsam is a mixture of forced labourers, ex-prisoners, ex-concentration camp inmates, and the Diaspora, from Germany's eastern provinces. They are all moving southward, as if believing their homes still existed, or that they still had relatives alive to give them shelter. If the Netherlands and Belgium are any examples to me, there is little left of Europe. What has not been bombed has been looted, and what has not been looted has been burned to the ground.

14

The landscape of Europe's lowlands is pitted and scarred from the movement of giant armies slithering their fat bellies against the land; while their hydra heads tore and destroyed the countryside, the villages, and the cities before them. The nameless throng of people opposite our slow-moving trucks is expressionless; their mien stolen from five years of war and untold privation. Their eyes are cast down at their feet, stamping towards a dirty, dusty unknown road. Do they have any thoughts and emotions left? Or, are they automatons who instinctually force their legs left and right onwards towards their birthplace like diseased salmon spawning against a dammed river?

The air is warm and the smells of fresh earth, petrol, and spring mingle together. A hundred kilometers north, Soviet infantry and stray remnants of Wehrmacht divisions still clash. The Germans, we are told, are fighting in a panicked scramble to come westward rather than face retribution from the Russians. Four days ago, Hitler shot himself in his concrete bunker below the depths of Berlin. Above ground, Red Army forces pitched their flag on the Reichstag and leveled the Prussian city. We have been on the move for almost a full day lumbering up the northern spine of Germany. We do not know what we will encounter. We do not know if there will be resistance, if we will meet an enemy refusing to surrender. At lunch, we lost two men to drowning. Foolishly, they went for a swim in a swollen roadside canal. Their names will be etched up on a monument to the fallen instead of being remembered as mocking chance moments before peace.

Suddenly, on this journey into the enemy's land, our trucks stop. Word has reached us from HQ. Last night at precisely 18.20, Allied Forces accepted the surrender of all German armies, all German military, navy, air, ground, and anything that could, would, or should carry a gun in the northern part of Germany. Field Marshal General Montgomery Heath received the instruments of surrender in a tent at Luneburg from a clean-shaven General Admiral Hans-Georg von Friedeburg. He was the last supreme commander of the Krieg's Marine. The rigid infantry General Hans Kinzel put his hands high, for all German forces in this area. The surrender is for Holland, and northwest Germany, including Denmark. The rest of the Third Reich still resists, even with Berlin and Vienna burning and under Russian control.

In Northern Germany, it is complete and total capitulation. The city we are approaching is open and free of hostilities. The war is on its deathbed. It has only a few days left to maim and kill. But I am safe. The city is open. We are now occupiers and I am alive. We approach Hamburg, a modern-day Carthage, brick dusts billows against our uniforms. The grey faces of the 'master race' scurry around like rodents upon our approach. They are in search of food, missing relatives, safe housing, or happier days. They scatter in confused fear as our truck horn sounds. They shun our looks. Germans' cast their heads down as one of us stands at the edge of the truck to curse them with cat calls and hollers.

Two years previous to my arrival, Hamburg was set ablaze. The metropolis and its citizens burned and baked for three nights. It was 1943 and the war's outcome was still uncertain. It was the time when men in charge of this conflict's direction were resolute; total war was our only passage to victory. Russia, our ally, demanded we do our share of defeating the Nazi war machine. The morale of the enemy must be crushed. So the men in charge of the war asked the men with slide rules and mathematical minds to calculate an exact dropped bomb tonnage to create enormous civilian carnage, panic and chaos in the city. The scientists set to work and after many sleepless nights, they solved the equation of explosive-to-death ratio. Their discovery was handed over to the RAF who used it as if it were an instrument of

God's vengeance upon the wicked and sinful.

On a summer's evening, when the air was humid, languid, and sluggish; on a summer's evening when children were playing in the streets and their mothers were gossiping on their door stoops, Hamburg was set alight. Incendiaries fell from the July night sky above them. Hundreds of Lancaster bombers opened their bellies and spewed out ton after ton of high explosives packed with phosphorous. The sheer tonnage of TNT and humid weather created a firestorm. It reached eight hundred degrees and brought winds that swept across streets and lane ways, alleys, parks, and industrial zones with hurricane force. As the RAF, my RAF, crept eastward bombing the city, 133 miles of street footage was burning. The conflagration reached ten square kilometers and affected 16,000 thousand apartment block buildings. Some said only 15,000 thousand civilians died on that mission. Others said over 50,000 thousand people perished. There were some who did not say a word as they licked their vengeance for London, Coventry, Rotterdam, and Warsaw.

Today, May 4, 1945, the fires in Hamburg have long since been extinguished. Here, the war is finished. Germany is kaput. I feel nothing as from the truck I survey the crumbling brick skeletons and the grey ghosts of buildings. I am alive. I have been through Holland and Belgium and seen Germany's legacy; emaciated children, looted homes. I have seen both national socialist collaborators and German army deserters dangling from trees. I have seen mobs savagely beating women. I have seen women with their heads shaved, tarred and feathered. I have seen justice done in the streets.

I have no feelings, except perhaps relief. I am twenty-two and will now see twenty-three. Perhaps I will get a life; maybe even a different life from the one I had before the war. I am in the back of that truck with my cigarette firmly between my lips, and my stomach is full. I am cook to her elder brothers and younger sisters. It was also ordained that Lillian would be her mother's rock and right hand. It was a role Lillian could not play without complaint. She let it be known to both her father and her mother that she had not been put upon this Earth to be a servant. Nor would she be maids to her brothers and a nanny to her younger sisters.

Much later on, Lillian shared her revulsion about how courtship to my father had led us to starvation's cul-de-sac. When I was a small boy, my mother, drunk on cider, lamented her fate. She moaned and carried on about being chained and married to this lifeless rock, this old load. Lillian riled on about her husband. She ridiculed his family with their pretense of belonging to a much better society than the Deans.

"Serves me right for rubbing a turd and thinking there'd be brass," she said.

During these viperous downpours, Albert would sit on a stool beside our cold fireplace. My dad, with a warm pipe in his mouth, tried to escape from us and his own misplaced guilt. He fixed his gaze onto the living room wall, which had grimy, smoke-stained wallpaper loosely hanging from it. Perhaps he drowned out her tirades with the imaginary sound of his ancient hammering against subterranean cliffs. Perhaps he saw himself young, fit, and free, farming coal out of narrow seams. Perhaps he saw himself when he was younger, and Lillian and he still had illusions to be lost.

Lillian was a beauty in her teens. She had long hazelnut hair and cheeks that were high and rosy. She was a reckless and fearless, Yorkshire lass that tore through suitors like a lioness on an antelope. Most, she alienated because of her sharp tongue and animal intelligence. Her reputation was solidly wanton in the village of Hoyland Common. It stretched beyond the hills and moors to Rotherham, some ten miles southeast. She swore she would follow no man unless it was out of these suffocating hamlets.

How Lillian ended up at my father's pub was a mystery to me.

Rest assured, it was no doubt in pursuit of a suitor, a miner, or a farmhand that brought her into the small, public house by the Barley Hole Pit. The public house over looked a series of workers' cottages, all of which were squat, lightless building with broken slate roofs. The tenements had been used for generations to house underpaid miners in substandard, disease-laden buildings. For the miners and their families; it was a troglodyte existence of easy disease, early death, disfigurement, or illness that led one to the workhouse. Rewards for them were found in heaven, never on this Earth.

The New Inn was laden with tobacco. There was the smell of ale and the musky aroma of working men, unaccustomed to the luxury of a bath. To the side of the pub's entrance was an old upright piano where my father played jaunty songs, made popular by the music halls. The room wore a bodice of dark Victorian paneling. Its wooden floors were warped and creaked with any footstep. The floors, although swept daily were coated in a black sheen. It was coal dust banged off the hobnail boots of the miners as they walked through the front door. There were sturdy chairs made to hold the weight and girth of miners. While upstairs, there were rooms rented to merchants on the way to wool markets or business calls to hock mining machinery. Behind the bar there was a Versailles-like mirror that illuminated the soot-stained men in rough clothing and hard talk. Some played skittles off to the side, others talked to my father, tending bar. It was a simple task as there was only cask ale and cider available as per their two-guinea-a-year publican's license. My father, however, was disdainful of his bartending tasks as he was no drinker, no social gad fly. He preferred his own company rather than a room of boisterous men.

Lillian was a breath of fresh air in the stagnant pub that housed men so old, they remembered the time before steam and their grandfathers recalled the fight against Napoleon. Lillian always arrived at the New Inn in a fresh dress while her uncovered skin smelt of perfumed soap. Her breasts were exposed just enough to make men notice that an alluring youth had crossed their threshold. In 1913, she damned convention by visiting the New Inn and drinking light ale while mixing with men. She pointed her finger at fate and challenged it for good or ill.

When she entered the New Inn, miners lifted up their tired heads from stagnant conversations and pulled their pipes from their mouth, catching the scent of sex, of youth, of wanton rule-breaking. With her easy wit, her adolescence, and sensuality, Lillian aroused a desire in my father, which like the moth's addiction to the flame, he could not resist. At the same time, she was flattered by the attention paid her by an older, muscular and powerful man who had some refinement and some capital. She knew from local gossip about Albert's family and their climb up the slippery, economic ladder to publican. Lillian was aware of the history behind Benjamin Smith's bawdy Beer House he had opened in the 1840s. She knew that Albert's granddad, when alive, counted his profits and kept a club to bash down the more riotous drunks or malcontents who desired political change through unions and socialism.

At least Lillian admitted that cash flattered her vanity and brass could always be used to buy things that fired the furnace of her ego. Albert treated her well with outings to Rotherham and walks around Barnsley. He showered her with reverence and softness, and endless compliments as to her looks and dress. Honestly, Lillian was not accustomed to this manner of courting and she liked its feel. Lillian fell in love with the notion of being loved and cared for. My mother was seduced by the simplest and emptiest of fairy tales: the one that ends happily ever after.

Like a siren, my mother sang in the pub and encouraged my father to accompany her on the piano. Lillian sang the songs of the music halls from Blackpool, the illuminated city filled with chintz, carnival barkers, and organ grinders. She sang with a lusty, throaty voice that made the male patrons grin, while it made Albert's father grow alarmed at her attention to his eldest son and his reciprocal consideration. The housekeeper, Mrs. Mcheter, warned the New Inn's scullery maid to be mindful of Lillian and avoid her company.

In the pub's parlour, Lillian sang a risqué ditty, and when it came time for the chorus, in a loud and jaunty voice she defied all those around her to sing better, to sing with more abandon.

"So why should I drink corfee or tea, when there's plenty of ale for two."

From songs about beer, about times at the seaside, about spring and summer, and all things that had to do with youth and hope; Albert was easily beguiled. It was easy to love life if it were above ground, beyond the coal pits and beyond the flagons of hard ale for thirsty workhorse men. For Lillian, it was easy to feel the craving and hunger of youth that wanted to devour everything in its way, to be free and blissfully happy. It was easy to see how Lillian loved the attention of the miners and the landlord's son. It was easy for her to dream of one day being the chief mistress. Lillian swam in the imaginary praise she would receive as wife to a publican. She could feel the strength of her own money jangling in her purse if she married Albert. Lillian reasoned money could buy her freedom. There was a twenty-six year difference in age between them, but Lillian deduced he was the finest catch for her. At least, he was solicitous to her needs and he was prosperous, with an ever-expanding future.

So one evening, it was natural and effortless for their respective desires to seduce them into each other's arms. After the final beer had been poured, the last notes of the piano had drifted away, and the gaslights along the wall were extinguished, Albert and Lillian went up the back stairs, drunk, to his bedroom, hand-in-hand. They slunk into the room, as they had no wish to wake Albert's brothers or the housekeeper. They were fortunate that Albert's father had gone to call on his married daughter Mabel and was not at home. The room overlooked the low depressing cottages that housed the after-birth of the industrial revolution. From the window, they saw the spires of the colliery, with its giant, two-wheel pulley that hauled coal baskets up from a darkened world below. If they looked beyond the houses and the pit, there were some woods, and beyond the trees were the moors; at least it was something that had not been dug or crushed or dirtied by the pit owners.

Inside the room, there was darkness that was slightly illuminated from the outside night sky, lurking through the window. Albert's long sensitive fingers fumbled while unbuttoning his shirt and pulling off his suspenders and trousers. Nervously, he folded them and placed them on a chair. He cautiously slipped beneath heavy woolen blankets where Lillian expectantly waited. Either by design or lack of birth control, she conceived with a man almost as old as her father, and far clumsier than her other blokes.

It did not take Lillian long to realize she was pregnant. At the time, she was not sure whether it was a misfortune or a blessing, but she would know after informing Albert. Lillian reasoned that since he was her only dance partner; he better sort this out or else the entire village would know that Albert was putting very young girls up the spout.

Albert was warned by his siblings that Lillian was no good, a bad seed, and a bad bet. His brothers were not pleased with this romance and warned him their father would snuff it out, as he did with the coal gaslights every night, with a twist of his hand. Albert ignored their warnings because he believed the future was his to own.

In early summer of 1914, the district was prosperous and beer sales brisk, the world looked optimistic, and the future bright. The mine worked to full capacity and there was plenty of spare cash. Albert was in his forties and his father was still head of the household. Surely he would understand, Albert wished to start a family and continue on the family business and name. Francis Smith, however, was neither young nor optimistic; he was a pragmatist. Francis remembered his father's stories of a life without steam, without gaslight, and men in silk breaches who ruled the known world. He remembered that the walk up the stairs was long, but the tumble down from another man's boot was quick and painful. Life was short but money was long to Francis. One built a history by stacking a penny upon a penny until it was a mountain of money.

Francis Smith had raised nine children into adults, into miners or wives, and he wasn't going to allow his dominion to be attacked or assailed, not by an outsider and especially not his own son. He demanded his daughters marry, as they were a burden on his budget, but he schemed that his sons remained in his house, unmarried. They were used as his iron hand in pub dealings. He told his boys there would be time enough for marriage and money when he was dead in his grave. Since 1885, when Francis' wife died delivering the last child to Francis' dynasty, there was little room in the pub for emotion, compassion, or tenderness.

Francis held his family and his small fortune together with the intensity of a despot. He allowed no truck or trade with gold diggers or interlopers. For his family to survive in the unforgiving environment of pit mines and pubs, iron authority was exercised and used without mercy.

The only son to defy Francis' edict was Hamlet, who suffered from the disability of being named after a Danish prince. It was an odd choice to call one's son, to say the least. It was a strange whimsy, considering Yorkshire had long been cleaved clean of sentimentality. Decades of enslavement from errant aristocrats and the tyranny of the industrial revolution had erased any false notion that right could overcome might. Nevertheless, Hamlet was the one son who struck out on his own and raised a family; he was banished from the family home and like a curse, his name was never mentioned.

My grandfather believed the only child in need of protection was the pub and that his boys must defend the New Inn from all threats, like worker bees in a hive. His other sons, Albert, Benjamin, Edgar, Basil, and Colin, all took their instructions from their father. Any regret they may have had for not marrying was allayed by the feelings of duty and responsibility to their father and their small legacy, the New Inn.

Indeed, Francis would have sent Lillian packing with her story about a child out of wedlock, his son's responsibility, and the supposed ill-repute that this would bring on his family, his name, and his family's pub. After all, this was Yorkshire, England's north, where bastards were as common as sheep. It was a region where unwed women noted down in the church registry, "It was the woodman that made the baby with me." Yorkshire was England's bastard child, right down to the last person. It was expected that Yorkshire worked like bastards, unrecognized and without recompense. Yorkshire, from its stomach that created coal, to its muscles that weaved the country's wool was chattel for the moneyed men in the south and the landed aristocracy.

After toiling and plotting for seventy-two years, Francis took to his bed in early April complaining of fever and chills. My grandfather, after making deals with the pit owners to shop out unruly or revolutionary miners for decades, was now weak and sick. During his illness, he requested that his brother, Larratt, and his wife, Laura, come to tend to the pub. As the days progressed, Francis was more febrile, confused, and delirious. My grandfather refused either medicine or a doctor. The infection in his body spread to his lungs and developed into pneumonia. His body burned and Francis dreamed he was back in the pits, underneath tons of smoldering coal. A doctor was summoned, who after listening to his chest, knew Francis' chances for survival were slim. It was best that Francis make amends with his god. It would be wise, the doctor surmised, for the patriarch to say farewell to his family. Francis, who was seemingly indestructible, called for his brother, Larratt. In delusion and in the madness of fever, Francis begged his brother to look after his sons and the pub.

"There is no will," Francis told him, his eyes bright with fever. "I wrote no will. I did not do," he whispered, "what Father did for us; put on parchment what is for thee and what is for thou."

Terrified, my grandfather cried out; he had misgivings and forebodings that without his brother's assistance, doom would befall his sons and daughters.

"Take hold off the pub," he begged Larratt.

Francis repeated the ordination in front of all his children, the housekeeper, and the doctor. Francis, delirious from the illness, implored Larratt,

"Protect them, until they are ready."

"Ready for what," Albert asked, puzzled.

"Lad, the business needs a steady hand," Francis responded, his eyes, unfocused and hazy, looking for death. "You need the guidance of your loving uncle to preserve the pub."

The daughters wept as Francis' fever and cough grew worse. Francis' sons clasped each other's hands stoically and wondered about his strange pronouncement.

Finally, on the eighteenth day, Francis began to hoarsely suck his last breathe into his rotten and fetid lungs, his last scrap of air, while Albert and Larratt stood by his bedside. Late in the afternoon, while tea was being prepared, Francis turned his back on the living. My grandfather choked to death on his own bodily fluids. Mrs. Mcheter, the housekeeper cleaned and dressed his body. His sons lifted Francis' corpse and placed him in a solid pine coffin. They carried him downstairs to the pub where they propped his coffin up along the wall beside the piano. He had one final day, in Earth's sunlight. For one last time, my grandfather oversaw the day's taking. Miners arrived after their shift for a memorial drink; they removed their caps and bowler hats and raised their glasses of ale to the passing of a publican.

Together, Larratt and Albert stood off to the side, greeting the miners and pit bosses, accepting the silent sympathies for their brother and father's time on Earth. Larratt told his nephew not to be dismayed by the strange last pronouncements of Francis.

"His commands must be embraced," Larratt told him. "It was an ultimate directive and who are we to judge a man's final wishes?"

Albert's uncle pledged that anything not his by law and deed would be relinquished in good time. The uncle argued that although Francis' reasons might be undecipherable to them, the decree should be honoured and the publican's license temporarily transferred to him. Albert struggled with a conflicting sense of betrayal and trust for his father and his uncle. After all, he was the rightful successor to the pub. Should he blindly and obediently accept Francis' desires? But there had been many witnesses to his father's decree and perhaps he was over-reacting. Silently, Albert relented; he was a dutiful and loving son. If it was only temporary, so be it, Albert concluded. He had lived many decades waiting for his turn to take his father's place in the world. A month or half a year was a blink of an eye to wait for his legacy. Eventually, Albert reasoned, he was going to be the publican.

All of Francis' daughters and sons came to his funeral, including Hamlet. The whole village attended his interment whether they despised him for his thrift or for his close relations with the pit bosses; all the villagers came out and bowed their heads in respect, for his sheer force of will to keep the pub and his boys successful and prosperous, both beneath ground and on top. Only one person was asked to not attend and that was Lillian. Larratt and the rest of the family considered her an opportunist. Albert reluctantly accepted the prohibition to keep family peace. However, Lillian never forgave him for his misguided loyalty to a family who was soon to betray him.

Albert and Larratt led the funeral procession. Francis was laid to rest beside his wife and near his father, Benjamin, at the Holy Trinity graveyard, in Wentworth. Albert truly grieved his father's passing and followed the proscribed duties as first son. He told his brothers there was no need to be alarmed that their father had not left a will. They were protected. Their claims were assured because Albert and their uncle would shortly attend the probate court in Wakefield. For the time being, Larratt was innkeeper. It was only temporary, a month or two at most before Albert and his brothers and sisters would be rightful titleholders to the New Inn.

For several weeks, Albert felt as free as King Edward upon the death of Victoria. May came and spring returned to the moors. The air seemed cleaner around the mines as the rains cleansed the soot and dirt that erupted out of the collieries. On the 26th of May, loving brother, devoted first son, and an auctioneer named Job presented themselves to the probate court. They assured the representative of His Majesty's Government that Francis died without a will. The men swore that Francis' estate comprised no more than £219 and 19 shillings. It was a modest but tidy amount. The testimony of Larratt, Albert, and the auctioneer satisfied the court, who released Francis' estate to the rightful and natural heir, Albert.

The license for the New Inn was not considered part of the estate as Francis had transferred his rights to his brother in his last moments on Earth. The Brewery that controlled the pub also had no care if the license went from father to son or brother to brother, as long as there was continuity and the taps kept flowing, drowning the thirst of paying customers. Furthermore, the local municipal council, during their quarterly hearings, had accepted the change in license holder and duly noted it in their registers.

Albert returned home to inform his siblings that in due time, Larratt would transfer their legacy back to them. For now, their uncle would remain innkeeper. Albert explained to his brothers that no harm would come to them. They were all guaranteed what was rightfully theirs. The brothers were also informed that Larratt, his wife, and two children were now permanent residents at the New Inn. It was compensation for their assistance to Francis. Everyone just had to make room. Unfortunately, the scullery girl and Mrs. Mcheter had to go; there was no money to pay for their further services.

This was certainly far from a perfect solution that Francis had devised before his death, but it seemed to Albert to be an acceptable temporary resolution. *Eventually,* he thought, *full and rightful ownership of the public house will come to me.* Albert did not see that Francis' death was not liberation for him and his family; it was a talisman marking the end of time. It was the passing of old England and the beginning of a fearful, new world whose grammar and structure was alien to the past.

A little while after the probate hearing, Lillian told Albert she was carrying his child and that her life would be ruined if they did not marry. Albert never paused or blinked to this announcement; he understood it was a moral imperative and an act of love towards Lillian to accept her and the unborn child. Immediately, he proposed marriage. It was an inevitable conclusion to the dilemma in a time without proper birth control. My parents' sexual encounter initiated events that would ruin both of their lives.

Albert believed his upcoming marriage was an improvement to his old bachelor life. My father thought he was his now own man, charting his own course. He reasoned his family's past diligence would keep his financial sails billowing and travelling towards new and greater prosperity. My father believed his life was set like his watch, and it would keep ticking as before with his brothers, with the inn, and the Barley Hole coal pit. Every day, except Sundays, they went down the pit and broke coal for the nation. Every afternoon, they ascended towards daylight and poured beer to their brethren. Albert was just adding to his future by including a new wife and a new child to the pub in Barley Hole. Albert thought that finally after two generations of grim dark work and struggle; his family had prospered enough to soon be above ground, where they could dispense with the drudgery of mining.

Lillian developed an increasing affection for the growing creature within her. It was more than just a stepping-stone from her parents' crowded home on Beaumont Street. It was her baby to nurture and mold into a beautiful child. Lillian only dreaded that the child inside her, made her belly swell, making her look unattractive and old. But she knew it was better to suffer the bastard inside her; as it was the down payment, so to speak, for a new house away from her parents and her siblings. At the New Inn, she was going to live by her rules and her rules alone. Lillian had already planned that Albert would buy her posh furniture, posh clothes, and in summer, they were going to the seaside on holidays. When she was married, Lillian thought she was going to be far out of the reach of her father, who was ever ready with a fist to beat down anyone who dared to defy him. With marriage, Lillian was going to be far away from her mother's sermons on Jezebels, Salome, and the Queen of Sheba. My mother desperately wanted to finally show her mother, father, and siblings that she had risen above their station and she was a woman to be respected.

What Lillian did not understand was that the money, the so-called wealth of the Smiths, was slight and tied to the pub. Moreover, Larratt was now the legal licensee of the New Inn. The money from the pub was supposed to keep all of Francis' progeny in pocket. It was to hold them all in good stead and in good respect with the people of Thorpe Hesley. Lillian saw Albert's inheritance as an enormous spoil, a treasure won through the war of sex and conquest. My father, Albert, was a boastful and prideful man and he liked the comforts and affection provided to him by a younger woman. Albert liked the superficial admiration he received from the pubs customers for having such a young woman at his side. So Albert obscured the limits of his wealth to Lillian and himself. He ignored the obligations he owed his brothers and sisters. Foolishly, he dismissed the influence his uncle had on the New Inn and on its residents.

In May of 1914, the New Inn was pumping ale to a steady crew of thirsty miners; beer was cheap from the brewery. There were no hour restrictions on the pub and miners found more cash in their pay packet, which they spent on the entertainment of drink. Barley Hole, the mine and the pub prospered as the nation grew fat and rich in peace. Whether they had any forewarning of the impending disaster to their lives and fortunes was anyone's guess. Did anyone in early

June 1914 hear the distant peel of thunder, signaling the approaching storm?

Lillian told her parents, Walter and Mary Ellen, that she was betrothed to Albert Smith and they wished to marry straight away. Lillian did not tell her parents she was pregnant. Walter forbade the marriage; he knew his family was not the proper sort to be mixing with the Smiths. It was well known that the Deans were several steps below the Smiths in economic security and status. In fact, Walter had to join the army when he was eighteen because there was neither work nor enough food for him at home.

In the army, he was assigned to an artillery regiment that had sent him to India as a private. With neither war nor uprisings in the Far East, he bathed in colonial splendor and comfort for six years. He indulged his passions in garrison towns across the sub-continent and at night, he lurked in the wild streets of Calcutta. It was there in some back ally that he dropped some coins into a prostitute's hand, dropped his pants, and caught the clap. While Walter Dean was in India doing his part for imperialism, his wife, Mary Ellen, my grandmother, was having an affair with a butcher's boy. Mary Ellen's time in the haystacks produced a son, Albert Edmond. Even though Walter forgave his wife her transgression while he was in foreign parts serving the Crown; Mary Ellen never forgave herself. She took to regularly attending the local Anglican Church to help clean away her sense of guilt. Pregnant with remorse and a feeling of criminality, Mary Ellen hid her shame by pointing out the moral turpitude of her daughter Lillian at any opportunity. And so Walter knew that any relationship between his daughter and Albert was an invitation to destruction.

"He be too old fer ya, lass. Why, I ave only seven years on im. Look at uz. Ready for the bone yard, I am and Albert can't be far behind. "Lil, it's not proper. Francis asn't even warmed the dirt in his grave."

Even more aghast at this proposed union was Albert's Uncle Larratt who asked, "How are we supposed to all fit under, one roof?"

Albert's siblings never grasped or fathomed why their brother, the son of Francis, the grandson of Benjamin Smith, cast his lot against his kin. Was it the furtive pleasures of the flesh that drove their brother away from them? Why would Albert take up with this crass woman; who could not conceal her selfishness, her lack of breeding, and her ambition? No one outside of Albert and Lillian deduced that they were just simply and stupidly in love with each other.

My uncles might have tolerated my mother joining the family, and they might even have held their noses at her becoming head of the household. Perhaps they would not have lived happily ever after; but there would have been peace because the pub dripped a small pool of wealth to them like a leaky faucet. However, it was Larratt and his wife who spread discord and rumor about my parents. Larratt told Albert's siblings that this proposed marriage was irresponsible. The marriage would defy Francis, as he never thought highly of Lillian or her family. Larratt continued that Francis was wise to have left him in charge of the pub. It was fortuitous that this occurrence had been designed by god. Who could tell what Albert would do to the pub and their fortunes while in this childish state of infatuation?

In early summer 1914, at the Barnsley Registry office, Lillian and Albert were joined together in matrimony. As my father and mother both courted a lie in their wooing, why not continue it into their marriage. My father subtracted seven years from his actual age, on the marriage certificate and wrote down that he was forty. My mother added seven years and wrote her age as twenty-six. Perhaps by one subtracting seven years and the other one adding seven years, they were both trying to cancel out their mutual deception. They wanted to obscure from the curious and the meddling that one was too young and the other too old for this marriage bed. The formulization of Albert and Lillian's marriage was a brief perfunctory affair. No family members or friends attended their marriage ceremony. It lasted only slightly longer than the sex that had led them to the marriage altar.

Outside the registrar's office on June 29th, my parents walked out onto wet cobblestone streets, as Mr. and Mrs. Albert Smith. There was no wedding feast, no wedding toast, and probably no wedding bed for my parents.

It was a Monday and the day before, in a sleepy Serbian town of Sarajevo, the Archduke of Austria and his wife were assassinated by an unemployed Slav nationalist. On the day of their wedding, the news was printed on the front page of every major European newspaper. But who on the day of their marriage paused to buy a newspaper? My parents walked past the cries of newspaper headline as millions of others did that day, consumed by their own mundane activities, unaware that a murdered royal had any significance to their lives. For most, dead princes and princesses in faraway countries was just a foreign fairy tale for night-time story telling.

It rained long into their honeymoon, and in July, armies across Europe mobilized their troops and set off to war in August. Britain promised the boys would be home from the fields of France for Christmas. They were not. And as the first British troops were ushered off to France, my mother miscarried. It was the first of many omens signaling their life together was cursed.

In Rotherham, my father saw droves of army recruiters seduce fit and hungry miners to join the local regiments. Fat, balding men sold tales of adventure in foreign climes. Army recruiters were no better than carnival barkers, regaling the callow youth about the rewards awaiting a man who picked up a rifle for the King. Men far beyond the age of enlistment admonished the young not to miss a chance in the dust up. It would be a shame, they said, to lose out on the fun and adventure. Battle would ennoble the spirit. Pit owners financed their own regiments. They encouraged their employees to take the pledge and be purified in this just war. My father saw beer sales plummet as more miners made their way to France. *No matter,* Albert thought, *the war will be short and everyone must roll up their sleeves.*

"We all have our part do in this war. Larratt should soon relinquish the pub and its license to me."

My mother and father handed out free drinks and offered glad tidings to the departing boys of Barley Hole, Thorpe, and Rotherham; brothers in the pit, soldiers in arms. In 1915, my mother became pregnant again. This time, Lillian felt the birth of a child would assure her claim to be mistress of the house.

In 1915, while my mother grew excited over her pregnancy, her brother, Thomas Arthur Dean, downed his miner's pick and donned a soldier's uniform. He was determined to be part of this big show and he wanted to do his part for King and Country. He enlisted at the local regimental barracks, where a medical examination discovered his lungs were like burnt and hollowed out villages, left by retreating soldiers. He was discharged as unfit for service. My uncle's lungs resembled a victim of a mustard gas attack, except he had seen no combat. The mines did that to his lungs. He had to sit out the war, for a while longer. Tom would have to wait until the bleeding of men and resources became so great that he was called upon again for King and Country.

The war, the Great War was measured in feet and yards. It lasted longer than anyone had dreamed. It drained Europe of its youth. It swept away old deceits of empire of duty, of patriotism to one's motherland. At the Somme in 1916, 58,000 British soldiers fixed bayonets while their officers blew whistles marshalling them over the top of mile upon mile of trenches. When nightfall approached, some twenty thousand men had died of their wounds. No objective was reached, except the dispatch of telegrams back home to loved ones, announcing the loss of another and another and another in this great and noble cause.

In 1916, Thomas Arthur Dean was again called to enlist; men were growing scarce for the killing fields. Again, the military found his lungs too feeble to be gassed. He was discharged back to the mines, where he coughed and spluttered, breathing in foul coal dust. Finally in 1917, he was deemed fit for the Veterinary corp. The army allowed him to tend and groom horses. Yet for Thomas, even the simplest of tasks of brushing the mane of a horse was too great. After only five weeks in the army, he was asked to report to the infirmary where a medical officer listened to his lungs, which sounded like a dry, brittle, paper bag. The doctor was compelled to discharge him from active service because his lungs were afflicted by chronic, debilitating bronchitis. He was immediately transferred to a Sanatorium in Collingham. Thomas Arthur Dean, on June 11, 1918 succumbed to his wounds and suffocated to death at the Tubercular Hospital, in Collingham. He was twenty-seven. His mother, Mary Ellen washed and cleaned his dead body to prepare it for burial. Thomas left a young wife and two daughters, who were banished forever from Mary Ellen's mind. She gave to God her second son to punish her for her first son; the bastard Ted. Thomas was honored by the military as a fallen soldier. It could be said that his war was waged underneath the crags of Yorkshire, hauling black silicate to the surface, scarring his lungs beyond redemption.

During the war, Maggie Spooner Dean lived in Thorpe Hesley with her husband, Herbert, a miner. She was my mother's cousin. They had two small children. Maggie was susceptible to the government's anti-Kaiser propaganda. She was immersed in stories about Germans bayoneting children, ravaging Belgian farm girls, gas attacks, and merciless zeppelin raids. She grew fearful for the safety of her children. Maggie became obsessed with the notion Germany would invade Britain. She was terrified that German soldiers in spiked helmets would march on Thorpe Hesley. Eventually, it drove her mad. She began to see apparitions and hear their voices coming from her back room. She could hear Germans whispering under her bed. Her delusions overwhelmed her.

On a July day, in the late afternoon in this small village, Maggie Dean heard someone knocking on her front door. Terror and fear struck Maggie because she believed that banging on her door was coming from an advance guard of invading Germans intent on raping her and murdering her children. In her delusion, Maggie was relieved that at least her husband and eldest son were out taking a stroll and safe from the imaginary Germans. However, her youngest not yet a year old lay resting in his bassinet, near the coal fire. Delicately, she bundled her young son into her arms and rushed into the scullery with him. She laid him on a butcher's block and found a hatchet used for chopping wood for the fire. As if she were Abraham commanded by God, Maggie shadowed above her young son and brought the hatchet down across the boy's head. When the police arrested Maggie outside of her home; she was calm, almost peaceful. Neighbours circled her in shock as they looked at her smock covered in the blood of her son.

"Is it dead?" she asked.

A gawker told her, "I think so."

"Good," she responded. "If it had lived, it would have been an imbecile."

Unfortunately, the infant was not dead and suffered a painful night in a hospital ward before succumbing to his wounds. Maggie Dean was charged with infanticide but during her trial she was found innocent by reasons of insanity and committed, for life, to lunatic asylum at Broadmoor prison.

As the war dragged on, The New Inn and my parents' marriage began to suffer. The war was eating up more and more raw materials, including barley and hops, used for beer. Lloyd George's government imposed beer rationing. It was introduced to stem drunkenness, which was hampering munitions production. The government drastically reduced the hours a pub could operate and therefore how much a pub could make. With fewer miners, fewer hours, and less beer, the Inn was slowly growing broke. Albert's dreams of building from the strong foundation of his ancestors was being shaken and torn apart from shells falling hundreds of miles away from them in France and Belgium.

Larratt and Albert had increasing disagreements and arguments. Primarily, they were about when Albert would take control of his inheritance: the New Inn. Larratt dismissed these entreaties as thankless. The uncle retorted that every day, he was investing in a losing pub. He would not hand over the pub until he could be properly compensated. His loyalty to his older brother Francis and his acumen at steering the pub through the troubled times of war were worth more than Albert could ever afford to repay.

Albert was lost in the unfathomable world of modern warfare, economic stagnation, pit slowdowns, and family betrayal. He hid behind his miner's pick and shovel .He hid behind the miner's tradition of stoicism. Daily, his kind stood in the face of cold rock, sudden death, and poor wages. Theirs was a life of endless stone-breaking and coal-hauling. Talk and complaints were for the weak. But the day-by-day toil of diving beneath the earth and farming coal could not erase the ledger in his head when he compared his present situation to the past. He was now a lodger in the house and Inn his father had built. He was now a tenant to his uncle, only seven years his senior. He was under the authority of an uncle who showed no inclination to surrender the pub to its rightful heirs. For Albert, the summation of these calculations was horrifying. He had relinquished his birthright; he had betrayed Francis' ultimate wish that he would continue to make the family prosper. Albert had trusted too much. He had felt too much. My father had given up too much because of misplaced family loyalty and his good nature.

Larratt's wife, Laura, and my mother clashed at the slightest opportunity. From the moment she took up residence at the New Inn, Laura assumed the role of mistress. Either by omission or failure of memory, she forgot the pub belonged to Albert and his brothers. When downstairs in the bar, Laura referred to the New Inn as "our pub, our home." She ingratiated herself with the miners with free pints of beer. Laura looked for any reason and issues to disagree with or disavow

Lillian. She spread word around the village and pub that Albert's wife was not to be trusted. After all, Lillian was cousin to that, "Beastly child-killer Maggie Dean."

"These Deans," she gossiped, "are nothing but bad blood. It's in their blood to be wicked mams. They're rotten to the core and mad to boot. "Can any of these Deans be any good if they allow murderers, baby-bashers into their family?" Laura intensified her campaign against Lillian. She questioned the validity of the marriage to her nephew.

"She's a gold digger. She got with child to steal from our ouse. Laura made jokes to the other village wives. "She be his bairn, naught his wife."

For Laura and Larratt, Lillian was a country girl with bad manners. The pair invoked Francis' name. They uttered that the former innkeeper would not have approved of this match.

Indelicately, Larratt inquired, "Albert, how are we going to live under one roof with this new baby? There is just no room," Larratt reasoned to Laura and Albert.

My father demanded to know when he would receive his legacy. It was now September 1915 and his wife was seven months pregnant. Albert had no time to waste if he was to properly provide for his new child. The uncle waved away Albert's pleas. Larratt declared vehemently that the pub would never be returned to him.

"Never in this day, nor in the days hereafter will thee Albert have t'pub. Lad, you chose wrong, you picked a filly over a mare. Thy father, Francis, would be ashamed of thee. A steady hand as mine is needed to take your dad's work, my work to greater riches. It's just not in ya, lad. Best you and thy woman be gone from here. Naught but trouble."

In the end, Larratt convinced himself that his brother, Francis, had bequeathed the publican's license to him. It was his legacy being the last surviving son of Benjamin Smith, the first publican in the family. Larratt declared to my father, "You received all your father's worldly assets but the pub. What you were given at the probate court was a tidy sum. You have done with it as you wished, to set you and your brothers and sisters right."

Albert threatened to take his uncle to court. No court in the land, Larratt rejoined, would accept Albert's title to the pub, as there were witnesses to the death-bed bequest. He added with smug satisfaction that even the town council had tabled and accepted the motion to change the license to him eighteen months before.

My father knew then that the seam of his argument for restitution, for return of his suspended bequest, The New Inn, was lost. Albert had no allies and no witnesses. His brothers and sisters, although sympathetic to Albert, had no interest in the battle between uncle and nephew over a title they could never garner. They took the proceeds of Francis' lifelong efforts and they had spent it for good or ill on themselves and their own families. Albert, they all agreed, should move on and accept his uncle had the right to the pub.

My father quit his job at the mine where he had toiled for over twenty years, and with my mother, seven months pregnant, fled Barley Hole. They left the village on a cart drawn by an old dray horse which carried there scant possessions along with the painting of Albert's father. My parents held hands and looked away from each other, terrified of what might await them in exile. They went as far away as he could from Thorpe Hesley and the memories of his former life. They found a one-bedroom cottage in Brampton Bierlow called Fernlea. It was here that they hid and tried to raise a new-born.

The winter of 1915 was one of the coldest in Yorkshire's history. Rivers and canals froze over while farmers' fields were tightly wrapped in a burial shroud of snow. At Fernlea Cottage, the atmosphere was resentful as my parents adjusted to the new order of life as exiles from Barley Hole. My father placed Francis' portrait on a wall in their small sitting room. The painting looked scornfully down on its new surrounding and the past generations of workers, who had lived and died in that threadbare shack.

On November 29th, my mother, with the help of an old village woman, gave birth to my older sister, Marian. Her birth dampened my parents' gloom. They saw her arrival as the turning of the page from the old world they once inhabited to the new world they were compelled to live in. If a baby could be born healthy and Albert could work at the new mine, their life could continue with quiet, but proud determination.

It was only that the never-abating war was starting to reach into their lives. Daily published casualty lists reminded them that death was all around them. They scanned the broad sheet and recognized endless names of the dead and wounded from their old community. It was said the best of England was lost in the First World War. The statement usually referred to the upper classes; the rich and privileged. But the brawn and guile was also lost in the mud of Flanders, Ypres, and **Passchendaele**. The uneducated, the mill workers, the factory workers, and the farm workers all were sent to their slaughter. The children of the industrial revolution, who had given their strength and their youth to build Britain into a mighty economic engine, were now sacrificed for the benefits of the rich and over-fed privileged classes.

Four years of war passed. The younger men that Albert had toiled with in the mines died in their multitudes in the trenches. When the war ended in 1918, Albert and Lillian felt their passion for each other diminish. Their love for each other was now static. Without knowing it, hard circumstances had declared an armistice on their desires for one and other. Now, my parents' simply coexisted.

The New Inn had suffered during the Great War. The conflict had strangled the business with tariffs, shortages, fewer miners, less work hours. The pub, although wounded, would be able to gather strength and prosper again in peace. The miners returned to the pit at Barley Hole. When the war ended, Albert understood that the pub was forever lost to him. My father was forever lost and abandoned from Barley Hole and its environs. From now on, he would have no allies, no friends, and no family in Thorpe Hesley. In either war or peace, Larratt poured bitter and lager. He washed away any trace of his brother's family from the house and pub, standing like a sentinel before the entrance of the pit.

The fireworks celebrating peace soon dimmed. The soldiers began to return home to England and to Yorkshire. My sister Marian was diagnosed with spinal tuberculosis. It was a relentless disease that humped her back and crushed her spine as if she were being subjected to extreme pressurization from beneath the ocean. My sister's illness required that my parents move to Barnsley to allow Marian treatment for her tuberculosis at the local hospital. While Marian languished with TB, my sister Alberta was born in 1920.

2

Birth and Death

As I have written, I came with no fanfare, no glad-handing in February 1923. I was born in Headling Prospect, a not so well-to-do neighbourhood. My parents moved there with the slim proceeds my father had saved from mining. The remainder came from the money left to my father from Francis, nine years previous.

I think my older sister, Alberta, was the only one enthused by my arrival. She could now have a companion, a partner in this lonely world of distant and imperious parents. Lillian and Albert were now too consumed with my elder sister Marian's painful and long death. Money was an ever-present problem for them. Coal prices were collapsing. Miner's jobs were not secure. Pit owners believed they could turn the clocks back to the days before the war and reap giant profits. We lived as close to hand-to-mouth as possible. As a family, both economically and emotionally, we were only slightly above the water line. My parents had little time to tend to the emotional needs of healthy toddlers.

In May, 1926, the first of several General Strikes were called. It was to protest the brutal practices of mill and mine owners against their employees. England saw two weeks of pitched battles that almost dissolved the country into civil anarchy. The British Army was called out to quell the uprising. There was an overall gloom in the clubs of London, a fear that revolutionaries could take the country. For the workers, there was dread that that their demands for fair wages and better working conditions would be denied them. Winston Churchill railed at the worker class as if it were scum and rabble. The bright young people of Soho, Kent, and Sussex danced until dawn and drank champagne. They cynically joked about the workers and the new war to come against them. Did they know how their wealth was created? Did they know or care to see row-house poverty?

When the strikes were quelled, it caused more strife for the miners and millworkers than when they had put down their tools and taken up their pickets. The workers lost more rights when they returned to work than when they had taken strike action. Their pay was cut almost in half and their hours of work increased to Victorian times. The General Strike showed to many that England had won the Great War, but sacrificed its young to fulfill the greed of a few mighty families.

Until the General Strike, my father worked as a hewer and spent his weekdays in Elsecar. He returned home on the weekends, scrubbed clean of coal. I never saw him come back home from the pit, pitch-black. I did not see him scrub off the grime with carbolic soap while sitting in a tin bath heated with warm water from a kettle. Instead, our house was clean of a coal miner's sweat. It was filled with the warm smells of my mother baking currant cakes and loaves of bread. However, by the time labourers strife became an all-out battle, my father, because of age and perhaps unionist sympathies, was reduced to surface labourer. It paid far less than for those who worked beneath the black coal ocean. My parents lived off his wages and the ever-dwindling hopes that his uncle might see his error and return the inn to them.

At that time, I was almost four but I can recall a feeling of unease in our household as my parents slipped further into poverty and my eldest sister grew more infirm. She was treated like a delicate porcelain doll because her bones were brittle and easily fractured. Marian was so weak she spent her days marooned on a basket-woven bed which was on wheels to allow my mum to take her outdoors. When the bed was pushed outside, the thin rubber tires squeaked mournfully but Marian remained silent and still as she took in the fresh air.

I could never see Marian whilst imprisoned in her invalid's landau, unless lifted up by an adult or by my other sister, Alberta. It was Alberta who lifted me up to say good-bye to Marian when she became too ill to be cared for at home. Since my parents were near destitute, Marian was taken to the work house for medical attention. The infirmary easily admitted Marian as we had barely enough money for rent or food. When Marian departed our house for the last time, she was like a wordless crippled angle sheathed in a blanket and imprisoned in a caged chaise lounge.

My sister was transported to the poor house on Gawber Street in a horse-drawn ambulance, which was also used as a hearse. The work house was erected in the 1850s. It possessed a grim façade created by Victorian rectitude and moral certitude. Its outward appearance declaimed that abject poverty was a sin. Its thick, impenetrable black doors said: want and need must be kept barricaded and hidden behind ominous and threatening walls. The three-story prison for the poor also acted as an infirmary for those that had no other means to find medical assistance.

At the poor house, Marian was attended to by the resident surgeon, Edward Bernard Collingham. He was not only an excellent physician, but also a man well regarded in the community. Over a decade previous, he risked his life and jumped into the Barnsley Canal to rescue a mother and son who had fallen into its frigid December waters.

At the poor house my mother watched over her Marian for weeks. Lillian acted as both nurse and mother to her daughter by changing and cleaning her bedclothes soiled in her bodily waste. My mother held

Marian tightly in her arms when she moaned in pain and could find no other comfort than her mother's love which was incapable of stopping her decent towards death. My father, still dirty and dusty, came to visit Marian after his shifts at the mine were over. He would touch her forehead. He ran his hands through her long chestnut hair. He sang to her. No matter how jolly his tune; her tuberculosis trundled on, paralyzing her limbs and speech. Near the end of Marian's life, Alberta and I were looked after by our grandmother. Although no one told us our sister was dying, we knew from the clamouring sadness enveloping our house that a transformative event was occurring.

My mother kept vigil for three weeks. Lillian knew that her first child, born in a dank cottage on the fringes of Elsecar Road, was dying. With leaden silence, my father kept his own watchfulness. Albert was overwhelmed with regret for what he had already lost and what he was about to lose. On the morning of October thirtieth, Marian left this world at the age of ten after being physically tormented and tortured by TB for most of her life. For her brief interlude, her short journey on this Earth, Lillian and Albert had attempted to communicate to her that she was loved and wanted. Desolate as my parents were, Marian's body was committed to a common, mass grave. Parental love alone would never pay the church warden's bills.

The day before Marian's death, the General Strike was broken. All workers were ordered back to their jobs with reduced wages. The day after Marian died; EI Milne's Winnie Pooh was published. Marian's demise was wedged neatly between the ruin of the working class and an idealistic wood called "Pooh Corner." It was an optimistic place, a bed-time story for middle-class children to keep their imaginations warm and comfortable. Happy, well-fed children were allowed to dream; while children in Wiggin, Glasgow, Barnsley, and other far-afield places craved breakfast in the morning and a thick blanket at night.

With Marian dead; it was left to Alberta and me to struggle on and suffer the loneliness of hunger. It was a cruel name to christen a girl born in 1920. My father, perhaps fearful he would have no son, bequeathed his name to her. She was cursed by errant school boys and bullies chanting and mocking her down the narrow Yorkshire streets straddled with row houses. They chased Alberta while coming home from school and they cried out, ".Bertie, Bertie," as if calling after a fat, middle-aged man. After Marian's death, Alberta told me, "From now on, Harry, my name is Mary."

By the time Marian quietly died from TB, my father had run out of his capital both in strength and finances. Just after my sister's death, I became very ill with whooping cough. It left my tiny frame grasping for air and hurling out the familiar sad sound of a crane. My father, already having lost one child to Tuberculosis, used whatever energy he had to make sure I would survive. He cradled me in his arms. Biceps and forearms that had once been like steel and smashed solid rock gently brought me downstairs to my mother. Lillian prepared a steaming bowl of menthol and water. She placed my head underneath a towel to soak in the vapors to ease my lungs and push air back into them.

On Christmas day in 1926, my parents put on a brave show for my sister and me. I suppose they wanted us to believe that even though our sister had just died and money was running out that we were safe and loved. In the parlour, my father played carols on the piano while my sister and I sang the well-worn festive jingles with abandon. On that holiday, my mother cooked an enormous goose and we gorged ourselves as if knowing this day would never come again for us. After the meal, I lay on a warm throw rug on the parlour floor. I was lost in preoccupation with my gift, a small miniature railway set made in Japan. Beside me Mary played with a new doll: her gift from Father Christmas. My father and mother were allowed a respite from grief for a few brief hours that afternoon in 1926; peace would not come to any of us after that for decades.

Soon after the holidays, my parents started to loathe each other as our economic situation worsened. As the coins ran out, love exhausted itself into contempt from my mother and guilt from my father. Both my parents were shell-shocked from the horrendous reality that Albert was an old man of sixty. He had no savings, no property, and no real potential to continue earning money. My mother must have been startled to realize she was a young woman in her early thirties with two small children. Albert was a rapidly aging husband, who no longer resembled the strong, strapping, confident miner she had loved before the world went to war. At sixty, my father was working at the local mine, too old and weak for the work beneath the ground, he slaked out a living on top as an odd-job man. What shame, what sadness this wrought upon my father, I do not know. It must have been a humiliation and a sad recognition to him that he had been reduced to an old work-horse. Albert must have known he would be used until he was maimed or killed in a mining accident. He had become the very penurious, enslaved creature of pity his family had fought to escape for over two generations. There was little silver in his weekly pay packet and we often did not have enough coal for the fireplace.

As there was no money for coal, Lillian engaged her children to scrounge for fuel. Mary and I were enlisted by my mother to steal coal. Carrying a small bucket, my sister would drag me along to a nearby mine. Outside the colliery, mountains of slag were heaped high and heavy. It was thick granules of coal dust thrust together. It formed shifting coal dunes. Afternoons far from school, Mary and I scratched through the dust like ancient birds foraging for seed. We sifted and crawled and dug like child-miners. We looked for the stray bits of coal that had become lost in the black, gritty dust. Day in, day out, we filled our bucket with broken coal. In the evening, we sat beside a low warm fire, before cold parents dimming the heat in their loveless and loud resentment. My father must have been cruelly ashamed to see his two children no more than seven and ten, scraping coal from a slag heap.

By the late 1920s, my father was sixty-one and prematurely aged.

The strain of using a shovel or a hammer to put food on the table was grinding him down. At the mine, there was no time for pity. Either a worker was up to his job or he was not. If he was not up to his task, there were others that would quickly take his place. To preserve his employment, my father took every menial order with patience and silence. He accepted every demeaning command to shovel coal or pull broken equipment away from the mine entrances. Albert did not complain. He would lift. He would carry. He would fetch for the few shillings that kept his family away from the poor house. But his body could not keep up with the six-day work week. The physical demands, the sheer stamina and strength required to work nine hours a day, lifting and dumping scrap were too much for my father. Soon enough, he was lifting and hauling too much for his body to bear. He was forced by the pit foreman to haul broken machinery, iron and scrap too heavy for a younger man. One day, he ruptured himself, throwing his intestines and internal organs askew. It crippled him. He was dismissed from the pits as a has-been. My dad was pensioned off with twelve shillings a week.

Albert, the first son of a publican, was now Albert the invalid. He lived with the disgrace that he could no longer keep his family fed and clothed or in a warm comfortable house. Albert was physically and financially broken. Our family was expected to survive on less than a pound a week. Lillian's low ember of love for Albert cooled. The arctic airs of financial necessity blowing in through our windows and doors were seeing to that.

I was not yet seven when the stock market crashed in 1929 but I had already witnessed my share of ruin. Tuberculosis had claimed my sister Marian while my father was pensioned off as broken goods by a colliery that couldn't protect its workers. My mother was emotionally wounded by the loss of her daughter and the decline of our family's fortune. Our family's fall from grace in the 1920's was a prelude to the destruction waiting to befall working families across the world in the 1930's. We were on the threshold of the Great Depression and the leveling of the poor, the middle class, and the downtrodden in Europe and America. In the coming global economic turmoil, my sister and I and our disconnected parents were to spend years ducking debt collectors and doing midnight runners from landlords. Hunger was ever-present. Like an abandoned dog, I was compelled to forage for food in the refuse bins of restaurants and grocery stores to feed myself and my sister.

3

Bradford

From Barnsley we moved to Bradford. My sister and I, because we were children, had to rely upon my mother's dubious moral compass, dubious map of the human heart. Her directions suggested we keep moving and not look back. Perhaps that was because she too was hungry. My father was no use to us as he just clung on to our mother and us, dependent and silent. We were like migratory beasts of the plain, moving forward to find a safe savannah to graze. Lillian also knew there was more chance of remaining anonymous in a city rather than a village. Nobody's fool, Lillian Dean's instinct for survival at whatever cost was renowned to her siblings and reason for shame by her parents. My mum had little money but with cunning, sex appeal, and the ability to assume vulnerable airs, she was able to let a three-story house from a naive house owner. My mother quickly went about transforming a relatively respectable house into a workman's squat with three beds running aside each other in narrow bedrooms. She took in Irish Navies, as they were lowly paid and in need of cheap digs. Drinkers and fornicators were welcome as long as they could pay their daily or weekly rent. She suffered no abuse, but handed it back liberally.

A tenant of ours pissed his bed. My mother accepted this nightly nocturnal occurrence for several weeks as he paid his due on time. But the smell of urine became too strong and she grew tired of the complaints from the other lodgers. Lillian tossed him out of the house, telling him not to return. When he pleaded for his possessions; she returned to the third floor bedroom and thrust open the window. Lillian hurled his meager belongings including the piss-stained mattress to the small garden below. My mother cursed his belongings and him.

"Go fuck yerself to high heaven," she screamed. "Fuck your pissed stained mattress and your piss-stained money," Lillian grumbled at him.

On many occasions, my mother sent my sister and me to procure pullet eggs from a nearby store. The pullet egg was half the size of a regular egg. It was cheaper by half and was imported from Poland. They were packed in large wooden crates with only moldy old straw to cushion the egg. Most eggs were broken and rotting by the time they had completed their long journey from Poland to Bradford. The shattered and smashed eggs hidden in the straw emitted a foul damp smell like farts trapped in a sofa. Poor customers like my sister and I gagged from the disintegrating smell. Our stomachs turned as we rustled through the straw, saturated in rotting methane, hoping to find a few eggs that could be taken home and fried for our tea.

By this time, our father had given up all hope of being a hunter gatherer for his clan. He preferred to sit on his stool beside the fireplace. Silent and morose he smoked his pipe while my mother flirted with the lodgers and degraded him in front of the paying guests. Whatever turmoil, whatever regrets he may have had, they were wordless. On the wall above his chair was an elegant portrait of Francis. In the painting, Albert's father appeared with a giant handlebar mustache. He wore a morning coat adorned with the tie of a prosperous merchant. I wonder if my father sensed disappointment glaring down from the portrait over how much had been lost. Or perhaps Albert stared upward to curse Francis for invoking duty and family loyalty only to betray him with his uncle.

My only real contact with my father was to watch him put on his hat and coat for his many daily solitary walks. I saw him leave glum and return home morose with few words for me. After working for over four decades to become an invalid must have been an overwhelming shame, one that my father shouldered alone. Yet on several occasions, and I am not sure what warranted it, he would take me up to his room to show me his prized possession.

It was the *Harmsworth History of the World* in eight volumes. They were bound in leather embossed with gold leaf. The books were elegantly mounted across his writing desk. When I was allowed to leaf through the beautifully bound books, vast treasures awaited me. For a boy of seven not used to exotic worlds, the books were stunning. With me on the floor and my father near me, I opened the book and felt the silky pages between my fingers. My father warned me to be careful as these books were special, ancient books. They were not playthings. They were to learn and to improve oneself. With my father close by, the noise of boarders below, and the catcalls of my mother seeping up through the floorboards, I became lost in the "The Seven Wonders of the Ancient World." I saw magnificent illustrations, exact drawings of faraway places, unheard-of kingdoms. I dreamed that I was before the mighty Pyramids of Egypt. I imagined myself walking through the Hanging Gardens of Babylon, which soared seventy-five feet above the ground flush with a bounty of flowers. On another page, I was at the Temple of Zeus at Olympia conversing with ancient Greeks, or sparring with Alexander the Great. I lingered at the temple of Diana, breathing fresh, clean Ionian air. On another page, I stumbled upon the Mausoleum of Halicarnassus and felt a million miles from the boarding house and boarding room. Only the smell of my father's pipe or the harsh sound of his throat clearing to indicate that I was too rough on the book brought me crashing down to kith and kin. But there were more pages to explore and I sailed between the Colossus of Rhodes while the lighthouse of Alexandria guided me into safe

Egyptian shores. On many weekends, my father offered me this rare treat, this passport to escape our present discomfort.

On one such day after our excursions through ancient lands, my father said to me, "One day, lad, one day, you might go out into the world and see some fantastic, magical places."

It was the tenderness of a father that believed he had nothing to give his son, no legacy, no trade. Albert gave me a far-off prospect of another land, another country, another hope. I would have given up the vague promise of new horizons, of anything if my father could have let me linger a little while longer, with him near. I desired that he would protect me for a little while longer, while I rummaged through the history of the ancient world. These Sunday respites were not to last between my father and me; events below the room would banish him from our house soon enough.

Perhaps my father knew that that our money was running out along with his time with me because, for my birthday he took me to the Alhambra Theatre. It was my first time, and I was proud and overjoyed to be in the sole company of my dad, who treated me with sweats and attention. On our way home, Dad held my hand as we crossed the busy street and hummed musical hall tunes to me. I exploded with delight when I recounted to my mother our day at the theatre. Fairy tale characters came to life for me for the first and last time in my youth.

Where we now lived, the other residents hardly resembled the characters from a child's bedtime story; unless it was from Brothers Grimm. The other inhabitants were transient navies. Their faces were forgettable. The road workers were rough and ready, quick with jokes and song. But they were always being replaced by the next crowd of workers and down and outers. When the workers moved on, fewer came back because Bradford was shriven by the great depression. As menial jobs became scarce, there were fewer men able to pay for cheap lodgings which meant our family would also have to move on because

Lillian now had no means to pay our share of rent to the owner. So before suspicion was heightened, before her charm could no longer buy a reprieve from the rent, midnight came. And under black, cold, Yorkshire skies, we slipped from our doss house lodgings and on to the unfriendly streets. Lillian found another house, another owner, and inveigled him with a sob story of hungry children, broken hearts, and a promise to pay as soon as we were on our feet again.

By this time, Lillian had exhausted all means to buy food or clothes for her family. We lived through many hungry mornings to many hungry nights, when for once good fortune seemed to shine down upon my family. While walking on the High Street, my mother happened to spy a giant brown bag with a chain clasp around it. She picked it up and noticed that it had the name of a department store stenciled across it. Curious and hungry, she proceeded to open it. Inside were the day's receipts for the store. There was fifty pounds in notes and silver in the purse. It crossed her mind to pocket the money and not say a word to anyone. Fifty pounds would provide for us for many months. The store could easily accept this loss if they were careless enough to lose it in the first place. However, my mother's conscience and knowledge that she was many things but not a thief wore her down.

Lillian walked over to the store and asked to see the manager. When he appeared, she informed him of what she had found. The manager sized up my mother. She was not of his class. He thanked her for her honesty. As a reward, the store presented her with a bag filled with day-old broken biscuits. Ashamed, Lillian left hurriedly. She was furious. Honesty had unjustly paid her. Civic duty meant her children went hungry, went without toys, went without clothes, and simply went without. Her good deed had been returned and valued at the sum total of broken biscuits. She brought them home and placed them on our kitchen table. Lillian stared at them in bitter silence. No one was to disturb her as she sat, arms crossed, glaring at the bag. Mary and I went to bed. We left our mother alone in the kitchen with her reward for honesty: stale biscuits.

The following morning, before we awoke to go to school, Lillian returned to the department store. My mother carried in her hand the bag of broken biscuits. At the store, she demanded to see the manager. The obsequious attendant asked if the manager would know the reason for her visit.

"He bloody well will," my mother intoned.

Several minutes passed. The highbrow manager, who had looked down upon my mother the day before, greeted her with cold, officious, politeness. He inquired as to how he could be of assistance to her today.

My mother slammed down the package of broken biscuits and said, "You can start by taking these bloody things back."

Aghast, the manager repeated, "Back? But why?"

"I found fifty pounds of yer money yesterday. You think broken biscuits paid for my kindness to your store?"

The manager stammered.

"Bollocks," my mother retorted. "Five pounds," she blurted out mysteriously.

"Five pounds?" inquired the manager.

"That's right," my mother replied, "five pounds, for my service to you and your store."

"But that is a lot of money," the manager told her.

"It's a lot less than losing fifty pounds," my mother replied.

"I can't possibly ..." the manager responded with haughty disgust.

"Look," my mother told him, her face pushed up close to the manager's face. "A fiver or I am going to scream at the top of me lungs what shite this store gave to a poor ungry mam. It's a grand store to throw garbage to a poor mother, with two little kids to feed and a sick husband to care for. Broken biscuits, by gum... after I saved the day's receipts from more unscrupulous kinds of folk?"

The manager, with reptilian lips, was standing ramrod straight as he answered, "You will have to go to the book-keeping office. I will have someone issue you five pounds under the condition you never come into this store again."

During our time in Bradford, I changed schools as many times as I changed homes. The schools I attended were Catholic. It seemed my mother, having lost her belief in my father, found faith in Catholicism. More to the point, she was told Catholic institutions were more generous in their alms. My mother came to this revelation after she developed a deep fancy for one of the Irish men who came to lodge with us. His name was O'Sullivan. Lillian thought she could entice him into her heart with Catholic children. As for her husband, Albert, Lillian passed him off as her own father. It gave her free reign to date and flirt with the men she thought could assist us. My mother told me that should anyone ask about my dad, I was to answer that he was my grandfather. My father made no protest because either he was ignorant of this change in status or because he knew he was on sufferance. Without my mother's stamina for loosening stray bobs out of other men's hands, Albert would be out on the streets, a wanton beggar.

So both Mary and I entered the Catholic faith as mendicants and to permit my mother her carnal desire with more ease. Mary and I learned our catechism without devotion, except to avoid the cane. I went to school wearing the only pair of shoes I possessed; hard workman's clogs whose design had not changed since the beginning of the industrial revolution. The rigid fitting shoes were alms for the poor. The shorn, corduroy trousers I wore came from another charity house that specialized in destitute, off-the-rack fashion. Every day, the tides of the economy, my father's surrender to the fates, my mother's greed, envy, and anger at her destiny drove us further beneath the waves of life in Bradford.

The staggering effects of the 1929 stock market crash reaped total industrial collapse in the North of England. By 1930, mills and mines were closing on a daily basis. The dole was only temporary.

Unemployed workers could expect fifteen weeks of substandard government assistance; afterwards they went hungry. The North, along with Scotland and Wales bore the full strength of this economic maelstrom. The industrial North had been stripped for centuries by the South for raw materials. The counties that built the foundations of the empire were abandoned during the depression. They were left to whither and rot like fruit falling to the ground. While drinking champagne in London nightclubs, middle class youths from the South danced until dawn; while miners marched in protest to Parliament over shoddy wages that were starving their children to death. The literati spoke ominously about the rise of communism as a scourge that would envelope and destroy Britain. There were some who spoke of the shame the South should feel over the protracted rape of the North. Orwell denounced and fulminated against the unimaginable weight of poverty industrialized Britain had to bear. Oswald Mosley, before he became a Nazi, railed at the government's blindness to poverty and unemployment.

The country's unemployment rate exploded to 2.5 million. In Bradford and many other Northern towns and villages, the effects of malnutrition began to creep across every street corner. Rickets, TB, death from starvation were not freak occurrences, but living experiences for many, including my family. Disease was rife in all the towns across the poverty-racked North. Mary and I, followed by other children, chanted down squalid streets blanketed in want and hopelessness:

"Mother, Mother, take me home from the convalescent home.
I've been here a month or two, now I'd like to be with you."

I was marked by my clothing as a beggar. I was deemed an untouchable at school. Amongst the poor, I was considered the lowest of the low because of my rotting corduroy trousers. I had few friends. Other children were afraid to befriend us, as if our hunger and poverty could be transferred like an airborne plague. There was little time for friendship anyway. There was only time to run from landlords and scavenge for food. My sister and I were hungry in the morning, hungry in the evening. We went to sleep in cold lightless rooms, our stomachs sick from hunger pangs. We suffered from excruciating chilblains, which were only soothed by rubbing our warm piss onto the wounds. I was pursued by famished nightmares in my sleep. I dreamed I was drifting through the air. I was floating and soaring only to look down and see my legs were bound with metal straps tethering me to a wooden board on the ground. Wherever I soared in these night terrors; I could never be free of the ground, of my home, and my family. Even in my sleep, I was to be always locked and chained.

When the frost-chilled morning arose, Mary and I hurriedly dressed underneath our dirty bedcovers. We crept unwillingly downstairs to be greeted by a cold grate fireplace, its hearth empty of warmth. Mary was the one person that made my hunger less lonely. My sister made life a little more optimistic. Mary was good at finding another lodger's bread, which we shared, and if we were lucky, drippings from the previous dinner. Like a little abandoned animal I would sing;

"Old Mother Hubbard went to the cupboard to give the poor dog a bone.

But when she got there the cupboard was bare and so the poor doggie had none."

Before getting out the door, I would throw on two oversized jackets to keep me warm. Mary laced up my boots and stuffed a piece of her bread in my pocket. "Fer later, Harry, when you're at school and good hungry, like dog down lane."

Outside, we faced a walk of several miles to a new school or an old school. It did not matter: what awaited us was taunting or physical violence from our teachers. Trudging to school, we found no comfort in our thoughts. We knew we had slipped beneath the waves and were lost. As transient Bradford gypsies, Mary and I had no time to do our school work, our arithmetic, our history, our grammar; we fell behind the rest of our classmates. We realized we were falling behind and we were ashamed. We were embarrassed by our threadbare look, and humiliated by our hungry stomachs and hazy minds. And should we have forgotten that we did not know our lessons, that we did not know our catechism, that we did not know Jesus, we were beaten with the cane. It was the inscrutable instrument of Catholic education used liberally, but never judiciously on Mary and me.

The priests at our school had swinging big bellies that moved like pendulums. Their faces were whisky-red from too many nights of cards and cigarettes. On Sunday, Bradford's downtrodden would turn out to mass. Holding their last farthings, the poor in the back rows of the cathedral placed their coppers into the collection plate as if they were buying a lottery ticket to heaven. The fat silver plate represented to me one thing: the priest could eat good roast at tea and bugger the poor with homilies about the eye of a needle and the travails about a rich man trying to enter paradise. And on Monday, the blessed Father would have the strength to whip the malnourished and the unloved back into God's dominion. It seemed the good priests of Bradford generally started with me and ended with my sister.

The nuns were just as thin as the sticks they used to beat us with. They moved as silently as creeping Jesus and their faces were expressionless. In Bradford, the sisters were the Earthly instrument of God's wrath. They took pleasure in the pain they delivered upon me as it was a daily occurrence. For my failure to memorize the multiplication tables, I was beaten. For my failure to remember the martyrdom of some saint, I was beaten. I instigated anger and displeasure to the nuns by simply being artistically uncoordinated. Sister Christine was my drawing teacher. She was a dour, unhappy character, who took no joy in beauty or in children.

She instructed our class to draw an apple that sat upon a table at the front of the room. I produced a lousy reproduction. It neither resembled the forbidden fruit of Adam and Eve or anything slightly tempting. Sister Christine crept around the room on rubber-soled shoes inspecting and approving or disapproving the students' representation.

From behind, she descended, laying a mighty and painful slap across my head with her hand. Obviously, my apple was smudged and imprecisely created, for the nun felt such esthetic revulsion, she thought it necessary to exercise my lack of form with physical pain. The strength and ferocity of the blow almost made me lose consciousness. For the whole afternoon, that side of my head hurt while my pride stung from humiliation for much longer. Even my mother noticed my injury when I returned home from school. My mother said nothing to me, but the following day she arrived unannounced at the classroom of Sister Christine.

Lillian told the sister, "I hear you've been disciplining our Harry for not meeting your fancy apple approval." Sister Christine obfuscated. She claimed I had been acting out in class.

"Sister," my mother said, "mark my words, you touch my boy again; if there is the slightest scratch on him; I will beat you with my very hands."

The sister looked stunned.

My mother departed, telling the nun, "Justice is mine sayeth the lord."

Eventually, the Catholic schools were able to provide a hot meal for the most destitute children at lunch. I stood in line, aroused with joy at the lingering smell of stew, potatoes, carrots, or mutton. While I waited in the food procession, I dreamed about when it would touch my plate. I ravenously imagined the substance crossing my lips. When I could finally sit down with my lunch, I gorged upon the food like a half-starved mutt. I licked the plate dry, knowing I would not see a real supper until the following day.

Mother became unhinged by our family's rapid descent into poverty and hunger. Emotionally, she felt shock at our situation. Also, my mother had to withstand the critical eyes of her siblings. Lillian's sisters and brothers cast a disdainful eye towards her for marrying a man in haste and mortgaging her future. They did not approve of Lillian's forlorn love for my dad, or her dim hope of hidden riches from her husband's family. Lillian began to despise her responsibility as mother and wife. She began to despise herself. There was an element in her that became feral and never returned to normalcy. She fought for food for her family. She fought for lodgings for her family. However, her acts of resilience and struggle were always orchestrated, almost operatic. Lillian's overtures cast the root cause of our misfortunes upon me and Mary, as if our existence was a mistake. Sometimes, Lillian was just wantonly cruel. Stridently, despairingly, Lillian noted her life would be easier if she just abandoned us to an orphanage. Lillian, who had witnessed the cruelty of the work house and experienced the indignity and death of her first-born at the work house, expressed a reality that she feared would befall her other children. Her ominous proclamations were warnings to us children that nothing was secured in this life and love does not outlast famine.

Baggage my father, Mary, and I might have been to my mother's ambitions, but Lillian did get on with her life. Mr. O'Sullivan, the man who introduced my mother to the Church of Rome, also introduced her to adultery. O'Sullivan was tall and carried himself like a soldier. He dressed better, a little more dapper than his profession warranted as an everyday workman. Even though he no longer lodged with us, he still frequented our house. Although not rich, O'Sullivan worked every day, knew how to laugh, and was as youthful as my mother. He was not like Albert. He was strong and filled with optimism for both the present and future. He did not seem worried by all the poverty, stagnation, and rot around him. Mr. O' Sullivan's frequent appearances precipitated a change once again in houses. We moved to Chesham Street, but this time, my mother took in no lodgers. Also, my father's good furniture was returned from pawn to decorate the parlour.

A large solid, oak cabinet decorated our parlour. It had two carved openings on either side of the cabinet. They were adorned with two-foot-high, hand-painted porcelain ceramics. Beside the fire was a comfortable mohair chair. It was where my mother reclined to spend her evenings, with her feet resting on a leather footstool. Two husky men laboured up our narrow stairs to return to my parents' bedroom suite to their bedroom. It was solid, dark mahogany, which was a remnant from the days when the New Inn was held by my grandfather.

Mary and I were happy to be in better surroundings. We had a bit more to eat and a bit more coal in the fire. But we were also filled with the uneasy feeling that this plenty was temporary. Experience taught me hunger always returned. Although the surroundings had improved, domestic bliss eluded my parents. My parents engaged in nightly screaming bouts, nightly fits of pique. They raged over lost illusions, wanton wives, and rudderless lives. Mary ensured Lillian's wrath by standing up for our father when he was let low by an endless torrent of sarcasm from his wife. Their sixteen years of marriage was based upon the hope that things could only get better. Whereas the opposite occurred; the longer they stayed together, the worse things got. The emotional plates that had held my parents together through so many mutual failures and defeats finally shifted. My father moved more to the periphery of my life, and perhaps his own as well.

Lillian took to frequenting High Street dress shops that accepted payment on weekly installment plans. Her credit was confirmed when the shop sent a man to our house. The man saw our posh furniture and presumed we were solid, debt-fearing Christians. It seemed Lillian was shopping for a meal ticket. There was an outward appearance of domestic bliss in our house, but it was all theatre for my mother to get clothes on tick and capture a new man. Perhaps Lillian was looking for a man like my father. Well, a man like my dad when he had money; when he was younger and had a little more spark of live and vitality. She needed a man to resurrect her dormant desires as a woman. Lillian needed a new man to feed both her body and her imagination. Ultimately, she was looking for a man who wouldn't mind feeding some extra children.

And she presumed that man was Mr. O'Sullivan. My mother believed O'Sullivan would give her a life complete with both leisure and pleasure. She had thought the same when she accepted my father's hand in marriage in 1914. Time had not eroded my mother's acumen for self-deception; in 1930 my mother disappeared into the night with Mr. O'Sullivan. She fled to St. Albans, near London. My father gave us no explanation for my mother's disappearance. She was just gone. Mary said, "Mam didn't go with the milkman because he still comes round looking for money." Through the spring, we waited for news of my mother and none came. Mary tended house for my father while I rummaged for extra food in the High Street tips. Albert locked himself up in his rooms. Perhaps he was lost in *Harmsworth's* eight-volume encyclopedia looking for enlightenment to his lot. Or perhaps he was just in his room staring at the walls, smoking his pipe, waiting patiently for ten-year-old Mary to serve him his tea.

At the end of spring, close to my parents' anniversary, Lillian returned home from St Albans. She came back wearing a new dress, a new coat, and carrying presents for the whole family. Lillian held in one hand a pineapple, as if she had just arrived from Captain Cooke's expedition to the South Seas. In the other hand, she held "authentic Irish soda bread." It was from the emerald shore itself. Lillian also proclaimed she was many months pregnant. She left no doubt that O'Sullivan was the father. Upon hearing the news, Albert went out for his daily walk. He said nothing to my mother. That night, Mary and I ate large portions of the Irish soda bread with a weak and meatless broth. The pineapple, it seemed, was for decoration. Lillian took it to various locals to demonstrate the wonders and oddities London had to offer.

4

Arrivals and Departures

That summer was easier, dare I say it, happier for Mary and me. Even in this damp and wet part of Yorkshire, the sun came out, warmth returned; optimism budded and left little time for us to brood. Summer was also better for food scavenging at the back of restaurants. The rubbish bins found in alleyways behind Bradford's cafes and hotels on its High Street were a smorgasbord of half-eaten delights: jellied hams, semi-fresh bread, and half-eaten cakes. For the near starving like my sister and me, we supped well. For Mary and me, there was no shame in dining on food cast away by overfed stockbrokers, bankers, and mill owners. The bin at the wholesale fruit market was like King Solomon's mine for me. There was so much slightly damaged fruit thrown to one side. Mary and I always came downtown prepared with a paper bag to hold our booty. We ventured home loaded with apples, oranges, and pears. There was enough that we stuffed ourselves until our bellies were full and our emotions content, knowing we would sleep sated.

Through July, the days fell upon one another like the footfalls of a newborn lamb, clumsy and spry. Our street, Chesham, ran onto Great Horton, which ended up in a large open field called Trinity. One afternoon, we heard rumors that a circus had set up their tents on the common. Mary and I made our way up the street and discovered erected tents in the clearing. In the distance, you could hear the sounds of exotic animals bellowing from the field. Mary and I went to the opposite end of Trinity field, where we were camouflaged in the long, tall grass. We crouched on our hind legs. I gazed towards the circus to see if I could catch sight of this strange and mysterious world of carnivals. The sound of hammers and workman straining to construct the circus was all around us. The odd elephant trumpet made our mouths drop open in surprise. I was tinged with mild fear, wondering if the mighty beasts could break loose and trample us hidden in the brush. An hour had almost passed, and I grew restless. I became bored having seen no wild creatures, no clown, and no strong man. I was about to ask my sister if we could go when suddenly, Mary began to shake my shoulder,

"Harry, Harry, come and look." It was as if I had been transported right into the middle of *Harmsworth's History of the World*. Parading outside one of the tents were three beautiful, lithe Burmese women. Their necks were wrapped tightly with gold bands, making them appear as thin and graceful as giraffes on the African plain. They walked in front of their tent and appeared to me like princesses of Asia. The Burmese women of the circus were enticing, forbidden, and utterly foreign to the world as I understood it.

As my mother's pregnancy progressed through the summer; I was considered a nuisance and sent to live with my grandparents in Barnsley. My mother packed a cheap suitcase for me and took me, dragging behind her, to the bus station. When the bus to Barnsley arrived, she pushed me through the open door and advised the driver to make sure I got off at the right stop. "Wait for Uncle Harold," she admonished. "He will walk you to Grandma Dean's house."

My mother's family lived on Beaumont Street in a two-bedroom tenement house. It had a ginnel leading onto a back plot for gardening or storing equipment. My grandparents, Walter and Mary Ellen Dean, had arrived in Barnsley twenty-five years previous. Walter was from Harley, a village near my father's pub. Mary Ellen's family, the Hoylands had been part of the Barnsley landscape for over two centuries. They owed their meek and meager existence to my grandmother's great-grandmother. She had been born deaf and dumb, but the local lord, the Earl of Fitzwilliam, took her into service. It was rumored that the Hoyland girl was a mute beauty who caught the eye and wandering penis of the Earl. In due time, she sired him a bastard.

The Fitzwilliams ruled this part of Yorkshire since the 16th century. They treated the Earth and what lay beneath it as their private treasury. The Earl was not known for his kindness. However, he was widely credited for his thrift and greed. He was renowned for sinking dangerous mines that killed or injured many workers. The mute's bastard child, according to family legend, grew into a strong young man who loved his speechless mother with great profundity. Upon hearing of his aristocrat lineage, the mute's son demanded recompense from the Earl. He demanded honour be shown his mother for lifting her skirt and obliging the master. The Earl and the woman's son were able to come to an arrangement either by guile or threat of physical harm. The man was granted stone and land to build a modest house. Over the years, the house remained in the family and was now the property of Mary Ellen's father, George Hoyland.

I arrived at my grandparents' house and was greeted by gluttonous silence from my grandfather. From a child's perspective, he looked like a large, gruff walrus who laboured to either stand or walk. Walter Dean had long since retired from the mines and spent his time silently remembering the glories of India and his youth as a soldier in the Far East. He said little if anything at all. At dinner, he sat at the head of the table and ate in oblique silence. I was not afraid of him, nor did I court his affection. He was several years older than my father and seemed as distant to me in age as Albert. My grandmother, however, was an extreme opposite to her husband. Mary Ellen was blunt in speech and held strong opinions on everything, including religion, which she was very keen on. She always wore thick, black boots that were obscured by her dress trailing across the floor. Underneath her clothing, she wore numerous petticoats and a huge grey corset. She was usually silent around me. I think she thought it best to speak no ill of me or my mother. If she despaired over my mother's dalliances, I was not informed. If she regretted me as a grandchild, I had no way of determining it, as my visits to her house were without Mary. I had no yardstick to measure her affection. She never raised her hand or voice in my direction, nor did she hug me. Yet her food was always plentiful, warm, and delicious. At the dinner table, the only noise was the squeak of forks against porcelain plates. My mother's sisters had already been married off. So our table was occupied by my grandparents and their two sons, Harold and Ted. Ted was illegitimate, but asides from Mary Ellen, no one else seemed concerned. In fact, Walter got along well with Ted and greatly enjoyed his company.

Ted showed modest affection for me. He had a gentle quietness about him that I found appealing coming from a household filled with so much hidden noise and anger. He seemed to be a man content with the daily plodding of life. Later on, he obtained a hand-painted gypsy caravan. It was decorated as if it were direct from some oriental bazaar. In summer, he would live and travel around the local country as if he were a vagabond. Ted was the only one at the dinner table who would inquire about my day. In the mornings, my uncle was in the back carefully and solicitously tending his garden. He would let me take ripening fruit from his small plot. He did not speak much and everything was in short syllables to me like, "Mind this," or "Yer alright there." But it was spoken from a calm river of emotion and he made me feel relaxed.

Ted, however, could not abide my mother. If I mentioned her, he politely changed the subject. It was never explained to me why Ted had a personal grudge against my mother. Perhaps he did not approve of her life or perhaps he did not agree with the choices she made to endure and let her children survive. Ted's dislikes were always whimsical. He had great admiration for the entertainer Gracie Field until she married an Italian. From that point onwards, she was as popular as my mother to him.

Harold was much younger than Ted and was prone to be either easily annoyed or easily amused. One day, early on in my exile, Harold suggested I go with him to Sheffield. He had some business to attend to and he felt like company. Enthusiastically and without hesitation, I accepted his offer. It was an exciting prospect to travel to a large city for an adventure.

We came to Sheffield by means of a slow meandering bus. When we arrived, Harold went about his errands, stopping in several shops. He instructed me to stand outside, wait, and not be a nuisance. By about lunchtime, he had concluded his dealings. Harold brought me into a public house, where we stood by the bar. My uncle had me stand on the rails so the bar man could see me. Harold ordered himself a neat whisky and inquired to the innkeeper; "How bout something fer me nephew?"

"Orange cordial?" suggested the innkeeper.

"Make it an orange and gin," replied my uncle.

The afternoon passed with my uncle drinking whisky and I, only seven, was sipping on several gin and oranges. Both my uncle and I were thoroughly pissed by mid-afternoon. My uncle suggested we better catch the last bus back to Hoyland Common. Staggering, we both mounted the bus and fell into a fitful but drunken sleep until we reached Barnsley station.

Although Harold lived with my grandparents, he was married. His wife, Ida, worked on a large industrial farm as a book-keeper and lodged there. His wife came frequently to my grandparents' house. Ida was a nice, friendly woman devoid of Harold's flightiness or Ted's clumsiness. She sensed my increasing boredom. So she gave me a key to escape the slow and dull pattern of summer days on Beaumont Street. She lent me her bike. For the first time in my life, I was free to roam further than I had ever been before. Before that summer, I had never ridden a bike. I took many tentative steps before I came close to soaring from Beaumont Street and escaping my old and sloth-like grandparents. I energetically and arrogantly hopped on this gearless bike, built for an adult and not a seven-year-old. My feet barely reached the thick wooden pedals. I slowly, laboriously started to pedal and feel my mobility. For a few brief seconds, I soared like Orville Wright at Kitty Hawk. Alas, the seconds were brief. I came crashing down on the hard cobbled street and heard the innocent chuckle of Uncle Ted.

Many attempts and many aborted take offs ensued in that first week. Gradually, by the second week, I developed my wings. I was able to pedal and remained balanced and aloft. I was ready to discover the hills and dales surrounding my grandparents' house. I spent my mornings and afternoons with this bike. I sensed that for the first time in my life, I was independent. I was free of the burdens of hunger. I was far away from my parents' despair and hunger for other lives. I was free from my own sense of shame. On this bike, no one was to judge me poor because I could pedal faster than their taunts. I could hide and reflect in fields empty of human gazes, only occupied by a few slow-grazing, pleasant cows. As with all things in my early life, these sheltered moments of calm were brief. They always signaled a downpour, a bad shower ahead. The summer winded its way through my grandparents' house on Beaumont Street as it had probably done for decades. There was a slow determined rhythm of breakfast, lunch, and dinner. Adults and children were free to conceal their thoughts from others. No one really spoke. Each of us obscured our happiness, our own memories and our own grief.

I still can find no answer, no reason why my grandparents had no picture, no remembrance of their first-born, long since dead, a causality of war. His name had been inscribed on the local war monument, but his memory was carved in silence in their home. He was never talked about, at least not in front of children. But for that matter, did we ever have a picture of Marian in our house as a memento moiré? We had none. I do not know if it was because of our poverty or because my mother felt the separation so deeply that her only means to flee from it was by omission.

When I returned home to Bradford, Mary was patiently waiting for me at the bus station. We walked home in silence. I was afraid to ask if things had gotten worse with my mother and father. Now summer had turned into fall; it was September 1930. Breadlines increased as the dole dried up. For the unemployed, Ramsey Macdonald's socialist government was incapable of handling or managing the economic catastrophe. More workers were sent home from their jobs because the politicians refused to support reconstruction projects or stimulate the economy. My father's disability pension scarcely fed him, let alone a family of four.

By the end of September, my mother went into labour in our sitting room. A midwife assisted her in the birth. My sister and I played and scampered about the kitchen. Outside, we heard the screams and pants of rage from our mother in childbirth. My father was mute to our games or his wife's long labour with another man's son. He sat limply on his stool before a low coal fire in the kitchen. Albert was quiet and perhaps mourned the death of his first-born, Marian. After much effort and pleading from the midwife, my brother Matthew was born. My sister and I heard his loud demanding screams of despair when he was released from Lillian's womb to this cold and desperate house.

After Matt was born, my mother's hopes of being rescued by Mr. O'Sullivan evaporated quickly. It seemed he was no more than a bounder. He had done a better job at conning my mother than she had of him. Later on, she claimed that O'Sullivan had wanted to take her and the new child to Australia. In her story, O'Sullivan did not give a toss for Mary and me. We were to have been left behind as destitute orphans. But according to Lillian, she could not agree to such a sacrifice.

Not long after Matt's birth, our unhappy family was forced to leave Chesham Street. Rent arrears caused us to move into another series of tenements. Our new neighbourhood, St Andrews Villas, was fraught with itinerant labourers, unemployed mill workers, and struggling pensioners. My mother somehow purloined a truck and a work man to haul the flotsam of our existence to our new refuge. The house was in the north-west of the city. It was a much further walk to school then the last residence.

My mother had been contracted to transform the house into a doss by the landlord. Assiduously, she prepared its many rooms into dank sitting room squalor for elderly down and outs. For her efforts, our rent was reduced and my mother was in charge of collecting rents from the hapless tenants. Mary and I tended to general cleaning duties. This included washing the bog out back, which held turds recorded in the Doomsday book. The house had a giant banister. I used to slide down it with much excitement. It caused a great deal of irritation to the other aged guests; caught off-guard by this small boy rapidly logging down the staircase.

My parents shared their room with our new baby brother, Matt. Mary and I occupied the attic. It had been divided into three shabby compartments with low beams, rotting floorboards and a twelve-inch square window cut through the roof to provide oxygen. The rooms in the attic did not have doors. We were the first to know when it rained, as the slate roof was in need of repair. Water dripped down the sides of the walls and gathered in puddles on the floor. The five other bedrooms were let to indigent married couples who had lost their lodgings. The rent was cheap. But nothing is cheap when you are on Queer Street. My mother was in charge of collection; it was a weekly ordeal. Lillian knocked on the residents' doors and made sure they did not attempt to dodge their debt. Once collected, my mother would deliver it to the landlord, who lived at the other end of town.

The residents enjoyed the parlour to read a newspaper, smoke, or play endless games of whist. The portrait of my grandfather took prized stage above the coal fireplace. Francis looked down in puzzlement at these ragged, hungry guests that were refugees from the economic storm outside. The tenants, like my family, were tired and shamed by their circumstance. Most of them were quiet and hid their former lives from the prying eyes of their new companions in this leaky lifeboat. No one wanted to be reminded of better days, and they were old with skills no longer required, in an ever-wasting economy.

One lodger, Mr. Brown was not as reticent. His wife generally remained upstairs nursing a drink from a flask. He sat downstairs smoking Kensington cigarettes. He was trim and always meticulously shaved. I used to time my visits to the parlour based upon his presence. I would corner him and beg him to tell me stories of his exploits in the Great War. He obliged. Brown sang to me marching songs and told me abbreviated tales of the trenches, cleansed of dirt and death. He always concluded his story by presenting me a silk card that had a different flag of the world on it. The flags were a promotional giveaway provided by the cigarette company. So that I could collect more flags, I encouraged him to smoke with more urgency. His stay produced a hundred foreign flags. I pinned those global ensigns up on the wall near my bed. Each night before I turned out the light, I stared at them and dreamed about one day traveling to those faraway lands. Before falling asleep, I imagined worlds far from doss houses and dirty slums.

Six months shy of my eighth birthday, I took my first job. My mother explained to me it was necessary I accept some adult responsibilities because we were so destitute. The money I earned at seven was to assist in keeping us fed and alive. There was an off license up the street from our house looking for help. When I approached the owner behind the counter, he gave me a disdainful look. He was a man quicker to blame than praise, quicker to berate than compliment. But the owner was wise enough to know it was cheaper to hire a child than a hungry adult to do general cleanup. I worked for him three days a week, after school and did a half-day on Saturdays. I scrubbed floors and stacked shelves for tuppence and leering glares from the owner. I worked quietly and diligently. Apparently, I showed enough aptitude for my position that I received a promotion of sorts. The owner now wanted me to deliver crates of beer to local customers. I weighed no more than eighty pounds and I stood less than five feet. But I was the captain of a steel-wheeled handcart, wide enough to fit three crates of beer containing nine, one half-pint bottles. I maneuvered my wares up and down the narrow industrial streets of Bradford. The weight of three beer crates was too great for me. So with much criticism from the owner, I was compelled to make three deliveries instead of one. The pay was not magnificent, but my wages were able to assist my parents. It was a great humiliation for my father to watch me return from work and place my wages into the family's piggy bank. My tips, however, I hid from them. With those pennies, I bought treats for Mary and myself. At bedtime, my sister and I rushed upstairs to our cold attic bedroom, where under our bedcovers we shared a Cadbury's chocolate bar, cut into enough pieces to last us the week.

From our new squat, school was now an hour away. There was now little time for lessons and homework with my part-time job pushing crates of beer and my chores around the rooming house. Exam time came in November. Rather than face both the verbal and physical beatings from failing my exams, I played truant from my tests. I spent most of my days loitering in the city centre of Bradford. I walked myself to distraction. Generally, I was lost in a day-dream. Sometimes, I met my father on the High Street in a similar state of truancy. Both of us wished we had not run into each other, spoiling our day-dreams. My father would fish into his trouser pocket and give me a penny.

"Be on your way lad. Make sure your mam is none the wiser of our encounter."

I then trundled off lost in a dream. My fantasies about pirates and treasure seemed far better than my present surroundings or what was awaiting me at home. After being absent from school for several weeks, the truant officer paid a visit to my mother one evening. I told him I was not prepared for my tests. I preferred not to write them. The officer let me off with a warning. However, my lenient sentence had not been received by the nuns. With great delight, they set upon me with the cane. Once corporal punishment had ceased, the good sisters unleashed a verbal maelstrom regarding God's vengeance on lying, deceitful boys.

On Saturdays, I treated Mary with my tip money and took her to the movies. We watched a multitude of short films starring Laurel and Hardy, Charlie Chaplain, Buster Keaton, Harold Lloyd. For a few pence, my sister and I disappeared into a celluloid dream. At the Odeon, everything was funny, everything ended with a smile or a kiss. At the pictures, everything was different from our way of life and those who occupied our rooming house. The cinema was a place of refuge for a small boy like me. It was as alluring as an opium den. Movies and serials let me fantasize and drift away into a world filled with adventure and rewards. On the giant screen, life was indeed larger and everyone was beautiful. Sadness could be overcome and justice was always delivered.

It was at the Odeon where I developed my first film screen crush: Sylvia Sidney. She seduced me with her sensuality and her maternal aura. The starlet melded desire with safety. I dreamed that if only she were in my life, everything would be different. If she knew me, I thought, my days would be exciting and free of the fever of hunger. I would protect her against thugs and gangsters. For my reward, she would smother me in warm kisses and hugs. But the furtive escapist dream melted like film against a cigarette when I got home to St Andrew's Villas. I opened the door to discover the sitting room full of the residents. Their heads turned away from me to shield themselves from unwanted conversation or irksome and troublesome children. My father sat in the corner, pipe in mouth, staring forlornly at a wall. My mother was slightly tipsy from bottles of beer she had drunk in the back scullery. My brother fed on her breast. Irritated by my entrance or my calls for attention, my mother pulled out her engorged breast from Matt's wet lips and pumped her milk across my face. It ran down the sides of my cheeks as if I was sobbing cream.

Lillian laughed and said with contempt, "He looked hungry too!"

Dejectedly, the residents raised their heads from day-old newspapers and sighed. I dashed from the room. I hurried up to my attic refuge, humiliated and angry, consumed with shame as I wept. Upstairs, alone and angry, I knew all too well how far my life was from the movie fantasies I watched at the cinema.

Not long before Christmas 1930, my mother announced to my father that she had taken a lover and her fancy was moving in with us. Economic necessity forever relegated Albert to a secondary, off-stage role. Forced from his marriage bed, Dad moved upstairs to share the attic with his children because rent was free in the loft.

That night after my father's warrant had been writ by my mother, Albert lingered along while in the sitting room, alone. He remained sitting in his chair; his father's painting above him. My dad smoked and tapped the stale embers out of his pipe. Albert stared at the wall. It was his final indignity, the final shame. It was like a pick into his broken spirit. It cut and tore at his insides until he was raw and bloodied with self-scorn and self-loathing. After sixteen years of marriage, after sixteen years of watching the shore around him disappear from the pounding economic waves and ill-timed and mis-calculated strategies; my father snapped and displayed his long, mute suffering, for the first and last time.

Everyone in the lodging house was asleep, but my father and mother. Upstairs, my mother called to him. She said that it was best he come to bed. Albert was now a man who had been reduced and subtracted year in, year out, by nameless actuaries. The events in his life summed up his entire existence to zero: no legacy, no money, no youth, no family. He screamed out. He lashed out against this indignity. How could he be under the same roof as my mother? How could she share his bed with other men? Albert called out, "I am betrayed; I am cheated." Albert charged up the stairs. In his hand he held a small knife; he used it to clean his pipe. It resembled a tiny shoe. The noise quickly got my sister and me out of our comfortless beds. We rushed down to witness my father lunge at my mother. I saw the knife in his hand. It was a blade that would have trouble causing a paper cut, let alone wreaking jealous rage against a betraying lover.

Lillian easily over-powered my father and pushed him to the floor. He was left a wounded animal, quivering and shuddering with adrenalin and spent anger.

"Nothing here to see," my mother said to us. "Off to bed with you, there is nothing to be seen."

The commotion stirred the other tenants and their doors crept ajar. I saw their ears and eyes pressed to the fragmented opening to their rooms and heard them whisper and gossip as they returned to their beds.

Mary and I left our subjugated father on the floor. Shamefully, we went upstairs. My sister and I pulled the covers up over us, as if blankets could hide our own sense of shame and disgust. The next day, my mother sent me to the butcher's to get two ounces of roast beef, "For your father." It would be the last time I heard my mother refer to Albert as my father. I can only surmise the gift of meat was kind treatment to those that had surrendered to the waves and were now drowned. My mother's new lover and provider was Bill Moxon. He came from the same surroundings as my father. Lillian and Bill had known each other since their teens and shared a long mutual fancy for each other. He was now a cowman at a prosperous farm not far from St Andrew's Villas. He was a tall, thin man in his early forties. Moxon was one hundred and eighty degrees different from Albert, who had grown stunted and squat with age, infirmity, and poverty. Bill was confident but not overbearing. He took up residence in the house and my mother's bedroom with an ease suggesting their romance had been a long-standing affair. Lillian had also inferred to him that he was Matt's father.

For Christmas 1930, my mother ensured my sister and I received some yuletide treats to compensate us for our father's familial demotion. She put us on the list for the diocese festive charity. It was for the very poor and it was arranged by the St. Vincent De Paul Society. On Christmas morning, my father found enough money to buy my sister and me some penny candy. Lillian gave us a toy each, which she had received from the church. Bill hovered in the background and wished us good tidings. Then Mary and I dressed for our journey to hear mass and receive the church's bounty. The priests and nuns told us it was important to give thanks for the birth of baby Jesus and the eternal life he granted us in the hereafter. Our parish was very insistent on hammering into their charity cases that Christ was our savior. Every time you received food from the church or alms from the church, "Say a wee prayer in thanks to Jesus for his kindness and love to you." I was told he protected Christian children all over the world, and was especially watchful on his birthday. On this Christmas Day, I gave thanks that the sermon would be brief and the hymns at least joyful.

Following mass, we made our way to the meal for indigent children. The feast for Bradford's poor was held in an open type gymnasium. There were long bench tables where we sat and ate our Christmas goose and pudding. We were told to pray, and we, the poor, the destitute, the unloved and unlucky, gave thanks again to the ever-watchful Jesus. Silently, I prayed that the nuns were in a forgiving mood this day and that my ear would not be pulled or my backside bruised by their love for discipline in the name of the Lord. After the meal, a Father

Christmas appeared, with a tubercular cough, and presented to each child an orange, and a pair of socks.

At home, I found my father upstairs in the attic.

"Happy Christmas, lad, sorry there weren't much for thee and thy sister. Next year, hey son, next year…"

Downstairs, my mother and Bill drank festive beer until the approach of Boxing Day. On New Year's Eve, Mary and I went mumming. We earned some cash for treats and handed back a few shillings to our mother and father. I asked my sister if our dad would stay with us up in the attic and if the new man, Bill, would be our new dad.

Mary told me, "Never you mind about that. It's grown up doings. Harry, you and me," she added with conviction, "will look out for each other. I won't let you fall out of my hands. The only thing that matters is us two." She stared straight into my eyes as she continued. "Bugger the lot. Remember, Dad is our dad and nobody can take him away from us. Even if he goes away, he will be our dad always."

I felt happy; I could trust one person not to leave me, not to scold me. There was always one person to make sure that I was washed and loved and it was Mary.

During the first week of the New Year, my father quietly moved out of our house and out of our lives. Albert took up residence across the street and only took with him the grand portrait of his long-dead father. Before I reached my eighth birthday, I stopped speaking about my father. I was shamed by him, I was ashamed of myself, and I was ashamed of my mother, who survived the depression by following the sound of small coins falling from another man's pocket. I did not see my dad for a long while. But I knew he was across the street. I knew he was near and keeping a furtive eye on my sister and me. When I went to school or played marbles in the street, I sensed him watching over me.

When my father slipped out into the night and out of my life, his Uncle Larratt toasted another prosperous New Year for the pub and his family; who were well fed and warm living in comfort at the New Inn. The pub withstood and prospered during the dark economic times because poor or rich, funeral or wedding; everybody needed a drink.

After spending fifteen years at Broadmoor Prison for the criminally insane, Maggie Spooner died at forty-five. Behind bars, Maggie spent decades tearing oakum as therapy and penance for her mental illness. The post mortem report stated her death was from natural causes. If she had hung herself, the verdict would have been the same: natural causes. Her life was effectively over when the voices overcame her.; when the imbalances in her brain's chemicals commanded her to sacrifice her newborn like Abraham before God.

Mr. Brown and his wife, who preferred to drink alone, departed the rooming house soon after my father. They moved to an even cheaper part of town; where they found more amenable accommodation for the gentile detritus of Bradford. Now for me, there were no more friendly chats by the fire with Mr. Brown while he inhaled deeply on his Kensington filter tip cigarettes. The chair where my father used to sit by the fire was now occupied by Bill Moxon. To me, this shift in personnel did not seem right. But I was too young to protest except through escaping into fantasy and dreams. When I was older, I told myself; I would be independent from fickle families.

My sense of detachment and apartness from the rest of the world was only enhanced by my father's disappearance and my mother's new love interest. I trusted no one but my sister, and reluctantly and with reservations, my mother. Lillian still held our family together with whatever resources she had or could obtain, but it was hard for me, as a child, to comprehend or forgive her actions that allowed my father to be set adrift from us. My father became to me like Marian; a vision without real form. My dad was a ghost who visited my night dreams and left a shadow upon my soul.

Now Bill Moxon was the central male figure in my childhood. Bill was able to provide us with milk and meat from his job as a cowhand, which was a considerable improvement to living off drippings and hope. One weekend, he asked me if I would like to go to the country and see his cows. I gladly accepted. Secretly, I was thrilled that an adult had taken enough notice of me to want my company. Moxon and I got to the farm by taking a bus as it was on the outskirts of Bradford. The dairy farm was a modernized production unit with automatic milk machines for the cows and a giant pasteurization vat. Bill carefully explained the intricacies of this modern farm to my eight-year-old ears. For my troubles, Bill gave me a fresh bottle of milk, laden with butter fat. The top of the milk was as sweet as candy. When we left the farm, he tousled my hair and said, "Good lad," in the manner he would to a terrier.

Eventually, Bill was promoted to pig handler. In the mornings, Moxon travelled across Bradford with a horse-drawn cart. He collected slops from the restaurants and pubs for the pigs to dine on. On occasion, he brought Mary and me a large formless mass of discarded toffee from the Mackintosh candy factory. It had originally been intended for the pigs, but Bill thought it better suited children. With a hammer and chisel, Mary and I chipped away at the mound of toffee until our hard work transformed the mass, into shrouds of thick brown treacle. We sucked the sweetness from it as a carnivore licks the marrow from a bone.

Not only was Bill in charge of feeding the pigs, he was also responsible for cleaning the sties of their shit. Every day, he shoveled, washed, and scraped away the effluence of four hundred well-fed pigs. After his shift, he rode the bus home stinking of shit while the other passengers gave him a wide berth. When he returned home, his stench enveloped every room as if we lived right beside the pig tip.

One day, Bill needed me to give him a hand at the pig farm and he bribed me with the promise of Macintosh toffee waiting for me at the farm. When we arrived, Bill furtively explained he had come to kill a pig. I was required to assist him. I was terror-stricken. Blood-curling images danced in my head about having to slay a giant pig. Bill calmed me down. He told me where I could find the toffee. Later, I learned it was intended for the pig's dessert. So I enjoyed a condemned animal's last treat. By mid-morning, stuffed with treacle, Bill found me and said, "Come on, Harry; wait in shed over there while I get the pig for killing."

The shed had a tin roof, cement sides, and a stone floor. Across the back of the shed were two large steel rails. There was a hook with a rope attached to it. The hook rode the rails by means of a metal wheel attached to it. On the floor, there was a giant sledge hammer, which appeared to be the same height as me.

Suddenly, Moxon approached me with the largest pig I had ever seen. The hog was unhappily in tow behind him. The pig struggled against his rope lead. Bill dragged the reluctant pig forward towards the shed. Its wails grew louder, more shrill and frightened as it got closer to me. In one hand, Bill held the pig's lead and in the other, he carried a tightly knotted noose. "Right, Harry," he said, "I'm going to put this noose against pig's mouth on top of teeth. Come quick, I need you to hold rope as tight as you got. Piggy's head has got to be high to the sky. Don't let go of im, lad, because I am going to clout im from behind with hammer."

The pig struggled with every turn to break free. I was terrified that the pig would escape and attack me for threatening his life. I stammered, "I can't do it, Bill... he's too strong."

"Better lad or you be for dinner tonight."

I grabbed the short rope; the pig's teeth were yellow and threatening. The rope held his mouth open while its giant tongue slapped back and forth in its giant jaws. Its breath was full of Mackintosh toffee sweet. The pig cried out in fury and fear. Its back end dropped dollops of shit.

"Higher, lad, higher," Bill instructed.

I felt I could not hold on for much longer. Finally, Bill smashed the back of the pig's head with the sledgehammer, with an executioner's strength. The pig collapsed. The rope went loose. Bill attacked the pig's neck with a strong, long blade and slit its throat. Blood exploded from the jugular. I felt sick to my stomach and rushed away to retch. Bill struggled to bring the pig's carcass to the shed.

He called out to me, "Job's not done yet, boy."

Moxon hoisted the pig up onto the rail trolley to let the blood run clean of the carcass. "Good work, lad," he told me. "There be plenty of crackle for you on Sunday's roast… good work, lad…"

My family lived at St. Andrew's Villas for more than a year, which for my family was a record of permanence, rarely to be achieved again. It was the result of Bill Moxon sharing the household expenses and the rent, along with my father; who gladly gave his meager shillings to Lillian in the hope his children were being looked after. Everything fell into a steady pace. Gradually, it was explained to anyone who dared to inquire about my mother's living arrangements that Bill was our mother's new husband. My father, if anybody cared to ask, was long dead. Both Mary and I would get enough to eat as long as Bill remained the breadwinner. We accepted Bill because hunger was left outside for a while. For extra money, my sister and I collected beer and soda pop bottles and spent our Sunday afternoons at the movies with the proceeds. Mary and I, once again, could afford to lose ourselves on screen excursions to pirate islands, gangster's hideouts, or pratfalls and laughter.

Equally, my mother's life with Bill was spent in diversion. They drank on the weekends until drunk and argumentative. In slurred voices, I heard them bang into the doors and landings. Mary and I heard them cursing the house, cursing each other, damning themselves. Over time, my mother and Bill passed out. The next morning, they greeted each other sullen, hung-over, and more resentful than the night before.

Chapter Five

Sowerby Bridge

One Friday evening, Bill returned from the pub and announced he had quit his job. "There be no more shoveling another's man's pig shit and muck, for me. Down Sowerby Bridge way; they built a sparkling new rendering plant. Everything bloody modern and they promise good wages."

Lillian looked concerned because Sowerby Bridge was near Halifax and miles from where we lived in Bradford. She grew more anxious when Bill retorted that he would write when he was sorted. Lillian thought Bill had either found another woman or had grown tired of living with her and her menagerie of children. My mother was aware that Bill was no more likely to write to her than he was to purchase a pair of false teeth; which he was in desperate need of as he had lost most of his teeth from decay and brawling. That weekend at the pub, my mother held her tongue to ensure that Bill's last memory of Bradford was pleasant. My mother understood that without Bill, our future was very precarious. She had only one aim now and that was to follow him to Sowerby Bridge and make him feel responsible for us or hunger would quickly return to our household.

On Monday, Bill left and my mother made began preparations to follow him. Mary and I were taken out of school on the excuse there was a near and dear relation on death's door. My brother Matt was deposited with our aunt Alice's because he was far too young to assist in our nomadic search for Bill Moxon. Mary and I were told if the other tenants asked where we were going, we were off to see our ill grandfather.

"Why go so far, Mam; he's just across the street according to you," my sister declared.

"Shut it," Lillian told Mary.

Just as we boarded a bus to Huddersfield, Mary declaimed: "here we go again, the Smith merry-go-round."

Upon our arrival in Huddersfield, Lillian deposited us in a dilapidated and seedy rooming house. A miniscule kitchen was shared by all of the lodgers. The landlady did not question why a nine and thirteen-year-old were left in the care of the forsaken; she just took the rent in advance. Our mother left us with two loaves of bread and some jam. Lillian told us to make do.

"Don't scarf it all at once; I might be gone a couple of days. Mind yourselves," she warned. "Be good. Don't get under anyone's feet." She left us each with a determined hug.

Our room had one bed with a lumpy mattress. It was right beside the kitchen, which worked to our good fortune. From our insignificant and dark bedroom, we smelt a simmering stew. A resident was preparing their dinner. We heard her slip out for a cigarette. Abandoned on the stove was a wonderful thick, meaty broth, its aroma beguiling us. It was only natural that my sister and I snuck into the kitchen. We took with us our bread and soaked pieces of the thick spongy loaf into the pot of hot and succulent meat, potatoes, and veg. My sister and I ate our bread dipped in the stew and felt content. It was more like a holiday than a search party for our absent meal-ticket.

Mary and I went back to our cramped room, our stomachs full and our spirits content. Our brief adventure had been joyful so far, absent of parents and adults. However, when my sister and I slipped between the covers and turned out the lights, we were left like roped and baited prey for bed bugs. The rooming house was rife with the noxious, blood-devouring insects. They burrowed underneath our skin. The bugs sucked our blood with as much relish as we had stolen another woman's meal. Itching and dejected, we spent the night squashing them with our bare fingers and our shoes.

The following morning, Lillian returned to collect us and told us the news that her hunt for Bill Moxon was successful. She located him at Stand Evens meat processing plant. The plant manager believing that Lillian was Bill's wife allowed her to wait for Bill at the foot of the plant's entrance. Just after the shift whistle blew, my mother pounced on Moxon and used all her feminine persuasion to charm Bill. Lillian dropped vague hints about Matt's paternity. She said that we were all a family and he must, as head of the household, protect her and her children. She would be loyal to him and if necessary would follow him to the ends of Yorkshire, if not the Earth to be with her man. My mother said there was to be no more talk of her former life with Albert, he was history and Bill was her present and her future.

As for Albert, my father he was left alone in his tiny room across the street from us at St. Andrew's Villas. Albert's consolation for losing his family: he retained his eight-volume history of the world. This compendium of history and natural events, however, had no illustrations or chapters on great depressions, hungry workers, and men deemed too old for work. It did not have a page index to reference 'men thrown onto the slag heap of life.

Bill accepted Lillian's pleas to return and resumed his role as breadwinner in our lives, out of guilt and a genuine affection for my mother. From now on, if we wanted to eat, we had to follow Bill Moxon's orbit. Bill instructed my mother to find a suitable home near the rendering plant for us to live in.

Lillian's elation at saving her station in life and ours as well was short lived. When our mother returned to collect us, she noticed the deep bite marks from the bed bugs on our arms and faces.

"Bed bugs, vermin, and shite don't ride for free," she declared. Lillian commanded, "Leev everthin, but what thee are wearin."

She then swept our hair and clothes clean of any contagion. We would not return back to Bradford with bugs and vermin, confirming our lowly state to others.

We returned to St Andrew's Villas, dawdling behind our mother. She claimed to the other tenants, "Our granddad is poorly. It's best we move closer to him as he needs our luv and help."

The following morning, Lillian left for Sowerby Bridge to secure lodgings. The next day, she returned home and announced we now had a new home. Unfortunately, it turned out to be an old, broken down house attached to an outer building of a farm. It was convenient for Bill to get to work, but for us it was torture. It was situated up a steep mountainous incline; it was like scaling the heights of Mount Kilimanjaro.

Within a day, Lillian arranged a beat up old truck to collect our belongings. The lorry carried them to our new rustic and poor environs on the outskirts of Halifax. While the truck was being loaded, Mother lectured both my sister and I not to be in the way. We stood on the street abject. We saw my father concealed behind sheer curtains in his dank room across the street. Mary and I looked away, frightened. We were both embarrassed that he was not stronger to protect himself or us.

Whatever questions I might have asked my mother about our new home were quickly answered upon our arrival in the nether reaches of Halifax. The town, since the middle ages, was a crossing point between the rivers Calder and Ryborn; in the industrial revolution, wool merchants erected grimy, squalid weaving mills. The effluence from the factories spilled out, poisoning and choking the water way.

We marched through the High Street, which contained a series of shops and professional trade windows. Large matronly women with net mesh bags and loud voices blocked the street. They made note of us, the new arrivals in this small town; they looked unimpressed. I looked back at them uninterested in their condemning glares and complained bitterly to my mother for having to hold onto my uncooperative baby brother Matt.

Our Mother encouraged us to move forward by saying our destination was not much further. We were now at the end of a brick lane way which meandered behind tenement housing for the poor and unskilled workers of this settlement. As the lane way opened up, we discovered an enormous, forbidding hill. My sister and I paused and rested on top of our suitcases. Panting, we looked at each other and demanded to know if our mother was serious. She surely did not expect us to climb up that hill with Matt in my arms. Was she joking? Did she really want us to live on top of a mountain peak? My mother told us both to be quiet.

"Never mind the hill. At top is a house, all to ourselves. There be no other tenants. There be only we and Bill. Our Bill be bringing us fresh meat every day for our tea."

We struggled up the hill beside our mother; Matt held in my arms, while Mary dragged our stray luggage along. It was an ordeal of curses, out of breath pleading, and sheer condemnation to our mother. Surprisingly, Lillian took it all with good humour. She knew that if we were not satisfied with our new home, Bill would be. The distance to the rendering plant was only minutes by foot. Atop the hill was a cross-road where we turned right and proceeded to a farm building. It was connected to a small, stone house by means of a ginnel, similar to my grandparents 'house on Beaumont Street. Our new home, however, did not even contain the dilapidated charm of Beaumont Street. It was a cold, miserable dump.

The entrance to the building had no door and looked as if it had been constructed in the medieval era for washing. The cement floor through time and erosion was now a broken mess of debris and gravel. I learned later that a previous occupant had hung himself in this vestibule. His suicide, no doubt, was from the dread at living in such a squalid location. Every time I came home, past dark, the thought of the dead corpse hanging off the beam sent shivers up my spine. The door to the living area was made from old and thick wood. My mother turned over the lock with a long key, probably manufactured in the 18th century. The tumblers sounded as if it was a prison door being swung open, only to be shut again.

It was dark inside the farmhouse that was only slightly alleviated by a small window in the scullery. In this house, there was a feeling of decay and damp like a cave. A long, narrow stone stair, covered in cobwebs, led upwards to our bedrooms. The rooms were insignificant, as if the builder had included them as an afterthought when told workers needed to sleep. They contained bald, slanting, stone walls that were off center, as the house's foundations had shifted for a century or more in the clay soil around it. Our view from the narrow window upstairs was barren fields and a few craggy trees bent against a grey sky, dripping down cold, wet rain. Below me, I saw scrawny chickens pecking and scratching in low scrub surrounding the farmhouse. The truck arrived several hours after us. The driver was irate as my mother had misled him about the actual distance to our new abode. The driver fumed about taking an ancient truck up a steep gradient and he demanded more money. My mother told him to stop his complaining because he would take what he got and not a penny more. The three of us unpacked our belongings and squared away the house as best we could. Thankfully, Lillian had the foresight to have stolen a bag of coal from our last house, and we were treated to a warm fire to accompany our dinner of cold sandwiches and hot black tea.

For the present, this was the best my mother could do to keep us alive. We survived, but our mother wasn't permitted to salvage even a small sliver of dignity for herself in the process. It was a small price to pay considering the alternative was life on the street. Our new home was far from an oasis, in either natural abundance or beauty. It was a place to hide. It was an exile's location, far from the world and hope. We would remain there until society mended itself or accepted us back in civilization.

We had abandoned our natural father to eat. We had fled to a rundown farmhouse. We had accepted Bill Moxon as our bread winner. What else could have been done? Lillian had no skills to offer the working world. So all she offered her children was a new a man who might keep us under a roof. She tendered the offer with the sad pretence we were a family. Yet outside our home there were worse consequences. There was greater hunger outside our doors, but not by far. Sometimes, my sister Mary stole herself away from home to visit Albert. Mary told me that he had less than us. He could barely afford tea or a bun to eat. Mary said the council helped him out a little.

My father was means-tested by the government and they judged him adequately poor to receive a meager ration from the state. It was the manner in which they treated him which was so sad and appalling. One day, government inspectors came to his lone room and measured his worth. They calculated Albert's value by his clothing, his father's portrait, and his paltry pension. They humiliated him as they had humiliated the nameless faces all across the country. It was necessary, said the ciphers in Whitehall. There was no other way to assess who was truly destitute, who was truly a shirker, unless the test was so horrific that only those starving would permit it. The assessment results could determine if you lived or died from hunger, cold, or exhaustion. Evidently, my father passed the test with colours and received his 'O' level in poverty. What my father received from the government was enough to keep him alive. Labour's first Prime Minister, Ramsey Macdonald, saw to it that his electorate, the disenfranchised, would be the one's punished for the great depression. Britain's poor paid for the outstanding debts of the First World War.

I turned away from Mary's dire pronouncements on our father. I looked at my own sad life and pitied us. I wondered if there was any escape from this sentence of servitude and penance. It appeared that my sister and I were paying for sins we neither committed nor created.

I was promptly enrolled in the village school. At first, I was thankful it was not a religious institution, but it was a mistaken impression. The school may have been free of God, but it was still bountiful in secular, corporal punishment. On my first day, I realized that the majority of teachers enacted physical violence as a means to punish the weakest around them. It somehow balanced out their lost illusions and spoiled lives.

Being a small village school, my teacher was compelled to teach three different grades at once. He did it with equal disdain for anyone who disturbed his hectoring and brow-beating. He was a nameless, formless, middle-aged man with flakes of dandruff running down his jacket. His broad Yorkshire accent rolled out the tedium of existence with every remonstrance to his pupils. His teaching method was to harangue. He showed his loathing for all children who could not grasp what he perceived as profundity with sarcasm. It was a hard, lonely term for me. I dreaded each morning as if it were my last on Earth.

Even with Bill's full-time employment, we were short of money again. My mother was also reluctant to ask Bill for the full upkeep to provide for us. She feared Bill would soon find enforced fatherhood a burden. My mother advised me, "Time to find another job, lad, the fairies don't bring milk at night for ya."

It was apparent to Mary and me that Bill's outward kindness masked a fair amount of bitterness. He did not enjoy being saddled with a family not of his own design.

My past experience as a seven-year-old delivery boy helped me secure a similar job at Jubb's Grocers. They were a fairly large chain of food stores and had been visible in Yorkshire trade since the 1850s. The Sowerby Bridge outlet was managed by a fearful man. The manager feared making a mistake and losing his job in a climate of unemployment and economic destruction. He warily measured me up. He stated his regular boy was moving on to other pastures; therefore, I could start on a trial basis. It would be a test to see if I could handle the responsibility of this manual job. Every day after school, I was required to arrive promptly at 5 p.m. to stock shelves and scrub the floors. I was expected to do a half-day on Saturday. I was paid five bob a week for my services.

The manager threateningly told me, "Master Smith, you are on probation. Our store believes in high standards. Any transgression from my instructions and you shall be shown the door. If you cheat me in anyway, you will have no reference and no prospects in life."

I was proud to be taken on as stock boy even if the manager had been supercilious and mildly pompous to me. He offered me work and showed a trust and interest in me as few others had to that date. My teachers certainly showed no interest in me except as an object of derision or a target for their paddle. My father's interests in me waned as he became consumed by his own economic, emotional and physical destruction. By the time he left us, or we left him, Albert watched from the side lines and hoped all would turn out well for me and my sister as he no longer had any power over our fates. Bill's interest in me was measured by the fact that I was not his son. He fed me because he enjoyed my mother's bed and company. As for my mother Lillian, her interest in me was cold and brutal like a bear toughening up her cub to survive the forest. It was only Mary who during our lonely trek through poverty loved me totally, without reservation or selfishness.

After I accepted Jubb's offer of employment, I trudged up the long elevated road to our grey farmhouse home. I proudly announced to my mother that I had a job again and could assist in providing food and other necessities. Lillian, ever pragmatic, asked what I was to be paid. Without hesitation, I lied, "Four shillings per week," I exclaimed.

My mother was pleased by the amount and did not question me further. That evening, I told Mary that I made more per week:

"Mary, I've got a shilling spare per week for us to share. We can spend it on whatever we like and Mam and Bill know naught." My sister beamed at my ingenuity and our mutual riches.

Our landlord was a farmer who tilled the surrounding land and he lived just up the road from us. His farmhouse was even more dilapidated than ours. When Lillian had the money, she had Mary and I buy our milk and eggs from him. It seemed every time, I knocked on his door, there was a long silence until eventually the door creaked and broke open a fraction. On the other side was the staring eyeball of the farmer's wife or his half-wit daughter who would demand. "What ya want?"

"Milk, mam," I boldly proclaimed. The door slammed shut. I heard the sound from the lock bolts closing again. Minutes passed and the door opened just enough for me to thrust the money into the hand of the farmer's wife's. A bottle of milk was forced through the tiny opening and into my hand.

At first I found the farmer a fearsome man because he had a long shaggy, white beard that made him look like a biblical patriarch. But one day, I saw him out in his fields and when he noticed Mary and me, he called us over and gave us permission to play on the haystacks in his barn. It was the best carefree diversion my sister and I experienced during our long and lonely days imprisoned in that desolate community.

It was now 1932 and after many months in the desolate farmhouse, Lillian began to feel the isolation. She was nearing forty. The ceaseless days spent in search of food and money ground her down, both emotionally and physically. She lost her good looks. My mother took to drinking; either to create a false sense of hope or to keep Bill distracted down at the pub. She had to hold a vigilant eye on Bill, or else he would stray into another woman's affections. As time went on, they both began to drink themselves unconscious. Whatever pride Lillian had was stripped away and she ignored her looks and grooming. She was constantly being fished out of the pub drunk and rambling. One time, my sister and I dragged her home from a night of boozing at the pub. Her voice was hoarse from cigarette smoke and the coarse shanties she sung. She was barely able to get up the hill to the farmhouse. My mother stumbled on the ground laughing and cackling like a mad woman. Mary and I grunted with exertion from lifting Mam horizontal and we progressed upwards with her dead weight.

We were almost home when I heard my sister call out, "You dirty bitch."

Lillian was in the middle of the road, her legs akimbo. She took a piss wantonly, without remorse as if she were a dog on the street. My sister and I were mortified and shrunk in disgust. I was revolted that this woman was my mother. Quietly, we brought her home and put her roughly to bed.

Hours later, we heard Bill Moxon roll in like a bad storm. He swore, banged doors, and yelled at unknown ghosts from his past. The sound of the wind and rain whipped across the barren moors as Mary and I made a pact by candlelight inside our tiny room. We pledged, one day, we would run away from this sad madness. We would live in houses filled with food and laughter. There would be no self-pitying drunks in our adult life.

The Bill and Lillian show was now a regular weekend occurrence where both of them consumed liquor in gin madness. Rat arsed, from Friday tea time to Sunday bedtime they verbally vomited forth their distrust and paranoia about each other. Bill's general lament was to accuse my mother of entrapping him with bastard children.

"You caught me, Lil, with lies, a mountain of lies, nothing but rubbish from yer gob. What a useless cunt, you are. You and your useless children are naught but trouble fer me"

Plates were smashed. Glasses tossed and drawers emptied of their contents. In the morning, Mary and I surveyed a kitchen of broken glass, up-turned chairs, and shattered dreams and hopes. The floor resembled a beach after a tempest had tossed a ship and broken its spine, spilling its contents into the tide to wash up on shore.

Within time, Bill and Lillian destroyed or damaged every cup, saucer, and glass in their mutual war of attrition. We were left to drink out of jam jars as we had no money to replace the broken crockery. Bill and Lillian were in a death grip, not strong enough to break free of each other or strong enough to kill each other. They were only capable of hurting and maiming the other.

Their weekend ordeals were a nauseating spectacle. Mary and I were forced to listen to their endless tirades that exhausted them into a dreamless sleep. We were consumed with fright. We knew our little lives were hostage to their regrets, their drunkenness, and their violence to themselves. For us children, it was like being forever in a trench, suffering heavy bombardment from enemy guns. Silence moved to shrill voices, tears to accusations, love to vitriol and contempt. We were like specters, loitering upstairs in our rooms. We tended to our little brother; whose first years were nurtured by two children. Lillian was not a mother to Matt because her moorings had slipped and she sunk into a sea of alcoholism.

After weeks of storming and fuming, it reached a fever pitch and the yelling and the threats crossed over the unmarked border to violence and assault. It was another miserable night. We heard Bill and Lillian downstairs in the kitchen, arguing over Bill's philandering eye. They had spent their evening pouring their money, our money, away at some narrow, smoky pub in Sowerby Bridge. Their voices downstairs grew in crescendo, as reason was lost and affection killed by too much drink and too much petty resentment. Bill thrashed my mother.

We heard the screams and we heard the beating; we heard my mother pleading for him to stop. Mary and I fell over ourselves to get downstairs and protect our mother from Bill. Lillian may have evolved into a drunk; who for a time had abandoned us emotionally, but at that moment, she was on the floor being beaten and she was our mother who deserved protection.

Mary and I pounced onto Bill Moxon's back, while he kicked my mother as she lay on the ground in the corner of the kitchen. Our young fists beat his back. We pulled his hair and bit his shoulder, but Bill was like a giant animal stung by a wasp. He threw his shoulders to and fro trying to toss us from him. Bill moaned and threatened us to get off him or face a beating ourselves. He punched us, but we did not let go. We held roughly and firmly onto his back and shoulders. We were not going to let go until he released Lillian. Eventually, Bill's writhing stopped and as if woken from a night terror, his breathing calmed and his anger simmered off his body, like beads of water evaporating off a skillet. Moments later, Lillian was up and on her feet. She was unsteady, a little crouched, and defensive. Her eyes were blackened and blood dripped from her lips.

In a whisper, she said, "That's enough, Bill. Mary, Harry, get off him. Stop this now."

I was crying. Mary was crying. We were broken vessels; we were like the bits of crockery shattered and unrecognizable on the floor. I cried out for my dad and knew he was not ever going to be with us again; he was never coming back, but I still cried out for him. Mary cried out in fear, in anger, and loss. She wept loudly; remembering a better time, before the famine, before the economy collapsed, and our father was sacrificed. Mary shook and could not be comforted. Like two prized fighters in their corners, my mother and Bill panted, waiting for the bell to send them back into their skirmish. The night ended in the ejaculate of violence with lost mothers, lost fathers, and forsaken children. For a long time, everyone remained on the dirty, stone floor like discarded gun casings.

In the morning, after the tempest of ale, anger, and poverty, Bill met his nightly deed of aggression, unshaven and hung-over. He acted contrite and sheepish. He was ashamed of the violence the night before and left early. Moxon hoped he could clean away the stain of his violence with more butchering at the rendering plant. Lillian was quiet and cold in her guilt. She served up a breakfast of thick and lumpy oatmeal for us.

Bill and Lillian's drinking stretched and meandered from one weekend to the next. My sister and I fended for ourselves and kept a watchful eye on our younger brother Matt. Mary and I grew despondent at our new responsibility. We terrified Matthew in sleep with threats that the boogey man was under his bed. We told him if he did not close his eyes, we would release the fearful phantom on him. The sad part was Mary and I knew there was a boogey man lurking inside this desolate farmhouse; it was alcohol combined with despair. As long as beer was plentiful and money short, the fighting between Bill and Lillian continued. Like sentinels, Mary and I waited in our beds for our mother and Bill's physical battles. We knew as the light grew less and as the hours crept away into the darkness, they would come home pissed and violent. We knew Bill would throw punches at our mam. We knew we would rush downstairs and join the melee hoping to separate the two. Our only luck was that sometimes before Bill released all his fury and rage; his shoulder dislocated. It left him writhing in pain, unable to strike my mother or throw wild punches at us.

After a time, Bill lost his job at the meat packing plant. We were on the move again. We were like a herd of animals that only traveled in the dead of night, to avoid the carnivorous landlord. Leaving the bleak farmhouse, crucified on the top of the moor was a relief for me and Mary. We deluded ourselves into thinking that wherever we now travelled, it would be better than where we had last settled.

6

King Cross

We ended up in King Cross, which was a suburb of Halifax. The city was a smoldering cauldron of mills and factories. There was endless steam and smoke vomiting into the sky, from the industry churning out carpets, candy, and cloth. Somehow, Bill Moxon convinced a landlord to let him a small store. Bill opened up an undersized butcher's shop. Lillian found us a house just off of King Cross Road. It was a row house built on a steep slope. It was a relief to be back in a larger community with streets and lane ways. It was a municipality one could disappear in for hours.

I must have been through five different schools by the age of eleven. Bolton Brow was my last. The primary school was built with an aura of Victorian dourness. Every school I attended previously, I was either brutally hazed or assaulted by irate nuns and priests. This was not the case at Bolton Brow and from my first day there, I had a reputation as a tough guy. I can only surmise it was my work house looks, or maybe my hard image was caused by gossip about my mother and her brood of children from different fathers. At Bolton Brow, I finally began to take a keen interest in learning. I found the teachers there were willing to instruct and guide young minds.

Mr. Stokes was my history teacher. I enjoyed his early morning lectures. They were filled with tales of Roman Britain or the crusades. The other students were less enthusiastic. Stokes was too timid to discipline. At times, the students' din would overpower his tales of long ago Britain with errant knights and mighty battles against the French. I lost my patience with the other students.

I clamoured, "Shut your gobs. Let the man talk."

The ruckus ceased and order was returned to the classroom; my reputation as hellion intact. As I found a new appreciation for school, Bill's butcher business was rapidly failing.

The store front was too small. The meat selection was too sparse, and the hygiene nonexistent. The customer base dwindled down to a few pensioners who could afford no more than offal. Our meals at home were rationed and there was little money for extras. Hunger returned as an unwelcome lodger in our lives. The new business, the lack of money, and debt collectors looming at every corner was not improving Bill and Lillian's relationship. Their brawling continued and their drinking persisted. Our lives continued to wither as our money situation devolved.

Now, we were no better off than when our father was with us. Once again, my sister and I were in need of hand-outs to sustain our meager rations. My clothes were worn and hung loosely from my skinny, undernourished body. As fall turned to winter, my shoes wasted away. I had preserved my shoes through two years of midnight dashes and they were now moribund. The soles had rotted through. I stuffed old newspaper and cardboard in them to keep the snow and sleet from touching my feet. In the end, the shoes were no better than socks. I could not go to school anymore when the weather was snowy, slushy, and wet. I felt dejected and ashamed and I was angry. I was brassed off that my life, such as it was, could be ruined because my family was too poor to put shoes on my feet. I was resentful that I could not get an education or be free of this drudgery because we could not afford enough food or decent boots.

As the weather improved, I returned to school. I hoped no one might see the empty bottoms of my shoes and my torn socks. I slunk into the back of my math class, knowing I had fallen behind again. I feared a thrashing or the jeers and jibes of the other children at their desks.

Mr. Dawson, our math instructor, was known to the students as "Froggy" because he resembled a giant toad, sitting on a leaf at the side of a river. He called out my name.

"Here, sir."

"You are to remain until the other children have left the classroom," Dawson intoned with slow deliberation.

For the hour, I sat in silent dread. I imagined the lecture I would receive; the moral condemnation I would get for once again being a truant. After the other students left, Dawson called me up to the front of the class. He sat behind a thick wooden desk. Distracted, he flipped through homework papers. I quivered in silence.

"Now," he started.

Pausing, he reached into his upper waist coat pocket. He produced a silver snuff box. Dawson opened the box. He tapped snuff onto his finger. He deeply inhaled the ground tobacco into his nose. There was a sneeze, from him.

"Why were you absent from school yesterday?"

"Not my fault, sir, my shoes," I blurted out.

I lifted my foot upwards so that he could see the gaping holes plugged haphazardly with leaking newspaper and soggy cardboard.

"Ah," replied Mr. Dawson. "That is a dilemma. Go home," he told me. "Complete today's assignment and see me again after class tomorrow. Now go straight home, boy, and no dawdling."

That night, as best as I could, I did my math assignment. The following morning, I trod alone to school. I hid in the back rows of Mr. Dawson's math class. At the end of lessons, I approached his desk as I had done the day before. Mr. Dawson took my homework assignment and placed it carefully on his desk. He pulled open the top left-hand drawer of his desk and took out a bag. Inside the paper bag was a pair of sturdy, brown shoes.

"Try them on, boy," he said, expressionless.

I slipped off my rotting shoes and slid into these new shoes. The fit was far from perfect. I would have to put newspaper into the toes, but they felt warm, strong, and nondescript. Wearing these shoes, I was no longer the poor boy who came to school as Huck Finn.

"They are fine," I told him. I was about to thank him.

"Not a word," Dawson replied.

He turned his head downwards to his desk and fumbled into his top pocket. Dawson pulled out his snuff box and repeated the ritual of inhaling the ground, white tobacco. I left with the new shoes wrapped around my warm feet. Outside the class room, I was able to walk with pride and confidence. I was free from the ridicule and the stares of others more fortunate; made cruel by their gluttony.

Bill Moxon's business quickly collapsed and he and Lillian began jousting daily about money; until one day Bill got up and left us. He abandoned Lillian, us, and the house. He just got up and left.

"Bugger off. I'm better off without thee and wee kids," he told my mother.

Lillian was now alone with three children and no source of income. My mother found respite from our inevitable destruction and ruin in drink and denial. Lillian's weekend and weekday forays into oblivion were stark reminders of our incessant and seemingly inexhaustible descent into poverty. In the evenings, Mary and I remained awake in dread, pondering what state our mother would be in on her return from the local. One night, she left in a stage set of theatrics, claiming, "Poppets, if there be no brass in my hands soon, it's the workhouse for thee. There's naught in the cupboard, there's naught left." Lillian left slamming the door.

Mary and I were left to scrounge for dinner for ourselves and little Matt. At eleven, we heard milk bottles rolling down the lane way. There was a dull sharp thud as if a bin man had tossed a sack of heavy rubbish on to the sidewalk. Mary and I rushed down the stairs. I reluctantly peeled the door open. There was Lillian, lying face down, dead and silently drunk. Grabbing one arm and Mary grabbing the other arm, we hauled our mother through the door. We were like fisherman on a trawler pulling in an enormous haul of near-dead fish. She did not stir as her body was dragged roughly across the front entrance into our house. Once safely inside, we closed the door. Both of us prayed that no neighbour had either seen her approach, witnessed her fall, or spied us transporting our mother into the house as drunk and lifeless as a street derelict. I found a blanket and dropped it onto my mother's intoxicated snoring and farting body and went to bed, shivering with shame and emotional exhaustion.

I cannot imagine what humiliation Lillian endured that night at the pub. She was trying to raise money for our rent and our food money. I do not know what desolation she endured that night. I do not know if other patrons laughed and sniggered at her wretchedness, at her knees scrapping rock-bottom. I do not know and am fortunate that I was never told what transpired that night. All I know was she failed in obtaining the much-needed money and that my mother felt the shame of that night, alone, for the rest of her life. Whatever deed done or promise made signed in gin would go to her grave unspoken. Mary and I would also hold secretly and shamefully the disgust of dragging our mother from the street gutter, drunk and lifeless.

The following morning, she informed us in a distant voice, "We're in shite. Without our Bill, there be no meat for tea, no milk, no pudding, no tea for tea. We are good and proper buggered. I've got enough brass to last a fortnight, maybe a month. Then, my ones, it's the poor 'ouse. We'll be vagrants. For us to survive, wee kids of mine, must be tough and work like grownups."

My mam said if Mary and I found work; we might keep this roof over our head. Lillian concluded in a monotone, "I'm with child. There's another nipper on the way."

Evidently, before Bill left us, he deposited a parting gift for my mother and gave her and us his own bastard. The child inside my mother was the saddest of creations. It was conceived amidst strewn and spent ale bottles, discarded remnants of fried bread and middle-aged desperation. I will never know if this pregnancy was deliberate to keep Bill within Lillian's orbit. Even if the conception was an accident, it caused unwanted suffering to the child and to the rest of us in this doomed household. At the news of his coming heir, Bill did not return. Most likely, he thought it was a ruse to keep him under our roof and under Lillian's grasping hands.

Lillian's revelation opened up new rivers of disgust and anger for me towards my mother. Were my sister and I to be in perpetuity taking care of Lillian's growing menagerie of spare children? We were children ourselves. It was depressing and disheartening enough to try to look after oneself. Now Mary and I were called upon to fend and protect not only ourselves, but an increasing brood of runts in the litter

Mary quickly found work at a local wool mill as a spinner. I located another outlet of Jubb's. It was on the High Street of King Cross. A sign was placed in their front window of the grocer requesting the need for a delivery boy. I went inside and inquired about the position. The manager asked if I could ride a bike and whether I had any issues with heavy lifting. I said confidently that I was good with both as my previous jobs had given me experience. He gave me the post of delivery boy. For a young boy, it was arduous service, bone-breaking servitude. I was tasked with loading and delivering baskets of groceries. The basket was mounted on top of a bike's front tire, which was two feet by three feet. The front tire was half the size of the back tire. This allowed for a larger basket to be attached to the front. The woven basket was laden with an enormous amount of groceries.

It added upward to thirty pounds to the bicycle's drag. My delivery route took me miles away from the store in King Cross. I biked to the suburbs, profitable farms, across the dales and through every hill and dip imaginable. My course took me as far away as Rishworth.

The contents of my basket consisted of flour, potatoes, meat, produce, jams, bread, milk, and a wide assortment of dried goods. I did my duties energetically and without complaint. Yet secretly, I was ashamed that I was compelled to work no better than a dog. It was because my family's fortunes by either caprice or poor judgment had left me enslaved to child labour. If I saw another kid walking or biking to a social event, while I was left to toil with weighty, cumbersome, food deliveries, it humiliated me. Young girls walked by me dressed for a birthday party and I felt their indifference to my enslavement. Their party shoes quickly tapped across the cobblestone streets to get away from me. Sometimes, they tossed me the same awkward and uncomfortable glance as one would to an animal, over laden with equipment and gear. They maneuvered ahead of me, distracted by thoughts of parties, dances, or happy homes. Their furtive eyes fell upon me for no more than a teasing moment, until they recognized that the human before them was not of their class, not of their milieu.

After some time, the manager at Jubb's trusted me enough to let me work behind the counter. It was feat of mental acrobatics as all items, sometimes up to twenty separate goods were priced out loud to the customer. The amount was calculated in one's head and hopefully the correct tally was blurted out to the customer at the end of their purchase.

The manger was a French man named Voicey, who still had a very strong accent. Voicey was more interested in chasing female store clerks than handling the mundane affairs of the business. I caught him, on numerous occasions, in the back store room. He would have a woman planted on sacks of sugar while his pants were draped down across his shoes. The carnal desires of Voicey allowed me to take on more and more responsibility. My manager willingly discarded his responsibility to me to pursue his true vocation; back room shagger. While he was in a state of undress in the backrooms; I was permitted to decorate the store's front window display. The store window arrangements were a source of pride for me as I was able to create some impressive and artistic displays. One even took second place in a local competition. However, Voicey took full credit for the display, even though he was busy romancing on the sugar sacks. I was still pleased that my unaccredited work was held in esteem.

Although only twelve, I took up smoking and bought Woodbine cigarettes, weekly, for two pennies a packet, which held five, filter-less smokes. At break time, I stood outside and lit the rough fags with Bryant matches. The match box displayed a pompous-looking Captain Webb. Webb had been the first man to dare to attempt to and succeed in crossing the English Channel. The matches spluttered to life and I soaked into my callow lungs the coarse tobacco. Standing with my cigarette in hand and a green feeling in my stomach, I believed I was quite the man.

Next door to Jubb's was a very high-end chocolate confectionary store. It had an enormous window display dripping with brightly coloured bon bons and chocolates created in all manner of shape and sizes. They were all hand-crafted and presented in rich, beautiful boxes. The store's clientele were affluent and ignorant of the want around and behind them. Elegant women, their fat children in tow, fashionably dressed wearing patent leather shoes, entered the confectionary shop. They left with boxes of chocolate; their calorie count exceeded the weekly intake of food for me or my sister.

Flush with sales and a reputation for excellence, the chocolate shop routinely discarded entire boxes of chocolate. If the first tray showed any hint of mold, they were dumped in a bin behind the store they shared with Jubb's. Out back, I discovered amidst the rubble and the refuse, perfect, exquisite boxes of chocolate. Bows and ribbons were still delicately wrapped across them. I tore off the chocolate box lid like I was a buccaneer. The chocolate and candy was blanched in white mold, destined but rejected as unfit for the moneyed class. Yet if I were to lift and discard the first tray, I would find underneath perfect chocolates, edible and sweet. I uncovered delicious chocolate motifs. The craftsmanship was pure artistry. The taste was exotic and delightfully edible. After my shift was finished, I scooped up the boxes and brought them home. I shared them with Mary, until we were sick on the riches of chocolate.

With the combined salary of Mary and me, we were able to keep ourselves, our mum, and little Matt in the house in King Cross. In the new year of 1935, pregnant and desperate, Lillian rushed to Bradford and took a room in the doss-house where Bill was staying. He had moved back to our old haunt of St Andrew's Villas. Lillian hoped to shame him into accepting his namesake but it did not succeed. It must have come as quite a surprise to Albert, my father to witness his wife's fecund return as he still lived in the same squat across the road from our old address.

My mother gave birth to her new child on January 13th 1935, in the room that she had once occupied with Albert. Moxon was initially unmoved by the child or Lillian's demands for recognition of his new son. It took Bill several months to agree to register the child in his name and accept it as coming from his blood and bone. It took well over a year for Bill and Lillian to fully reconcile.

When Lillian, returned child in hand but sans Bill, I felt revulsion at my new brother; who was another mouth to feed. He was not like Matt, who I saw as my brother, blameless for his condition. Irrationally, I saw Bill Jr. and my mother as conspirators in our family's unraveling. I was never able to accept the child as anything but an impediment and an intrusion into my life. He was a nuisance; especially since I was beginning to enjoy my experience at school. At Bolton Brow, I was enduring less embarrassment and humiliation then I had in other establishments. Also, I was absorbing a little more learning. I was not kindly possessed to having more responsibility thrust upon me, with this desperate child, in this desperate household.

Fortunately, I had found a means to escape the cries of a newborn and Lillian's half-drunken cries for assistance. It was my introduction to the library in King Cross. It was my university, my comfort, and my escape from the greyness and the emotional hunger in my life. On my off time, I trudged over to the library, which was housed in an antiquated, Victorian building near our house. I perused the shelves of books filled with strange titles. There was a multiplicity of authors from Aesop to Toynbee. I grabbed novels that caught my fancy and indulged my mind and my imagination. With Victor Hugo's *Les Miserable's*, I suffered another man's sorrow, his poverty, his love for his sister, and compared it to my own sorry state. In *The Count of Monte Cristo*, I witnessed injustice and the fight to right the wrongs of birth and legacy. I endured the pain of romantic, unattainable love through the writings of Dumas. In Ryder Haggard's *King Solomon's Mines*, I was pitched into a fast-paced world of thieves, daring archeologists, and intrigue. Or in *Montezuma's Daughter*, erotic desire was aroused for foreign beauties and distant shores. I lost myself in the world of the Lake poets and became entranced and enmeshed at the pure ethereal beauty of Wordsworth's sonnets. His odes to immortality and the refulgent daffodil left me dumb and awestruck at the immense beauty his words delivered to me directly.

For the price of a few pennies, I was transported across the world and sat at the feet of great men, great thinkers. I read and imagined tall adventures and I absorbed wondrous riches that the world held out for those that could break free of their provincial, dusty lives. I took my weekly selection of books from the library and selfishly kept them to myself. I read them underneath my bedcovers, long into the night with a dimming electric torch. I woke up bleary-eyed and hung-over from words. I was exhausted from a night of reading the deeds of swashbuckling adventurers. I was comforted by other books, whose words spoke to me and to my loneliness. They told me there was a world outside my house, there was a world outside my hunger, my mother, Bill, and outside my father, Albert. There was a world waiting and maybe there was love to be found.

Eventually, with some money I had saved from the watchful eyes of Lillian, I bought an old bike. I used it to escape into the country. On my only day off, Sunday, I biked to a quiet spot and underneath a tree, with a sandwich, a flask of tea, and an apple; I read or let my mind wander. I day-dreamed about my future and wondered what would happen to me when I grew older. My imaginings slipped into fantasy and I dreamed I was with the most beautiful woman and living a thrilling life, replete with houses and grand banquets. I dreamed of travel and faraway lands.

I dreamed so much of great voyages and grand discoveries that I set upon visiting the medieval city of York. I was determined to make a pilgrimage to the Minster. I was not wandering to the great church as a religious supplicant; I wanted to go as a servant to beauty in a disfigured world. It was decided; the following Sunday, I would ride my bike twenty miles to York and I would break free of the gravitational pull of King Cross, my mother, Bill, and all things blighted and superficial.

For an entire week in between school and work, I studied maps in the library. I plotted my course and the exact time I should leave. I purchased puncture kits for my worn tires, which I knew would face much abuse on the journey. I bought a new satchel to hold a rain coat, my thermos, and sandwiches. On the following Sunday, I left King Cross and felt like Charles Lindbergh departing New Jersey to fly solo across the Atlantic. I told no one of my plans for fear they would thwart my desires with impediments and arguments.

After a quick breakfast, I left my house at seven in the morning. Hurriedly, I wrote a note to Mary and told her I would be back late but not to worry. My route had been planned to avoid Bradford and

Leeds. I skirted up a secondary dual carriageway that had less traffic on it. Presumably, it was the quickest and easiest method to reach my destination: the Minster. Before long, I realized that my chosen path was through some of the hilliest and bent roads towards the ancient city. My tires punctured every half hour. I was quickly using up my puncture kits supplies of patching rubber.

I was caught in a rain shower. I took cover underneath an elderly, roadside tree and sipped tea from my thermos and took deep bites from my cheese bun. I began to doubt myself and cursed my arrogance at attempting this stupid venture. Turning back was not possible as I was past the half-way mark to York and it was now closing in on noon. The storms past and the skies returned to a greyish blue. I folded up my raincoat and stored it back in my bag. I mounted my rickety bike and pushed upwards to the city.

By two o'clock, I approached the great walled city. The spires of the Minster towered before me. They were a fulcrum in the landscape, the tallest structure in a hundred miles, since the 12th century. I pedaled my bike to York's main gate: Bothan Bar. It was also the ancient entrance to the roman fortress, built by the Roman 8th legion. I walked underneath its stone ceiling. I saw the slits cut into the masonry, where archers defended the city in the 1300s. I pushed my bike up through the shambles, where hawkers battled to grab my attention to their stalls filled with all types of meat, cheese, fruit, or sweets. They shouted, imploring me to come see their fresh produce, the best apples, and the most magnificent pies or jam. The shambles was like a Moroccan bizarre that took me on a long winding, incoherent ascent to the cathedral. Suddenly, out of the shadows of the vendors, the roadway parted and uncovered a wide expanse.

Finally, the second largest medieval cathedral in northern Europe was exposed to me. It stood like a colossus, powerful and silent as the sphinx. The sun draped down and swept around its peak and fell across the stained glass windows. To my left was part of the old Roman road constructed by legionnaires of Caesar Claudius. A thousand years ago, that road would have stretched to London in the south and to Hadrian's Wall in the north. Above me, the bells pealed, announcing the passing of the quarter hour. I approached and entered the church and I pulled open the gargantuan, oak doors.

I had no love of religion. I had no love of the cold-hearted, cruel, impiety of the nuns and the priests I had encountered at school. I had no affection for my church or my religion. I had no respect for the celibate hypocrites who doled out physical punishments for my alleged imperfections as a Christian. I had no reverence for the superstitious who seemed more interested in their petty prejudices than God or Jesus. I had no devotion to a Church that employed sadism to subvert its flock into meek obedience. Yet while I walked through the majestic silence of the Minister; its life stretching back to the Dark Ages in the 600s; I felt the magnetic draw of open and honest belief. I perceived the majesty, the solemn beatitude this cathedral held over life in Yorkshire for close to 1500 years. I felt reverence for the workers, the stone masons, the carvers, the glazers who had toiled in creating such a wondrous place. I felt awe at the simple and great lives that had passed through this cathedral, held together by a belief in a higher authority I no longer accepted.

I had lived and grown up in cramped and wet houses. We were stifled with too many hungry people, too many angry, poor, people. We were choked with too many people lost by war and the depression. I lived with people forgotten by God and missed by beauty. They were condemned to be like the poor mule, forever pulling a weight upon a circular stone. My people were the ones always promised that if we obeyed, riches in heaven awaited us. If we were meek and obedient, paradise was ours. If we allowed the mighty to plunder the Earth, here and now, we would find eternal happiness on the gossamer clouds of heaven.

Until that day, I had never seen physical beauty created by men. I

112

had only read about it in books or dreamed about it in my head. I came to York to see majesty, to see history, and to feel that I was part of this great tapestry of life, in Northern England. Looking upwards against the vaulted ceiling and across to the silent saints of the church, I finally knew I had worth. I knew that despite my past, my family's lost legacy, my father old and absent, my mother holding on to what little we had, with desperation, anger, and fear; that I was not eternally condemned to a life empty of purpose. I knew that my sister Marian's death or my lost innocence, my stolen childhood could not be cleansed or purified from me. I understood, that day at York, that I was destined to carry all those memories, all that pain with me, for as long as I lived. But I was granted the right to ascend and try to escape my backward existence because I was different and unique.

I spent another hour exploring York and found an inn where I had a half pint of bitter. I jumped on my bike for the long journey home. I did not reach home until well after supper. Twilight was fading into dark when I arrived back to the streets and laneways of King Cross, where a lone man with a tall, burning shaft lit the gas street lamps. I was exhausted, elated, and unable to explain to anyone why I had ridden my bike to York. My mother thought I was daft and Mary laughed at my folly. But I went to bed and fell into a fitful sleep that night. I dreamed of my eventual escape from King Cross, Halifax, and Yorkshire.

My escape was short-lived as Bill Moxon returned back into our lives, brusquely after my pilgrimage to York. I came home one day and found him sitting in the parlour. He was banging the out of tune piano and singing mournfully:

"Down in the Deep, Sailor, Beware, Down in the Deep, Sailor, take care."

It was the only song he knew how to play. He had learned it in the Royal Navy, during the First World War. Seeing him sitting in our front parlour, I froze in horror. The last few months had been peaceful for Mary and me. We seemed more like a family again, struggling and hungry, but at least united in some form of bond or love for one another. Bill's return signaled to me that yelling and fighting would begin with more vigor. I was disgusted at his return.

By 1936, the world outside my horizon was growing as cold as my existence. With the death of King George V, Edwardian England perished. As the final clock stopped for the King, the abdication crisis was born. Boys from school and me paraded in hordes singing at the top of our voices, "God Save our gracious King, God Save our noble King… send him to heaven in a corn beef tin… God save the King."

Within months, Edward the Eighth renounced the throne and his brother Bertie took the scepter to become George the 6th. The new King was crowned the following year.

In February 1937, I turned fourteen. I would be forced to leave school at the end of term. It was the age to leave formal education, unless one had money. It was the age for one to take up a trade and earn one's keep. Although it could be said I had been contributing to my share of the living expenses since the age of seven. I despaired about my prospects for full-time employment. I desperately wanted to work full-time so I could earn enough money to move out on my own and perhaps find a girlfriend. Maybe I could have what I considered a normal life.

Off the High Street in Halifax there was a used clothing store called Copley's. It was a good store to pick up decent work clothes at reduced rates as the suits were either pawned or donations from the newly dead. I stumbled into the store and found some better pants and a jacket that were suitable enough for job hunting. The coat and jacket were a little too big. I was able to hide it by riding the waist further up my abdomen and closing the jacket.

I spent several days stopping in store after store, enquiring about full-time employment. Dejected after days of rejections from prospective employers; I went into down-town Halifax. I entered the

114

Arcade, which was a building enclosed in glass and steel and possessed about fifty different businesses from tailors to butchers. I was fortunate to find a sign posted on Grosvenor's looking for help. I explained to the owner that I would be leaving school at the end of term. I was able to work part-time until summer when I would be available full-time. The owner, a Christadelphian, with strange ideas about God and charity, agreed. However, he explained that my position would again consist of me pushing a heavy barrow. I was to transport freshly butchered meat and giants wheels of cheese from their main store to the Arcade. I was devastated. The last labour I sought was that of Sisyphus, rolling rock upon rock up steep and dangerous slopes. As far as I could see, I was no better than a horse in a shuck being beaten by merciless masters. I was like the pathetic dray horse being forced to haul unimaginable loads of goods across the expanse of Halifax. Everyone was to witness my servitude.

"As much as I would like a job, sir," I explained, "I'm getting plum tired of being relegated to hauler and loader of food stuffs."

"It's temporary, lad," the owner assured me. "It is a test to see if you are up to the task to work in my store. In time, Harry, if you show me your mettle, I will give you a better job. And that is my word as a Christian."

There was little else I could do. I accepted and counted the days and months until I would be released from my bindings at both home and on the barrow.

My fourteenth birthday passed without fanfare. Mary took me to a tea shop to celebrate my becoming a man. I was a grown up indeed; in a world caught in economic collapse and the stench of world conflict raging around us. She treated me to butter cakes and gossip about the girls she worked with at the mill. Mary told me, "There are quite a few comely ones down at my mill. They would be dead proud to have you on their arm. I can put a good word in fer ya, Harry?"

Although I feverishly wanted a girlfriend and desired the sensuous affection a female could provide I was too shy and self-conscious about my poverty, my poor education, and what I considered my underprivileged upbringing.

"No thanks, Mary. I am doing alright with the lasses on my own," I lied.

I thought I was always to be alone. Instead of going and looking for romance, I locked myself in my room. I read my books, which were filled with beautiful woman. The suitors were all brilliant, intricate, and attractive; leading lives replete with purpose. Their images in my head contrasted bitterly to the coarse and foul work girls and work men inhabiting the mills and factories of Halifax. As for the other young women, secretaries, teachers, nurses; they were beyond my orbit. They spoke and acted too sophisticated for me. I could never reach their elevated plain. Their parents were able to pay for their education beyond the age of fourteen. Little did I know; all of it was role playing marked by centuries of tradition; it was a play between those that have and those that are destined to have not.

In spring of 1937, every schoolchild was presented a box of chocolates, in celebration of the coronation of George VI. It was our reward for our loyalty to the new King, the empire, and God. The box was painted in the colours of the royal family. On its lid was a photograph of the new King and Queen. "Let them reign happy and glorious." Chocolate was given to the lowest of the low. With my royal token, I was expected to look upwards and respect and love our rulers and accept my humble lot. I cared nothing for kings and queens or games at court; in those early days of spring, the world was divided into those that were served and those destined to serve. I had no more understanding of the new King than he had of my poverty.

Mary was now seventeen and for three years had worked full-time at the mill. Since she began working, Mary had saved her money to move out of Lillian's orbit. It was her objective to leave our house for good. She wanted to start her own life somewhere else. She needed the company of people who could profess love to her; if only in words enhanced by lager and lime. Mary needed self-confidence. It was something I was not able to give her as I lacked it myself and our mother stole it from her with indulgent neglect. Mary needed to break free of our mutual past, but she was still caring enough to lavish some of her precious escape money upon me.

Mary realized I was lonely and feeling wretched and pubescent, slaving away at Jubb's. Mary suggested we go on a day journey to Blackpool. It was my present for leaving school.

The next Sunday, we took an early train from Halifax to Blackpool. It was my first train trip and I was enthralled at the prospect of an adventure. The giant steam locomotive pushed itself out of the station with blasts of grey smoke and a giant cry from its whistle. Mary and I sat on wooden benches in the third class compartment. We pulled the heavy window down and breathed in heavy, sooty air as we were propelled towards the sea. On our voyage, we passed innumerable, identical hamlets and villages. We saw the same grim and dour people enter or exit the train. Mary and I made fun of the stodgy, old people while we passed the time eating apples. For me, it was like I was leaving my homeland. In my imagination, our train could have gone to Zanzibar or Tashkent, instead of Blackpool, the mythical northern seaside town to the poor crowds from the north. It was a city filled with diversion and amusement where, throughout long summer nights, the town was set ablaze with a multitude of illuminations, and cheap romance was found between cotton candy kisses and the Ferris wheel. Always present, in the back ground was the noise from the crash of the sea waves and the thunderous roar of the death-defying roller coasters.

"Harry, Harry," my sister called out to me, waking me from my dreams. "Don't you worry; one day, Harry, we will grab a train and never look back, never come back. Bye-bye Mum, bye shite life... Hello world..."

Enthusiastically, I cried out, "Yes."

When the train rushed into Blackpool station, Mary took my hand and we hurried out of the station waiting to find fun and adventure.

"Remember, Harry, no rainy day thoughts. Now, brother, it's time to go find some fun!"

Outside, the sky was clear and blue and the temperature mild and refreshing. We were lucky because we found a cheap fish and chip shop on our way to the beach and boardwalk. We treated ourselves handsomely to two orders of battered cod and chips. Our lunch was wrapped in yesterday's newspaper. Mary and I found a bench near the shop and we sat down to eat. We tore through our meal. We laughed and joked in between bites of fish drowned in malt vinegar. Feeling stuffed and sated, we crunched up our spent lunch and dumped it in a bin. We walked down to the beating heart of Blackpool, the boardwalk beside the sea. As we approached, we heard the noise, the electricity coming from the amusement rides. We saw the giant Ferris wheels turning on the horizon, with loud and boisterous occupants. We heard bells clanking while men barked into metal tubes, magnifying their voices.

Our first quest, we decided, was a walk on the beach as we had never in our lives seen the sea or smelled salt air. We hopped off the boardwalk and our feet sank into voluminous sand. Looking out towards the water, I observed tiny breakers riding up against the shore. Above us, seagulls frolicked and shrieked, spying stray bits of trash to eat. I had brought a ball with us and we played toss on the cool sand. We both thought we were on holiday, in our version of paradise. After a while, we stopped playing catch. We traipsed down the wide expanse of sea and surf, kicking the sand upwards, while walking astride each other. We were arm in arm, singing childish lullabies.

"Once upon a time, when birds shit lime and monkeys chewed tobacco…"

Mary said, "Let's go to the Blackpool Tower."

She had heard it was the most reasonable place for games and diversions. The tower, built in the 1890s as homage to the Eiffel Tower in Paris, stood 520 feet high. At its base was a giant building that housed a circus, zoo, and aquarium. We gained admittance for a couple of pence and immediately found the animal enclosure, where we laughed at the monkeys. I made silly faces back to them and imitated their gestures and their antics. The lions in their cage looked proud and indifferent to our entreaties to roar as kings of the jungle.

In a quiet moment, Mary said, "Not a bad life eh, Harry? For the lion that is… all he has got to do is look fierce and tough. Scare the shite out of people. But at tea time, he knows a man will come along and throw a nice bit of meat his way. A roast beef or a leg of lamb, we wouldn't even see on Sunday. For that big pole cat's supper, I'd roar and snarl and bark."

Suddenly, she let loose a giant growl as if she were a lioness. We left the animal den and rode the elevator to the top of the tower, eating a piece of rock candy. We stared out across the sea and I told Mary, "If you stare a little further out, there is France."

"And a little further back is Leeds and bloody Manchester," she replied. "One day, Harry, and never you mind, one day we will get out."

We descended the tower, our cheeks whipped by the wind as we raced to the fairground.

"My treat, let's ride the dodgems," I called to Mary.

We jumped into our separate cars and chased each other around the ring, while sparks of electricity traced the ceiling. We drove into one and other and bumped other cars. We laughed until tears ran down our faces and our turn and our money ran low, ending the ride.

The day was quickly done. We made our way back to the station and our train, which would take us to Halifax and home. On our return journey; we were both exhausted from joy. Mary and I hugged each other.

"Promise," I said, "that we can do this again, real soon."

"Sure, Harry, sure we will."

Separately and forlornly, we stared out of the window while outside, cloud and darkness descended.

A few weeks later after the magic of Blackpool had evaporated, Mary told me she was moving out of the house. She had found better employment at another mill in Low Moor, near Bradford. She was not going to stomach another year living in this house watching Bill and Lillian drink and brawl. She was not going to look after our younger brothers, nor clean up the debris left by Bill and Lillian's pub carousing. My sister told me about her plans to flee and swore me to silence.

On the quiet, Mary left that Saturday to look for a place. She returned on Sunday and told me she had found a suitable rooming house. It was quiet and not too expensive.

"I will be gone by the following Friday."

It was said with a dreaminess and selfishness of the newly paroled. Mary's leaving filled me with dread. She was my only friend and confidant and I truly did not know what I would do without her. Together, my sister and I shouldered the same burden and the same memories of years spent fleeing debt and hunting for food. We preserved a burning ember of love for each other, our father, and even our mother. Her leaving made the glow dim and flicker. I would be left utterly alone and without any ally in this house.

Mary tried to comfort me and said that she would visit me often. She said seductively that my time to leave was soon. When I was just a little older, I could come live with her. I too would be freed from Mam and Bill Moxon. Her words were as comforting as treacle. I felt a little resentment that she would escape the altercations and blow outs destined to occur between the ever-drinking Lillian and her Bill. I also felt a creeping uneasiness about what would happen to Mary and the rest of us once Lillian knew about her irrevocable departure.

Each week, Lillian expected both my sister and I to contribute a portion of our pay to the house and food expense. It was two thirds of our pay packet. Before Bill had returned, my sister I and handed over ninety percent of our wages to our mother. However, Bill now made decent money as a butcher with Grosvenor's, the grocer shop that had a couple of outlets across Halifax and where I would soon be working. Presenting our money on Friday afternoons before tea was a ritual. My mother appeared to be an Egyptian overseer counting the grain harvested, offered as homage to the pharaoh by the enslaved Israelites. I placed my money into her hand as she sat reclined on her favourite chair. She counted my coins to make sure it was the correct amount. Lillian never allowed the house to be cheated. Normally, after me, Mary followed with her wages. That Friday, she was not behind me and our mother enquired where my sister was. I acted indifferent and ignorant. Tentatively, I said, "Upstairs, I think."

Moments later, with light footfalls, Mary came downstairs, holding a small bag. Her coat was already wrapped around her.

"What's this then?" asked my mother suspiciously. "What are you up to, Mary?" Lillian asked in a puzzled tone.

"Nothing, Mam," Mary sheepishly replied.

"Come on then, Mary get into parlour and give me thy wages," my mother demanded impatiently.

"Can't, Mam," Mary replied defensively, almost meekly.

"Can't?" Lillian barked. "Why can't thee? Why the bloody hell can't thee?" she said with rising anger.

I melted into the furniture and the wall paper. I was terrified of what would happen to my sister now that Lillian had been roused to anger. If I could have tip-toed out of the parlour, I would have.

Mary entered the front entrance of our parlour. Her body was tall, thin, and foreboding. My sister's legs stood firmly apart with her arms to her sides, in stiff pride.

"I am moving out," she said defiantly.

My mother rose from her chair. She lurched forward to within inches of my sister. She raised her right finger and began wagging it as she ranted.

"Like hell you are… How dare you move out."

"Dare?" Mary replied. "You fat bloody cow, I can do what I want. And there's no one to stop me. Do you think we are just here to feed you? Do you think I work at bloody mill to pay for you? You are a lazy fucking cow. Your man is now back by hearth, by your bleeding lap. So you're doing alright," Mary continued defiantly. "You're great, big, bloody man can pay his way. Butcher man can pay your way and anyone else's bloody way, for all I care. But from this very second I, Mary pays for bloody Mary. And Mary takes care of herself because not thee or your man, can do it, could do it, or would do it."

Lillian bellowed, "You ungrateful bitch, you little grabbing, mewling bitch."

"Me?" Mary demanded in rising anger. "Me, ungrateful?" she repeated. "Since I was four, Mam, I have been serving you. I've been feeding you and working like a fucking dog, for you. After your fights and boozing, after the debt collectors had gone, after dad was chucked and Bill buggered off, who was bloody left? Me! Mary! It's always, dependable bloody Mary I've had no bloody life because of you. I've gone to bed cold and fucking hungry because of you. I took care of Harry and Matt because you were not fit to help. Look at you now with another little bugger on your tit."

"Fit to help," Lillian retorted. "Fit, you know naught about what I've done for thee. I've ad no bloody life; I've lost my bloody life to you fucking kids, to your fucking needs," Lillian said desperately. "Without me, you'd be in workhouse or on the streets. Your dad, with his igh 'n mighty family; he was no bloody help to me or to you. Did any of them raise a finger when we had less than naught, when we were so bloody skint we ate shite from rubbish bins? I've got blood on my hands, lass, from scraping and fighting for food for you and your bloody brothers," Lillian retorted, her anger rising. "And now you come to me and say here's the thanks, Mam, for all your work; I am moving out. You are moving on and out like you have bloody airs or something, like you're better than us. Mark me, Mary, life will soon have you sorted and sorted well and good.

"I tell ya good bloody luck; cause you're going to need it; because naught is coming from here. Bugger off then, leave your bloody mother, and leave your bloody brothers and good riddance to thee." Lillian's face was flushed, her eyebrows arched in a Mephistopheles' grimace.

Mary reached into her coat, found her house key, and threw it to the ground. She looked at me and said with a weary smile, "Never you mind, Harry. When you're ready, you can come live with me. Take care of yourself because Mam is going to be no bloody hope to you."

Her words trailed off like an echo coming from the dying notes of a phonograph and fled out the door with her. Outside, Mary walked alone to the bus station. Hopefully, it took her to a brighter future. But with her flight, my friend, the one who kept me warm at night, left. My sister, who made me feel strong; made me feel love instead of hate; who shared my hunger, my tears and my joy, left our house. She was gone, like Marian. She was gone, like Albert. She was a phantom.

Lillian returned to her chair. She fell into it, subdued by the storm that had just passed. I remained quiet and waited for Bill to return home. I fetched up Matt so he would not fall under the angry feet of Lillian. The baby cried and wailed for his dinner and Lillian dejectedly flung out a withered and tired breast to calm the infant. Bill arrived home from work and Lillian prepared our tea; runny fried eggs and fried bread. We ate in silence because no one dared utter dared aloud about Mary's departure.

7

Moving Out

After Mary left, I counted my time until I could flee my mother's house. I felt no warmth or attachment to this lodging, to my mother, Bill, or his toddler. I felt some remorse to be leaving Matt behind. However, I needed to escape this weary life that clung like a hungry orphan, on to me and on to every repetitive day spent watching my mother and Bill argue each other into sleep. It was probably from the time Mary lifted me up to say good-bye to Marian or the moment my father brought me downstairs to my mother while I was sick with whooping cough; but we were a family silent in love and outspoken in hate and shame. If there had been any chance for us to love each other, it was wrecked from the dark forces around us. Outside catastrophes inflicted famine, industrial collapse, and strangled any remote possibility that our family could survive as a healthy, caring, and adoring unit.

Growing into a teen, I could not help but blame my mother for our sorry plight. I could not help but look at Lillian as an object of disgrace and embarrassment. She drank too much and she brawled too much. She had sex outside the marriage covenant and cuckolded my father, at least twice. Sadly, the man she found as a lover was an imperfect provider, and he was also coarse and treated us children as liabilities for sex and a warm bed. In the deep recesses of my mind, Lillian was the principal cause for my father's destruction. She was the reason for our expulsion into a dark and unfeeling world. It was as if Lillian had wrought and manipulated our downfall from her vices; be it drink or the need to enjoy being admired. I did not recognize that she was neither evil nor a bad mother. It was a world turned on its side that drove us to cannibalize love. Our struggle for food and housing discarded affection, love, and decency as unnecessary luxuries, and Lillian never explained to me the workings of her mind. She never voiced to me the humiliation she endured down at the pubs where she begged for extra money, for a loaf of bread, or to find Bill and drag him home before he drank all the food money away. I was fourteen and could not square in my heart that Lillian and Bill were anything but old, decrepit objects for my ridicule or my blame. To me, they were the sole and unforgivable origin for us being poorly dressed, uneducated peasants, who only earned their keep through brawn and not brain.

Shamed by both my present and past, I developed anger and disgust for my Northern poverty and my Northern broad accent. My voice was like a mark of Cain. It condemned me at every syllable I uttered as uneducated and unsophisticated. My accent only made me fit for manual labour and labeled me from the North. Actors and actresses on the screen all spoke with the diction of the South or in North American flatness. The only actors with loud, yobbish voices were comedians like George Formby. The Northern yokel was also popular as a peasant or on screen scenery to allow the hero or heroine to pass. I was determined to forge my way out of poverty and out of my social class.

I signed up for elocution classes at the Athenaeum Working Man's academy. I paid for the tuition with some of the money I had saved to leave home. The Athenaeum was a cooperative learning centre for languages, pronunciation, diction, and self-improvement. The school was established by a group of utopian cloth cutters in the 1890s. They hoped to advance education to the down-trodden. Entering the school, I was greeted by an attractive, middle-aged woman with a middle-brow accent. The woman offered her hand in a polite, gentile greeting.

"My name is Miss. Florence Haynes."

Awkwardly, I took her soft hand and I held it too tightly as if her good breeding could infect me like a tactile infection. I explained to her I wanted to speak proper, educated English. I wanted an accent to escape the North. I needed a voice that no one could recognize sprang from Barnsley, Bradford, or Halifax.

Florence explained, "This is a finishing school, primarily. Young men and women enroll at the Athenaeum to improve their chances of gaining entrance to college or university. At the very least, they come here to improve their chance of success in business. A modulated tone is the passport to your future, both in business and in love," she concluded. "You don't look the sort to be going to either university or joining the banking profession."

"Suppose not," I replied. "I still ave a right to succeed and make summa of myself."

"Too true," Miss Haynes noted. "Sadly these days, there are too many of you wanting more and getting less." The administrator sighed. "I am reluctant, but I will make an exception in your case, as you seem earnest. Be here next Saturday afternoon," she instructed. "Class begins at two. Don't be late. Don't forget, it is a shilling a lesson."

Quite a fair deal, I naively thought to become a polished and sophisticated gentleman for a shilling.

When I arrived the following Saturday, I was greeted by a teacher named Agnes. She was in her twenties. Agnes wore a grey, pleated skirt and looked as far removed from sophisticated society as I was. There was about nine of us in the class. They were mostly young men, around the ages of seventeen or eighteen. We also had two brunette women who were about twenty. They all looked at me curiously when they saw the state of my used clothing. Shyly, I smiled at them.

Immediately, they recognized that while my accent might have been as broad as theirs, we were miles apart on the social evolutionary chain. The other students were children of mill supervisors, green grocers, and the developing mercantile class. The other students viewed me as someone who had mistakenly entered the room and forgotten to bring the tea trolley and biscuits. Agnes began the lessons. Each of us was to read a piece from a nursery rhyme. All of us failed miserably in imparting any voice but broad Yorkshire. It would take weeks to see any improvement. I spent hours whispering to myself in my bedroom, fighting against generations of breeding. I manipulated my tongue and jaw trying to erase the beer halls of Wentworth, the pits of Barley Hole, and the servitude of the Hoylands.

Gradually, my speech pattern developed to a more neutral accent, which resembled the 'neither from here nor there' county. My work mates thought I was taking the piss out of them with my newly developed speech pattern. The owner, with his profound reverence for God and self-improvement, applauded my efforts. As my speech became less my own, I became bolder. I was able to erase my past as if it were a ritual cleansing with each vowel and syllable that sounded less like my mother's speech, Bill's bold as brash utterance, or Albert's long-ago, almost musical solicitudes. Now, when I spoke, there was cloak of strength and anonymity that surrounded me. I felt less like a servant and more like a master. I was able to conceal, if only for brief moments, my poor education and my impoverished upbringing. I was able to repudiate my history for good or ill.

Still shy around girls, I pretended I was more sophisticated and cosmopolitan. I took to smoking Kensington cigarettes as they were slightly more expensive. Hopefully, they displayed my newly acquired cavalier attitude. When I met Mary for lunch or a lime and lager; she looked on in amused silence at my futile attempts to erase my identity. To her, I was like so many from my class who had attempted this deception before. We soared, briefly, like Icarus through the class structure of England, only to be discovered to be a peasant from the North. The hierarchy burnt our wings by their power and privilege and we tumbled backwards to Earth.

In September 1937, I was fourteen and no longer considered a child by my society. Now, I was a full-time employee of Grosvenor's, hauling their cheese and meat cart like a serf. I was a full-time pack animal. I was the grocer's mule; albeit a burrow with a more refined and softer accent. I do not think the women who saw me in the streets labouring with the weight of my barrow either recognized or acknowledged my efforts to improve myself. Nor did the bankers and businessmen who demanded I give them right of way on the street reflect and think; 'There goes a young man with a bright future.' Like the rest of my kind, the working class, we were background noise. We were like the buzz of an insect you cannot see.

Thankfully, on the weekends, the manager set me to work at their store located in the Halifax Market. There they sold butter, bacon, ham, and hot and cold meat pies. I transported these delicacies on a pushcart from their storage unit a block away from the Arcade. I wheeled in this giant gurney of victuals, which resembled the cheese carts of Gouda. Friday and Saturdays were the busiest hours. I worked with the other market girls and boys from seven a.m. to ten p.m. The other employees were slightly older than me, but they took good care of me and allowed me to make mistakes and learn on the job. There was a tremendous amount of electric energy in the market, as we sold vast amount of goods and wares to an ever-hungry public.

As the autumn progressed, Lillian informed me we were moving to Boothtown, which was a suburb of Halifax. The new residence was quicker for me to get to work and it gave me a chance to make some friends. For me, there was no despair in this move; we left in the dead of day, our rent proudly paid in full.

Moving to 24 Boothtown Road was neither a move up nor down the ladder . It was a sidewise maneuver. Our house was the end unit in a row of fifteen tenement houses. The backyard was insignificant, sunless, and contained a cramped, reeking privy for our bodily needs. My bedroom was on the first floor. If you stood straight up and extended your hands out in both directions, you could touch the sides of the walls. Upstairs was another bedroom, for Lillian, Bill, and Bill Junior. Above them was the attic, where Matt slept. Boothtown was a grim and drab neighbourhood that over looked the mills and their grey plumes of smoke. Our neighbours were spinners and weavers for the factories that manufactured carpets for the floors of both the poor and rich of Britain and her many dominions.

Boothtown afforded me the luxury of finding friends. For the next few years, as governments prepared for war by either ignoring it or advancing its cause; I chummed around with the likes of Erick Whitely. He was a year older than me and an apprentice engineer. Eric was all-modern, quick-witted, vain, and boastful. Whitley extinguished my valuable free time with declamations of what bird he had bagged. With a thin terrier face and a wispy-haired mustache, he exuded cynicism. His personality was on the take. Being around him, I felt the cheap excitement of a lie told brazenly. Eric introduced me to Roy Broadbent, who lived in a village called Sydall. Broadbent resided with his elderly mother and aunt. Roy and me had something in common we both lacked fathers. Roy's died when he was an infant and mine died emotionally for me when I was almost eight when he was shown the door. Eric's father, on the other hand, was very much alive. Eric spent a lot of time boasting about his dad, which was an irritation to both Roy and me. It was not the fact that Eric had a father that bothered us; it was because he insisted on talking about him. This made us keenly aware of our own absent dads. With Roy, we both did not have to talk about our fathers. They were in the past tense, dead or deserted.

Broadbent always dressed in the manner of a 1930s American gangster. He wore a fedora hat and sported wing-tipped shoes. Eric called him "boss" in mock deference. Roy as "boss" was ironic; the

129

moment Roy opened his mouth or extended his hand, it was obvious his character was soft and kind. He was incapable of malice, except for the sin of vanity.

The final element in my trinity of mates was Doug Butterworth. He lived near King Cross with his mother, brother, and sister. Like Roy and me, Doug was fatherless. I do not know if it was by design or convenience, but we three became fast friends. I believed it was a relief to all of us that there was no shame in being fatherless. We had no need to speak of our dads, who were either dead or gone from our lives. It was the first time in my life that I felt accepted me as an equal and these friends never judged my dodgy background.

My friends' households were a study in contrast. Butterworth's was in a perpetual state of chaos with people charging in and out and tea cups cluttering tables while clothes for mending were heaped around the four corners of their parlour. In the scullery, dishes were piled high in the sink. But I was welcome to whatever was there.

"Help yourself luv. Don't mind the mess. Fancy a cup of tea," were Mrs. Butterworth's encouraging words to me.

The welcome and affection held true at Roy Broadbent's house but his mother and grandmother controlled their domestic affairs and finances with a no nonsense commonsense. Roy was dotted on and lived with a motherly love which appeared to me both appealing and smothering considering my mother's haphazard approach to love and affection.

I tried to avoid visits to Eric's house because I found his parents asked too many questions about my background and asked too few about their son's ethics. I found the Whitley's had too much sense of their own perceived self importance for me to enjoy their scones and their judging stares.

When we were not working, my friends and I trawled for girls in the evenings. Trying to find a girl to kiss our walk home was our constant pursuit. On Friday nights, we met at a dancehall above Jamison's Tailors.

There was a live band and the musicians played dance favourites, from America. My greatest impediment for finding girls was I could not dance. Instead, I circled the perimeter of the dance floor and chatted up stray, partner-less girls. I would inquire if following the dance; they wanted company on their way home. If I was lucky, a girl accepted my advances. While walking her home, we stopped at the park to kiss or grope each other in furtive and futile attempts at lovemaking. There was more failure than success, in my youthful sexual attempts, as I was petrified over the outcome of sex. I had seen all of its sad consequences with my mother. She was chained and bound by unwanted children. I had witnessed, too many times, adults' love wrung from them as passion deserted them for the cruelties of economic reality.

With a willing girl in evening darkness, in a quiet secluded place in the park, I fumbled and stumbled in crude mimicry of lovemaking until she grew tired of my indecisiveness and stopped our mutual frustration, jumped up, and cleared the twigs and dirt from her skirt before demanding to be taken home. But it was far safer to be thought a fool. It was far better than the full weight and responsibility of a pregnant shop girl who wanted restitution for her ruined live and the ruined lives to come. Sometimes, I tried to buy a safe at the chemist but it was a long and embarrassing procedure. I had to request the said prophylactic from a young female shop assistant that I probably met at a dance in the past. It was abject humiliation to wait in a long line of old women looking for liver pills. There I stood at the chemist's sweaty, pimply, and shifty while in front and behind me; women tightly held their handbags and eavesdropped to hear my request for a bridle for my lust.

If we were short of cash and ideas, we ended up at a pub. My friends and I nursed half-pints of beer until our jokes and ale grew stale. Whereupon, we departed to make endless circles around People's Park. We ran into other friends, acquaintances, and strangers, and generally loitered away what little free time we had bumming cigarettes, picking up girls, or making jokes.

At home, Bill Moxon had raised enough scratch to purchase a used, wireless radio. It was operated by a huge wet battery. It took central position in our living room. If I had the chance, I listened to news with Bill. Unless it was about a cut of beef or a Barnsley chop, Moxon was ignorant of most things. Yet Bill was astute enough to know Hitler was no good. During the Munich crisis, Bill listened intently to the deliberations over the Sudetenland. While my mother yelled at him to do something productive.

"Get off your arse and clean the grate."

"No good will come by this Fritz," Bill intoned to me. "No bloody good."

I was not sure if there was going to be a war and if there was a war, what would change for me? It seemed to me to be the same old dance, if there was war the soldiers would be promised better lives and better living conditions, after the battle was won. The same promises were made to the men returning in 1918, from the Great War but I knew that was cobblers. The men never got anything because as a child, I saw a great many war veterans living in the same run-down doss-houses as us. Legless, armless, and homeless; they were no more victorious than the German soldiers. As far as I understood it, wars were conducted for the rich and powerful and fought by the poor and hopeless. So I certainly did not want to end up in a war because of Hitler, nor because of Czechoslovakia or because those in charge had bungled the economy and society through blindness and greed

In late September 1938, Neville Chamberlain came back to Britain waving a piece of paper and proclaimed peace in our times but Lillian never received the information. My mother's war with her children and her lover were never to have an armistice only brief ceasefires for the combatants to collect their dead. After Bill Junior's arrival and Mary's departure, Lillian hoped I was on her side, in her battles against Bill. But it was a bit too repetitive and a bit too much for me with

Lillian's boozing and her unfortunate flights into melodramatics. In the past, her theatrics may have worked on me, when we were truly at the work house door. Now her pleas for assistance made me cynical as I was convinced she had failed constantly to attend to my needs to be nurtured and loved. Moreover, Bill now worked with the same employer as me, where he was well regarded as one of their prized butchers. Money was tight for Lillian, but even tighter for me. She insisted on increasing my room and board and refused to understand that I also had to pay for work clothes, my entertainment, and the books for my self-education. Lillian's demands were greater than I could bear. She wanted me to sacrifice for children that were not of my doing and not from my father. They were from men who had brutalized and victimized my mother. I did little for my mother now to assist her emotionally and resented the financial burden she placed upon me. For me, she became like my dad: a liability that must be abandoned or I would be lost.

On an ever-repeating Saturday evening after spending twelve hours at work; I ended up at a neighbourhood pub. I had arranged to meet a shop girl for a date. I thought she would not show as it was well after ten when I finished work. But when I arrived, she was there, patiently waiting for me. Her name was Silvia. She had an earnest look and she wore only the slightest hint of makeup. Her accent was soft and the harsh Northern tone was absent from her vocabulary. Silvia was mature in her thoughts, but liked to laugh. She seemed generally interested in my company and my inane tales about work at Grosvenor's. As last orders were near, we did not linger long in the pub. Silvia accepted my offer to walk her home, which was at the opposite end of town from where I lived. She resided in the comfort and relative prosperity of Saville Row. We approached her home and sat down at a bus shelter opposite the park. We held hands for the better part of two hours and made plans for another meeting. Near us, the church bell peeled. Silvia said it was best that she be off home. I accompanied her to her front door. We kissed and said our good-byes. As her door closed, I pirouetted.

Gleefully I began the long trek home to Boothtown, elated by the evening and the prospect of love. In my ignorance, I was always on the hunt for emotional connections. I cast love out not because I loved any of these village and city girls, but in the hopes they would return my love, denied me throughout my life. Over the decade, my family had fled hunger and degrading poverty. My memory erased any tender moments my parents showed me before the infinite maelstroms and disasters pulled us all apart from each other. I was an empty vessel who needed the fuel of kindness, devotion, and affinity to charge my soul.

As I grew into my teens, I erased my recollections of my dad holding me tightly, or singing to me on the piano, or holding my hand while we crossed the street to go the Alhambra. I washed away memories of being alone with him and his prized encyclopedia of the ancient world. I replaced them with a hundred other memories of nauseating hunger and humiliation. I remembered him forsaken and leaving our house. Any trust or love I had for my father dissolved into anger and despair at his departure, and at our failure to not properly hold on to each other or even bid good-bye. I closed my eyes to my mother's hapless love, demonstrated to me as child, when she bounced me and my sister on her knee. I denounced her attention to me as a child and condemned her hugs or kisses as fake theatrics from a woman who intended to survive, no matter how dirty the business. I banished from my mind, the fear she endured every time there was no money for rent or food. I negated her courage when she begged for a loan, or pawned what little we had left. It was forgotten by me as I weighed it against her boozy melodramatics where she proclaimed she had withstood and fought the flood against us alone and unaided, during the troubled times. Perhaps my mother did hold back the tidal wave of total annihilation. Yet there were a thousand tiny hairline fractures in the mirror on her soul from enduring so much pain and so much disappointment in her own life.

She never articulated why we made the choices we did to survive the depression. She had, in her disjointed, raw visceral manner, made us survive the tumult. However, we emerged like fools and paupers, naked and unprepared for anything but daily, brutal survival.

So when I arrived home early that Sunday morning, elated from holding tender hands that had the scent of Palmolive soap; I was not expecting to find my mother standing behind the door. It was not the moment Lillian should have chosen to present herself as a wise and sober, suburban mother. Indeed, Lillian didn't say anything to me as I swung open the door. Instead, she used her fist, the size of a small ham, to crack the side of my head. It was such a blow that I stumbled and saw stars for several seconds before I cried out.

"Fuck, what did you do that for?"

"Watch it or I'll give ya another one, you cheeky bugger. Where have you been? It's well best bed time. Why, it's the wee hours of the new morning?" Lillian demanded, hissing like spittle evaporating off a hot iron.

"It's none of your bloody business," I exploded, trying to get a hold of my faculties and restrain my anger towards my mother.

"Dus thee know the time?" she enquired, her voice leaping an octave.

"Fuck the time," I replied, struggling to get past her. "You don't hit me, get it," I screamed.

She grabbed a hold of my collar and told me, "I am your Mam. I still can take you over my knee and give you a walloping."

I struggled free from her grasp and leered at her.

"Fuck you, you boozy bitch. Take a look at me, Mam. I am not pissed. I am not in the gutter. But, Mam, you've been in the ditch. I've seen you there and you have never dragged me into house dead pissed, before the neighbours can see. So fuck you."

Lillian snarled, "On your bike, lad, get on your bike and bugger off."

"I will," I answered as Bill opened the bedroom door and bellowed out.

"What's this racket about?"

"Nothing Bill," I shouted back. "Lillian's just been promoted to night watchman. I'm going to bed. I'll see ya in the morning for breakfast." I turned back to my mother and added, "Don't worry, Mam, I'll get on my bike and not bloody look back, just like Mary."

I left her in the hallway and Lillian spluttered out half-sentences and accusations. I slammed my bedroom door shut and collapsed into an angry, disjointed sleep.

The following morning, before anyone had woken, I was up and out to work. I mentioned my desire to move out to one of my workmates. He suggested a family whose son had married and moved on. They had a spare room for let in their house on Melville Place, off Gibbet Street, in central Halifax. Gibbet Street, several generations previous, had been the executioner's ground for traitors, murderers, and thieves. It was on this street that the guillotine was first used, long before France and the Bastille. Common criminals were held in stocks on the side of the street so that the passing citizenry could jeer and mock the condemned. When I arrived at 26 Melville Place, I was greeted by a polite woman in her fifties. She explained that her husband and daughter lived in the house and they were only looking for a quiet and hard-working boarder.

"I don't need any trouble-makers or drinkers."

The landlady quickly accepted me, after learning about my position at Grosvenor's and after I presented a written recommendation from the owner. I told her I would be able to move in a week's time.

My departure from Boothtown and my declaration of independence from Lillian were not as hard won or dramatic as Mary's departure. By the time I got around to telling my mother, she was resigned to the fact I was leaving. She wished me no hard feelings.

"You are allus welcome eare."

I sarcastically agreed and went up and collected my meager belonging. They consisted of a change of clothes, some books, and a handful of silk flags that contained the ensigns of various countries. I left with no pictures of my mother, my father, or of my siblings.

136

We either had none or they had been lost or misplaced, after so many evacuations in the dead of night. As I left my mother's house, I shook Bill's hand, patted Bill Junior's head, and said something cavalier to Matt like, "I'll see ya in the funny papers."

I kissed Lillian's cheek and handed her the front door key. I left relieved and elated thinking I could kill and bury the past by walking forward and taking the bus from Boothtown to downtown Halifax. I would never look back, I thought. How naïve I was because my past was always lurking and beating the bars of my soul. It was like a prisoner in solitary confinement, dragging his drinking cup against the iron doors that held him firm and fast.

As I jumped on that bus, my father Albert was probably making tea in St Andrew's Villas. His Uncle Larratt still chortled behind the bar at the New Inn. He counted his cash that balanced out the soot he must have felt covered his soul. Mary still worked as a weaver and she was getting serious with a boy named Priestly, whose family were plumbers in Bradford. Outside of the west Counties, Winston Churchill, the enemy of the general strike, was politically exiled. He had been deserted by his party as he foretold horrible things would befall the world if we did not prepare against Herr Hitler.

The storm clouds blowing across continental Europe neither dimmed nor curbed my enthusiasm at being free from my mother. I was convinced I was sailing on the right course to love and happiness. By 1939, my work with Grosvenor's had been recognized and the owner made me an assistant manager to the store in the Arcade. I was moving upwards and perhaps my future was assured.

8

The Phony War

Summer 1939 was long, lazy, and filled with abundant sunshine. In between work, I spent my time aimlessly chasing girls or loafing outside with friends in city parks. My mates and I were admirably unconcerned with the atmosphere outside Halifax or Yorkshire. My world was now safe, well fed, and routine. After sixteen years of incessant flight from creditors, hunger pangs, cruel teachers, and absent parents; I felt reasonably comfortable. I was still self-conscious about my upbringing and my deficient education. But I had found friends who liked me and enjoyed my company and this was a new comfort to me. However, Mary and I were now emotionally distant from each other as she worked far away in Bradford and developed a circle of friends that were outside of my interests. To an extent, I reconciled with my mother, and on occasion, I went to Boothtown for a meal or to spend the odd night amidst familiar arguments and discord.

On September 1st, at seven in the morning, I was at work preparing the food displays for the end of week customers. By eight, the store was packed with women, their hair wrapped in kerchiefs, their faces bleached white from sunless days, their lips stained blood-red, while their hands tightly gripped empty, mesh bags ready to be filled with weekend treats. I was in my white smock, pencil in hand carefully filling orders for the customers. Neither the women nor I knew that earlier in the morning, the German army had launched an unyielding assault against Poland. As I joked on my tea break with other staff, Stuka bombers tore apart Warsaw. While I thanked an elder woman for her patronage, panzer divisions chewed up Polish cavalry. The Poles were too foolhardy to realize the saber was no match for an eighteen-inch gun mounted on a steel-reinforced tiger tank.

It was not until late afternoon that news about the German assault seeped into Halifax and Grosvenor's. The implications were still uncertain to us. After work, I met up with Roy, Doug, and Eric. We briefly talked about the German invasion, but dismissed it as more smoke and shite. The blowhards in government would solve it as they had in the past, through endless talk and endless blather. I was more interested in hearing about a dance coming up the following week in Bradford. It was not until Sunday morning that I learned the true extent of Friday's invasion. I was at my mother's, huddled around the radio with Bill Moxon. This time, even Lillian was quiet while the Prime Minister explained to an anesthetized population that we were now at war.

Bill Moxon said, "We're in the shit now, lad, we are in the shit."

Outside, I heard neighbours opening their doors as if the cold-water shock of war's declaration drove them to be with their fellow citizens on the streets.

Within weeks, we were issued national identity cards, which tracked our residences and our movements. Barrage balloons obscured the horizon while below, tons of sandbags were positioned around government offices and important buildings of commerce. I was now sixteen and manager of Grosvenor's Arcade store. I was responsible for maintaining a constant supply of goods and stock in the store. I balanced the day's receipts, and nightly, I delivered the day's take directly into the owner's hands. But I saw that my good fortune was not to last. Those two years older than me were already signing up for the services. They were being trained for death and combat. I knew the war was not going to end before my eighteenth birthday. I dreaded the notion of becoming a government number pushed out to defend our homeland and end up maimed or dead.

As for my friends; Eric knew that being a tool and die-maker, he was considered essential to the war effort and would not be required to don a uniform. Eric tried his best not to upset any managers, as he preferred to remain at his lathe grinding the instruments of war for the Army, Navy, and RAF, rather than hold a gun. Doug Butterworth's heart was literally not in it for war. He had a slight murmur that left him bedridden for days on end. So he knew he would serve as best he could at home. As for Roy Broadbent, the gentle giant who stood over six feet four inches, he insisted the only choice for him was the Cold Stream Guards. When I was asked what branch I would join, I said I did not know. I honestly was not sure. But I responded that it would probably be the Air Force because I couldn't swim, which cancelled out the Navy, and I disliked the notion of walking to my death.

The atmosphere in Halifax during the first few weeks and months of the war was relaxed. The population was almost in a party mood as this phony war had altered the city's drab, nomenclature. It added a sense of excitement and danger, without the preconditions of pain and suffering. We now lived with air raid wardens, blackouts, and sirens that announced phantom bombings raids that never blemished Halifax. Most of us thought it mad that the Luftwaffe desired to bomb Halifax; how strategic was a drab, mill town? But the British government dictated that all buildings of importance were to be guarded against the Teutonic danger droning above the clouds. By government decree, Grosvenor's organized civilian air raid wardens to protect their warehouse against fire and destruction caused from explosives dropped from the sky.

As we were short-staffed, I was recruited to be one Grosvenor's air raid wardens. I worked in shifts with six other employees, during the heightened threat of attack. Provided with gas masks, tin helmets, and buckets of sand to battle against the mighty Nazi Air Force; we smoked impassively, in the shadows of the warehouse. I spent the evening in split shifts with another worker. Outside of the warehouse, I looked upwards at a clear, cloudless night sky; empty of an airborne armada, while my compatriot dozed on a cot inside.

The war progressed through its phony stages while I managed the store, played fireman, and wooed girls down at the pub. For now, I was insulated from the war. It had escaped my friends and I but eventually it came for us and enveloped us as it had done the others. In 1940, my sister married an infantryman. He went off to basic training while she remained at Low Moor, working at the mill. I watched time drip and relentlessly splatter on the floor as I waited for the inevitable letter from the government calling me to battle. In some dreamy moments, I looked at the war as an escape, a diversion from the world of my parents and my ancestors. However, I watched the newsreels and heard the gossip on the street; this war was deadly business where most of us were to either end up dead or broken. While the newspapers clamoured, the politicians declared this was a just war. The people of the British Isles were asked to stand against an enemy who threatened our way of life. The question for me was did I want to fight and likely die for a country that had forced millions of people into destitution in the 1930s and destroyed my family? If I was to go to war, I was going to choose the reason I considered right to sacrifice my life and, at that point, I saw none.

My employer, the Quaker, was bound by his faith to reject every war as unjust and unnecessary. He came to me in 1940 and offered me a bargain. If I became a Quaker; he would stand before the military and attest that my religious beliefs deemed me a conscientious objector, and therefore unfit to serve. My employer begged me that this was God's will. Not only would I be safe, but my employment at Grosvenor's would also be assured. For several minutes I contemplated his offer, but in the end, I refused it. I knew I was going to do my best to avoid being killed over Hitler, Churchill, Poland, and France. However, I was not going to stand before a military hearing and swear it was Jesus and my love for the Almighty who commanded me to refuse the King's shilling. After years of physical and verbal abuse at the hands of nuns and priests, I would rather take my chances in the amoral world at war. My odds of surviving the war seemed greater than the blind hypocrisy and cant force-fed to me as a hungry child by a predatory Catholic Church.

In spring, the Low Countries were overrun and German troops poured into France and battled to the death with Britain's Expeditionary army. I knew then it was the RAF for me. I was going to volunteer before I was conscripted on my 18th birthday. Hopefully, being a volunteer might improve my chances of surviving the war with fewer scars than I endured during Britain's black decade of economic Gotterdammerung.

In late autumn, I asked my mother if I could return home until I was called to war. She happily agreed. The extra rent money jingled lovingly in her purse. My mother enjoyed boasting to the neighbours about me, her eldest son.

"That's right, luv, he's a manager at Grosvenor's. My lad is no fool. He's a brave one too. Went and joined the RAF. You know the never so few lot. Not like the rest of the lazy sods around here waiting for Hitler to come knock on their doors."

The month of December 1940 was very cold and miserable, but I made my way by bus, three days before Christmas, to the Recruitment Office HQ in Huddersfield. I was intent to place my name down as willing lamb to slaughter. I arrived at the drab Recruitment Office located on the city's main street. The regional headquarters was filled with banks of typewrites and sallow men in woolen uniforms. I showed the duty sergeant my resident ID and proclaimed loudly that I was volunteering for the RAF. I was ushered into another room where I was given a brief questionnaire about my education, my occupation, my residence, and my religion. I wrote: Left school at 14, Grocer's Assistant, Roman Catholic. I was five feet four inches and 130 pounds and the RAF gladly took me as a volunteer. There was little else they could choose from as our island was being strangled to death in the Atlantic and in Africa. It was scarcely six months before I took the Kings shilling that France fell and surrendered to Hitler. All of continental Europe was either in the hands of the Nazis or the Soviets, who had signed a non-aggression pact with Germany. The war effort needed anyone who could walk into a recruiting center and sign their life away on the dotted line.

In 1940, I spent my Christmas at Doug Butterworth's home because I couldn't stomach my mother's drunken antics over the holidays. I reasoned this might very well be my last Christmas and I may as well enjoy it with a real family. Over Christmas, I briefly saw Mary and I brought her a present of fresh meat from Grosvenor's. As she was waiting for her new husband to return home from leave, we did not spend much time together. My father spent Christmas by himself. He accepted the Yuletide greetings from his landlady and supped alone with his memories.

The New Year passed without excitement and after the holidays, my employer begged me to reconsider my moral opinion on the war. "Stay with us and be a conscientious objector," he argued. Why should I not be spared? Why should I not be given God's grace of both a long life and a white smock serving the over-fed of Halifax? I politely declined. I only asked that he keep my job open for me when all this war nonsense ended.

My birthday was a quiet affair. Roy had already left to join the Cold Stream Guards and Butterworth was ill again and had taken to his bed with a quivering heart. I did not want to spend my last birthday, perhaps my last days on Earth with Eric. His fast talk about the money he was making in selective war service sickened me. Instead, I decided to indulge myself with a visit to the public baths. They were located at the top of Boothtown Road. I arrived and paid an attendant 50p. It was a privilege to soak in a warm bath rather than a tin tub filled with tepid water in a kitchen. A female attendant led me along a narrow passageway until she found an unoccupied room. Inside the narrow, wood-lined space was a hanger for one's clothes, and a deep, porcelain, bathtub. The attendant placed a plug into the bath. She turned the taps on until the bath was filled with warm inviting water. When finished, she closed the door behind her. I undressed and submerged myself in calm, cleansing hot water. I was empty of thoughts or cares until the water grew cold and it was time to dry myself, dress, and depart.

Afterwards, I spent some hours with Mary, who had come down to Halifax to bid me farewell. We did not talk much. We sipped our ale. We held each other's hands on the table. We looked into each other's faces, seeing if we could read our past upon them. She joked and bantered more than me because I was withdrawn and frightened about what tomorrow would bring for me. I was as scared as I was as a child when the nuns beat me because my future was as ominous as my past. I experienced the same form of loneliness when Albert left us. There was no one and nothing which could ease my sense of apartness from the civilian world. When it was time for my sister to leave, she got up and kissed me.

"Come back safe, Harry, just come back."

The following morning, I awoke with a jittery feeling like it was a school morning. I dressed warmly and went to the kitchen. My mother was sitting alone, warming herself by the oven. Bill had already gone to work and Matt and Junior were at school. She made me a cup of tea and cut me a large slice of fresh bread. There was a generous lather of butter and jam on it.

"Go on, tuck in. Well, lad, this is it. Keep your head down, Harry. Don't do anything daft because life is short, my boy, life is short."

I hugged her with mixed emotions. I mumbled farewell and made my way to the train station.

The platform was deserted while I waited for my train to take me to Padgate for induction. It was cold, damp, and grey; sweet smoke from the McIntosh candy plant fell like drizzle across the station. I reached into my overcoat and found a near-empty packet of cigarettes. I placed one in my mouth and furiously struck a match, quickly inhaling the harsh tobacco. In the distance, I heard the whistle of the train. I smelled the coal burning off its engine. I breathed in the coal that had been dug from the pits of Barnsley, Elsecar, and Barley Hole. I tasted it in my mouth, around my teeth, and on my tongue. It was the soot of my father, my grandfather, and all my ancestors who laboured beneath the ground. As the train drew its way into the belly of the station, another passenger approached the platform. He was a man in his fifties, long past the time for war, and he was whistling the tune, 'Run rabbit, run rabbit, run, run, run…"

PART TWO
WAR & PEACE

9

Square-bashing at Padgate

I was expelled out of the train at Padgate Station, which is near Warrington. Numerous other bleary-eyed boys followed me out of the train's carriages. There was a confused and harried look on our faces. No one introduced themselves to each other. We all turned and shuffled in the direction marked RAF Padgate.

Some carried small bags filled with gifts of food from their mothers, wives, or girlfriends. I held tightly onto a cardboard suitcases fastened together with coarse string. These boys and I lazily ambled towards the gates of the base. As I strolled along with the rest, I encountered a surprising sensation welling up inside me. It was almost elation at the prospect of something new. It charged excitedly through my blood. It was the sheer novelty of this experience; the nation would take care of me if I helped take care of the state. But in the back of my mind, the euphoria of change was tempered with a dark thought that this new experience could include a letter sent to Lillian telling her I had died for King and Country. Reluctantly, we crossed over into the camp and each of us moved in our own individual way, until we reached the recruitment building.

We loitered outside, until one of us in the crowd got up the courage to open the door.

"Have your enlistment papers ready," bellowed an RAF sergeant like a wolf hound. "Stand in a neat single file. No talking," he hollered, as he pulled young men in through the entrance.

We resembled riders about to enter a carnival ride renowned for its fearful journey through the underworld.

Eventually, the sergeant grabbed my paperwork. He scanned it. Cursedly, he bellowed, "In ya go, Smith."

From those fierce words, I was inducted into the RAF. Inside the stone building through a narrow hallway, I was led to a large windowless room filled with banks of desks. Corporals and lowly LACs typed, filed, and wrote on long sheets of paper. It all recorded: the day's fresh batch of recruits. My papers were assessed and a clerk looked up and told me, "When you volunteered, you indicated that you want to be a wireless operator. Is that what you still want to do?"

I thought for a moment and agreed it was my preferred choice. It seemed like a safe enough assignment and a rather exciting position. The terminology Wireless Op filled me with prospects of learning a new and, I presumed, innovative technology. Considering my previous encounter with a radio was the one in my mother's living room, operated on unreliable, cumbersome wet batteries, I believed I was to be led through an electronic wonderland. The clerk looked down at my enlistment paper and with a thick fountain pen put his initials on them. I was dispatched to another section of the building where a medical doctor ordered me to strip. I was prodded from all directions. My pulse and blood pressure were taken and I was measured and weighed like livestock at a fall fair. They inoculated me against disease with injections that made the muscles in my right arm ached. While the physician motioned me to dress, I looked up and noticed a clock face staring down at me. It dawned on me that in less than five minutes,

I had been deemed fit for combat. Pushed out of the medical exam room, I tumbled down the hallway. It was marked with arrows pointing me towards the next station of my transformation, from civilian to cipher. I was pitched into a room where barbers made quick work of my hair. They trimmed it back to my skull in a short, back, and sides cut. Stunned, I left that room. Down the hall, a sergeant spat orders at me to be on the double and get kitted out.

A short, bespectacled boy behind a cage screen door read my measurements off my recruitment papers. He was like a professional clothing salesman. The clerk went from piles of shirts to heaps of pants, coats, and boots, and then neatly presented them to me. I signed that I had accepted: one shirt, one belt, one overcoat, boots, hairbrush, boot brush, cap and one kit bag. I agreed; it was my responsibility to keep, in good order, the clothing and accoutrements given to me by the King. Loss or malicious damage to this uniform was a breach of regulations; the punishment was forfeiture of one's pay. I was also given my service number, which I was to memorize. Upon request, it was to be repeated, immediately: "Smith, AC 1777…." From now on, the numbers tumbled out of me, as if they had been given to me at the baptismal font. I was presented with my pay book. It recorded my weekly stipend awarded to me for service to the war. I stammered a very civilian, "Ta." The clerk ignored me and he wanted to get on with the next fitting, for the chap waiting patiently behind me.

Outside of the recruitment building, I turned in all directions. I swung round to all degrees of the compass wondering what I was to do next. Where was I to go? There were ten other teenagers who performed the same delicate movements as if we were radar beacons. I was broken from my lassitude with the strangeness.

"Get a move on, you lazy lot, on the double," a sergeant howled. "Follow me," cursed the sergeant.

We were led to a pile of dry straw heaped up in a covered shed. We were ordered to fill a cloth paliass until full. This was my mattress while in attendance at Padgate. With one hand, I dragged my hay-filled mattresses, which resembled a straw man for Guy Faulke's night. In the other hand, I clasped tightly onto my kit bag.

We marched out of step to a Nissen hut; it was to be our sleeping quarters during our time at Padgate. It was our refuge from square-bashing, or how we learned to march; either in advance or retreat of the enemy. I asked what bed was mine.

"Anyone you can find, sunshine," bellowed the sergeant. "And don't be shy or else you will be kipping on the floor."

I hastily found a cot with thin wire springs that held my straw bedding. I threw the paliass down and placed my duffle bag on the bed. The bed sunk into a curve with the inconsequential weight placed upon it. Not knowing what to do next, I stood around my cot, still wearing my street clothes.

Unfortunately, the other recruits followed my example and when the sergeant discovered us still dressed as civilians, he screamed out with loud disgust, "Do you think those clothes are your Sunday best? "You are the biggest bunch of gob shites I've met this week. Wakey, wakey, rise and shine, you are in His Majesty's Royal Air Force. You wear that bloody uniform until Mr. Hitler and Mr. Mussolini are on the bloody gibbet. If you die before them because of your own bleeding stupidity, we will put you in the ground wearing your blue uniform. So get bloody dressed, you are air men now."

The sergeant smartly turned and his boots methodically hit the wood floor of the hut. He marched out, slamming the door behind him.

"I don't think we will be calling him Dora," said a Lancashire man who had the cot beside me. "Name's Robbie and I'm down from

Wiggin. I used to peddle fish now I'm in this fine fucking kettle."

Robbie was very small, almost scrawny, and he wore thick, round glasses that made him more insect-like than human. I introduced myself while fastidiously putting on my new uniform and dressing for my new role as ACH 2 or "Aircraft Hand 2."

The woolen uniform itched and was tight and smelled of moth balls. The boots cut roughly into my feet. They were more suitable to a Chinese woman with bound appendages. I placed the cap on my head. The others in the room played soldier with each other. They bantered to one another and greeted each other with sloppy salutes until the sergeant re-appeared and gave us a bollocking for being tardy and not properly dressed. Our belt buckles were askew, our caps not at the proper tilt and angle, and we were utterly and as hopeless as, "Tits on a bull." We were told to stand at attention, at our beds. The sergeant passed across the room like an ominous battle cruiser. An N.C.O. appeared and told us to designate two men from the hut to fetch coal. Because we were closest, the sergeant nominated Robbie and me. Our hut was allowed two large pails a day, which would be fed into the two inefficient stoves at either end of the hut. The shed was located at the far end of the camp. So I was once again being employed as a dray horse. This did not make me optimistic about the future. Robbie and I left to fetch the coal.

On the way, Robbie confided, "I'll be buggered if the RAF is going to get me killed. I'm getting out of this war in one piece."

"How?"

"Never fucking volunteer for anything. Best thing," he said, "is to melt into the scenery. Don't give the buggers a chance to remember you."

"Mate," I said, "I don't think we've been that successful if on our first day, we've been already volunteered to haul coal."

Robbie rejoined, "Stay to the back of the room, Smith. Stay so far back that no one remembers you." He asked if I had volunteered.

"Yes."

"Bloody marvelous, Smith, it was brilliant to volunteer. Everybody is thinking you were some gobshites, patriot, or hero. They thought the same of me back home. If I had waited until they called me up," he put a finger to his throat as if it were a knife, "I'd be drowned in the North Atlantic or running from the whole fucking German army in Libya. This is the only time, Smith, that volunteering might save our lives. Let us bugger on through this merry-go-round called the RA bleeding F. I plan to say my yes sir, no sir, and two bags full if asked, otherwise I am stum. I reckon I can get home in one fucking piece from this fucker's war. I reckon I'll be back in Wiggin with all my fingers and toes. My cock'll be pointing in the right direction, skywards."

We returned to the hut with our ration of coal and received cheers from the other recruits. The sergeant returned for us at five o'clock. We were all marched to the mess hall. We were fed an inedible stew, which consisted of boiled meats and animal parts even unrecognizable to me. "Gaud," said Robbie, "it's like the C.O backed over a vagrant and they just plopped him in the pot."

To me, having had both worse and less, I consumed it without complaint. I knew there would likely be a day when the RAF would not be able to feed us; very much like Lillian and Albert could not always provide for their children.

There was loud talking, laughter, and hoots and hollers running down the mess hall. The new recruits were taking this more as a day's outing, until a row of sergeants ordered silence. It reminded me of my days spent in the food halls of the Catholic school. There, the nuns disciplined me and other students for poor table manners with a swift backhand to the head. At Padgate, the only element missing to remind me of my blessed time with the church was a giant crucifix hung beatifically from the walls. Instead, it was replaced with Jesus' Earthly representative: a portrait of King George the Sixth.

After completing our indigestible meal, we were herded back to our sleeping quarters, where the sergeant hammered at us about the morrow's bone-breaking itinerary.

"You love birds," he barked, "get your shut-eye because when the sun sticks her head up out of your arses tomorrow, It is rise and shine for you sorry lot. I want to see your smiling faces in the morning with your beds made, your uniforms clean and tidy. I want to see those uniforms on your skinny little backs and your boots polished. After that, you will shit and shave. Be on the parade square at eight o'clock sharp. The RAF has decided to see if you've got any brains. So, tomorrow, my sunshines, we are going to test your skulls to see if you can handle a radio or a shovel. After that, ladies, we squad bash all ficking day. So, lights out and pull off your socks, and keep yer hands off your cocks."

The sergeant doused the lights in our tin shed on his way out.

"Gran'night, mate," said Robbie.

Around me, twenty-five boys from Yorkshire fell into rambunctious sleep. Our slumber was interrupted with loud snoring and farts that resembled the sound of distant anti-aircraft guns. Far away in Cardiff while we slept, the air raid sirens sounded as Luftwaffe forces pounded the Welsh city. Henkel bombers attacked and gutted the university, the warehouses, and industrial housing that hugged the port.

The next morning, we awoke to our sergeant's explosive shouts as he kicked the side of our beds and exhorted us to get up. Bed covers were torn from us and our skinny legs and arms emerged out of our warm cocoons un-coordinately. We stood by our beds as under-developed airmen. I dressed quickly and along with Robbie, I made my way to the privies that were constructed out of tin and warped wood.

When I swung open the door, I realized I was to share this space with another recruit. I quickly looked over and saw his pants dangling around the bottom of his legs. I discerned shitting noises coming from his body. I tried to turn, but was met with a congenial voice. "How are ya?"

I looked the other way and said, "I was doing alright." I loosened my trousers. Like the man beside me, my pants were crumpled around my boots. I squatted on top of a rough hole and emptied my bowels. I lit up a Woodbine, which slightly camouflaged the stench of a thousand airmen's turds, piss, and vomit.

Afterwards, I met Robbie at the washing up hut, which was in an old, brick building. Grey lights cast shadows against row after row of metal wash basins that had long copper taps hanging from them. The water was cold and fell out sharply. The soap was hard on my face as I tried to lather up and shave with an RAF issue razor that made my face bleed. Robbie waited for me outside and he mocked his new-found indentured servitude to the RAF.

"They think this is hard? They say this is difficult? Try living in Wiggin with four brothers. We kipped in the same bed. We were like snug fucking fish in a tin. Except when you pulled the blankets off, for your troubles; you got one big, giant, warm fart. I tell you, this is a walk in the park, next to Wiggin. And you know Churchill is going to balls it all up, anyways. Fight them on the beaches, my arse. So I am going to do as little as possible and hope the bastards forget about me."

Inside the mess hut, I grabbed my breakfast of fake eggs, a rasher of greasy bacon, and toast. I washed it down with watery tea that Lillian would have referred to as "witch's piss." Robbie dug in to his yellow breakfast and said he wished he could have a fag. But smoking was forbidden in the mess hut. We finished our meal and Robbie and I went outside to walk towards the parade square. I tried to finish my Woodbine that I had started in the bog but the sergeant marched up towards us. Quickly, I dropped the cigarette and hid it underneath the sole of my boot.

The sergeant screamed, "You lazy sods, good for nothing layabouts. Follow me to the testing section."

We marched haphazardly into another building. A different NCO proceeded to unbraid us as to our slackness and shuffling appearance. There were fifteen of us and we were ordered to sit on a wooden bench with a long table straddling beside it. The NCO placed in front of each man a series of blocks, cubes, wooden circles, and jig-saw elements. We were to arrange, attach, and connect these asymmetrical designs within three minutes. I found the exercise perplexing and somewhat complicated. Others around me handled this assignment as if a dismembered human skeleton were placed before them and they were timed to put the old bones back as a human being.

"Time's up," said the NCO.

He walked down, inspecting and marking our ability to make spatial judgments. I looked at Robbie and asked him how he did.

"Piece of cake, I just copied you."

The sergeant frantically marched us out of the room with curses and damnations. He directed us down the hallway to a similar-looking room. In this room, there were rows of headsets on the tables. Another NCO explained this test would determine if we could proceed to wireless school or if we had to find another calling in the RAF. The NCO made us listen to Morse code over a loud speaker. It was a cacophony of noises, scratches, beeps and blips to me. "That, lads," he explained after a long impulse emanated from a speaker on the table, "is a dash. The short blip is a dot. Simple, isn't it? One long sound, one short sound and we are making music.

"In a moment, you are going to place the headset on. I am going to send out some Morse code. I just need you to count the dashes and dots. It's easy peasy, like counting sheep in a pen," said the NCO, self-assuredly.

My confidence deflated. I remembered I was never good at exams. I feared tests. I was never prepared and thought they showed me as stupid or the slowest. I had an uneasy feeling I was going to fail. I dreaded the notion that these new people, including Robbie, might make me the butt of their jokes. I would be considered an imbecile. If I could have walked out of the room and said this was all a mistake, I really wanted to be a bomb loader, I would have. However, the rest of the men in the room looked equally uneasy. Robbie joked that it all sounded Japanese to him.

I was given a pencil and a piece of paper where, at the top left of the foolscap, I wrote 'dashes' and on the right, 'dots'. I placed the tight black headset on over my ears. I looked over at Robbie, who appeared ridiculous with the headset and his large wire rim glasses. With an explosion of electric notes the test began. Everything moved at an almost indecipherable speed raining inside my skull, until it all went white inside my mind and body. Now, each impulse sounded like an echo, distinct and unique. I visualized them as they floated past my ears. That one was a dash. This one was a dot. So went the examination for three minutes. The quiz was terminated by the NCO. He collected the papers and began marking them. Wait outside, we were told. After ten minutes of shuffling and nervous jokes, the NCO came out. In alphabetical order, he called out the names of those that had passed. I was the last one to be called, but I had passed. Robbie also advanced. "See, I told you; it is all Japanese," he retorted.

The rest of the day, I was marched with my fellow recruits upwards and downwards. My legs and feet ached in the tight boots provided for me. The sergeant, with threats, abuse, and humiliation, taught us to about face, right turn, and to march double time; until it was time for tea. When, we prepared for bed, there was less talk in the hut. We had been stripped of our energy from mindless, numbing marching. I quickly fell asleep, pleased that I had passed my first two days as an ACH 2 with no complaints and some progress. I reasoned if this was all the war had to show me, it wasn't going to be too bad.

Robbie spoke to me before turning over in his bed. "I've had harder ways of earning a pound. We get food, beds, and clothes. Outside of prison, this is the next best thing for staying safe," he mumbled in a sleepy voice.

It certainly was better than civilian life for me. At least in the RAF, I was hidden by a number. My past was blurred and unseen like everyone else in the Nissen hut; we were anonymous. My old life was obscured and unimportant to anyone but me. Here, my present existence was identical to everyone else's. I wasn't judged as poor or rich, educated or uneducated. At Padgate, I was just a number locked in a filing cabinet, with thousands of other eighteen-year-old boys.

Our third morning at Padgate was a mirror image to the second morning. We woke from warm beds and placed our feet onto cold floors. We pulled on our uniforms and rushed to the latrine to shit and shave. We ate the same breakfast and fell out for inspection at the exact same time. The sergeant taught us how to salute and what to salute.

"If it moves, salute it."

Outside, it was barely above freezing, but we ran until sweat dripped down the crack of our asses. We about faced and stood too and we shuffled. We formed neat identical lines. They were all symmetrical lines of unsmiling acne-scarred faces from all parts of Yorkshire. Each day, breakfast, lunch, and dinner were the same. There were always heaps of food, an abundance of meats and steaming boiled potatoes. The sky above us remained constant. It was always wintery grey only broken by the sound of RAF turbines overhead, practicing flight maneuvers.

During the evenings, we were provided free time. We had the option of playing endless, ceaseless, monotonous games of cards. I never had the leisure in my youth to learn the games of chance, so I observed Robbie and the others play trump or lose their bid. We were free to write letters home or to girlfriends or a wife. It was stipulated that all correspondence was censored for information that might be helpful to the enemy. What information could we have possessed that would raise the eyebrow of German spies? Was it that we all thought this war was a lark? The conflict had no real meaning to us. Our experience was limited to newsreels showing defiant defeat in the desert. Our reality was the chocolate soldier routines on the square. The blitz was long past. Air raids were as threatening to us as the sound of distant thunder that promised rain in the next village.

In the evenings, we were at liberty to lie to our hut mates about how many girlfriends we had, or how many women we had fucked. Most boasted but I was quiet. I was not sure if my silence was a sign to them that my conquests were few, or that I was one who preferred not to kiss and tell. As long as we were back in camp before ten p.m.; we were free to leave the enclosure. We usually went to the local pub where the regulars treated us as irritants and show offs. They generally mocked and derided our proud piss and water Air Force attitude.

The fourth morning, afternoon, and evening, fell like the third and second morning, afternoon, and evening. Our lives were as routine and as anticipated as the moving of a loom at a mill in Halifax or Bradford. We followed a predictable pattern as if our marching, saluting, and shitting in meticulous order would protect this island from Teutonic efficiency. By the tenth day, we were presented with wooden guns. We were taught to march into battle with timber as a weapon. Later on, we were given Lee Enfield's; relics from the First Great War bereft of ammunition. The RAF believed it made our square-bashing more realistic. Our ultimate purpose, after all, was to attack, defend, or run away with dignity. By the second week, I was all for running away with dignity. There was a dull tedium, like a headache that never left you, to all this walking up and down a parade square with five men abreast, ten men deep.

I pointed it out to Robbie. "I joined the RAF because my feet are flipping flat and that is all I bleeding do. Up and bloody down, across and bloody back; I've walked to fucking Manchester and never been out the bloody gate in front of us," I moaned.

Repeating the mistakes of the First Great War, they put gas masks on us. They sat us in cement, windowless building and let off smoke flares in the confined space. I felt the foreign sensation of inhaling and exhaling through a breathing apparatus designed for limited survival and not comfort. The goggles around my eyes fogged up as smoke filtered through the room. It was claustrophobic and panic-inducing. It was like drowning, without being in water. It was how the pig must have felt that day when Bill dragged it towards me for slaughter. I and several others began fiercely banging on the doors demanding to be let out. The sergeant laughed at us as we stumbled out of the building like Saturday night revelers leaving their local, weak-kneed and giddy. The last one out was Robbie, who apparently was not afraid of tight spaces because of his nocturnal bed-sharing with four brothers. I pulled off my mask and I sucked in fresh cold March air that felt brittle in my lungs. That exercise taught me that I did not want to die in fire or by gas, but in my bed, very old and very content.

I felt the ennui of the drills and drab skies, cold bunks, and strange young men around me. But it was also comforting to me because I felt responsible to no one but myself at Padgate. I marched, I drilled, I ate, and I shat. No was able to fault me because I was doing my duty to my country. I owed this nation nothing other than my obligation to march on the spot towards a battle that may never come for me; not if I had anything to do with it. I had already marched and fought alone, as a child, for food, for clothing, and for shelter. This present game of toy soldier was pure escapism. It was no more than a charade, a child's playground game for me. Looking around at the others on the square, it was probably no different. We all kept time with our marching feet. There were worse things we could be doing. I could be serving pork pies to the Halifax's middle class. Robbie could be flogging fish on Wiggin pier. We all could be unemployed and praying the dole would keep you alive for a little while longer. Politics, democracy, Poland, and Hitler never entered our heads except as a cliché. We were here because we were here. It was different from where we came from; it offered us a vista on new prospects and new beginnings. We were eighteen and did not read the fine print of our contract with the King. He could use us until we were dead if he so wished.

Three weeks into square-bashing and our squad was informed that we were moving to another base in a week. If we had any letters to write, we better do it now. Several days previous, I had gone into town and had my photo taken in my new uniform. I had a dozen copies made. I sent out letters filled with proud exploits of my deeds and my new life. I mailed one to Lillian and wished her birthday greetings. I wrote another to Mary, enclosed with fond wishes for her being well and happy. Off handedly, I added without much conviction that if she met up with our dad, "Tell him that I am in the RAF fighting the war for England." With the remainder of my photos, I posted them off to various girls whose addresses I had obtained before I left Halifax. I composed the same letter to each woman. I wooed them as a proud airman about to take up battle against the fearsome Nazis. I concluded each missive, "I truly hope and pray that I will get back safe from all this danger; so that we may spend some special moments together." It was bullshit and looking around the Nissen hut, the majority of recruits were repeating my efforts to get laid in Bridlington, Burnley, Hull, or Huddersfield.

On the morning of March 18th, we lined up on the parade ground and were presented with our travel cards. We were going to RAF St Athan in Wales for further wireless training. We marched to the rail station. The men and I joked and made light of the fact that we had advanced through our first stage of life in the RAF. It took us almost eighteen hours and numerous connections to reach Wales. When it started to grow late, we worried aloud if there were going to be trucks to meet us at the station to take us to the camp. Or whether we would have to employ our newly acquired marching skills and foot it to the base. As dusk fell, the blackout curtains were drawn and we were left to stare at each other while we were trapped in hot and sweaty compartments. The morning's optimism was replaced with the weary sound of the train wheels clashing against the tracks. Men shuffled out from their compartments to cramped corridors and tried to light up cigarettes to extinguish what little oxygen was left in the train. I was standing next to Robbie, who had grown mute and humourless by the length of the trip. My head bobbed up and down while my kit bag slumped against my right leg. I was by the carriage window. A heavy black out curtain was inefficiently strung across it. Along the side was an insignificant opening to the outside world. If I squinted, I could see darkened homes, silhouettes of villages empty of life as we move southward into Wales. I perceived the shadows of the terrain that even in darkness presented itself as more lush and verdant than Yorkshire.

Outside of my tiny optic vision, in the Far East, Tommy Doolittle with twenty over-laden bombers began a daring one-way raid over Tokyo. His bombers took off from aircraft carriers. The bombers were not built for long missions and ran out of fuel over the China Sea, where most of them ditched. The damage to the city was slight, but Doolittle's guile at penetrating deep into Japan reverberated within the Samurai nation. By the time we reached the station, an Executive Order had been signed by President Roosevelt that allowed the American government to round up and incarcerate enemy nationals living in the United States. Japanese Americans were sent to relocation camps and stripped of their property. Innovative England had enacted legislation in 1939 to imprison all foreign nationals at war with us, which included Jewish refugees from Nazi-land. German provocateurs and Jewish refugees bunked together until myopic bureaucrats were able to tell the difference between the two.

10

ST. Athan, Wales

When we neared the station; sergeants clamoured for us to listen up. Upon de-training, we were to form into our assigned units and await instructions. I thought we were always awaiting instructions. Whether I turned right or left, it was decided by another and double checked by another higher in authority. It was a chain of command that stretched from me to the Air Marshall, so it seemed. But that was only fantasy because in this war, like the last war and any war to come; the left hand never knew what the right hand was doing.

The long, unruly train slowed down to a trot and then stopped as we reached the Cardiff terminus. The carriages recoiled and threw everyone askew. We opened the train doors and spilled out like waste water from a washer woman's bucket. Robbie tried to light a Woodbine. In the distance, a voiced screamed, "Put that bloody cigarette out. There is a blackout in effect."

Robbie groaned and stubbed the heater out with his thumb and then the two of us mutely moved along to where the vehicles awaited us. On the way, the kit bags felt on our backs felt as heavy as the dead. It was a thirty minute journey to our camp at St Athan and when we arrived everyone was tired and morose. Driving through the new camp gates, it was apparent this was a bigger and more industrial type of base. It was more like a giant factory or mill, with many buildings, annexes, warehouses, workshops, and sleeping quarters.

We were ushered out of the truck and ordered to march over to the first building on our left. We presented our travel documents and assignment orders. Being moved about like a snooker ball irritated Robbie, but it left me unimpressed. I had been banged around and made midnight dashes all through my youth. As a kid, I left many doss-houses through the back window or front door in both confusion and haste. At least in the RAF, I knew I'd always find warm food and a bed waiting for me. Inside the building, an orderly greeted us in a decent manner.

"You must be knackered. I'll have someone show you to the mess hut and then to your billets. Tomorrow, lads, you are on oliday. Get familiar with St. Athan because it is probably bigger than most villages you were born and bred in," the NCO told us.

The mess hut was four times the size of Padgate. The menu was identical; plentiful food rich in meat, spuds, and watery tea. But it tasted good as we had not eaten since leaving Lancashire. It was also pleasant that we could smoke in this mess hut, which Robbie did with abandon. I lingered, drawing on my Woodbine and wondered how this could be war. I was feeling sated and comfortable from a good meal and a hearty smoke. But in Poland, probably, at the moment I exhaled smoke contentedly from my fag; intellectuals, Jews, and communists were being butchered in a camp called Belzec. They were shot before enormous open pits where their corpses fell with calculated precision as if they were match sticks being tossed into an ashtray.

Fed, we marched gingerly to our billets. It was an improvement on Padgate. We had real, if lumpy, mattresses that had reluctantly embraced the sleeping bodies of untold airmen before my weary bones lay down upon it. An airman deposited a bucket of coal into the stove to cut the damp, Welsh chill blowing off the nearby sea. Until today, the furthest I had ventured was to York and to Blackpool to bid my sister and our childhood good-bye and good riddance. Now as a man, I thought foolishly, I had traveled from the Northern coal fields of West Yorkshire to the southern coal-belt of Glamorgan, as a reluctant warrior.

In the morning, I was awoken by the clashing sound of a new sergeant; who bitterly antagonized us to rise from our dark slumbers and make ourselves presentable.

"Some oliday," I remarked to Robbie.

"Some war," he answered back.

After dressing, we meandered to the privies, which were greater in size and stench than Padgate, and quickly did our business.

Breakfast was a busman's feast of seemingly unlimited bacon and scrambled eggs. We poured tea freely into our RAF-issued mugs. We smoked liberally as we talked amongst our mess mates about our proud home towns and villages. I was the only one who found no urge to boast of Halifax, Bradford, or Sowerby Bridge.

"It's all right," I would say generically.

If prodded I invented my home life. I made it sound as broad and humdrum as the rest of their pictures of home. My life to them had the football pitch, the pub, the dance hall, the cake shop, and the prettiest girls in town. And for them, I had a mum that made a Sunday roast that did herself proud. If someone asked about my father, I said he was a butcher and we had a normal and happy home that I shared with a sister and a brother. Unfortunately, Billy Jr. did not appear in the movie of my life and was erased from my narrative, along with Albert, my real father.

Following the fry up, a veteran LAC sat down on the benches beside us. He had been at ST Athan for the last three months. He introduced himself as Pat and he painted a cubist picture of what we were to expect: a shit storm of work and discipline. He was our Virgil for the day and he led us through the nether-world of St Athan. The

165

LAC, who was maybe a year older than us, had sage wisdom stenciled on his face. It was from his extra months of training. We were warned to salute with rigour.

"The officers, sergeants, and NCOs are all bastards here. They will put you on report for any shoddy displays of discipline. Be alert," Pat told us. "Work and don't sod off or it is the glass house for you." He reminded us, "There is a war on."

As if it had slipped our minds and no one could muck about anymore because we were taking a thrashing.

"We lot," Pat continued, "are in the RAF. Some of you are going sky-borne and others are staying feet on the ground. But our mates in the air are taking a beating."

They were being shredded to bits by German fighter planes and anti-aircraft batteries across the occupied continent.

"No one wants to be up there," and he pointed skyward "because it is closer to God than anyone wishes to be at the moment."

Like a sibyl portending evil days, the LAC told us Bomber Command squadrons took off from airfields all across England and returned in battered formation, their flock thinned and damaged. The ratio between life and death in the air was thin.

"So learn your courses," Pat warned. "Follow the rules and you will be done right by the RAF."

The LAC took us on an extensive tour of the camp. It was the largest training base for signals, wireless operators, bomb aimers, navigators, and other journeymen in the business of delivering death on our fortress island.

I was overwhelmed by the immensity of the camp and its various sub-directories and mazes of military protocol. It had the efficiency and icy formality of the rendering plant where Bill Moxon butchered pigs and cattle. The LAC showed us the building where we would spend the greater part of our days; it was where we would earn our keep by perfecting Morse code. The remainder of our time would be spent in square-bashing drills, until our names were cleansed from our memories and only our service number remained. After the tour, I returned to our billet with the rest of my wireless training unit. I made confidence-building small talk with Robbie and some others. When it came time for lights out, I quickly fell asleep. However, I had an uneasy night because I was fearful that I was going to bugger it all up and end up in a front line fighting air division. There was no quiet inside my brain but outside of my bunk and our hut was a hushed silence. There was a creeping darkness that smothered the breathing and snoring of others. It made me only aware of my expiration and respiration as if on an operating table.

On our first formal day of wireless training, we met our instructor. He was a cynical, chain smoker with deep nicotine stains which ran up on down his left index finger. There was an overwhelming damp stench about him as if he was dragged from a coal cellar every morning to provide us guidance. While our training books were handed out; he informed us that his method of instruction was the best. He wanted us to learn our vocation as quickly as possible, so we could get on with our true purpose, fighting the war. It would take us six months to become fully functional in Morse code and for those that failed his course; there was an ominous threat of worse professions. And so I set to work learning, memorizing, and studying the intricacies of this new, electronic language. My Morse knowledge advanced, day in and day out as our instructor took us through the monotonous world of keyboard work, signal identification, speed, and message retention. It was slow, repetitive, and painfully dull progress. Yet outside of my classroom, there were thousands of messages being transcribed, sent, and coded each day. They detailed bombing missions, troop advancement, and endless bomber command casualties. They were coded lists of men lost over enemy territory, or terse reports about crashed aircraft. They spoke of planes being too shot up to land safely and men dead upon impact.

In my dreams each night, I bashed against an imaginary keyboard and made long and excruciating dashes and dots. I sent out distress calls to release me from this infernal camp, this idiotic war, this pallid life. I was only saved by our weekly foray to the local pub for a piss up. I headed off to the village pub with Robbie and another hut mate, Brian. He was from Salford, Lancashire. He was a big lad, with a giant mop of hair, when not shaved by the RAF. At the pub, we immersed ourselves in watery ale and harsh cigarettes. Around a table overflowing with other recruits from St Athan, we took the mickey out of the camp, the instructors, and the war. Brian was an excellent mimic and precisely imitated the eccentricities of our wireless instructor.

Robbie broke into song and ironically bellowed out, "We'll meet again don't know when… don't know why."

The pub, like the camp, like the RAF, was just moments of piss and vinegar for me. I may have marched in step on the parade square but inside my brain; I was overcome by confusion and panic. In those early months of my war, I felt free of personal responsibility. I felt more connected to these strangers who shared a hut with me than I did with my family. I felt more of an attachment and a greater sense of community to the rest of those blue-uniformed kids than to anyone in my youth; I eagerly plunged into the river of uniformity. It cleansed me of my individuality because I despised what I saw reflecting back at me from my grimy, shaving mirror. I feared that if I thought too deeply, probed too much, I would uncover behind it all an overwhelming, fearful, intestine-grabbing sense of waste and futility. As I sat in the pub with my new mates, my new life, I was nauseated that this was the prologue before I ended up dead and forgotten. I thought to myself; *If I cheat death and keep my head down, will life cheat me? Will it just throw me back into the dung heap from which I came?* But I continued with the songs and mock camaraderie. Perhaps, I didn't know how to play poker, but I was good at bluffing and concealing the thoughts inside my head. Years of hiding my emotions from adults had taught me well, and it would serve me well in the RAF.

As time dripped wearily away, my RAF schooling became a drab routine. I was perfecting the skill, the art of being considered neither wet nor dry. Even Robbie acknowledged my supreme gift.

"Smith," he said, "you have a knack for being liked, but not too well liked to draw attention to yourself."

Three of us in the back row of the class passed our wireless exams and became LAC WOP, which was a land-air crew wireless operator. My marks were above average, but not too above average to set myself out as anyone special. I had successfully faded into the scenery and I would hopefully find a comfortable spot to spend the rest of the war.

I was awarded a signal badge for passing the exam. It meant I now had something to place upon the left sleeve of my uniform. Proudly, I sewed on my new designation and jauntily marched off to the nearest photographic shop. I got a handful of photos made to send to a group of shop girls I had romanced back in Halifax.

Having graduated, I was permitted leave to go home to Halifax. Holding my travel warrant for home in my hand left me with a dead sensation because it was a destination I wished I could abandon for good.

It had been six months since I stepped away from the Halifax train platform. And now I was back for seventy-two hours. It was raining; miserable, sad Halifax rain. I had let no one know I was returning and I was ambivalent about staying at my mother's house. I decided to first go up to the White Swan, the grandest hotel in Halifax and treat myself to a beer like I was Odysseus' returning from Troy. I stowed my kit bag at the station's left luggage section and plowed my way up to the hotel. I wanted to prove to the rulers of Halifax that I was a man in uniform. Along the way, the newspapers cried out that in distant Russia, the battle for Stalingrad had begun. Another newspaper screamed that the Eighth Army hammered away at the iron grip of Rommel's Afrika Korps in the African desert.

In the gleaming bar room of the White Swan, I lingered and savoured my half pint of beer for as long as I could. Vainly, I hoped that a stray civilian would pitch in and buy a serving man a proper beer. The men in suits, the men of commerce, and the merchants that could waste their time in The White Swan were not going to indulge my fantasy. I left discreetly after the bar man became irritated by my loitering. Long sips on short beverages were never appreciated at the White Swan. I returned to the station to retrieve my gear and made my way to the Arcade.

When I sauntered into Grosvenor's, I made a big show of myself. The girls were happy to see me, but I also encountered the lad who had taken my place as manager. His good fortune at assuming my position was apparently divine. He proclaimed to the owner and the military that he was a devout Christian, a pacifist, and a devotee of Jesus Christ. He greeted me in a nervous and fearful manner. In my opinion, his faith was a curious and opportunistic one. All things were bright and beautiful, for him, because he stood on a stack of bibles and swore to the government that his god forbade him to shed blood. Strangely, his god said nothing about the pilgrim who profited from war by remaining behind to sell meat at a good profit to hungry civilians. I did not idle long at the shop, only long enough to make a date for the following evening, with a bubbling, witless girl. I left in haste and dread for Boothtown and Lillian.

My bus was filled with middle-aged men in drab raincoats and elderly women with colourless kerchiefs hiding their hair. Along the interior of the bus, propaganda posters shouted out to tired riders to be vigilant for spies and saboteurs. Within a couple of minutes, the conductor called out my stop. Regretfully, I slipped off the bus and into the persistent, Yorkshire drizzle.

To my disappointment, the street was deserted as I wanted the locals to see that my family had righted itself in me. I wanted Boothtown Road to observe me walking down the block and witness that I was in RAF blue. And we, the Smiths, descendants of Albert, owed nothing to anyone in this community or this country. When I came through my mam's front door, it seemed quiet and forlorn. Bill was still at work and Matt was out with his young mates. Only Billy and Lillian were there. Indifferently, I greeted my distant younger brother, who returned my indifference with a negligent shrug of his shoulders and a quick good-bye. Billy disappeared out the door to find things that were more amusing than me. I was not disappointed by his exit. I considered his existence a hindrance, another spot on our already gravy and soup-stained name. Lillian greeted me in the same manner as my departure; with guarded emotion. Her warmth suggested a cold front was on its way.

She noted that I looked well fed and fit. The RAF, according to her, had cleaned up my slouching attitude. Lillian put the tea on the boil. She informed me that Mary was doing well as could be expected as a new mother with a husband away in the army. In the early part of my training, Mary had sent me a brief note that said she had given birth to a boy. I sent congratulations, but I didn't understand the enormity of her problems. It was daunting having a baby in war time, with few resources and a husband in the services. From my induction in the RAF, I wrote Mary twice, three times at most, and I received from her the same amount of post. Our letters were banal, stilted attempts at hiding our emotions and distorting the present with clichés and pleasantries.

As I sipped my tea, which was brewed strong and thick, I munched on a biscuit that Lillian had prepared for me. It was odd; everything in the house seemed as normal and worn as I had left it. However, my family had shifted from me like an uneven load on a lorry. They seemed so unimportant, almost trite because I believed I had turned into a man after six months of keeping in step with a parade sergeant. Mary, I adored and loved, but now only from afar. I felt we had both packed away our childhood pain for adult adventure. As for Lillian, sitting before me, her hair wrapped into a tight, neat bun; I grudgingly and resentfully mustered up some love for her. My emotions for her were as fixed as Greenwich Mean Time because I both loved her and loathed her for what I considered her base character. In reality, Lillian's flaw as a mother was that she made my sister and I survive childhood in spite of her transgressions, her failings and a world gone mad in economic despair.

Lillian encouraged me to go to Low Moor the following day. "Try to get acquainted with yer new nephew."

My homecoming with Lillian was expediently interrupted with the arrival of Bill.

"Let's have a look at you. You did alright, lad. There's no muck on you, Harry."

Lillian fished around in a kitchen drawer and presented me with a spare key.

"Doors always open for thee at any time of night, as long as it is not past bloody midnight." As I stood up to leave, my mum and Bill said in unison "Tara."

Outside, Bill Junior was playing with some toy trucks and making loud engine noises. I stepped over Billy as if he were the family cat. I walked straight down the road to take the bus back into town.

I ended up in a pub that I had frequented with my Halifax mates. As fortune would have it, Roy Broadbent was granted leave from the Guards the same weekend as me. We encountered each other at the pub. Roy and I spent the night comparing our training, our sergeants, our grub, and our new mates. Roy's schooling in the vocation of infantry and cannon fodder was near complete. He said they would soon be sent overseas to take up in the fight against Germany. Broadbent said it half-heartedly. It was my opinion that the uniforms, the food, the birds were all nice. But the end result of killing or being killed was not the best conclusion for any of us. My other two mates, Eric and Doug, were doing alright by the war, he told me. Especially Eric; he was earning extra money and rations as a tool and die-maker. For the time being, Eric was cock of the walk in Halifax. He flashed his cash around while he escorted brightly rouged tarts to dance halls.

Roy and I left the pub. I explained I would be at my sister's the following day and on a date in the evening. I spoke gravely to him, while putting my hand to his arm.

"Be careful," I implored. "When they send you overseas, don't stick your neck out for no one. We have to come home safe. We can't let Eric have all the birds for himself."

I left Roy to make his way home to the safety of his worried mother and doting aunt. I got in just before the crow of midnight. I dropped off to sleep in my old bed, amazed at the silence emanating from the house. It was if all the past animosity had expired from exhaustion and age.

I was up early the following morning to catch the bus into Bradford to see my sister. Even though Albert lived in Bradford, I did not visit him. What was I to say to him? I had not seen him since 1930, when I was almost eight. I was a now a young man with a hazy memory of my dad and only remembered his failings, never his virtues or his own suffering. I found it best to leave him locked away in my subconscious as a dormant nightmare.

Mary's house was on the outer reaches of Bradford. Low Moor was buried in smoke stacks and green hills. It had angular steep streets that led up to barren row houses. Her dwelling was a one-up- one-down residence connected to a multiplicity of similar units. I knocked on her door. Inside, I heard the wail of a small child behind the entrance.

I called out; "It's your brother; open up, love, and get us some tea."

Presently, I heard the turn of the bolts and chain falling off the latch and Mary was before me. She had a radiant grin but my sister had a worn look around her face as if she had been carrying the weight of the barrow I pushed when I was seven.

"Get yerself in here," she said, and hugged me warmly. She

173

brought me over to her child's crib.

"I'd like to introduce you to the youngest and newest member of our traveling circus, Derek."

He was a beautiful, healthy boy. He was loved and well looked after.

I told her, "Hey, Mary. He is a luckier bugger. He's got a proper Mum and Dad."

Mutedly, she agreed, picking up her child and holding him tenderly. After a while, she put him down to sleep and made us tea. We spent four hours together and we did not say much to each other. Mary seemed reluctant to talk about her life and her husband. I was hesitant to speak about my RAF days as I thought it insignificant.

She said, "You men get all the bloody luck and glory. Look at you in the RAF, it's a life of adventure, no dull days down at mill for you."

At the time, I did not know what she meant. I never fully understand her words until many years later. My sister was far more trapped by the bonds of earth, kith, and kin than I was as a man. Men ran away, while women were forever tied to their primal obligation and responsibility towards their offspring.

When Mary and I were children, we pledged to survive and love each other. We were like marooned sailors clinging to bits of wreckage being tossed on an angry and lonely sea. Now, Mary had too many others desperately holding onto her and she had to keep them from being washed overboard. So she remained silent about her problems, her worries, and fears. Both she and I had learned as children to bury our hunger and our fear because there was no one to save us but ourselves.

When I was leaving, she told me, "If you need something, just holler. I will help."

"Ditto," I replied, kissing her cheek.

Sadly, I left knowing that neither of us would call upon the other if we needed help. We both believed, wrongly, our problems were burdensome and added weight to the other's responsibility. So we parted, loving each other, but no longer able to share ourselves with each other. For that stupidity, we were both rendered far more desolate and lonely.

I went straight from Low Moor to meet my date at the appointed pub. For my last night before returning to Wales, it was an embarrassing, paltry night. It was replete with piteous small talk to a woman who, as the night wore on, became more repulsive to me. I walked her home with self-disgust. We sat down on a bark bench on a quiet street and fondled each other. I grew sickened at myself and what I considered my bestial nature. There were so many people I would have rather been with at the moment. And while I kissed her; I tasted the stale bitter back wash of desire that contained neither affection nor respect. I wondered if I could ever find someone who loved me, and in my thoughts, I cursed the woman in front of me as a cheap scrubber, when in fact I was no better than her.

I returned home to Lillian's house. I slipped quickly into bed as I wanted to make sure I would be up and out before anyone had arisen. The follow morning, at six a.m., I left the house. On the kitchen table, I left a scribbled a note for Lillian, apologizing for the brevity of my visit but I was now under another's command.

I rode the train back to St. Athan. It was over-flowing with weary, dejected faces of soldiers, sailors, and airmen returning from leave. At the train station near Cardiff, I grabbed a bus. It took me directly to the base. I presented my travel papers and was signed back into the camp by an absentminded NCO. I went directly to my bunk and got underneath my covers. I tried to warm myself from the clawing cold trapped in my body from all the despondent emotions Halifax created in me. Robby attempted to talk to me, but I turned my back to him and slipped into dark slumber. Most in our hut, the following day were transferred to another RAF camp. I was thankful that Robbie and Brian were on the same list with me. We were scheduled to go to White Waltham, near Maidenhead.

11

White Waltham

Our camp at White Waltham was situated in a wooded area about two miles from the airfield. The aerodrome was the central hub for marshalling aircraft and airplane parts from around the nation. Throughout the day and night, the bucolic surroundings were being continuously disturbed with the ceaseless drone of Wellington, Lancaster, and spit-fighter planes The aircrafts were primarily ferried by female pilots and retired or injured RAF personal. The grass fields were in such bad condition from the wet winter the year previous to my arrival that an officer attempted to requisition two elephants and a mahout to act as tractors to plane the fields. The officer's novel approach to runway maintenance was rejected. It was feared if there was an air raid that the pachyderms would bolt and cause mayhem in the surrounding villages.

At this base, we had one sergeant major. He was master over our unit. He designated his minions to be in daily charge of us. His name was Sergeant Meade and he had a fearsome memory and easily held grudges. Later on, I witnessed firsthand his memory and his resentment when I tried to enter the camp after curfew.

On our second day, Meade had our unit on full pack march. After several miles, we reached a meadow where we rested. Ominously, Meade hollered, "Take a good look round, lads. Take a good long look at those green fields. Paint a pretty picture in your heads of England's green rolling land because pretty soon, all you are going to see is miles of sand."

Robbie looked at me and said, "I was hoping we were going to see Glasgow. Don't like the beach, don't like the sea-side, and don't like this musical ride."

Places with sand; I recoiled in dread. The notion of searing heat, no water, and being face-to-face with the enemy was a dismal prospect. It was not a destination that emboldened me with confidence.

Hectoring Meade said, "Full pack marches every day, lads, it's time to trim the fat off the roast."

Another NCO was to be designated for these RAF rambles.

"You'll thank me when you are in the Sahara, fit as a fiddle."

We began our hike back to camp sullen and forlorn at the threat of combat. Compared to St Athan, White Waltham was insignificant in size. Our quarters were identical to the last two stations; Nissen huts. As in Padgate, our mattresses were stuffed with straw. There were some new men from the South billeted with us. Their diction and accent indicated that up until now they had led a very charmed and easy life. They looked particularly effete. They were incapable of the labourious monotony actively promoted by the RAF during war. They clung together in the hut like kittens. They seemed afraid of us from the North, with our rough voices and harsh jokes. Generally, I felt contempt for them. I hoped they would be punished by brute work and mindless tasks. Most of us looked on our current tasks as a luxury compared to our civilian lives and backgrounds. However, one of them was unique: Clementine. He possessed an eccentric intelligence. He was always disassembling equipment to see how it operated. Nevertheless, he was incapable of taking the strays bits of his enterprise and reassembling them. He was considered reckless and a day-dreamer by the top brass, who refused his request for pilot training. The RAF believed Clementine was more inclined to wreck more planes of ours than down enemy aircraft. Therefore, it was safer for our side to have him as a common LAC with his feet firmly anchored to the ground. Clementine was also remarkable to me because he came from a wealthy family, but he was untouched by any sense of entitlement or class consciousness.

The following day after breakfast, our assigned sergeant formed us into our marching units. The sergeant was named Greene. Judging from his accent, he was originally from Sussex. Greene was built like a farm-hand that was used to working in the fields. As other sergeants had in the past, he inspected us on parade. There were the usual humiliating insults, cat calls, and intimidation. With this one as our band leader, I thought we were in for it. I was not looking forward to endless days spent in marches designed to break not only one's spirit, but also the arches in one's feet. Thus, we began a quick march out the camp gates. Our packs weighed heavily on our backs and silent blasphemies were on our lips. About three miles up the road was an open field. Beside it was a small building that turned out to be a tiny shop.

Before the store, the drill sergeant halted us and screamed out; "Right, lads, time for a brew up. Get your kits ready. If you want a bun or biscuit, go inside. You can buy one from the lady."

With our sweets, our tea, and our packs used as pillows, we laid out on the grassy meadow. We talked in loud tones as if we were on a church picnic.

"Steady on, lads," called Greene, "keep your voices down. Gather round," our commander announced. "Let me give you the lesson for today's sermon. I don't much care for walking. I don't much care for marching. I don't much care for trouble. So anyone grasses me out, you know what I am talking about… this, our afternoon holiday, I will crucify the bastard. I will have their bullocks thrown to the camp dogs to eat." He paused and looked at us all before continuing. "Secondly,

178

the most important rule of marching. Lighten the effing load."

He opened his kit bag and it was full of straw.

"Like our leaders," the sergeant noted, "it's filled with bloody straw. If you want to carry the weight of England on your back, so be it. If ya want to get through these days, lugging the least amount of shite, take my advice. Straw is not only good for cows and horses; it's good for us. It's as light as a fucking feather."

I wasn't too sure if he was serious or whether this was some intricate maneuver to get us all into trouble. Every day, our marches ended exactly at this juncture in a comfortable meadow drinking tea and eating biscuits. Robbie and Brian deduced that the sergeant had a relation in the shop.

"He's just making a quick bob or two because we are a lazy bunch of buggers."

It did not matter to me what profit Green might have made. We loafed in pleasant surroundings without care or concern.

Several miles up from our resting spot was Maidenhead. In the evenings and on weekends, we were allowed to travel to town. Robbie, Brian, and I made the walk up to the picturesque town, which was situated on the banks of the River Thames. We walked about town trying to find girls or a pub to gamble away our time. Maidenhead was as beautiful as a slender woman with large round eyes, porcelain skin, lightly draped in soft perfume. Its charm was so delicate; I thought one could almost break it with clumsy hands as if it were made of blown glass. This town was so unlike the villages and cities of the North, constructed with brute force for utilitarian needs. It whispered to you and beguiled you with its charm. The town was gentile to its inhabitants. Its population showed its affection back to the village with loving appreciation and civic pride. I wondered how these inhabitants would fare if they were forced to change places with the people of Sowerby Bridge. I was equally curious as to how Sowerby Bridge would cope in the gentle breezes of Maidenhead. I thought the Northern folk would muck it up like a farmer walking into a fine house with shit on his Wellies. As for the southern residents, if forced to migrate north, they would need to be hospitalized for apoplectic shock after breathing in the foul industrial air and seeing damp grime peeling off municipal buildings, housing and ordinary residents. Indeed, England's North and South were polar opposites which repelled and could never attract each other.

In one of my multiple sojourns to the village, I met a young woman. Foolishly, I took her on a date to go punting down the River Thames, as if I was a privileged boy from the South. Elocution classes may have taught me to soften my vowels. It did not instruct me on how to steer and chart a course in a flat-bottom boat with a pole employed as a propellant. We both ended up in the river. We thrashed about like two black bears. On the river banks, a fellow airman stationed at our base observed my predicament with much amusement. After initial laughter, he made his way to the water's edge to assist me and my companion out of the tributary. The female ascended the river bank with infuriating disgust. She was enraged at me, her chivalrous date, for tipping her into the Thames, whilst my air force compatriot fell onto the ground in fits of glee.

I said, "It's not bloody funny. I had to rent that punt and it cost quite a bit of money. Look at my uniform, it's buggered. I'll be up on charges."

"Never you mind," he said, "I'll help get you cleaned up and back to camp without a hitch." While the man spoke, my date angrily waddled off and up the road, never to be seen by me again.

The airman helped me out and on our way back to camp, he introduced himself. "Jack Williams. My mates call me Taffy seeing that I'm from Wales."

Taffy was situated two billets away from mine. On the long walk back to camp, we became fast friends. He was the most open and honest person I had met thus far in my life. He spoke of Wales and his life before the war, near the docklands of Cardiff. Taffy spoke of his family, who for generations had been dock workers. As his story continued, his voice sang in the dulcet manner of his countrymen. Even sad and harsh tales rolled off Jack's tongue in a cadence that was beautiful and haunting. Even though Taffy, like me, came from a callous environment, he had a wonderful appreciation for poetry. Jack generously shared his knowledge of English poets and Welsh folklore with me. By the time, we reached camp, I was dried off and I was starting to feel fortunate because that day, I found a loyal and true friend.

Over the next few days, I did not encounter Taffy as our unit was scheduled for assault training. Fortunately, my Welsh friend had given me prior information about this course, providing me with some valuable tips. Sergeant Greene had us forge into a river with a rope strung overhead. We were to cross this limpid but deep stream as if we were in the wilds of Borneo. The rope was to navigate ourselves to the other side. Our feet were wrapped around the suspended cable like the tails of marmosets gliding down jungle vines. I warned Robbie and Brian to tie their money into their handkerchiefs; otherwise it would fall into the water. Brian balked at the daft suggestion. Halfway across the river, he cursed as he saw his coins drop from his pocket like a donation to the riverbed far below. Brian let go of the rope and plunged into the September cold stream to retrieve his money. He drove his head underneath the cold brook many times, searching for each errant shilling. He swore each time he came up for mouthfuls of air. Brian then plunged down into the water as if a treasure was on the riverbed, deposited by fleeing highwaymen.

Across the river, our sergeant congratulated us on another mindless and pointless task accomplished for the air ministry. "If you are in the RAF and crossing streams, it means you got no bloody plane. It's time to put your hands up," he noted, without a hint of defeatism, but wet with sarcasm.

In the following days, we learned to bayonet straw men. We acted as if they had angered us by being enemy straw men out to rape our country women. Enthusiastically, I ran up and energetically tore open the bowels of the scarecrow tied to the wooden plank. The Southern lads, with the more upper class accents, were exceedingly delicate in their bayoneting. Their stabbing technique resembled deboning sole at a restaurant in the finer parts of London. When it was his turn, Clementine showed an almost homicidal determination to plunge the bayonet into the straw replica of Nazism. It was as if he had missed his calling in disemboweling. Later on, our unit was provided with loaded Lee Enfield rifles to fire at targets many meters away. For me, it had, a similar feeling to being at Blackpool and aiming at milk bottles along the promenade. Very much like at the amusement ground, I walked away with no stuffed animal. I received a stern lecture from Greene.

"Bloody brilliant, Smith, we'll thank you when my kids great me with *Guten Tag, Papa,* because you were left defending the beaches."

I improved my standing with the sergeant by my deft and quick manner at hand grenade tossing. As I fully understood it, the device in my hand was a weapon that could easily maim, kill, or disintegrate me. With quick resolve, I pulled the pin and chucked the bugger several yards in front of me, right into a hole barricaded with sandbags. A muffled explosive groan burped from the pit.

"Bloody marvelous, Smith, you have just killed a German paratrooper," congratulated the drill sergeant.

Robbie looked at me and said, "More likely the milk man."

The recruit following me tossed his into the parapet without the same effect. There was no explosion, only embarrassed quiet. It was like a wet fart that slowly trickled down one's trousers. Unfortunately, his curiosity was greater than his sense of danger. He jumped up and out of our secure trench and walked over to the repository for exploding grenades.

The sergeant screamed, "Fuck."

He chased after him and tackled him before he ended up badly injured from an exploding shell.

At White Waltham, our bands of reluctant airmen were also charged with learning the witless task of guard duty. I was not the most effective defender of Britain when posted as sentry. We were ordered to stand motionless with a rifle slung over our shoulders. The rifle's purpose was rather questionable as it was unloaded. Every base occupant and visitor was aware that the rifles were without cartridges, including the stray dogs that frequented our garbage tip. I stood during my shift as stiff as a mummy. I surveyed the open road ahead for enemy incursion, until my eyes developed double vision. I fell into a tantric stupor of a charmed snake. If a truck approached, I demanded the driver's papers. I would inspect them with pronounced diligence. But honestly, I could not and did not care to differentiate between what might be actual papers and what might be forged documents. As far as I was concerned, if someone was mad enough to want to be let into this base rather than let out; it was their problem.

During one of my ill-equipped shifts as RAF sentinel, a slightly intoxicated airman approached. He requested entrance to his unit. I let him pass with a nod. In inebriated friendliness, he attempted to strike up a conversation. I told him to move on.

"You better be in your bunk quick as its Sunday tomorrow. Church parade comes early."

"Don't have to do it, mate."

"What?" I queried, "Why not?"

"Because," he mumbled, "Jews and Catholics get to stand down for English Jesus on the Sabbath."

He was right; Jews and Catholics were excused from attending Sunday church services and could avail themselves to their papist or Hebrew past times. It was a revelation and until that moment, I had concealed my Catholicism. In my mind our faith was another indication of my family's oddness and lack of conformity with proper and well fed British middle class ways. But from that occasion until the end of the war, I wore my allegiance to Rome brash and bold. For the first time, I reaped the rewards of heaven on Earth; the simple pleasure of lying in on Sundays or being able to read at my leisure.

My new privilege to absence myself from Church parade was noted by those in charge of me. Sergeant Meade stored it away in his irreproachable memory and I was now on his radar for any infraction of camp regulations. It did not take long for me to run afoul of Meade. Within a fortnight of my proclamation of the faith, I found myself in Maidenhead with Robbie. We drank more than we ought to and lingered far too long in the company of local girls in a pub. Probably, we hoped for a shag, or at the very least a grope from them. For our troubles, we received giggles and a thank you very much for the beer and an empty wallet. It was well past the curfew when we arrived back at base. We skirted the main gate and entered the camp from an open field. We stumbled up over a drainage ditch. It took us to the main compound, near our sleeping quarters. Suddenly, Robbie turned to me and whispered, "Fe Fi Fo Fom, I hear Sergeant Major's on the run."

"Let's split up," I said hurriedly. "You go left, I'll go right and meet up at our billet. One of us should get back."

Robbie trotted off left and whispered, "I'll be in Scotland before yee."

I made a sprightly dash to the right. I turned a corner towards two long rows of Nissen huts. As I moved starboard, I collided into Meade who barked, "Name, rank, and serial number?"

I stumbled and hesitated, wondering if I could provide another name when the sergeant interjected, "Smith, I know who you are and I've got your number. Orderly office, first thing tomorrow morning, report there," he commanded. "Now be off with you. You are in a load of trouble."

I found my way back to the hut. Robbie said to me, "How'd it go?"
I told him.

"That's rotten luck. You won't tell them about me though, will you?" he pleaded. "You should have followed me," Robbie chastised. "I've dodged coppers before."

The next morning, I presented myself to the orderly office. I made sure that my buttons and boots were shined like a polished diamond. Beside me were two other airmen on similar charges. An NCO brought us to attention. He told us to quickstep into the adjutant's office. I was first in formation in the punishment file. Once inside, the adjutant officer received our salutes and stood up from his desk. His cigarette burned in an ashtray on the desk. It made a single, obese line of smoke that hung from the ceiling to the desk. The officer cleared his throat and read out the charge against me. It was as if I had committed the capital crime of murder, instead of breaking curfew.

"LAC Smith, do you have anything to say for yourself?"

"No, sir," I smartly responded.

The NCO came alongside me and demanded that I turn towards him. I snapped around and faced him directly. The NCO slapped my RAF cap off my head. He employed as much force as Lillian used when I broke her curfew. The NCO demanded that I retrieve my blackballed cap from the ignominious floor. The officer moved from behind his desk and he was about to pronounce sentence upon me, as if he wore the black cap of justice served. I thought he was about to intone: "You shall be taken here to a place of execution where you shall be hung by the neck until you are dead."

Thankfully, the sentence was more lenient, but the declamation was as ominous as a capital sentence.

"Two weeks camp confinement."

Afterwards, I was marched out of the office in quick steps.

After having learned to march with straw in our kit, scale inconsequential streams, bayonet bound dummies, shoot World War One rifles, and toss grenades, the RAF rounded out our squad's military preparedness with truck driving instructions. At a morning assembly, we stood to attention for an achingly long time. A slow-moving Leyland lorry from the First War pulled up beside us. It stopped in a jerky fashion, with steam brewing out of its bonnet. An NCO hopped out of the antediluvian cab and approached us.

In a weary voice, he announced, "You've got seventy-two hours to learn how to drives this truck."

Mastering this ancient combustible beast was akin to handling a team of horses if one had grown up in a modern metropolis. I sat in the lorry's cab where I was given scant, vague information as to where the clutch, accelerator, and brake were. The gears were manipulated with a cumbersome lever that could have changed gears on the Titanic. The clutch was located at the base of the floorboard. The driving column was an enormous wheel created without the slightest suggestion of suspension. Once I got the beast started and propelling forward, it felt as if I was Steam Boat Willy from the Buster Keaton film. The helm of the truck spun from right to left, without centering the vehicle. The Leyland bounced from one side of the road to the other, as if it were a drunk lurching home at midnight on a country roadway. It made me, the driving instructor, and Robbie, tightly wedged into the cab, nauseous from the undulating, uncoordinated movements. To change gears, you had to double de-clutch, which caused a deafening grinding sound like it was coming from a medieval torture chamber.

We were given little more than an hour of driving time. Our instructor informed us that in three days, more trucks were to arrive as we were to be taught to drive in a convoy. The exercise was breathtaking in its capacity to generate innumerable collisions, blown gaskets, and curses against the RAF and British Leyland. A day driving in formation left us with sore necks and aching arses from being roughly bounced in spring-less chassis. We damned these trucks for their uncooperative nature. We swore at them for being ridden into the ground by indifferent masters during their post-war years. Seventy-two hours later, we were indoctrinated and now considered to be ill-trained jockeys of intemperate, unwilling, and easily distracted animals that were called Leyland trucks. We referred to them as "Bollocks Busters."

After gaining our slight and incompetent driving acumen, a squad of beat up old trucks greeted us on morning parade. Our commanding officer informed us that we were to be dispatched on a map and orientation exercise. It involved us driving through the local countryside locating landmarks through coordinates transmitted to us in Morse code. This exercise was orchestrated to determine if one: we could find our way in the dark from the privy, and two: if we could send a signal to camp informing them that we had returned safely from the privy.

Robbie called it, "Operation shite in bush."

Our parliament of trucks set out from camp. Each vehicle was given different orders and dissimilar locations to detect and report back from. The lorries were each equipped with an RCA radio transmitter, bedding, and provisions for two weeks. The truck was also outfitted with a large bucket for us to shit in. For our comfort, the bucket came with a detachable seat. If there were any bashful or self-conscious ones aboard our vehicle, a canvass wrap was included. It could be erected around the bucket to protect one from the blowing winds. It also shielded us from the incredulous stares of farmers as they encountered RAF men defecating in their fields, resplendent with grazing sheep.

There were five of us in my truck; myself, Robbie, Brian and Clementine, along with a cook who was a more capable driver than me. I was designated the chief radio operator. I was to transcribe the orders from HQ and submit back to them our whereabouts. Our trucks trundled off like the beginning of the Dakar-Paris road race. However, unlike the French road rally, we were wholly ignorant of our destination or a true and exact explanation by the RAF for this weird navigational foray.

It took us the better part of the day to find our first map reference. The grid location was dead center in a church cemetery. It proved

187

our superiors were as useless as us when it came to fighting the war. Clementine noted, "Perhaps the RAF is giving us a sign as to our ultimate destination with them."

As we were supposed to set up camp at these coordinates, Robbie and I decided to go the vicarage. We wanted to inform the padre of our intent. It was not a promising start. The vicar greeted us adorned in his vestments, while beside him an inhospitable dog was growling. The padre had a long grey beard and a thin unsympathetic face. He clearly took a dislike to us, to airmen, soldiers, Christian or otherwise.

"Permission, permission," he grumbled, "to set up a circus tent in my church cemetery. I certainly do mind. In fact I take umbrage at the notion. You boys think that my cemetery should be used as your lavatory? Certainly, not, good-bye, goodnight to you, and please be off this land at once. Use a farmer's plot; use the common. But do not touch my church yard for your shenanigans."

After the door had closed, Robbie said, "I bet that dog of his has had a bleeding leg up on every grave stone in the cemetery."

I signaled back to HQ that enemy forces were being uncooperative and we reconnoitered to a new position. For several weeks, this was our modus operandi. The majority of positions radioed to us were placed in the middle of streams, pubs, or in woodlots, and all of them were totally inaccessible.

By the second week, our transmitter conked out. Without radio contact, we were lost. Aimlessly, but rather contentedly, we meandered around the back roads of southern England. There was no one to interfere with our slow and useless progress. Robbie and Brian believed that this was one big RAF cock up. I found some paint and in enormous letters wrote across the side of the truck "Fred Karno's Army." When a farmer or a group of women walked beside our vehicle, Brian called out to them.

"Hey, Missy, don't miss the excitement. Come join our motley crew. We're out to defend England from Jerry."

We would all sing

"We are <u>Fred Karno's</u> Army, we are the ragtime infantry. We cannot fight, we cannot shoot, what bleeding use are we? And when we get to Berlin, we'll hear Hitler say, 'Hoch, hoch! Mein Gott, what a bloody rotten lot are the ragtime infantry."

In the afternoons, we parked our Leyland in a meadow beside a brook. We would picnic on tinned corn beef and beer bought from an off license. Clementine had a gramophone and some record disks that his mother sent it to him, even though our officers thought it an indulgence not suitable to enlisted airman. The 78 RPM disks were mostly classical and Robbie always grumbled at the selection. When Chopin etudes were played, he said, "Sounds like the cat got caught by the dog, with the canary still in his gob."

As for me, I had never heard Chopin before that time. As a small child, my dad played musical hall songs on the piano for my family. They were melodies for a poor population craving cliché happiness. Until that day in the meadow, I did not know a piano was able to emit such delicate notes. With a piece of grass in our mouths, we lay on our backs. We heard the lithe movements of fingers against a keyboard and in the next field, cows grazed while their bells rhythmically made time with the pianist.

One afternoon, Clementine played for us an ethereal voice; Marian Anderson. She sang with ineffable beauty from Samson and Delilah, "My Heart at thy sweet voice." It was a balm to my spirit. It was spiritual seduction for me. It was like hearing the dimensions, the actual weight, and breath of love defined to my feral soul. When the gramophone needle scratched the last notes of the aria, the diva's trailing voice pierced my heart. The aria traveled with me like a candle, protected in a lantern, forever illuminated, searching for love.

A week late, we arrived back at White Waltham. We were unshaven, our uniforms worn and dirty. We more resembled Shackleton's crew marooned on Elephant Island than an RAF mobile transmission team. We were quite irritable as our glee had deflated after enduring numerous rainstorms, damp clothes, and diminishing rations on our travails. Sergeant Green greeted us with indifference.

"We were beginning to get worried about you lot. Some even asked if we should contact the navy to see if you and your truck were floating out in the channel. For sure, this is another fucking cock up. Unless I led you by the bleeding hand, you lot couldn't find yer arse for lemons. Get yourself cleaned up before the CO catches you and puts us all on charges. Bloody idiots," he called out to us as we headed for the wash hut.

While we were away, the German 7th army was being asphyxiated at Stalingrad with a dense pincer movement from the Soviet Army. In the African desert where Hannibal once roamed and prepared an army to attack imperial Rome; Rommel was on the run. Montgomery advanced against the Fox and swept him across the unforgiving sands of Libya to the Mediterranean Sea. Meade's first-day admonition to us that Africa was our destiny never transpired. We seemed, mundanely ignored. We were forgotten by the war and relocated to White Waltham to do schoolboy exercises. While I slept some nights, I discerned the hornet drone of Messerschmitt bombers on their way to London.

12

Chigwell

Near Christmas 1942, my training unit was moved to RAF Chigwell. The base was situated in the heart of Essex's Epping Forest. Before our arrival, Chigwell was utilized to deploy barrage balloons across the London skyline. Often, it was a futile attempt to thwart Luftwaffe attacks on the city. When I arrived, the base was a conduit for transmitting coded messages to other military installations across the country. Our billets were located several miles from the main base, which turned out to be far more pleasant as we were encamped on a private estate.

Now, I was a lodger on the well-manicured grounds of Sir Felix Cassel and his Edwardian built, but Georgian-designed manor house. Our squad was provided tents that we erected in a park on the estate. Within our tent city, it was complete chaos and resembled a squatter's encampment rather than an Air Force base. For the first few weeks, we were left unattended; like errant children, we quickly turned our quarters into a cesspit. Officers and NCOs appeared unconcerned with our living conditions or how we lived. On many days, Robbie, Brian, Clementine, Taffy and me would take a late afternoon train to nearby Leighton to visit the infamous Red Lion Inn. The pub's reputation boasted that within its establishment, there were the most unattached, attractive women in the town. Every night, The Red Lion was engorged with all manner and distinction of service men and WAFs. There were Brits, Canadians, Americans, and New Zealanders. Everyone frequented the inn's warm embrace and her abundant stores of beer. As there was a seemingly inexhaustible supply of lager, there was no shortage of fights. Brawls at The Red Lion could be divided into two categories; those about women at your table, and those about women at the table yonder. If a young woman glanced at the wrong time, at the wrong man, fists flew. If a girl happened to sit at a table filled with our American allies and paid too much attention to our richer cousin, a liquored up and enraged male from the British Isles would throw a punch at a dubious character either named Tex or Slim or Bubba. To quell any animosity or discord between soldiers, sailors, and airmen, The Red Lion employed a six-foot-tall female bouncer. She resembled a beer keg. The female bouncer deftly hauled out any miscreants who had pushed the boundaries of civility. She would grab their collars from behind and drag their bodies across the floor like a dog being pulled maliciously by a chain. Pissed service men saluted her as she passed them on her way to the door with a subdued customer. She heaved the troublemaker onto the street with the force of an artillery round.

The giantess warned the guilty party, dusting himself off by the curb, "Oi. better be'ave yerself or next time, I'll give ya a right bollocking."

At last call, we hurriedly drank up and caught the last train. On the way back, Robbie pulled open the blackout curtains against the widow. He would open the latch to allow blasts of sobering air into our compartment. Frantically, Robbie jumped up on the seat beside the window and undid the buttons of his trousers. He pissed wantonly and inefficiently through the open window.

"Shut the bloody window and come down," We screamed as we

were hit by the warm back splash from his urination.

The first month at Chigwell seemed to be a terminus for our training. We had no orders, no organization, and were encouraged to make ourselves scarce from officers and NCOs. Those in charge appeared to have no knowledge as to what to do with us. They were loath to find a solution to our idleness. The Baronet, whose estate we gladly loafed on, tried as best as he could to keep us occupied. He attempted to instill us with a bit of culture, with weekly piano recitals to balance out our boozing in Leighton. The recitals were performed by his first son, Francis, whose desire to play well was greater than his talent. Having more money than acumen, the aristocrat's son yearly booked Albert Hall and filled it with unwilling guests who were compelled to attend by social pressure and being natural ass kissers. Francis had a caged audience with us, as we were his father's guests and it was hard to refuse an invitation from a baronet's son. It was, however, an opportunity to experience all types of composers from Bartok to Saint Saens. Francis was a very accommodating host; if a less than perfect pianist. It was said much later on that he was so eccentric, he boasted to have taught his horses French, German, and to count to ten backwards.

I was accompanied to the concert by Taffy and Clementine, while the others declined a night of culture for the more mundane pursuit of finding a shaggable WAF in the NAAFI. After the concert, we joined up with them. It was very enjoyable to round out the evening with a cup of tea and talk about the young women providing beverages, biscuits, and comfort to distressed airman in the recreation tent. The WAFs as tea matrons were generally in their twenties; they looked to find a bit of excitement or a husband while contributing to the war effort. It was far better to serve cups of tea than suffer the dreary existence of life with Mother and Father.

It was rumored and believed by the majority of airmen that the tea was laced with bromide. The theory was the Air Ministry laced our tea to lower our testosterone to keep our dicks in our pants. Clementine remarked how the government would be better off.

"They should cut out our hearts rather than our member. It's muff, lads, since the days of Helen of Troy that drives a warrior onwards, while it's gold a King lusts and fights over." The RAF never tried to dispel the myth. We accepted this tale of enforced sexual dysfunction as true. It did come in handy if a young airman couldn't satisfy a woman; it was blamed on the tea and not the drink.

At Chigwell, there was no inspection, no parades, and no work ever done by us. Even Robbie found our absolute freedom cumbersome and uncomfortable.

"It really is like the lunatic asylum where the inmates are running the place," he noted wearily. Sometimes, we slept late. Discipline was so nonexistent that when a pay officer came to settle our weekly wages with his orderly, he found us hung over in bed.

"Get up, you lazy bastards," the officer screamed. "The Air Ministry is here to reward you for a job well done," he added sarcastically.

Full of sleep and the beer from the night before, we shuffled over to the paymaster. We were like hospital residents receiving their medication. We yawned and mumbled our appreciation when we signed for our pay. The RAF may have left us with the illusion that we were at play and forgotten. But just as soon as we were almost lulled to sleep by the drab beat of purposelessness; we were informed we must return to White Waltham.

Our group felt forlorn as we returned on the train to our former base. It was as melancholic as leaving a favourite holiday camp after a long and pleasant holiday, knowing that drudgery awaited one at home. In our absence, White Waltham had not changed except it was now winter. Sergeant Meade's memory was as acute and cruel as ever.

"So you ladies have returned." He mocked us when we sauntered through the camp gates in broken, cynical, individuality. Within days, he had us sorted. We easily returned to the regime of automatons and marched, saluted, and slept when ordered. While in our hut, we groaned and complained as to the cruelty and whims of the RAF. One moment we were deluged by purposeless sloth and the next moment, we were inundated by the dullness of activities designed without rhyme or reason. But our imprisonment under the watchful and punishing eyes of Meade was not to last for long. The RAF had returned us to this base to complete our mission. We were ordered to wander again as a lost truck convoy equipped with radio receivers transmitting and obtaining messages from every possible church yard, farmer's field, or pub within a hundred-mile radius of London. This time, we left at night as they hoped it would develop our nocturnal senses. Perhaps they wanted us to be the owls of the RAF. In the dark, our trucks groped the roads like old men fumbling to take a piss at midnight.

Within a week, we were lost from the convoy. Dejectedly, we set up camp in a farmer's field some three hours from White Waltham. As before, our truck had Fred Karno's Army written bold and large on the side. I strung up a makeshift transmission cable across the roof of the lorry. We spent our morning sending out distress messages to our base. We were adrift in England without knowing which direction to turn to. It was cold and Clementine set up a small stove in the back of the truck. The weather was not promising and it was not as enjoyable as our autumn voyage round the countryside.

Suddenly, a staff car pulled up and I thought we were in the shit. An aristocratic captain of about twenty-four approached us. He enquired as to our success in this training mission. It turned out he was also attached to White Waltham. After we had responded, he said, "I say, chaps, this seems like awfully dull work, anyone fancy a drink?"

We all eagerly volunteered.

"There is a spot of bother about this," the captain said. He touched his nose with his right index finger and explained, "The Indian chiefs don't like us running about with cowboys. So does anyone have a spare LAC jacket? Much better to go native than in full mufti," he said.

"No one minds our boys having a bit of rum, but everyone gets bent out of shape when they see an officer raising a glass. Not done, bad form. What example are you leaving for the ones you lead and all that rubbish."

Brian handed him his coat and we all piled into the officer's car and drove off to the nearest pub. The captain stood all of our rounds. He showed complete disregard for the RAF except to say, "Mind you, we are winning. You do know that." The young officer continued, "And you do know," he paused, "a bit of blood has been spilled."

Exhaling smoke from his cigarette, he continued, "And more is going to be shed next year and the year after that, but we are showing Jerry what we are made of."

"Lots of young men," Clementine happily responded.

"Spot on, Clementine, lots of young boys. But right now with the Yanks and us, we have more young boys then Jerry and the Ities have."

The officer put out his cigarette and excused himself to go to the toilet. When he stood up and left our table, I noticed he walked with a limp. He must have been a pilot who had been wounded. The flyer had been left to spend the rest of the war on the ground, like a falcon with a broken wing, an animal without purpose.

The captain returned and announced, "Right, lads, time to go and fight the war."

We drove back in his car, to our lonely outpost.

For the better part of a year, the RAF divided our time between White Waltham and Chigwell. In the former, we were trained as a mobile transmitter signals unit. In the latter, we were schooled in indolence, sloth, and high culture provided by the imperfect recitals of Sir Fredrick Cassel's son, Francis. During the early winter months at Chigwell, I observed my squad mates play endless games of cards. They played sometimes for entire month's wages, which were staked on hands dealt whilst lady luck was out powdering her nose. Fortune never sat beside me. The only occasion I was foolish enough to join in,

I lost half my week's pay. From then on, I retreated from the mocking aces and gambled my time away reading books.

While card decks were shuffled infinite times and deuces were dealt, the Russians destroyed the German Seventh army at Stalingrad. British forces bombed Ruhr industrial factories to rubble. Bomber Command sustained enormous loss of life with these raids. In Norway, a heavy water plant was destroyed by British controlled saboteurs. While, we at camp moaned about the dull, steady routine of cards, tea, WAFs and Morse.

In the early winter months of 1943, Great-Uncle Larratt decided to pour his last pint and retired at eighty-three. He transferred his publican's license over to his son-in-law. Larratt saw his pub, obtained by stealth, grow stout and sturdy on the thirst of miners. Their mouths were always parched, no matter the circumstance; they always had brass for beer. The colliers of Barley Hole, in times of peace or war, and in times of austerity and economic depression, paid readily for their right to drink ale at their local. The well-worn wooden handles Larratt pumped to drown the sorrow of the poor and forgotten were an endless river of aqueous gold for him and his small family. Time had not changed the face or appearance of the pub. The wooden floors still creaked with the trod of hobnail boots. The pub was still ensconced in deep wood paneling. Its stairs still led up to the rooms where Albert's aging brothers slept. However, the hours, the days, the months, and years had washed away all memory of my dad and his lost legacy. Time had replaced him with a different myth and story, which had Larratt as narrator and hero. To the outsiders, too young to remember the time before the First World War, Larratt was the governor, the savior, and benefactor to his nephews. Without Larratt, the story said the brothers and the family would have been ruined and out on the streets, every last one of them. Myths Larratt created and maintained, but time was relentless and unforgiving to him and to all of us, regardless of our deeds or transgressions.

197

Larratt took to the identical bed where his brother Francis had breathed his last breath, three decades past. In early March, Larratt's arteries narrowed and weakened. They collapsed like a seam of coal miles below the Earth's surface. His heart stopped and he died believing that he had led a just and good life. His time on Earth was devoted to family, and the life hereafter would reward him. Like Francis before him, Larratt was laid out in the pub's main room. The New Inn's customers tipped their hats to their governor. My father, long since banished from the family, was not at the funeral. His name was only mentioned in almost inaudible tones by his sister, Mabel. He was the lamb that had gone astray, rather than the ram that had been beaten out of his fold by avaricious kinfolk.

After Larratt died, Albert's brothers, now into their sixties, were asked by the new innkeeper to find other accommodations. The brothers were considered relics of a by-gone age that were best disposed of and removed from sight. Albert's brothers ended up residing at Barley Hall, which was a lodging place for miners that had lost their family or drank themselves into poverty.

During those same winter months, when Larratt died and I sat droning out endless coded Morse messages; my sister sent me a quick cryptic letter. She indicated something was not right. Her family was disintegrating into the same chaos and dislocation we had known as children. I did not break the cipher immediately. I ignored the turmoil that she alluded to, veiled in the commonality of her phrases. I only discovered much later that her husband had gone absent from the army. It was Lillian who recounted Mary's ordeal to me, many months after my sister's tribulations had abated.

I never knew or was told why Mary's husband deserted from the army. I never cared to know, needed to know, or would know. But I could not judge her husband for his decision to leave the army without permission. Those of us in uniform, in combat, out of combat, behind the lines, in the air, on the ground, were either teenagers or young boys in their early twenties; we were scared shitless. The only reason we were all kept in line was a youthful naivety in our own immortality. It was our youthful belief that death would not come for us. It came for the chap down the table from us, or in the next room, but never for us. There were thousands like my brother-in-law, who because of an extreme sense of personal survival went underground, rather than have their blood spilt.

Military police harassed my sister. They came to her home and pounded on her door. They demanded to know the whereabouts of her errant man. While around the neighbourhood, female neighbours, hair in curlers with giant fags stuck on their lipstick-stained lips, fretted about how Mary and her man had put a black mark on their street. My sister's daily movements were dogged by determined military police fighting the war on the treacherous Bradford front, for deserters to the cause. Once, the military police even rapped on Lillian's door to enquire about her wayward son-in-law. When questioned, Lillian, who was as patriotic as the next person on Boothtown Road, crossed her arms. She looked at the young and healthy strapping young police officer and said, "Come again?"

The policeman repeated his interest in the whereabouts of her son-in-law. My mother had lived with little assistance and much government indifference during the depression. "Sod off," she told the policeman. "Go on now, find, yerself a real criminal, maybe a black marketer. Mary's man is none of my bloody business and certainly none of yer ruddy business. Better yet," she added derisively, "up the street is a recruitment center. Sign yourself up, lad. Do us and yerself a favour; go on now, off to the front, with ya. There ya can flash yer teeth at Hitler. Let's see you bold as brass staring the fucking Germans down, instead of poor defenseless women," she finished and slammed the door in the policeman's face.

As for my father, in war as in peace, he was emotionally ravaged by his sense of failure as a son, husband, and father. For thirteen years, my dad had lived alone in the same, small room in St Andrew's Villas. His father's portrait hung on the wall opposite his bed. However, by 1943, the frame and picture were coated in a blunt hue from the coal fire and my dad's pipe smoke. Albert always paid his weekly rent on time and he was polite and courteous to the migrating inhabitants of the house. But he was aloof with them as he once was to the patrons of the New Inn. Albert's demeanor was ancient and distant. His movements were slow, deliberate, and elderly. No one would have guessed that in his youth, he was a proud miner who ripped coal out of mines sunk deep into the dark, Yorkshire earth. If asked, he said he was a widower who had never been blessed with children. What else could he have said? No one cared to hear the truth. Everyone in that rooming house was an economic fugitive that had lost family, friends, and hope for better days. My dad was not going to lose what little dignity he had left by speaking to indifferent strangers and lamenting his vanished life.

He never said, "Take a good look at me. I was once young. I once battered and hauled coal. I once had a grandfather and father who traded their coal miners' smocks for the prosperity of a public house. Long ago, I had a family, and I was loved. I lost a daughter to disease and I was forsaken by another daughter and son because of raw, uncompromising hunger. My wife took up with a workman and a cowman and other men that I can no longer remember to feed our children."

For my dad, it was far better to stand apart and silent from the citizens of poverty. He kept his sagas of loss well hidden. My dad's only reminders of his past were the portrait, the encyclopedias, and dog-eared photos of me, Mary, and Marian. Our pictures were tucked away inside random volumes of *Harmsworth's*. Since his banishment in 1930, my dad lived a solitary, silent life. He took the bus to the outskirts of Bradford and walked the moors as a singular and lonely man. My dad ate alone in his room. He allowed himself one luxury: the odd pipe full of tobacco. His final years were exhausted in this singular lonely outpost, a bedsit in Bradford. My dad hewered his soul like he once mined coal: alone. He condemned himself and judged himself without finding a single reason to pardon his conduct. Albert never appreciated nor did others appreciate that he was not the executioner of his misfortune. He was merely a victim, like millions of men, women, and children who were suffocated by the weight of greed and the selfish actions of strangers, society, and kin. He was waste on a factory floor to be swept away after the workday. My dad's middle life and end life was the product of the great unraveling during the financial catastrophe of 1930.

By October 1943, British and American troops had fought their way to Naples and entered the vanquish port. Corsica was liberated by the free French. The RAF made bombing sorties over Hannover, Stuttgart, and Berlin. By this juncture in the war, Bomber Command had lost over five thousand aircraft due to enemy fire. During this war, the totality and finality of death on land, sea, and in the air war was staggering, humbling, and numbing.

While total war raged across the continents of the world, Albert, my father, was dying in inches. He developed a cough that was persistent. It was a racking cough that expelled sputum and blood fragments through his worn lungs. Even though his belief in the Almighty had been curtailed through more than seven decades of life; my dad did not fear death. Darkness forever was better than the ravenous regrets that gnawed at his belly. My dad welcomed death; it would extinguish his memories. Nothingness was a sweet respite from his life.

That month, my dad was admitted to St. Luke's hospital. He listed on the hospital form as next of kin his younger sister, Mabel. The day before my dad died, Mabel came to visit her brother who she had not seen for many years. Albert was still conscious; they spoke in hushed tones for a while. The hospital ward was overwhelmed with the indigent, who even at the end of live had to expire without privacy or comfort. Mabel asked what he wanted done with his possessions. He told her to hock them at the nearest pawnshop and burn what had no value.

"Wha' ever thou gets from shop, giv to wee kids, Mary and Harry."

On Oct 11th 1943, Albert Smith, loyal son, devoted husband, and caring father, died alone. Three days later, he was buried in unconsecrated ground in a plot stacked ten-deep with other forgotten people. Even in death, the poor shared eternity as if it was a cramped rooming house.

On the morning my father died, I was still attached to Fred Karno's Army. We were driving across Southern England looking for a map coordinate. At the time, I thought about brewing up tea and resting by the roadside with a Woodbine to keep me company. It was almost Christmas when I received the letter from Mary about our father.

She wrote: "Our Dad died in October. His heart gave out, Happy Christmas, Love Mary."

So that was it, I thought, sitting on my bunk. I read the letter over and tried to remember my dad, my father, but I couldn't because too much time was bartered since I was a boy and my dad was with me. I travelled with so much hurt since I last saw Albert and the only memory I recalled was shame. The day I received the letter, I again felt shame for my dad, for my family, and most of all for me. I quickly tore the letter up and I went to the pub alone. I did not want anyone to be with me, and besides I had told my mates that my dad was a butcher living with my mother, not a lonely lodger in Bradford. So I got drunk alone at a pub. With each mouthful of beer, I hoped I could wipe my dad clean from my conscience.

13

Invasion Preparations

By New Year 1944, England was preparing for the invasion of Europe. The island was swollen with Allied troops and equipment. Britain was like a pregnant woman coming ready to the end of her term. In January, American troops with British support landed in Italy at Anzio beach. They began a grueling offensive up through the Italian front. One bone-chilling night in the first month of the New Year, the RAF dropped close to three thousand tons of explosives on Berlin. The siege at Leningrad was relieved.

For me, however, our signals truck was on maneuvers, in Southern England. Our steady routine was as dull and hurtful as repeating the multiplication table out loud for one's entire waking hours. But we continued from map coordinate to map coordinate. I continued to send messages back to base as to our location, while I received in return from them confirmation that the grid was correct. To civilians outside and even cursory glances from other military echelons, we looked busy; we looked as if we were overweight with purpose. As far as I was concerned, I was being driven in ever-smaller circles around England. I knew that the invasion was soon. I wondered if our group was to be called upon to do something. Brian said probably not as we were just spare parts in case the invasion was a failure. If it fucked up, it would then be all hands on deck for a horrendous bloodbath to come. Brian was more worried about his brother. He was attached to the army and was going to part of that well-armed, liberation flotilla.

Robbie said it was probably best to keep our heads down and our mouths shut at this juncture.

"No point drawing any attention to ourselves. Keep to the back, lads, with the light well away from your faces. We don't want anyone getting strange ideas about dying."

I received and sent few letters home. I heard from Doug Butterworth. He wrote from his sickbed and informed me that Roy Broadbent was in the fight of his life with the Cold Stream Guards in Italy. Eric was happily turning his lathe and fashioning precision bombing parts for the air ministry. The dance halls, Doug regaled, were chock a block with every imaginable dolly bird looking for their man in a uniform

By March 1944, the American Air Force dropped a punishing amount of armaments over German cities during daylight hours. While at night, the RAF pounded and bombed what had not been obliterated by the Yanks. German cities looked like skeletons, bleached by the sun while their inhabitants were now mole-like creatures who cowered in the discarded brickwork. But underneath the torn buildings and piled up bricks, men with the death's head insignia on their black caps vowed total war and scorched earth against their enemies. As Russian forces recovered lost territory in the Ukraine and Belarus; they unearthed, like gruesome archeologists, a wasteland of death. They discovered massacred Jews, partisans, communist members, and the corpses of anyone the Nazis deemed beneath Germanic humanity. Whole villages were expunged, submerged and buried underneath the blood of the executed. The fields in Eastern Europe were moist with the blood of the dead. While in the West, the occupied countries waited, tight-lipped, expectantly, arms impatiently outstretched for the messiah of liberation. We knew in May that the invasion was near. There was nervous electricity amongst the officers. Road diversions were commonplace. Giant unwieldy convoys of trucks packed with instruments to either cause slaughter or protect one from slaughter were dispatched to the invasion marshaling area. Our ramblings were halted in the middle of May, We waited, idle, confined to base.

When the invasion was finally underway on June 6th, it was like the release of a violent orgasm. The skies grew dark as bomber upon bomber migrated towards their targets in France. From the comfort of England, we remained subdued and humbled by the news of hand-to-hand fighting occurring on Normandy beaches. I felt lucky that I was in the RAF. I was safe in England, while British, Canadian, Polish and American boys the same age as me at twenty-one were inching from beachheads to hedge groves with a curtailed life expectancy.

Brian's brother, Mark, was part of the third wave of invaders. When he reached Gold Beach, seventy-hours after the tumultuous advance, bodies still lay where they died on the pebbled shore. He was Brian's younger sibling and was more impetuous than his brother. Brian said later on, "He probably wanted to show me how grown up and responsible he was by volunteering for the army. Wanted to do his part, wanted to be part of the action, and have tales to tell his grandchildren."

Brian received a letter many weeks after D plus three from his mother. She wrote that the army sent her a telegram stating Mark died from his wounds early in June. He did not even have enough time to be kissed by a pretty French girl grateful for his part in liberation.

Our confinement to base lasted no more than a few weeks. We resumed our Flying Dutchman exercise by the time the King inspected landing troops in Normandy. During the summer of 1944, the RAF provided us with additional responsibilities. Our lorry was equipped with a primitive mortar to stalk German rockets. We were now Fred Karno's Army in charge of Doodle-bug hunting. A radio signal was sent to our truck from a tracking base; it informed us that a V2 rocket was in our vicinity. Once the transmission was received, we halted our truck and jumped out to look skyward. Our orders were to scan the horizon until we had identified the V2 rocket. Our sergeant nominated the cook to be in charge of both the bully beef and rocketry. So, Cook, with assistance from us, assembled the shell launcher far away from the Leyland. Once the lone deadly missile destined blindly for London was in sight, Cook lit a fuse beneath the cannon and a shell would burst upwards and punctured the sky in a bright colour that airborne spitfires spotted. Fighter planes raced towards the deadly payload until close enough that the pilot nudged the V2s wings, destabilizing the rocket and forcing it to crash and explode far away from populated areas.

Our search and fire team was created by the War Ministry as an inexpensive and perhaps useful method of destroying the winged bombs. Unfortunately, the law of gravity was a great impediment to the ministry's concept as the signal flare was held in a giant, metal canister. Inevitably, once empty of its starburst, the heavy container plunged to the ground with massive speed and weight. Prosperous farmers were not amused when their prized herds of cattle and sheep were felled by spent canisters crashing into their fields. One farmer approached us, outraged at our role in the death of his beloved bullock. He said he would have the local constabulary lock us up for willful murder. Our commander deduced that our efforts to stem the flow of human life being killed by the rockets should be left to the Spitfires because our assistance left an unacceptably high casualty rate for non-combatant livestock.

14

Transmission full stop

It was almost a year after my father's death when our caravanning across England was called to a halt. We were ordered to return to White Waltham. I was thankful that this venture had finally concluded. I longed for any new assignment that might remotely resemble war work. We were all curious to see if we were to be confined to England's shores, or whether we were to be sent to newly-liberated France or the Lowland countries.

When our truck arrived back at base, an NCO ordered us to remove our personal belongings from the vehicle. Moreover, our group was not only disbanded; it was being split up. Taffy, Brian, Clementine, and the cook were dispatched immediately to another camp and another assignment. A vehicle pulled up and hastily ushered them off. Robbie and I were left standing in an empty parade ground, watching as our mates' truck became smaller and smaller in the distance.

"Not even a kiss good-bye," Robbie ruefully lamented.

An officer then told me we were to be seconded to 13 ATSU near Luton the following morning.

Early the following morning, we left for our new assignment. On the road to Luton, it was cold and the ground was covered in frost. Thirteen ATSU was forty minutes away from our former base and forty years ahead in technology. This camp was a fully functional air traffic signals unit. It was responsible for the coordination and transmission of RAF cipher messages to its bases across UK and in re-conquered European territory. I was finally being called upon to utilize my skills. I was to send and dispatch messages that had some relationship to the fighting going on around us.

The duty officer received us and explained that we would be on a twenty-four-hour work schedule.

"So get used to late nights and early mornings without fond memories of a piss up."

I started work immediately. An NCO led me to a row of buildings that housed a massive leviathan of corridors and tight rooms packed with electronic, radio equipment. Robbie and I were both escorted to a small room equipped with radio and telegraph gear necessary to send and receive military messages. My work consisted of both transmitting and receiving ciphered notes regarding RAF business. I was content at my new occupation; it had purpose and consequence, unlike my old position as crew on a caravan that travelled like a vagabond provided with a government chit across the country's back roads. When I left my shift, the sun still beamed its lukewarm rays onto the ground. Outside, I heard in the bank of trees a wooden recorder emitting reedy Morse code. It was from a wireless operator who had gone gaga from the mental anguish at forever transmitting unreadable messages. In his spare time, he was always up in that tree whistling tunes of dots and dashes. The higher ups let him be as he never missed his shifts and it was not considered out of place to be eccentric in the RAF.

Much to my surprise, two weeks into our assignment, Taffy, Brian, and Clementine arrived at our new base. Robbie, first to notice them, called out, "I'll be chuffed-look what the cat dragged in."

Clementine explained, "Our transfer was buggered up. The bastards dispatched us to be bomb loaders until they realized we didn't know our arse from our elbow, unless it was sent to us in Morse."

Our old friends were assigned to our billet and our friendship continued on as it had when we vacationed for eighteen months across country dales at the expense of the RAF.

Shortly before Christmas, our squad of wireless operators was called into a meeting in the mess hall. There were a hundred and fifty of us in attendance. A captain told us in senatorial sentences with urgency in his voice that Christmas leave was cancelled. We were to form a new MSU across the channel, which caused us to send up a cheer. The war was drawing to a close, but finally we were going ashore into the newly liberated countries. At last, we were going to demonstrate our worthiness to this war, this cause, and to Britain. I was grateful that holiday leave was cancelled because Christmas in Halifax with my mother and Bill Moxon was a dismal festive cracker I dreaded to pull.

The captain said, "Lads, we can expect the ship with our name on it any day. But the navy is a funny lot. They may have other priorities before we are taken across the waves. So be patient, the time is near or far away, but it is our time."

Our departure was also heavily dependent on the advance of Allied armies into Germany.

Robbie and Brian rubbed their hands and exclaimed, "I fancy a bit of foreign skirt, a bit of parlez les vous, if you know what I mean."

The captain told us to pipe down.

"Men, this is an important endeavor we are undertaking for England. We will be in charge of an entire airfield. We shall be its central signals unit for the region we are assigned. Our bombers and fighters will depend on you for accurate weather, enemy troop movement, and air traffic control. We will be called to duty. It will be in days or weeks, but we will be called. So be vigilant. Know that you will only be given twenty-four hours' notice before you are sent to Harwich."

The captain walked off the lectern. A sergeant dismissed us and we returned to our normal duties. Later, I wrote to both my mother and Mary, sending my regrets for not being able to come back for Christmas. That night, I went to bed wrapped safely in my cot and thought of the excitement to come in Europe. I dreamed about the women of newly liberated Europe; the rumors said they were long on beauty and short on virtue.

I am not sure if it was because of Hitler's last gambit in the west, his armoured thrust into the Ardennes, but our deployment orders were not executed at Christmas. Instead, they sat in a pile of papers awaiting authorization at HQ. Christmas at 13 ATSU was a sad affair; we were a bunch of lonely, horny airmen packed into a drafty dining hall. Our only consolation was a few tots of rum that offered us slight festive greetings in our dour surroundings.

Clementine said, "I think only Hitler and his sorry lots are having a worse Christmas than us."

I agreed, "At least we got a Christmas cracker."

I excused myself and went outside, where it was lightly snowing.

The ground felt clean, but my mind felt cluttered. There was a time, I remembered, when my sister and I sang Christmas carols while my father played the piano and my mother sat on a chair beside us knitting socks or a sweater. I breathed in the brisk, cool air and forlornly exhaled it. Suddenly, a snowball cuffed me in the head.

"Come on, you lazy sod," Taffy called out, "it's time for target practice."

From the edge of the cookhouse, the other three appeared and I was ambushed in an avalanche of snowballs.

Confined to camp on New Year's Eve, we sang Auld Lang Syne at the chime of midnight and toasted the year to come. During the first days and then weeks of January, we waited in disjointed apprehension to deploy to Europe. After a while, we thought our captain had played a cruel prank on us. He promised us in December a mission in Europe and a greater role in this war, and it now seemed as fanciful as Meade's desert premonitions. We waited and asked our sergeants, "You'll know when you know," was the answer.

We waited and Warsaw fell to the Russians. We waited impatiently and the death marches began for the near-lifeless prisoners of the concentration camps. We waited while the Germanic retreat of *volks deutch* began, from the Eastern, Hanseatic fortresses of Lithuania, Latvia, and Pomerania. Over two million Aryan refugees limped across the snow or sailed in over-laden ships across the icy Baltic. While underneath the slushy sea, Russian submarines hungrily trawled the waters in vengeful wait. The Soviet Army liberated Auschwitz and we waited. For parts of Holland still under German occupation, *"The Hunger Winter"* was now in its fifth month and the citizens were reduced to consuming tulip bulbs and boiling shoe leather for nutrients. We waited anxious, ignorant, and callow for Europe.

15

Europe

Finally, our deployment orders were approved and in mid-February before dawn, sixteen trucks arrived at our camp to take us to Harwich. For one last time before departing, our sergeant made us stand on the parade square as he inspected us. While he walked amongst the rows of men, silently counting us, the cold air slowly crept up through my boots and numbed my body. When the tally was completed, the sergeant presented it to the captain, who ordered us to board the trucks. We leaped in and left our base; we felt a sleepy, grey midwinter excitement over our European destination.

It took us several hours to reach the port at Harwich. When we arrived at the dock's entrance, we were ordered to halt. While we waited, I got out of the truck to smoke a cigarette and stretch my legs. Ahead of us, there were hundreds of lorries, and all around me was bedlam. Ship whistles blew, claxons belched, stevedores cursed, while far overhead, winches screeched. All types of ships were moored in the, from freighters to battle cruisers. Each was fed by a symphony of cranes suspended in the air, gently lowering all manner of guns, crates, food stuff, and electronic equipment.

By nightfall, we were all too tired to curse. I was stultified by the limpid, inching movement of our truck to the boarding platform. Robbie complained, "If Noah had taken this much time loading his bleeding animals onto his fucking ark, he'd only have had two bloody baboons for company."

Suddenly, NCOs banged the sides of the trucks and cried, "Fall out, fall out, men."

The vehicles were the first to board. They were driven across steel bridges that led them into the ship's hold. We, the human cargo, were sent up a gangplank. We were packed like steerage immigrants to the new world below the main deck, which was above the engine room. Our vestibule had enough room for each of us to sit with our legs firmly tucked up to our chests. The compartment was frigid and airless. Low, yellow lights on the side of the walls cast a strange fog around us.

At around three in the morning, the harbourmaster gave final clearance for our transport ship to leave port. We sat morose, smoking, huddled in our great coats. The screws of the engine began a methodical rotation. Around me, I heard the slosh of water against the ship's hull. The smell of the ocean channel mixed in my nostrils with a heavy odour of diesel oil. The bodies nestled beside me provided warmth. The channel was rough and the swells moved the ship in a peeved and disgruntled manner. Robbie was sick inside his cap. I felt nervous, a static electric unease wondering if there were still U-boats lurking underneath the grim waters. Were they waiting for our transport ship? I surmised if the ship was hit, we would sink in mere seconds like a brick tossed into a river. I would be done for as I cannot swim and the winter waters would quickly drag me underneath. Of course, if we were hit, it was more likely I would be trampled to death in the dark, as confused men trapped below the decks of the steamer fought their way upwards to the surface. I slept for a while. It was a jerky, uncomfortable unconsciousness one gets on a rush hour bus cramped with the smell and noises of a multitude of different individuals. Sometime around five, I was awake.

Clementine, who was beside me, said, "We are going to Ostend."

"Where is that?" I inquired."

"Belgium," he replied.

By six in the morning, our freighter found its berth in the densely packed Belgian port. Overhead, I heard the trucks move out as they hit the ramp and jetty beside us; it echoed in our compartment. After a while, an NCO marshaled us from our pen. It was an effort to stand as our legs were cramped from the hours we were packed away like toys in a box. Getting up, we were like tired children at the end of long journey, and we cursed everyone in our path. We moved down the gangplank like pack animals coming to auction. My kit bag was firmly on my shoulder. When we were outside and on land, a blast of cold Belgian sea air burned my lungs. We marched away from the pier and moved to an open area where we found our vehicles and a Red Cross Tea Unit.

"Warm yourselves up," an officer encouraged us.

I headed off to the refreshment truck. Ancient, Belgian tea ladies greeted me with open smiles. They filled my mug with a warm and welcoming brew.

It was still before dawn at Ostend and grey light was splashed across the horizon. There was maniacal activity trembling all around me. It was like in Harwich except in reverse, unloading ships instead of loading them. Around me, I tasted destruction. Off into the distance, I saw burned and shattered buildings that looked like charcoal sketches of former warehouses dotting the wharf. Bomb craters were evident everywhere. Some were capped with the debris of fallen buildings. At war's end, this was my first experience with how the Wehrmacht marched back to Germany. They left for the victors a crumbling, broken, and torn infrastructure.

Having finished our tea and sandwiches, we were loaded onto our trucks to begin our journey into Belgium. I jostled to be at the end of the truck by its back gate. I realized it would be colder there, but I was curious to catch my first glimpse of a foreign country. The lorries rolled out of the port and we travelled onto a dual carriage way that was empty of traffic. From the back of my truck as the sun scrambled up over the horizon, I saw more than I wanted. Scores of dead horses littered the roadside. They were bloated and grotesque. In the distance, whole villages were torn from their foundation by fearsome hand-to-hand combat and aerial bombardment. We twisted around the outskirts of Ghent; its medieval skyline lying in ruins. Churches stood with their sides blasted open by cannon fire. They displayed a rough vivisection of the interior of lowland piety. Sad Bruegel looking families hung closely together on the sides of the road, dejectedly following a route to nowhere.

Our convoy bypassed Antwerp and by midday, we ended up in an abandoned insignificant aerodrome situated along the north coast. We dismounted from our trucks; our legs stiff from the journey. Cold and miserable sleet fell across my face. A slight wind was blowing up from the North Sea and through the deserted compound. The buildings situated around the airfield were in a state of decay. Doors swung open in the breeze and creaked disturbingly against their hinges. Windows were shattered and the interiors were vandalized. The retreating Luftwaffe had gutted their former base and left it teaming with garbage. They had strewn their bowel movements across walls and on the floor of the cookhouse, which over time had petrified.

Robbie looked around and said, "It looks like Wiggin on New Year's Day, only a little neater."

Clementine disappeared into one of the storage sheds. Minutes later, he emerged with two carbon rods both capped and connected by about a foot of insulated wire.

"What the hell is that?" I enquired.

"I noticed that the Germans paid the electric bill. This is our new kettle for tea."

We followed him into the kitchen. Clementine rifled around on the floor. The Germans had thrown the contents of the cookhouse on to the ground. Most of it was smashed and shattered, but Clementine found a large empty jam tin. We poured the water from our canteens into the tin. He stuck the rods into the container and thrust the wire ends of the carbon rod around a discarded plug he had found. He inserted the plug into a wall socket. There was a tiny cascade of sparks shooting from the outlet. Then the power heated up the coils sitting in the water to boiling point. We drank our tea, grateful for Clementine's ingenuity.

An officer found us in the kitchen. He advised us to quickly find a place to kip.

"Jerry's not the cleanest of guests," he said, "better go now before the others find the most comfortable berths."

In what appeared to have been officer's lodgings, I located a decent room for us. It looked like the former occupant could not be bothered to be messy for the Fuehrer. Brian and the rest dragged battered and misshapen mattresses from other sections of the camp. He also found some wood for the stove. It was cramped, but at least it was now warm and dry.

At teatime, a mobile food van appeared at the entrance to the camp. We were told by our commanding officer named Gibb, "Our sojourn at this abandoned airfield should be limited to no more than a week. Therefore you will only be served emergency rations."

I lined up with the rest for tinned pork and beans, which floated in watery gravy of liquefied fat. Gibb informed us, "You are permitted four-hour forays into Antwerp in five men relays." The officer warned, "If you think you will find any food or booty in Antwerp, you are deadly mistaken." "The Germans stole every last morsel of bread,

216

meat, eggs, and butter. What they couldn't take back home with them, they dumped into the sea. So the only well-fed Belgians are the collaborators and fish in the sea. The civilians have suffered and they will steal from you if given half a chance," Gibb continued. "So keep your eyes open. And remember, you are members of the RAF, so try to behave like Englishmen and not like some half-craved morons."

Dismissed, we went back to our makeshift sleeping quarters. Brian broke up bits of a door to keep the fire going and Clementine in his wanderings had found a half-bottle of German schnapps to keep us contented. Outside, I heard the deafening shuddering sound of Antwerp's artillery and rocket defenses go off. They tried to down desperate German Doodle-bugs blindly droning towards an unknown target and nameless victims. I stepped outside with Robbie. We watched with chilled awe at the flashes of light puncturing the sky to the south of us. It lasted no more than several minutes and then darkness once again descended and held quiet sway for the rest of the evening. Later on, I learned that over a million rounds of ordinances were used to protect Antwerp and London in the final months of the war. Even though the city was ringed with anti aircraft guns, close to thirty-thousand Belgians perished in these perpetual raids. Eventually I was able to doze on my emaciated mattresses. I fell into a silent and weary sleep after a long and fitful journey to the edges of the war.

The following morning, the five of us drove into Antwerp. I noticed our driver carried a side arm. I was sitting in the cab and asked him if the gun was loaded.

"Not bloody likely," he replied. "It's just to scare them away. The toffs would be in a right mess if I shot at a civilian for trying to steal his Majesty's tires."

We drove into Antwerp's main thoroughfare and it was easy to notice the erratic nature of the V1 attacks. A block of flats had collapsed onto itself while the house beside it appeared unfazed, as if sheathed in a protective coating. It was raining. Through the windshield wipers, I spied Belgian men pissing on the sides of buildings. It looked like it was Saturday night in Halifax and not Tuesday morning in Europe.

The truck halted on an attractive baroque street. The driver said he would be back in three hours. He expected there to be five us of waiting with no surprises. As he left, he yelled out, "Make sure you bastards don't catch the clap, the Belgians are riddled with it. They are dirty beggars."

For twenty minutes, we walked around and tried to get our bearings in this strange new territory. Belgian civilians ambled by brusquely and chatted in guttural Flemish, as they mocked us. Across the street, teenage girls passed and we waved to them and called out in English, "Come on, love, over here. Show an Englishman the way around town."

They giggled and hurriedly moved on while an old man with a wooden leg hobbled up to me. He gesticulated with his hands and mimed the act of smoking. I reached into my coat and pulled out a pack of Woodbines. He smiled and said, *"Ja, sigarette, bedanket sigarette."*

Handing him one, I tried to light it for him but he shrugged me off and limped down the street.

Robbie declared, "This town is as boring as piss on a Sunday after church."

Taffy suggested, "We should try to find a place that sells beer."

We agreed. We put our heads close to the window displays. We were like rude children trying to look for the toy section while out with a distracted mother.

After several angry or confused looks from the Belgians behind the glass, eventually a heavyset woman welcomed us. She invited us into her establishment with a wave and a large rotund smile. Inside the café were a couple of tables occupied by lone elderly men with grey stubble on their faces.

"Come, come," a woman, who was well past her Rubenesque prime, announced to us.

She directed us to an empty table.

"Zitten, zitten," she gestured.

We sat, pulling off our caps.

"Eten? Drinken?" "Eten, Drinken?"

We looked at each other. Heartily, we said, *"Ja."*

Brian pulled out a pound note and asked, "Money, good?"

"Ja, geld goed," she said with a laugh.

Then the woman hurriedly spoke to the other guests, who all laughed at our ignorance. Within moments, she brought over five bitterly cold bottled beers and some cakes that were packed with jam. Quietly, we ate our sweet and sipped our beers. I now felt like I was visiting distant relatives who were monitoring our every gesture. Outside, miles off, we heard a loud explosion. A V1 rocket had plunged into someone's flat and obliterated it in a flash. My friends and I jumped at the proximity of the violent noise. The old men at their tables laughed and said, *"Bom, bom,"* over and over.

Another one looked towards us and called out, *"Jongen,"* and put his two fingers below his nose, miming Hitler's mustache.

"Einde," he continued and wiped his hand in the air as if they were covered in muck.

We paid and left the café. The driver was waiting for us at the end of the street. He asked, "Did you fine the knocking shop?"

We spent five more weeks in Belgium and idled away our daytime hours with trips into Antwerp. At night we watched and grew numb to the artillery barrage against vengeful rockets hurled into the sky by a defeated nation. My birthday was spent on base watching the pyrotechnics. Robbie noted, "Probably the first time you had fireworks for your birthday."

During our time in Belgium, the Allies prepared for their last big push across the Rhine and into Germany. While soldiers slogged from west and east into the heart of Germany, "The big three" Russia, United States, and the United Kingdom met at Yalta. At the conference, the Great War lords established the continent's post-war boundaries, sealing the fate of Eastern Europe for generations to come. Soon after their meeting, Dresden, the birthplace of princes, the crucible of Germanic culture, was sacrificed as homage to Joseph Stalin. It was retribution against the nation that had precipitated so much violence upon the continent. In one night of bombing, the city teeming with refugees from the east, forced labour and allied POWs was offered as recompense for Germanic sin, over one hundred thousand lives perished in the firestorm.

On a very cold and wet morning at the end of March, Commander Gibb ordered us to decamp. We were moving north into Holland. We travelled like the baggage train of a Roman army, as we were near the rear, but close enough to hear the battle cries of the warriors ahead of us. Only days earlier, the push against the Rhine had begun, with division after division forging across the river. There were accompanied by salvos of artillery, softening the route for the Allied armies. The march into Germany had begun, while the Soviet army sat on the Oder poised like a panther ready to pounce on a wounded but still lethal prey.

For us, it was a mad dash along the coast of Belgium into Holland. Quickly, we passed remnants of recent battles that included flooded farmers' fields, abandoned houses, burnt out tanks, and dead animals parked at the side of the road. I sensed something more than annihilation in Holland; I smelled here the hunger from my childhood. It was painted on every sallow face looking mournfully at me from the roadside as we scrambled towards our destination, *Den Haag,* Holland's seat of government.

Shortly before reaching *Den Haag,* our team was issued loaded rifles. There were convincing reports from other British forces stationed nearby that *Wehrmacht* stragglers were everywhere, intent on resisting surrender. At a roadside break, Gibb said our new base would be outside of *Den Haag* in the town of *Wassenaar*. We were to occupy a former *Luftwaffe* airfield. It was a rich town and was the official residence for the Dutch Royal family. Yet the enforced starvation imposed by the Nazis even stripped this aristocratic enclave of wealth and arrogance. The road was lined with a sad welcoming committee of hungry children. Their arms were outstretched, begging for food. They were thin urchins, barefoot, wearing torn and well-worn clothing, thinning at the edges. I was sickened and horrified. I wanted to weep as I saw this famished parade of youth. In the past, I experienced this form of hunger that made one alone and as wild as a diseased animal.

A crude fool stood up in the truck and contemptuously tossed bits of a sandwich out to children on the sidewalk. The kids broke into the wake of our trucks and scrambled to grab bits of discarded spam from the ground. The airman said flippantly, "It's like feeding fucking ducks at home."

Enraged, I grabbed him by his collar and screamed, "You piece of shite, you fucking bastard,"

I let him go and took my rifle off my shoulder, lowering it towards his stomach.

"What's so funny now, comedian? What's so fucking funny now?"

Taffy and Robbie pulled me away from him. They got me to lower my rifle. I breathed in long, angry mouthfuls of air.

"I was jest having a joke, mate," said the airman, unconscious of his barbarity.

He was blind to any tragedy not occurring to his favourite football team or because his chips had been served up cold.

Late in the afternoon, our truck arrived at a deserted airfield and parked on the tarmac. The rest of our convoy proceeded to Wassenaar and our billets. The aerodrome hangars were behind us. An NCO told our group to fan out towards the storage sheds and hangars. We were to look for squatters and Germans who had been left behind to cause trouble. We divided ourselves into two teams.

"Bugger me," Robbie declared, "if I am going to get nicked by a Nazi when the game is almost over. I'll follow you, Smith."

Trying to recall my training days at Padgate and White Waltham, I drew a blank. We were never provided instructions regarding detection and seizure of enemy forces from newly liberated military bases. I remembered tuck and roll if landing with a parachute. I also recalled the catchall phrase, "Be prepared, and always carry a condom." But smoking out desperate Nazis was missing, from our wireless textbook. While we reluctantly approached the hangars, I told Robbie and Taffy.

"Let's do this with a lot of noise. If there is anybody in here, they are probably scared shitless."

"Like ourselves," replied Brian.

"Yes," I agreed. "Maybe we can bluff them out by saying there are more of us here."

Robbie screamed out by the hangar's entrance. "We got the whole fucking British Air Force out front, so you better come out. Even Winston Churchill is here, smoking a big fat cigar."

We pulled open the door to the main hangar, which squeaked on its pulley. Sunlight flooded into the darkened stale space while a startled pigeon flew up and out. We jumped back shaken and I saw we were not going to make it into dispatches. I suggested we keep the safety to our guns on rather than shooting ourselves to death. We agreed. Our team entered the crypt last occupied maybe three days ago by the German Air Force. It was a shambles. Robbie whispered, "Come out, come out, wherever you are."

"Oly, Oly oxen free," I responded.

To the far right, behind metal shelves we heard a paint tin drop with a thud. Beside it was a brown tarp that slithered to the far end of the building. Robbie and I charged forward towards the camouflaged movement. We put our boots onto the end of the cloth. Suddenly, two teen-age boys in military uniforms wriggled free from their cocoon.

"Hands up, lads," I screamed out. Hansel and Fritsel turned over as their bodies were still on the ground. In terror, the boys began speaking rapidly in German.

"Up, up." Robbie encouraged them with the tip of his rifle.

We got them to stand and with my gun pointing at their back, I marched them into daylight. They were no more than fifteen or sixteen. They were the last great hope of the German war machine. They were Hitler's child-soldiers. The two boys began to sob and I put a hand on their shoulders and tried to comfort them. The NCO started reprimanding us. He remarked they could be armed; they could be dangerous. I replied back, "Dangerous and armed? They probably have a sling shot and a Beano comic in their back pocket."

Robbie agreed, "Yeah, look at em, still fresh off the teat."

The military MPs were called to take them for interrogation and processing as prisoners of war. Satisfied that our airport was now secure, the NCOs had us board the trucks to travel to our sleeping quarters.

Our billets were situated ten minutes from the landing field. They were on a small crescent possessing a dozen homes that resembled large elegant Dutch sugar cookies. The pleasant homes and the street had a dream-like element to it. It was as if the war had passed by this neighbourhood, spared by a biblical pharaoh. Everything was unmolested with fresh paint and clean windows. In the middle of the street, a tent had been erected to act as our cookhouse. The rest of our squad was milling about the tent standing in groups of three or four. I found our sergeant and asked him who these houses on the street belonged to.

"No one now, the owners are all in jail for collaboration."

"Where are we to kip?"

"The commander wants you to sleep in the cookhouse."

"But look at all those lovely empty homes around us," I lamented.

The sergeant sighed and said, "Smith, do what you bloody well want, just don't muck about and treat them like a one-up-one-down in Manchester. Remember, I didn't give you permission if anybody asks."

I gathered up Robbie and Taffy, Clementine and Brian, and we proceeding like Goldilocks to find the bed that was just right. All of the houses on the crescent were detached villas. We requisitioned the most eye-appealing home. It possessed a giant entrance, massive full kitchen, vaulted ceilings, and bedrooms that I had only seen on the movie screen. I took as my own, an upstairs room that overlooked a wooded park. It had an enormous window that swung open gently, allowing a beautiful warm, spring breeze to traipse into my room. I could hear the nearby sounds of birds nesting in the trees.

Robbie clambered upstairs and told me, "If I fucking die, St Peter better send me here, because this is fucking paradise."

Taffy screamed out, "I'm bollocksed they have a bog inside. These dutchies really are clever, smarter than us by a mile. I've been shitting in the garden since I was wee one."

"Oi," said Brian, "there is someone at the door and we haven't had time to unpack and I've got me curlers in my hair."

I rushed downstairs to answer the loud knocking. I opened up the door to find three RAF guys who I did not recognize. The first LAC asked in a Welsh accent if they could kip with us. Taffy yelled out, "He's a Welsh man. Let him in. He's family come for a visit."

He stepped in and stood in the vestibule. He bent his head upwards straining to see the whole house.

"Blimey," he said, "sure is posh for Swansea." He turned to me and said, "Jack Bruton, glad to be your neighbour."

I shook his warm and kind hand. I knew I would become fast friends with this quick-talking Welshman.

It took me a while to settle in and get used to my surroundings. No one except perhaps Clementine had experienced this type of home before. Eventually, we called to the mess tent for our tea. There was a gathering of small children in filthy clothes on the street. Their shirts and pants hung loosely around their emaciated bodies. Some were shoeless, others wore wooden clogs. Some of them had their faces jammed against the canvas tent as if they looked for the circus in Trinity Fields and the mysterious women from Siam. The smell of food had driven them from their hungry houses towards the scents of cooking meat. They had been beguiled by aromas absent for far too long in their lives. I crossed the line of emaciated Dutch children who were so hungry that they received sustenance from the mere sight of food. Our group decided to ask permission from the mess officer to have the children fed before our squads. The officer did not raise a complaint.

"Let's get to it," he said.

Jack, Robbie, Taffy, Clementine, Brian, and I opened up the flaps of the tent. We gently ushered the children into the dining hall. The kids, maybe eighty in all, devoured the food and took second portions. They laughed and talked nonsense to us in Dutch. They kissed our cheeks and sat on our laps. I ate nothing for dinner as I felt stuffed by what I had just witnessed; I recalled a time when I had sneaked into a kitchen with my sister, and ravenously dipped my bread into another woman's stew and thought I was at the very gates of heaven.

While I was standing outside the tent smoking a cigarette, a pretty thirteen-year-old girl came up to me. The girl had long, tightly braided blond hair adorned, with colourful ribbons. She stood shyly a little distance from me. In halting English, she said, "I live on this street."

"You do?" I asked. "Show me where?"

The girl pointed to the largest and most magnificent villa.

"I live there. We are Koenigs," she claimed proudly. "My Papa is an artist. Please come visit us," she announced.

The girl disappeared quickly into the throng of children who were still licking their lips from their meal. Until we departed Holland; our cookhouse also operated as a field kitchen for starving and destitute Dutch citizens. Anyone, young or old, was welcome at our table.

The following morning, we were sent to the airfields to take stock of the equipment the Germans left behind. We assessed when the airfield could become functional. I asked an officer if we were to be permanently stationed at *Wassenaar.* He said it was most unlikely as our group was destined for Germany to maintain an airport.

"What about our job here?" I asked.

"Don't break a sweat," he warned, "because it will be all for naught. Germany is when your tasks really begin."

By earlier afternoon, we returned to the splendor of our villas. We lounged on the back porch on fine wicker chairs. We smoked cigarettes and our new flat mate, Jack, strummed on his guitar. The young teen-aged girl from the day before appeared from the woods, situated behind us.

"Hello," she called to me.

I went over to talk to her.

"My brother and sisters and Mama and Papa would like to meet you Tommies. Would you like to come for tea tomorrow?"

I agreed without asking the others. The girl skirted off quickly.

"Wait," I cried out. "I don't know your name?"

"Wilhelmina, just like our Queen's name." She then disappeared back into the woods.

The following afternoon, I showed up at the Koenig's' residence with my friends. It was by far the best mansion on the circle. It displayed an enormous amount of accumulated wealth and privilege. A servant

16

Hamburg

It was late afternoon when our trucks arrived in Fuhlsbüttel, a northern suburb of Hamburg; the neighbourhood possessed a functioning airfield we were to occupy. The area was bucolic and sprinkled with well-maintained, wealthy, middle class homes. This community received little or no damage from air raids. It appeared the RAF was exact in their destruction of Hamburg and it occurred in the city's central section, where industry and the poor lived. The rich of Hamburg were unmolested by aerial destruction. The German citizenry surmised that the British did not wish to ruin the mansions they wanted to occupy after the war. Fuhlsbüttel had a main square that was created in stolid Germanic tones. It exuded efficiency and conformity. Down a quiet street, off the promenade, the Germans had built a prison at the turn of the century. From 1933, The Nazis transformed it into a multipurpose, multinational concentration camp and transit facility for communist, Jehovah's Witnesses, gypsies, and Jews. The inner workings of the concentration camp were so meticulous and mundane that after the war, the citizenry at first denied its existence, and afterwards were incredulous that such a gentrified street contained a prison where Hitler's policy for a racially pure Germany was enacted.

Our squad was billeted on the airbase, which was a great disappointment to me considering the luxury we were used to in Holland. For the first couple of days, we were confined to base and given a strict non-fraternization order. It was easily enforced as most Germans hid behind closed doors out of fear or in pique at being defeated. However, on May eighth, everything changed because Germany's capitulation was official and hostilities ceased across the width and breadth of Europe.

On that day, to observe the war's end, our squad paraded itself in front of the Fuhlsbüttel town square. We wore our dress uniforms and stood smartly at attention. In front of us, a giant wooden platform was constructed, which was crammed with a military band, RAF officers, our wing commander, named Cox, and a padre.

While we stood at attention, waiting for a speech on high, it was warm and it felt like summer. I heard the wind whisper through the linden trees and discerned songbirds in the distance. There was no noise except for the stray barking of some dog, far off, who was displeased with the change in masters. On the dais, an officer strode over to the microphone and tapped it, causing feedback to revolve across the square. He introduced the padre, who asked us to bow our heads for those that had died in this brutally long conflict. It was coincidental, but the official ending of the war was remarkably similar to its beginning; they both were commemorated with a speech, a prayer, and a benediction. We sang God save the King and afterwards, and three cheers went up for our wing commander. A military band played *"We'll meet again,"* and the men in formation, broke into song.

"Don't know when, don't know how, but we'll meet again…"

Our wing commander congratulated us for a job well done, and our commitment to Britain and to freedom. Finally, we were dismissed with a blessing that God would keep our country safe. The ceremony was like a school leaving because there was nostalgia for shared memories, and happiness at the thought of a new beginning.

At the conclusion of the service, an officer reminded us that we were invited to a victory party across the road. This announcement brought thunderous applause from the men on parade. Once we were dismissed, my mates and I walked over to the building, a primary school, where the victory party was held. Entering the school, we made our way to the gymnasium, which had been hastily decorated with streamers and pictures of the royal family and Churchill. A WAF approached and told us, "In case you don't know, all the beer and all the food is on the ouse today cuz of the end of the war. Come tomorrow, though, when you are at the NAFFI, you will be paying for you pints again."

She kissed each one of us on the cheek and let us pass to join the party that challenged even the most abstemious to stay sober. The bar was an Aladdin's cave of looted drink from a *Wehrmacht* officer's mess; it included calvados, French champagne, German wine, beer, and schnapps. I drank copious amounts of beer, while I pounded the table to music played by an RAF band forced to entertain witless wireless operators and their ilk. As there were few women, airmen danced with other airmen in abandon and youthful joy. They knew that they now stood a chance to die in their beds as old men, decades hence. The day wore on while the beer, the wine, the calvados, and the schnapps were poured and drank in a ceaseless torrent, like a race to Lethe. Endless sentiments were espoused.

"No,, I was the better friend."

"No, he was the biggest shit."

Others on the table made blind promises. "As soon as I'm de-mobed, I'll marry her."

The heat inside the schoolhouse singed our words, which were now slurred, as sentimental and trite. Some of us stumbled into the washrooms to barf and then return for more beer. We all knew there would never be a day like this again, free drink and free license to get as pissed as you want, all on the RAF chit.

The band never seemed to stop playing and they appeared to know only five, maybe six tunes. Every time I was conscious of their melody making; it was *"Roll out the barrel"* being beaten to death by a tuba and a base drum. I went outside to get some air, as I was feeling sweaty and confused. With heavy hands, I felt through my tunic for my lighter, which I could not find. Propped up against the outside wall of the school was another airman with a cigarette burning on his unconscious lips. I pulled the fag away from him and uselessly, I attempted to light my cigarette from his, but my hands could not make the connection.

"Sod it," I slurred to myself and I started smoking the passed out airman's fag.

It was now dark and in the streets, I heard catcalling and whistling from drunken servicemen. I discerned stray gunfire in the distance, from RAF men discharging their Sten guns in the air. I stumbled away from the school to get a good drunken look at this nation and these Germans who had disturbed so many lives. But before I began my investigation, I urinated against a building. I stumbled alone for a while, calling out my name. I felt joyously, drunkenly, youthfully alive. In the shadows, I saw Clementine and I beckoned him over. He approached sheepishly.

"We did it, old chum, we did it, we lived, brilliant isn't it?"

"It is, Smith," he responded. "It really is good to be alive."

"Have a drink with me, Clementine."

"Can't," he responded, "I've got things to do," he added in a sobering tone.

"Do? What the fuck do you have to do except drink with me?"

"I'm looking for stray dogs," he noted mysteriously and left me.

I returned to the schoolhouse and sat down at my table. I felt very drunk and the room spun while the gymnasium's interior resembled a kaleidoscope to my eyes. Other people's words were as intelligible as rapidly transmitted Morse code. Slow down, I silently begged the room.

Jack and Taffy took one look at my jellyfish appearance and noted, "You've had your chips. VE Day is done for you, mate."

They carried me back to base, as if my body had been found wounded on a battlefield. To their laughter, I stopped and vomited in the bushes. Back at the airfield, they dumped me into my bed. Hours later, I was dimly aware of my consciousness and I sensed dampness at the side of my face. It felt like I was in a cold ditch made of china plates. When I opened my eyes, I discovered I was face first in an open urinal. I was taking shallow breaths of stale piss and wondered how I got into this mess. I lay there in the piss trough for a little while, until a sergeant major charged in and noticed me on the ground.

He looked at me and called, "Lad, unless you get up right now, a wee bit of Scottish rain is going to fall on to your head."

I rolled over and stood up slowly as I was unsteady on my feet.

"Get cleaned up, lad, the war is over but not your time in the RAF and there is work to be done."

17

Love in the Time of Occupation

For me, the war had more certainty than peace. The cessation of hostilities woke most of us up to an over-powering hangover. The coalition government at home collapsed soon after Germany's surrender and a general election was called. It pitted the solid old Tories and their quest for the status quo against Labour. We all had a lurking dread that de-mobilization would mean unemployment, the dole, and a half-life in the netherworld of Northern England. Churchill's victorious day in May, when he stood beside the royal family brandishing his trademark V for victory was short-lived. It was in occupied Hamburg that I voted for the first time and it was easy and natural that I cast my ballot for Labour. I reasoned that it was time for a change in my country and we should no longer be ruled by the few who enslaved the many to a lifetime of poverty and hopelessness. I wanted and deserved the right to work for decent wages, the right to join a union, the right to medical care and to education; in short, I demanded the right to live with dignity, which had been denied me and millions of other British citizens before the war. I wanted the right to change my life and put an end to my peripatetic existence; it was time to find a real purpose and make a future for myself.

The irrationality of my RAF existence was as normal to me as the chaos of my early years. As a boy, I was always on the move and slipped from one village, town, or city, to the next; like one changed into a new shirt in the morning. In the RAF, I was required to do the same, but there were some radical differences between my childhood and my formative years spent in the military. In the Air Force, we perpetually moved about but we were always guaranteed, a meal, a bed, and the security of a weekly pay packet at the end of our journey. Most importantly in the RAF, I formed close, youthful friendships with men who were sometimes very similar to me, but were often widely different from me. They generally possessed greater knowledge of the world and books, which they happily shared with me. I developed a bond and camaraderie with these men, whom I regretted losing when civilian life began to beckon all of us back to our homes. When my mates began to leave the service, it reminded me that soon, I would also return to my old existence as a grocer and nights at the pub, in cold and prospect-less Halifax. I was going to do my best not to end up back in Yorkshire, with only enough money to afford rock and chips for my tea.

Robbie was the first to leave, for home and he went without sentiment. "I'll see ya when I see ya. If you ever get to Wiggin," he told us while being loaded on the plane to take him home, "you know you've taken the wrong turn. Tara, Smith." He gave me a thumb up and disappeared into the aircraft.

Brian left soon after for Lancashire. Before he shipped out, we exchanged home addresses. I realized we would probably never see each other again and I reminded him to always keep his coins wrapped in his handkerchief.

"You might be forced one day to forge the River Calder, gorilla style."

Jack Bruton returned to Wales. He was overjoyed at being repatriated to the lush green valleys of his boyhood and rough streets of Swansea. From our original crew, it was only me, Taffy, and

Clementine who remained. The three of us became a shaky trinity, as peace had driven Clementine into more eccentric pursuits, which Taffy and I never fathomed. Clementine distanced himself from us as he developed an odd nocturnal hobby. He collected dogs' heads, which for the local canines who encountered him was quite a misadventure. Clementine hunted down a dog and it did not matter whether it was mutt or purebred, as long as it was a canine; it was fine for his ghoulish hobby. Once he captured the dog, he killed it with a knife, afterwards he decapitated it and boiled the pooch's head until only the skull remained. The headless dog's body was left where it had been butchered, as if it had been attacked by a deranged serial killer.

Roy Broadbent wrote me during the first few months of peace; he informed me he had returned intact from the Italian campaign. He was now married to an Italian woman from Naples and they lived with his mother in Halifax. Eric still worked and made loads of cash as a tool and die-maker. Doug Butterworth was out of work, again, because of his health. My sister Mary wrote to me and said the situation in Bradford and surroundings areas was bad. Even with the new Labour government, unemployment was high and housing scarce. Mary's letter confirmed to me that the longer I stayed in Germany, the better off I would be. I voluntarily extended my enlistment for another six months.

During that period, work at the airfield in Fuhlsbüttel was easy. My job consisted of either running wireless transmissions or air traffic control on weekends. Taffy and I joined up with a new group of workmates and we spent our off hours at a club set up by the NAFFI for officers and enlisted men. It was situated in the heart of Hamburg. Approaching the front entrance of the club, one was immediately submerged in loud American swing music. It was played from early morning until late at night. The club was jammed with all types of servicemen; Brits, Canadians, and Yanks all intermingled. Fights were a common occurrence and only controlled by a heavy MP presence. I constantly saw officers and enlisted men with German women hanging on to their arms. Some were legitimate girlfriends and others, driven by hunger or by deprivation, sold their bodies to the highest bidder for cigarette cartons and jars of Maxwell House coffee; the currency of the day.

Clementine, when not on the hunt for more dogs' heads, was scouting out Volkswagens as he wanted to bring them back to England and sell them for a profit. However, the government had banned their importation so as not to depress the domestic market. Clementine was not deterred as he had devised an idea for us to take a fleet of VWs and drive them across the North Sea in winter. He was under the impression that the entire sea froze from Germany to England during the month of January. He wanted me and a team of drivers to make a seven-hundred-mile trek across chilled arctic waters, until we reached the beaches at Bridlington, where we were to drive them ashore and sell them. No one would be the wiser, he reasoned, as we were coming by sea. I declined his invitation and Clementine was spared a Volkswagen burial at sea because shortly afterwards, he was de-mobbed and sent back to England. He left happy and smiling and inside his kit bag, all manner of dogs' heads, from dachshund to Saint Bernard were stowed to add to his collection back at his home.

With everyone leaving, I was forlorn at the notion I was also going to be discharged home. De-mob to what? I wrote to the Quaker about resuming my profession, but he politely informed me that my position was no longer available as times were tight in Halifax. So the Christian had rescinded his solemn promise to me and now I had no trade. There was nothing for me in Yorkshire but unemployment and limited prospects.

Feeling glum and alone, I moped around base, until one day, I was bored and loitered outside one of the makeshift black markets in Fuhlsbüttel. In front of the bazaar was a young woman who had jet-black hair that fell flirtatiously to her shoulders. It looked like she was in the market trading cloth to buy meat for her dinner. I watched her skillfully negotiate with the mobster who ran the bazaar. From my vantage, the black marketer tried to cheat the woman over the value of her fabric. But she held her ground and her body language intimated that she was uncompromising and not going to yield. Eventually, the seller relented and traded the portion of torn meat for an equal amount of torn cloth, and the young woman left triumphant. The woman strode up the strand, like a carefree schoolgirl who had just aced her examinations.

I was across the street and I do not know why but I began to follow her. I broke into a jog to catch up to her. She must have heard my footsteps because she stopped and turned around to face me; she looked startled, but not alarmed by my actions. I introduced myself in imperfect German, which I had picked up by spending an inordinate amount of time with German barmaids.

"*Frauline*," I asked, "could I carry your bags and escort your home."

She stopped and surveyed me to see if I looked dangerous and asked, "Are you Canadian?"

"No, I am British."

"*Gut,* you may take my bags up to the next street, but you can come no further."

I tagged closely beside her. I found out that her name was Elfriede and she lived with her mother. She did not seem interested in knowing my name but I told it to her anyway. She laughed and said, "You Englanders are always Tom, Dick, or Harry." We reached the end of the street and she said, "Well, Harry, this is your stop, *Danke,* for being so kind, *danke,* for your company. Now, I must go home."

I felt I needed to see her again. Frantically, I pleaded for another meeting. She hesitated and then responded. "All right Tom, Dick, or Harry, I will see you next week on Sunday at the park. Bring lunch for four because my girlfriends will be with me."

Elfriede turned and disappeared up the street, and for the rest of that long and impatient week, her words lingered like perfume to my ears.

I was able to convince Taffy and two other airmen to accompany me. Taffy was skeptical and dubious and kept on repeating the same warning. "She'll never show up, mate."

I purloined supplies from our cookhouse for the luncheon and I made sure we had an excess of smoked meat, cheeses, and good Riesling wine. As all things in Fuhlsbüttel, the park was not far from our billets. We walked eagerly to our dates and I was insistent with them that the raven-haired girl was mine. Taffy responded, "What if they all turn out to be dark-haired?"

"Well then, I guess, they are all mine."

We showed up at the appointed time and as promised, Elfriede was there with her friends. The women lazed in the sun like elegant cats in a luxurious garden, and they stared up at us as if we had disturbed their rest and sanctuary.

"Guten Tag," I said reverently to Elfriede and her companions.

Elfriede took off her sunglasses and introduced her friends, nonchalantly.

"Please sit down and join us," she said.

On the ground, we spread out a tablecloth and placed out our lunch. I opened the bottle of wine and poured a glass for everyone and we began to dine. It was a long, sensuous meal filled with broken conversation in indecipherable German and English. I watched Elfriede, in between our laughter and light-hearted conversation, devour cheese and savor the wine. Around us in the park were small groups of Germans, who were enjoying the free sunshine, but were too destitute to eat a meal. Elfriede suggested we share our dessert with two small boys playing near us. She called them over and fed them a portion of our cake, which they hungrily devoured, starved of sweets from years of war. With our meal finished, and our wine bottle emptied and lying on its side beside us, Elfriede invited me to walk alone with her. I noticed she was the leader in her group when she hastily spoke to her friends. Elfriede told them she was going for a stroll and she suggested they make themselves comfortable with my mates. Elfriede jumped up and used her hand to sweep away any dirt that had accumulated on her blue summer dress.

While walking away from our group, Elfriede made small talk, for a short time about the park, the weather, and the meal until she cautiously asked, "Who are you, Harry? "Are you one of the terror bombers that murdered my city?"

I said no I was on the ground, in Fred Karno's Army when the raids occurred.

"But if you saw what Germany did to Holland and Belgium, you might not call them terror bombers."

"I know," she said softly, "but underneath the rubble, my friends and my school mates are buried. So I am not going to be your friend if you did such things to my beautiful Hamburg."

I sheepishly walked beside her as she was, for me, utterly unique. I had never met anyone who embodied such intelligence, class, and sensuality; like a child, I was in awe at her beauty and her exotic thoughts.

"Let me ask you something? Who are your people and what did they do in the war."

She laughed. "Which family as I have two, maybe three. There is my real mother who gave birth to me. I was her love child between her and a chauffeur. Then there are my foster parents, my Mama and Papa who live in Hamburg. They took care of me when my mother couldn't or didn't want to anymore. And then there is my real father, Fritz the chauffeur, who I never much cared for because he was never around. The last time he wrote me, we were still at war and he was in Berlin. I don't think he is alive because our capital was destroyed by you and the Bolsheviks. Anyways, he is better off dead rather than being a prisoner to the Soviets. And today, I now live with my mother here in this town, outside beautiful Hamburg. She's looking for a new lover because her old one dropped dead of a heart attack just before the end of the war."

"A lover," I noted.

"Yes. I knew him as Uncle Henry. He helped my mother and me when I was just a little girl."

"Helped?" I questioned, intrigued.

"I was born a bastard because the chauffeur never married my mother; he just drove home to his own family. I was baptized Edelman, like my mother before me and her mother before her, because the women in my family, it seems, don't like husbands."

"So how did he help you?" I asked, puzzled.

"My family background was investigated because of my mother's bohemian lifestyle. They wanted to know if I was a Jew and from communist blood. Fortunately, Uncle Henry was some big-wig in the Nazi party and he stopped the investigation on me and my mother."

"A Nazi," I muttered in disgust.

"Don't worry, he was not some nasty man, quite charming and quite corrupt, but totally harmless. He had a business partner who was a communist. He could have denounced him and had the whole company, for not one *pfennig*. But he did not. So I don't think he was much of a Nazi. Anyway, it is all over now, he's dead, my real father's dead, and Hitler is dead; life goes on for the better. During the war, I got into a lot of trouble because of my name and my illegitimacy. But I am okay because my foster parents loved me and helped me.

"As for my real mutti, she helps but we can't help fighting with each other because we are like cats with our claws out, we scratch each other and then lick the other's wounds. "What about you, Harry? Where are your ghosts?" she asked coyly.

I lit both of us a cigarette and recounted my life to her, which was so dissimilar from Elfriede's, except that we were both social outcasts. I told her of Albert and Lillian and I conversed around the edges of my childhood, my hunger, and my mother's love affairs. When I finished, she took my hand and spoke softly.

243

"Harry, I want to live in the present. There is no past for me. There is only now and tomorrow. I have had lovers and some of them I think I was very fond of, but most, we were just amusing each other. I need more from life than flirtations because now the war is over and I might just live to become a very old woman. So, for now, Harry, my Tommy, we can be friends and we will see what time brings. I don't want any hearts broken, mine or even yours. So come visit me, take me for dinner, take me dancing. You can even take me to the moon and we will see what happens between the two of us because maybe there will be sparks or maybe nothing. But now it is late. And we must go back and collect our friends before they think we have run off with each other."

Since childhood, my emotions were crumpled and crippled by poverty of both the body and spirit. However, the time spent with Elfriede that afternoon opened up my heart to the possibility of being loved, wanted, and desired as if it were an unfolded origami bird. To pursue Elfriede was a gamble and I knew the outcome was uncertain. Failure was more assured than victory, but I ventured it was worth it; to change my life and its foretold destiny that was trying to exist in the mill towns of Yorkshire. I was willing; what other options were there for me except this, to cast my lot against my history and my sad ancestors and make this woman my wife, whatever the risks and whatever the cost. I thought with Elfriede beside me, I could renounce my past, my England, and my family's secrets, hidden like soiled underclothing, piled in a wardrobe. My future seemed fearful, but at least certain as long as she would be in it. A world with her in it was all together more interesting, more real, and more satisfying than anything that had come before in my life. I wished to orbit that bright star and feed off its light; from that afternoon I was beguiled. I set my ambitions on being with Elfriede.

I strolled back to base with Taffy and the other two airmen. I asked Taffy how his time went with the other girls.

"Bit of a waste," he answered, "they liked chocolate more than me. None of them have heard of Wales. What about you, Harry?"

"I think I have finally left Bradford and Boothtown behind," I told him.

What?" Taffy asked, puzzled.

"Nothing," I whispered.

When I got back to base, I wrote a letter to my sister Mary.

Do you remember a time when we were small, fed and happy? Do you remember a time, as children, when we weren't scared and lonely? I don't. I no longer want to remember hunger, abandonment, and fear of violence. I want a meaningful life and think I have found someone who shares my dream. I have decided to join the peacetime RAF and remain in Germany for as long as possible.

Hope you are well, happy, and free,

Your ever-loving brother,

Harry.

Book Two:

Hamburg 1947:   A Place for the Heart to Kip

By Harry Leslie Smith

With J.M. Smith

Author's Introduction:

To The Reader:

It is autumn and it is wet and damp outside. I can already feel the approaching cold and heavy breath of the frozen months upon the nape of my neck. If I survive, this will be my eighty-ninth winter on this Earth. Some say age brings wisdom, reason, serenity. I say bollocks; great age brings rheumatism, deafness, vascular degeneration, and organ failure. So far, I have been lucky and my body has endured my storm-tossed life, healthy and intact. It is a blessing I appreciate and honour every morning by performing the graceful movements of tai chi which provides me the balance to combat the punishment great age bestows on those who dare to live so long. We suffer the irretrievable loss of love, through death. We abide the profound loneliness of age as friends and lovers disappear from our grasp and are replaced with static photographs mounted high up on our fireplace mantel. I don't ask for condolences or your pity because I have felt an elemental chart of wondrous emotions during my life. I have experienced the very best and the very worst that mankind has to offer. I have loved and been loved and that is a great matter. It is all that should matter. It is all that must matter, even to you, dear reader. So as I walk into the fourth season of life, I say accept love as it comes and accept love as it goes because it is the only currency that never devalues us.

I leave you now with a small piece of my life; my time in Germany following the last Great War. It is a simple story about people searching to belong and survive in a world that was almost destroyed.

Cheers,

Harry Leslie Smith

Acknowledgments:

I would like to extend my thanks to Bundesarcihiv in Berlin, Germany, and the Hamburg City archives for allowing me to utilize their resources. Their assistance was invaluable in writing this book. I cannot express enough gratitude to my friends and my wife's closest confidants, Gerda Metzler and Ursula Overbeck, for their insights and assistance in my research about life in Hamburg during the 1930s. Your loyalty and your love, throughout the years to your friend Friede, is an inspiration. I am truly grateful to the kindness you have both shown me over the years.

I should also like to express my gratitude to the readers of my memoir *1923*, who encouraged me to continue my journey into my past. I extend my thanks to my children and my grandchildren for having supported me in my endeavors' to unravel our shared history. Vickie, Melanie and Cynthia, your thoughtful reading of my manuscript and your corrections have added immeasurably to the quality of my memoir. I am touched by the kindness and friendship you have all shown me.

I would also like to thank some men from long ago: Sid, Dave, Taffy, and Jack for being my mates. I hope you all found your way and grabbed some happiness out of this, all too short a life.

I must also acknowledge my appreciation and thanks to: Walker, Locke and Cox; who were not only decent officers, but thoroughly decent men. They always did their best and deserve to be remembered for their empathy towards their fellow man. Finally, I acknowledge my gratitude to all those people I have broken bread with while on this Earth. I hope your life was enriched as much as mine was by your company.

For Friede: 1928-1999

Who is my love, my faith, my heimat…

1

1945: The Conditions of Surrender

I don't know why, but the winter rains stopped and spring came early in 1945. When Hitler committed suicide at the end of April, the flowers and trees were in full bloom and the summer birds returned to their nesting grounds. Not long after the great dictator's corpse was incinerated in a bomb crater by his few remaining acolytes, the war in Europe ended. After so much death, ruin, and misery, it was remarkable to me how nature resiliently budded back to life in barns, fields, and across battlegrounds, now calm and silent. The Earth said to her children; it is time to abandon your swords and harness your ploughs; the ground is ripe and this is the season to tend to the living.

I was twenty-two and ready for peace. I had spent four years in the RAF as a wireless operator. I was lucky during the war; I never came close to death. While the world bled from London to Leningrad; I walked away without a scratch. Make no mistake, I did my part in this war; I played my role and I never shirked the paymaster's orders. For four years, I trained, I marched, and I saluted across the British Isles. During the final months of the conflict, I ended up in Belgium and Holland with B.A.F.U. My unit was responsible for maintaining abandoned Nazi airfields for allied aircraft.

When Germany surrendered to the Allies in gutted Berlin, I was in Fuhlsbüttel, a northern suburb of Hamburg. At the time, I didn't think much about Fuhlsbüttel, I felt it was between nothing and nowhere. It was much like every other town our unit drove through during the dying days of the war. Nothing was out of place and it was quiet, clean, and as silent as a Sunday afternoon. Our squadron took up a comfortable residence in its undamaged aerodrome.

While I slept in my new bed in this drowsy neighbourhood; the twentieth century's greatest and bloodiest conflict came to an end at midnight on May seventh. On the morning of the eighth, our RAF commander hastily arranged a victory party for that afternoon. The festivities were held in a school gymnasium close to the airport.

The get-together might have been haphazard and the arrangements made on short notice, but there were no complaints because death was now a postponed appointment. Our individual ends, from road accidents, cancer, or old age, were to be penciled in for a date in the far distant future. There was a lot of excitement, optimism and simple joy generated during the party because we were young and pissed on free beer. RAF officers, NCOs, and enlisted men marked the passage from war to peace, dancing the bunny hop in the overheated school gymnasium.

No one considered or asked on that day of victory, "What happens next?" That was tomorrow's problem. I certainly didn't question my destiny on that spring afternoon. Instead like the Romans, I followed the edict: *carpe diem.* I ate too much, I smoked too much, and I drank too much. And why not, I reasoned, the war was over and I had survived whereas a great many had been extinguished as quickly as blowing out a flame on a candle.

I still didn't want to think about tomorrow, even when our victory party was no more than a hung-over echo of patriotic songs and dirty limericks playing inside my head; I was content to wait and watch. I was perfectly happy to observe my mates plod onwards like dray horses trotting back to their old lives. I was satisfied to enjoy a moment that wouldn't last, peace without obligation. I relished the mundane luxury of sitting on a bench with a cigarette between my fingers. I indulged in the sensual pleasure of feeling the warm spring sun hover over my face. I was liberated from home and the dismal dull world of a mill town, where one's life was charted to end as it began: in a tenement house, under grey dense skies. I wanted to simply enjoy and savour my release from the threat of death.

During those first few days of peace, I was overwhelmed with a feeling of good fortune. It was really blind luck that I had endured. My survival was the mythical lucky dip at a fairground raffle. I was alive while millions of combatants and civilians simply perished in this long and brutal conflict.

It wasn't long after road workers had swept the streets clean from our victory parade that I began to realize my four years of service to the state hadn't altered me greatly. Perhaps I was a bit more educated and less naive about the world. I had certainly acquired some now-redundant skills in marching and Morse code. I was also more aware that suffering and hurt was not a commodity in short supply. Possibly an outsider may have even considered me more cynical and crass after my years with the RAF. Yet underneath my cocksure attitude, I was still the same, self-conscious, lonely, awkward teenager who had volunteered to join the RAF in December 1940.

No matter how relieved I felt with Hitler dead and peace at hand, it reminded me that my personal destiny was now my own responsibility. Considering that the war rescued me from the nightmare of my past life; I was a bit frightened by peace. I was comfortable in my RAF blue uniform, which made me look the same as Bill Jones, Will Sanders, or a multitude of other boys from counties all across Britain. I didn't want to be Harry Smith, from Halifax, former manager at Grosvenor's Grocers, son of a cuckold, from the backside of town.

So for as many moments as I could grasp, I took smug comfort in the anonymity of military life. I relished the new laid-back approach both officers and NCOs took to commanding our group. It was a simple decree to live and let live. As long as there was no scandal, we were allowed to pursue our own past times for amusement or profit.

As the spring dissolved into summer, I began to appreciate that the war had been relatively harmless and uneventful for me. My life must change, I ventured, because I was one of the fortunate few; I was healthy and alive. The question was how to modify my existence that had been chartered since my parents' rapid and one-way descent into poverty and rough living.

While shaving one morning, in the wash hut, I said to my mate Dave, "I don't know what to do with myself. I don't want to be working at a mill back in Halifax or be a grocer."

Dave took a while to reply because he was absorbed in taking careful strokes around his chin with the razor. "It's all in the cards you are dealt before you are born. Some get a lucky hand while others get shite. If all you get dealt is deuces, there's nothing you can do about it, except learn how to fucking bluff." Dave paused, looked at his clean face, and added as an afterthought to the rules for a successful life, "You also need a good fry up in the morning."

Was he right? Was it just down to luck? He might have been on to something. So far, every direction my life had taken was a simple act of chance or whimsy. After all, flat feet and a flaccid patriotic sentiment led me to the doors of the RAF. Most likely, had I picked another branch of the armed forces; I would have ended up as a name stencilled on a cenotaph to be washed in the indifferent rain falling on Halifax. So, for the present, I left my life in the hands of fortune reinforced by bullshit.

On the days I was permitted to leave our base, I strolled until my legs ached, exploring my surroundings as if they were the ruins of Troy. To remain alive in 1945, the Germans were reduced to the most primitive form of commerce; they bartered and begged, and they did it in every imaginable location. I encountered Germans in back alleys, street corners, or by the entrance to the train station, huddled in small groups trading their heirlooms for food.

In the beginning, I was emotionally detached from Germans and the destruction around me. Their suffering played as blandly as a sepia-toned news reel at the Odeon Cinema. The immensity of the pain endured by both the innocent and the damned was too much for me to absorb. What lay outside of my privileged life in camp was a festering sore that fouled the air. I tried to keep my distance from the Germans and their troubles.

Keeping my heart cold and lofty didn't last long because I was a young man looking for a bit of emotional adventure. Within two weeks, I was trying to start conversations with young German women. When I called out, "Excuse me, Fraulein," most walked by me or jumped over to the other side of the street. Some women smiled politely or giggled to their girlfriends at my bad accent and my limited vocabulary.

This game ended for me on the day I travelled up Langenhorner Chausee, in Fuhlsbüttel. It was a road populated with attractive two and three-story apartments, which were shaded by linden and cherry trees. It was a middle-class neighbourhood that stretched towards the horizon in relaxed prosperity. The street was a quiet and pleasant quarter that seemed immune from the tragedies unfolding all around it. It wasn't until I walked further up the road that I discovered no district in Germany was inoculated against hunger.

On the other side of the street, a commotion was brewing between an elderly man and a young woman. They were haggling over the value of a silver fork for a packet of cigarettes. I loitered and observed them struggling to barter their way out of starvation and ruin. Suddenly, I noticed a woman that made my heart and head stumble in aroused confusion. It appeared she was also bartering for food, but there was something different in her body language. It suggested to me a dignity and a pride that wouldn't yield to her circumstances.

Extraordinary, I thought and I said aloud, "You are beautiful."

Afterwards, I did something rash; I displayed a confidence I generally lacked, unless full of beer. I barged into the young woman's life. It was reckless, it was foolish, and perhaps it was even desperate. It also proved the extent of my loneliness or established my habitual foolishness to fall in love with foreign things. During our first encounter, she was moderately indifferent to my entreaties. Perhaps she was even amused by my stilted German and my pushy courteousness. On instinct, or possibly it was a girlish whim because I seemed harmless, she graciously allowed me to walk her part-way home.

"What's your name?" I asked.

"Elfriede Gisela Edelmann," she quickly responded.

I tried to repeat the name, but it jumbled out horribly wrong.

She laughed and said even though we weren't yet friends, "Call me Friede, it is easier."

I must have left a favourable impression because Friede agreed to meet me for a picnic the following week. So began my slow and irresolute courtship with this extraordinary German woman.

Perhaps the term woman was too advanced because she was only a teenager. However, at seventeen, Friede had more style, sophistication, and charm than anyone I'd ever met, dated, or simply lusted after. She possessed a sense of mystery because there was something unknowable and impenetrable about her personality. It was as if there was a sunspot against her soul. Perhaps Friede created this emotional no man's land around herself because she had encountered evil in Hitler's Germany, or perhaps because she harboured some unhappy family secret. Whatever the reason, she was an enigma who was hard to fathom, but easy to love.

It was primal, it was emotional, and it was natural, but I wanted to get to know her better. I also wanted to sleep with her and I would do anything to get to that end. At first; I took her on innocent picnics. I snatched food and wine from the RAF mess hut for our meals. I believed I was being cavalier. I thought Friede might even consider me cosmopolitan when I lit our cigarettes like Paul Henreid for Bette Davis, in the movie *Now Voyager*. She only smiled or laughed light-heartedly at my decorum. Initially, I didn't understand that she lived in a completely different world than mine. Her universe had more immediate problems and concerns than if the wine was chilled. After a while, I began to understand that her community was in serious trouble and was suffering from a severe lack of food and medicine.

It was during an afternoon lunch on the banks of the Alster River that some of her real misfortunes and sorrow crept up on me. While she sunned her bare legs, I noticed they were covered in tiny blisters and ulcers. Friede registered my awkward stare and smiled.

"We have no vitamins, liebchen. There's nothing left to eat: all of Germany will die from scurvy like we are on a polar expedition."

"Why don't you have any vitamins?" I innocently asked.

Friede explained that for most Germans, the last year of the war had been very difficult. Their cities suffered round the clock bombardment, while the Allied armies began a massive land offensive against their nation. In the final months of the war, food supplies for ordinary citizens ran out. Friede and her family lived off a soup that tasted like rainwater and ate bread made from animal feed.

"After the Russians crossed the Oder River in January 1945," Friede explained, "everyone knew the war was lost. It was only matter of time until we got a taste of our own medicine. I was terrified by who our new masters would be: Russia or America?"

"It was a good thing we Brits got here first before the Russians could get their hands on Hamburg," I replied.

Friede laughed at my simplistic response as she retorted, "It is sometimes hard to tell if Britain is the best jailer. You British treat everyone as if they are Nazis and deserve to be punished."

"How do we do this?" I asked.

Friede looked at me and smirked. "Our rations are table scraps for a dog. People are expected to remove rubble from the cities, but are allotted just 1200 calories of nutrition per day. Britain keeps my people on the edge of starvation. Have you seen the bread they give us?" she demanded angrily.

I had seen Germans queue impatiently for this almost-inedible food. At one time, I had even witnessed soldiers toss dense bricks of blackened dough to hungry crowds. It was a miserable ration to feed anyone. The ingredients were a dubious mixture of sawdust and salt, with a trace amount of flour that bonded the indigestible product together. The bread was baked in the morning and if you didn't consume it by late afternoon, thick green mould would burrow its way to the crust. Sometimes, I caught sight of vagrants in the shadow of bomb-damaged buildings, who had somehow got their hands on the thick rotten bread. Famished, they would stuff it into their mouths and wash it back with water scooped from the street gutters.

Friede continued and said that many believed the victors treated Germany like they did in 1918. "The Allies will let the German people starve to death."

"What do you mean?" I asked defensively.

"Unless you are wealthy, you can't buy food anywhere in the city. Mutti must travel north up into the countryside," Friede told me in a halting voice. "She sells our belongings to the farmers who give her a few eggs and a rotting turnip in exchange. How will we live once all of her jewels and silver are gone? Mutti says the farmers act like pirates. They have no pity on the city folk and will rob you of everything you own for a morsel of food. People say the farmers are rich from the city's misery and have Persian carpets in their pig sties."

Afterwards, I thought my invitation to a lunch by the river seemed nothing more than a cynical gesture. I blamed myself for not understanding her difficulties sooner because I had endured a similar hunger in my childhood.

My growing affection for Friede drove me to become a conspirator in her survival. I obtained food for Friede and her family by the old and reliable methods my mother had taught me: if you can't buy it, beg for it, and if you can't beg for it, nick it while God and the holy ghosts are down at pub. So, from storage units on our base, I snatched anything I thought useful to them, from food rations to soap and medicine. I wrapped up the contraband in a blanket and smuggled it out of camp in a haversack.

Perhaps I was correcting the wrong done to me as a starving boy? Perhaps I was buying love and loyalty with a loaf of bread? I didn't know or care. I knew winter was coming and without someone like me; her family would starve to death like thousands of other Germans, hobbled by this devastating war.

Looking back, I think the start of our romance; the picnics by the river, the afternoons spent loitering in river-front cafés were just a pleasant diversion for Friede and her friends. They were an excuse to eat delicacies and savour flavours long absent from an ordinary German's diet. In the beginning, Friede didn't appreciate the ardour of my passion, but enjoyed my diligence and loyalty in trying to please her ordinary desires and satisfy her most basic needs. I was able to provide Friede with food and protection in a nation that had been cast out of civilization. It was my sheer persistence to keep her sated and healthy with purloined wine, preserves, and medicine that allowed me to ingratiate myself to her. I was able to transform our relationship from the formal *Sie* to the more hopeful and friendly, *Du*.

It was easy for me to fall in love with Friede because she was as glamorous as a movie star. She had deep expressive hazel eyes, and raven hair that hung voluptuously to her shoulders. Her face was sensuous and, at times, mysterious as it expressed deep emotions and indefinable longing.

With my background of poverty, infidelity, and family betrayal, Friede was everything I couldn't aspire to in England. Her education, her taste, her style was utterly more sophisticated then my Woolworth's tuppence upbringing. Being arm-in-arm with her, I felt like I was a lead character in a Saturday morning movie serial. I fell hard for Friede and plunged into the deep end of German life under occupation. Yet the bottomless, almost un-navigable water of love in a ruined nation was my best option for a better future. It was certainly better than returning to a wet and dreary existence in Britain.

Unfortunately, Friede wasn't as easily convinced of my long-term suitability as either suitor or provider. In the beginning, my loyalty and my love were chided as unproven and a childish fancy. Besides, she said, "Tommies come and go; you too will leave for England and go back to your English girlfriend."

I protested but she was right, my time in the RAF was nigh. Demobilisation of soldiers and airmen was moving at a steady pace. If I didn't act quickly, I was going to find myself demobbed and marching in a victory parade leading me right to the dole queue. If I truly loved Friede as I so often claimed after a half-bottle of Riesling; I would have to find a means to remain in Germany. My only option was to extend my services with the RAF.

2

Staying On

Considering that I came from the rough streets of Barnsley, Bradford, and Halifax, extending my term with the RAF was an easy decision. There was nothing in Yorkshire for me except the dead footfall of orphaned hopes and dreams; I had neither an education nor a vocation. Before the war, I had been a manager at Grosvenor's Grocer in Halifax. Prior to my departure for military service, the owner had promised me that my position would be available at war's end. A lot can happen in four years and promises made in patriotic fervour are kept as seldom as New Year's resolutions. My old job was now probably firmly occupied by a conscientious objector, who dodged the draft, but never an excuse to make a pound.

By the age of twenty-two, I had an empirical certitude that there was nothing for me in England. Everything I cared for had been destroyed by the Great Depression. My father had spent his last years alone in a rooming house and died a pauper. As for my mother, Lillian, she was still alive, but our relationship had been tested and damaged by extreme poverty. She secretly defied the conventions of her class by living in a tenement lifestyle with a former cowman named Bill Moxon.

It was sometime between my seventh and eighth birthday, the

cowman replaced my dad in my mother's bed. In the thirties, outside our doss house, the Great Depression descended like a plague upon Yorkshire. My family, along with the rest of Britain's poor, was dumped on the ash heap of history. If it weren't for the war, the government would have left the working class to rot and fester. I had spent my youth running away from my family's ruin, disgrace, and innate sadness. I had tried throughout my teens and into my twenties to deny the hold our poverty had over me as a mark of shame and humiliation.

Dogma, fixed beliefs, or prejudices never reigned over my heart or my head, except for this one certitude; I didn't envision moving back to my mother's domicile. There was no sentiment or memory from the past to convince me that returning to her house would serve any purpose. It would have been as distasteful to me as returning to a nasty crime scene. The only emotion Halifax created in me was despair. To return to the tenement my mother shared with her cowman and my two younger half-brothers would have been a step backwards into the grey world of the 1930s. I didn't want to go back to twenty-four Booth Town Road, where I had lived as a teen. On that street or any other working class street in Halifax; the address didn't matter. Odd or even numbers; the tenements were all sadly identical. They were squalid, overcrowded, under-heated, privy out back, four-walled containers of despair.

In 1945, I had no attachments to Britain except for one person that still tugged at my shirt-sleeves, my sister, Mary. She was my true friend. She was my companion through my family's bleakest and saddest moments. But my affection for her wasn't strong enough for me to flee back into the oppressive and stifling arms of Britain's West Riding.

Besides, Mary didn't have the means to put me up even if I did want to return home. She lived on the steep hills of Low Moor, in a tiny row house with a young son and a troublesome husband. Nor did Mary have any influence with the local powers to find me employment; without a friendly word in a manager's ear; there was no possibility of a job. The mills around Bradford and Halifax were brimming with unemployed servicemen, all looking to return to their old positions. If I went home, I would be just another redundant cog in the broken wheel of British Industry.

Just to make sure I wasn't under any delusion on life back in Yorkshire, Mary wrote to me:

"Luv, there's nothing here for ya. There's nothing at all, no housing and certainly no brass. If you need it, I can always lend you a spare shilling. But I suspect you've got more than me being in the RAF. But I won't deny you anything I've got; which is love and a shoulder to cry on. Stay put and stay safe and stay out of our mum's way or she'll be asking for something from you. Enjoy your time abroad because you've got naught to come home to."

So there was nothing and no one to return to in post-war Britain. I knew I was more welcome walking outside the gates of our encampment down Zeppelin Strasse, than on Broad Street in Halifax. So I was content to be across the North Sea in a foreign and defeated country. In fact, I was better off stationed in this desperate and ruined nation than in Britain. At least in Germany, I was a member of the conquering legion. The RAF protected me from want and hunger. In exchange, I accepted that my life was theirs to waste in battle or in peace. However, in the spring of 1945, it was unlikely that the RAF was going to collect on the balance owed them. My life wasn't in any immediate danger in Europe and I wasn't going to remind them about the battles still underway in Asia.

Some of my mates had different notions about self-preservation and suggested I join them on an insane venture in the war against Japan. Their mission involved a self-propelled, one-man submarine in the South China Sea; the sub would affix limpet mines to the remnants of the Land of the Rising Sun's merchant marine. The scheme and their rationale - "Be a bit more of a laugh than hanging around 'ere," was lunatic at best and suicidal at worst. Considering that since my induction in the RAF, I had avoided volunteering for anything that might shorten my life with as much rigour as I ducked Sunday church parade, I wasn't going to break my lucky streak by accepting a suicide mission to the Far East, just to satisfy our dying empire or my more patriotic, testosterone-driven mates.

No, I wasn't going anywhere dangerous. I would remain in Germany because they were defeated, broken, and submissive, at least for the time. It was the safest place in the world for me and it also allowed me the time to pursue Friede. Staying on would give me the opportunity to win Friede to my heart, just like the crooners sang about over the wireless on Armed Forces Radio. I wanted to linger for a time in Germany so that I would be able to figure out what I wanted to do with my life. I knew I wasn't cut out to live as my parents did on bread, drippings, and lager.

Now that hostilities were over, the RAF had minimal expectations for the lower ranks. Their one simple rule was: keep your head down and your nose out of other people's business. I had no problem with this unwritten regulation as I had followed this practice since boyhood. As long as it didn't affect my immediate well being, the petty affairs of others didn't rouse any interest in me. It was safer to close my eyes to most everyone's evil or saintly exploits.

After all, if I wished to remain in Germany, there was wisdom in silence. I wanted to be known and relied upon for my indifference to the comings and goings of the world around me. Keeping out of trouble was one thing, trying not to witness trouble was unavoidable. Two weeks into our stay in Fuhlsbüttel and the profiteers were salivating at the opportunity to plunder an occupied country with no inventory list. Supplies from food to fuel were always going missing. One morning, a sergeant, put a friendly arm around my shoulder after I noticed a group of airmen hanging around suspiciously near a store house. The NCO said, "Lad, keep your eyes shut and whistle a friendly tune because there's naught to see here."

The men I encountered were shifting boxes of tinned meats,

preserves, and beer into an air force van, which when loaded took off for an unknown destination. Later on, I mentioned the truck with its cargo of RAF stores to a hut mate and friend named Sid.

"Oh that," he said. "It's a sergeant's fiddle. He's got some deal with a bloody Nazi who owns a restaurant. The sergeant provides him booze and meat. In return, good old Fritz pays him in gold coins and jewellery."

"What happens to the baubles?" I asked foolishly.

"The missus flogs it back in Leeds."

My mouth opened up to respond, when Sid said to me, "Don't even think of joining that party, mate. It's best we stick to what we know; getting pissed and getting laid, everything else is a big boy's game."

"Too right," I agreed.

So in the interest of self-preservation, I did what I was told. I turned a blind eye to my equals and my betters. I turned my back to anything that appeared out of sorts. I even closed my ears to the creeping sound of coins being counted in the darkness by those who were plundering the German nation or the British armed services. However, as the weeks progressed, it became more difficult to ignore the racket caused by the pilfering. It seemed anything of value, if it wasn't guarded or nailed down, was nicked. Some members of my squad acted as if they had found bits of a Spanish Galleon washed up on shore when they returned from a trip into Hamburg.

"Jesus wept, would you get a look at that watch. It only cost me a carton of bloody Lucky Strikes."

"Jim, if you'd spent forty years in pit as a ripper, you'd still not get a watch as fine as you traded today, for a bunch of bloody fags."

With a nation being hawked away for cigarettes, I wasn't going to be left out of this burglary. I took what wasn't mine, but I reasoned it was an all-together different type of crime. My larceny was innocent of profit or malice. I simply pinched food for the German girl and her family. My misdemeanor was insignificant except to those that received

269

my food parcels. I thought my actions were more akin to extending the hand of British philanthropy towards the less fortunate.

On base, there were a few others like me, unwilling to profit on the misery of others. We were incapable of seeing a reason to garner personal gain from the sunken and ashen faces of bomb-battered ordinary Germans. As for the rest, the temptation for theft and for sex without responsibility was overwhelming. It was too easy for them to suspend their morality while abroad. They believed that their ethics could resume upon their return to Britain. They thought their moral code was like a light switch; it could be turned on or off without ever marking their soul.

Within my barracks, a great many used food and cigarettes as a bartering device for nameless sex with near-starving German teenagers. Others traded food for gold, jewellery, and other valuable commodities, which they saved for their return home to Brighton or Birmingham as chocolate soldiers on parade. Their dubious earnings from fraternizing with the desperate provided a valuable addition to a down-payment on a house or a new car. Others just pilfered their money and morality away as if they were down at their local pub with their pay packet.

"For a bit of coffee or nylons, you can get those Frauleins to do anything you want."

"Smith, why don't you try it if only for a laugh? You'll never get a chance like this again, ever in your sorry life."

But I shook my head. I had already experienced life at the hands of ghetto kings back in Bradford to want to become a proper bastard in Germany. "Sorry, lads, I don't want anything from the bloody Germans because they're nothing but trouble," I remarked.

Someone at the far end of our hut shouted out, "We got Jesus of the Nazarenes sleeping besides us. Let's hope he doesn't go to turning tables at temple on Sunday."

I laughed. "Bugger you, mate. There will be no water into wine for you ungrateful lot." I went back to reading my book.

A few days later, I spoke with my friend, Taffy. "I wonder if things had worked out different in the war and Jerry was on our High Street buying us out for a thrupenny; how would we react."

Taffy was Welsh and as sentimental as me. I liked him for his love of poetry, whiskey, and his soft touch for hard-luck stories.

"Pack it in, Harry," Taffy said. "Most of those lads are like us; since the day they were born they've been beaten down by the squire, by the church, and by the foreman. All they want is to taste a bit of the good life after being cheated out of it for centuries by those Tory bastards back home. Sure, they shouldn't be filching, whoring, and acting like clowns on parade just because no one gives a toss. But I'll keep stum to their misdemeanours and leave it up to God to decide who's guilty and who's innocent.

"As for Ali Baba over there and his forty thick thieves; leave 'em be. Germany is a land of louts and I'll be glad when I am rid it and back home in Wales. You should go home too, forget this place; it's filled with bloody foreigners."

Even though it disgusted me, Taffy was right about the pilfering. So I kept quiet. I didn't want my larceny to be revealed, curtailed, or for me to be punished for helping the German girl.

It was both terrifying and exciting keeping Friede's family afloat, while the former German nation collapsed around us like a block of condemned buildings. It was also a giant fraud because my gallantry was circumstantial. I only appeared successful and confident to Friede because her country was decimated. Every day, I was frightened that Friede would discover my counterfeit, that my ability to save her was limited to my present circumstances. Anywhere else, I would have been just one of a hundred men, searching for work and shelter.

It terrified me to think Friede or anyone else might discover that my outward staged confidence was a swindle, a deception as devious as a cheque written on a bank account with a nil balance. So, there was no turmoil in my soul when I made an appointment with my superiors to extend my days in Germany. I had only one anxiety that perhaps the RAF didn't want me and were prepared to chuck me over the side, once my terms of service were complete.

Before my scheduled appointment, I made sure that I was properly groomed. A German barber cut my hair and shaved me with a straight-edge razor. My uniform was pressed by a woman who worked at the base laundry. I was determined that my outward appearance would convince any officer that I was born for the military life. After a quick cigarette behind a Nissen hut, I marched over to the wing commander's office where I was to meet with his adjutant. When I arrived, the foyer was littered with other men in similarly pressed uniforms. We looked like lackeys begging for favours in the Sun King's antechamber. The adjutant had a wiry LAC for a secretary, who acted more like a guard dog on an estate than an administrative clerk.

I announced myself to the secretary, who scanned a large appointment book looking for my appointment. Out loud, he called out a roll of names penciled in for upcoming meetings with the adjutant: "Benson, Hearn, Simpson, ah yes, and here we are, Smith. Your appointment is at 1.45, bit eager, aren't we?" he said.

"Pardon" I asked?

"You're early for your appointment."

"It's only five minutes away," I pointed out.

The clerk looked up at the wall clock, back to his wrist watch, and then smiled at me. "You're still early. Please take a seat."

The secretary returned to his duties and I was left to watch the minute hands from the clock make five slow revolutions. At 1:45, the clerk robotically stood from his desk and knocked on the officer's door. He entered and returned back to the foyer.

"The adjutant is ready to see you."

I stood up and the secretary admonished me.

"Come on now, let's get a move on, chop, chop. We don't have all day; the adjutant is a busy man. It's not like going to see the parson,

272

you know."

The secretary announced me to Flight Lieutenant Locke, the adjutant. "Wireless Operator Smith to see you, sir."

The officer was at his desk signing papers; behind him was a wall map of Northern Germany. He looked up from his work and said, "At ease, Smith."

The officer had a waxed moustache and was at least ten years older than me. It was a kind but weary face. I noticed he was wearing a wedding band. On his desk were framed photographs of a blonde-haired woman and a little girl.

He pulled open my file, read it quickly, and stated, "So you want to stay on in Germany. Any reason for this, I hope this isn't about a girl."

"No, sir," I said deceptively. "I like the air force and I enjoy the life. I think I can contribute to my country better in uniform than out."

He looked back at my service record. "You've never been up on charges and you've always passed your courses in the top percentiles. I've never heard anyone say a bad word about you. So you must be the decent sort. Well, I'm not going to deny this request. We are demobbing so many men these days, there is hardly anyone left trained to boil a kettle for tea. I'll have your request approved."

I saluted the officer. He returned it with a sloppy hand to head motion. I left the office, relieved; I had bought myself six more months of time with Friede.

When Taffy saw me, he asked, "So are you in or are you out?"

"Back in," I responded.

"Bloody fool," he said. "Everyone is begging to get out of this nut house and you are climbing to get back in. Well, Smith, since you know you've got a pay packet for the next six months, let's go out on the town and get pissed.

273

3

A summer in the ruins of Troy

During that spring and summer of 1945, history's forge was busy. Russia and America were intent on beating out a new and different Europe from the dead Nazi era. The Potsdam Conference formally divided Germany into four unequal parts. Naturally, Russian and America, being the strongest and wealthiest partners in the war against Germany, occupied most of the country's land mass. The smaller contributors to the war effort were offered a reduced share of the fatherland. Britain was given a small but meaty portion of Northern Germany. France was tossed some offal to assuage their Gallic pride. In this divided German, peace was strained between the Western powers and Russia, except when it came to reparations. On that subject, each occupying nation acted like an appellant at an insolvency court hearing.

Russia was by far the most brutal and vengeful occupier, having suffered greatly at the hands of Hitler's armies. So, without regret, the soviets gnawed and chewed into their share of the German carcass that stretched from Berlin on a north-south axis and eastwards to the rich farmlands of Pomerania. Trains left on the hour destined for Moscow, filled with dismantled factories, laboratories, and heavy machinery. Along with the spoils of war, these trains also carried former Wehrmacht soldiers and the SS, condemned to Siberian hard labour.

The situation didn't look much better for Germans residing in the Western-occupied zone of their country. The allies implemented the Morgenthau plan, which was created to neuter Germany's war-like tendencies and transform it into a pastoral society. The country's industrial base, its steel works, automobile plants, and consumer manufacturing centers were dismantled. The contents of Germany's economic greatness were shipped to the Allied victors in giant rail cars and ocean freighters. Like the communists, Britain, America, and France called the looting of Germany "reparations for the just."

As acetylene torches dismembered factories, steel mills, and ship yards across Germany, so the friendships I had built in the RAF were also being dismantled. One by one, my mates departed and their names were replaced on the sergeant's morning roll call roster with new and unfamiliar draftees. My friends went home to their old and familiar civilian lives, while I remained in Germany, beguiled by a fresh world emerging from the wreckage.

It wasn't meant to happen, but I fell in love with the German girl. Considering that our two nations had waged a brutal war for five years, it was astonishing that Friede and I even liked each other, let alone grew into lovers.

Before I met Friede, my knowledge of Germany was based upon propaganda posters and news reels displaying an endless sea of jackboots flood across Europe. I was convinced that Germans were evil and sinister after I witnessed the results of the Nazis scorched-Earth policy in Holland.

My black and white opinions about Germany changed when I crossed through their borders and encountered a civilization turned into a wasteland by aerial bombardment. On the ground, I witnessed emaciated German children living in appalling conditions in the ruins of their city. It was at that moment I accepted that both the damned and the innocent suffered in this war. The longer I stayed in Germany, the more I understood that Friede was both my Beatrice and my Virgil. She was the one who was to lead me through Germany's post-war inferno and perhaps towards our own paradise.

Friede was an excellent guide through both present-day Germany and her country's recent past, but sometimes the maps used were filled with errors created by the imperfections and the prejudice of the cartographers. There were moments when Friede expressed an overwhelming shame and guilt for the crimes of her elders, but at other times, she couldn't fully digest the totality of Germany's barbarity under Hitler.

Friede said it was impossible to fully comprehend the ever-expanding list of heinous acts her country had committed. She compared it to a child having a father that is wonderful to his own family, but is found guilty of murdering many people in the neighbourhood.

"You think to yourself; was this the same man that loved me and fed me and cared for me; yet did all of these wicked things to our neighbours?"

In many ways, Friede was just an ordinary teenager savouring the liberties of youth; discovering the pleasures of sex, and the exhilaration of being adored and wanted by men.

"I love the way you look at me when I wear that summer dress with my new white shoes."

Friede was nonchalant about male and female relationships and casually warned me that she saw other men.

"There are other boy's you know," she said in a carefree whisper one day.

"Oh?" I responded, acting as if I were cosmopolitan and blasé.

"Like you, they take me on walks or to a cafe," she added.

"Who are they? Anyone I know?" I asked suspiciously.

"Of course you don't know them. One is a German boy who I have known since I was four. And the other one is a Tommy who likes to talk to me."

I bet he does, I thought cynically.

Friede absorbed my silence and tried to explain her feelings about me and the other young men in her life. She said that her whole world had changed the day the war ended. Peace was difficult, hungry, and complicated, but it was also exhilarating. She wanted to enjoy the simple pleasure of being alive and young with few restrictions.

"Harry, you must take things slowly with me. Let our hearts grow for each other as we explore this new world," she told me, skipping slightly ahead of me.

"Sure," I said, "you're right." And then I lied. "You know I'm seeing other German girls, so don't get too comfortable with me, if you know what I mean."

I was no actor and my shoulders stooped and my face displayed a painful heartache. Friede noticed and became more serious.
"Those other boys are nothing to me. I am very fond of you. You are so... what is the word... gallant? I am very grateful to you. I just don't know yet what we will become, friends or lovers. So don't be cross, please understand." Friede added, "I shall always be your comrade. My heart will tell me when it is time to give it to you or another. Now stop pouting," she admonished me. "Buy me some flowers before you walk me home."

Friede introduced me to her past like I was the Sultan in Scherazade; there was a story every night that never finished and led further into her soul. She revealed her illegitimacy to me, her experience as a foster child and evacuee. She was adamant that if we were to continue seeing each other, she wanted, "No dark places in your heart, no jealously, and no anger in your soul. Between us, Harry, things have to be light as a Strauss operetta or as fun as the jitterbug."

Tentatively, we began to learn about each other's likes and dislikes to see if we shared anything in common, except surviving a war from opposite sides.

277

"I love to read poetry," I told her.

"Wordsworth, he is a good poet, but Goethe is more universal," she responded.

"I've never heard of Shiller, but everyone in the world knows Shakespeare."

"Shirley Temple, I loved the way she could dance."

"What about Harold Lloyd?"

"I don't know him, but you must know Dick und Dorf?"

"Who are they?"

"You know the fat and the thin man, who wear the bowler hats."

"You mean Laurel and Hardy."

"That's right, *Dick und Dorf.*"

During our first few weeks together, Friede and I didn't have much physical contact, except we held hands on occasion. Sometimes, she even let me kiss her lightly on the lips or play with her hair. I would sometimes catch her staring deep into my eyes trying to decipher what was greater, my lust or my affection for her.

Friede wasn't a patriot, but she was proud to be German. She knew her country's history and achievements in music, philosophy, art, and the sciences. Friede also admitted that Germany's character, its national greatness, was also the ember that sparked its evil. On one of our many walks, we strolled down an avenue showered in dust and demolition. Friede pointed to a group of women working outside their apartment block.

"Look at them, they have nothing and yet they will still sweep their stoop. They will always make sure the inside of their homes are clean. Even if they have no food to eat, Germans will always make sure they are dignified and clean. It is what we learn from birth. It doesn't matter if you are poor or rich, you must have discipline and pride in yourself." Sadly, she added, "This is what led us to this Gomorrah. Our discipline transformed us into criminals."

On another day, we were drinking wine at an outdoor river café, when she told me, "I think my emotions were created in the social clubs of Weimar Germany because they are so democratic, so contradictory. I am up and down and all over the map."

"You seem all right to me," I replied.

Friede shook her head. "No, I have so many anxieties. I am afraid a lot of times, for no real reason. It is a gift from the Nazis."

Friede explained that she was nervous and self-conscious because of her illegitimacy. She was confused by where and to whom she belonged. Was it with her mother or her foster parents? Did any of them really want her or even love her? She was afraid that people judged her because her mother took a rich lover and her real father was a socialist.

"That is why I read so many books," she explained. "I am looking for another character that might resemble me or my life, even if they are just fiction."

I confessed to Friede that I had the same fantasy as a boy and would hunt through novels looking for my identity or the cause of my family's misfortunes.

"Did you find anyone who was like you?" she asked.

"No, I'm afraid I have only found escape from the people around me. What are your favourite books?" I asked.

"Too numerous to count," she replied. "Many of them were forbidden under Hitler because they were considered anti-German. They even called Thomas Mann 'an enemy of the people'. But Mutti still had a copy of the *Buddenbrookes,* which she let me read. There were no books at my foster parents' house. They were simple people and didn't read much, except my foster father liked Karl Mai to drown out my foster mother's complaints."

"So you and your mother were anti-Nazi then?" I asked.

She looked at me with dark impenetrable eyes and said. "Before the war, everyone was pro-Nazi, even if they had doubts about Hitler. Now everyone is anti-Nazi, even if they have doubts about the British and Americans. My family survived like everyone else did in Germany. We had two faces: one for the world in black uniforms and another for life behind closed doors. You know," she added conspiratorially, "my mother even joined the Nazi party."

"What?"

"Yes, it's true. Her lover Henry said it was good for his business; it probably was considering he imported and sold tobacco products. Henry joined the party in 1939 because it was easier to sell lighters and humidors to officers' clubs if you could say you were a member of the party. My mother became a member of the Nazi party in 1942. It was a simple decision for her. Too many people were asking questions about me because I lived with a foster family and she lived with a much older businessman. There was always someone sticking their nose into our business and asking about my real father, Fritz. Funny how people stopped gossiping once she got her party badge."

Friede's illegitimacy tortured her. Being a bastard dug a deep furrow inside of her personality. It made Friede believe she wasn't complete, that her existence was evidence for a crime of passion. She believed she was just the product of a love affair that ended in shame.

"It is a stain on the child more than on the parents," she said bitterly. "Children made fun of me because I didn't have a father. I didn't fit in because of my mother's avant-garde lifestyle and my polar opposite life with my foster parents. Mutti's way of life made it hard for me to make friends. But even the lone wolf sometimes wants to be liked. So at school, I was a good National Socialist and said "seig heil" with the rest of my classmates." She paused and then continued. "Why do you look at me like I just said I followed the devil?"

"Did you believe in Hitler?" I asked.

"What a silly question. When Hitler came to power in 1933, I was five. I was too young for politics. I only knew what adults told me, or what I heard on the wireless and saw at the movies or at school. We were taught: "the Nazi party saved us from anarchy." So yes, I believed in Hitler because I believed in my mother and my foster parents and my teachers. Once, I even told my class that I met Hitler in Berchtesgaden on summer holiday."

"Did you?"

Friede looked at me as if I was a simpleton and said, "Sure and he shook my hand! Hardly, I was just trying to impress the class with a fib no one could contradict. If it makes you feel any better, I can tell you I hated the Hitler Youth. But that is because the girls were all bullies in my squad, so I tried to avoid them as much as possible. So," she added, while looking at her face in a compact mirror, "is the interrogation over? Am I now de-nazified enough for you?"

"I'm sorry; I didn't mean to hurt you."

"You didn't," she replied, snapping the compact shut. "I just believe you can't possibly know what it was like to live in Germany under Hitler. No matter what I tell you, you will never understand what it was like, and you will always say underneath your breath, 'Us Brits would never act like that.' Maybe not, but ask the Irish what they think of jolly old England. I am sure they have a different story to tell. Germany did horrible, unspeakable things to millions of people and we are rightly guilty, but I don't want to talk about it anymore because all of it just makes me sick inside."

In the time it took to change a phonograph, Friede could veer from extreme emotional brooding to playfulness. One evening, we sat on a park bench and argued whether occupational soldiers behaved no better than the Wehrmacht in France. Fed up with the conversation, she grabbed a box of matches that were resting on my cigarette pack. She struck a handful of matches and tossed them at me to see how I would react. Of course, I returned fire. Neither of us blinked in this game of combustible chicken. The competition only ended when the box was empty of flaming projectiles.

At other moments, Friede was guilt-ridden by the wretched circumstances faced by refugees. When we encountered a group of them slumped on the street, Friede took a fruit basket I had purloined from RAF stores, and she handed it out to them.

"They need it more than me or my family. Look at them; they must have travelled all the way from Lithuania. What is going to become of them? Who will help them?" she pleaded.

She began to hand out apples and pears to the displaced family. It looked to me like all the kindness in the world wasn't going to save them from annihilation. Caustically, she said, "You take everything from us, you English, and you think we should be grateful like a dog because you are a better master than Hitler."

I watched her feed the refugee family until there was nothing left to give. With the basket empty, she dropped it to the ground and swept their youngest child into her arms. "If only there were more people like us, there would be no war, no Hitler, no Stalin, and no hunger."

"Hush, Friede," said Gerda. "I have never been here, so it is all new for me."

It was a beautiful outdoor restaurant for a well-to-do crowd. Money, not ideology, was its political stripe. That was why it survived the Kaiser's abdication, the assassination of democracy, and Hitler's bloody end. Regardless of who was in power, the menu at the cafe remained the same: Vienna coffee, Sacher torte, and VSOP brandy. The cafe welcomed occupation as it did every historical event: with a cash-only policy.

It was a warm, cloudless day and the restaurant tables were crowded with loud British troops and their female companions. It looked like there was an equal portion of officers and enlisted men chatting and flirting with young German women. Although occupational command frowned upon fraternization, it was almost impossible to enforce. The occupiers were young men at the peak of their rutting age and had endured five years of war, privation, and the threat of obliteration. So, irrespective of HQ's fear that contact with the civilian population would lead to an outbreak of venereal disease, corruption in the ranks, and a diminished capacity to keep order in Germany, nothing was ever really done to enforce the regulation.

The atmosphere at the cafe was carefree as if it were a summer's day before the war. But that was because everyone was facing the river. No one dared turn towards Hamburg's skyline, where it was Gomorrah, the day after Lot had packed up and left. Hamburg was no more than a putrefying animal body where maggots and carrion fed off its carcass. Underneath the city's mountains of ash, cement, bricks, and burned beams were the mummified corpses of some thirty thousand bombing victims. They had perished during the RAF fire bombing raids in July 1943.

"Last year, you could still smell it," Friede noted while she put on fashionable sunglasses and got comfortable in her chair.

"Smell what?" I asked, while her friend Gerda looked out towards the river, disinterested.

"The stench from decaying bodies trapped underneath the city's wreckage," she responded. "Last summer, you needed to place a handkerchief sprinkled with eau de cologne against your face to stop the odour of rotting flesh from getting into your nostrils. It was overpowering. Even in the winter of 1944, how do you say, the taste, is that the right word? The taste of death overpowered winter's frigidness. Hamburg is a tomb," she concluded morbidly.

The waiter arrived and set down our order at our table. He was dressed in an immaculate white coat, black tie, and dark trousers. He bowed and scraped before me and fawned over the two women. Contemptuously, I imagined he displayed the same amount of servility when his customers had been Gestapo officers with their dates.

I offered the ladies a cigarette from my Player's pack, which they both hungrily accepted. I placed my cigarettes on the table. With Hollywood gallantness, I lit our cigarettes. I was about to bring the match to my smoke when Friede suddenly blew it out.

"Don't forget, it is bad luck being the third one to be lit."

"I don't think we have to worry about snipers anymore. Do we?"

Gerda laughed and responded, "Both of you should be careful of Cupid; he is the only one who will get you two into trouble."

Gerda slurped her coffee piled high with fresh cream, while Friede used a spoon to savour each mouthful of rich, butter fat. Her friend smiled and laughed at my jokes, even if she couldn't fully understand them. Friede intently observed how I treated Gerda and was obviously making mental notes of whether I was being kind or cruel. For some time, we talked about music. The two women were famished to know about American singers, swing bands, and whether I had any of their phonographs.

"Do you have Benny Goodman?"

"I adore Tommy Dorsey."

"What about Pennsylvania 65000?"

"Glen Miller," I told them, "is very popular."

I suggested we should all go to a dance held at one of the air force clubs in the near future.

"We can hear swing music played by some great bands?"

Considering I didn't know how to dance, it was a bold offer, so I quickly changed the subject. I suggested as an alternative that I bring some phonographs over to Friede's mother's apartment. "We can listen to some good music and make it our own private party."

"I would still rather go out dancing," Friede said with disappointment.

The afternoon passed quickly and pleasantly as everyone skirted unsettling incidents from the past or our precarious present. Only once did I let the conversation drift into uncharted waters, when I foolishly asked Gerda if she had any brothers or sisters. Gerda's eyes grew dark. "Two," she answered dejectedly. "I have not seen my brother Irvine since 1942. He was in the Afrika campaign. He was taken prisoner by the British. At least he is safe because he is a POW in Britain." Gerda stopped her narrative and asked. "Could I have another cigarette? Bitte."

Her younger brother, Hans, hadn't been as lucky as his older brother because he fought on the eastern front. When I closed the lid of my lighter, she resumed the story about her brother. He was at Stalingrad and couldn't endure the brutality. He tried to desert to the Russians. Unfortunately, Hans failed in his attempt to surrender to the reds. He was caught by his own side, who subjected him to a front-line court martial. Found guilty of cowardice and desertion; Hans was sentenced to death. The verdict was carried out within minutes of the judgement. He was strung up on a telegraph pole, like it was a frontier lynching. A sign was hung around his neck reading simply: *Coward*.

The story made me feel embarrassed by my good fortune during the war. Friede interrupted the heavy stillness.

"Do you now see, Harry? Not every German is a killer. It is our tragedy that in this war, we consumed our young like cannibals."

The waiter arrived with our bill. He presented it on a silver tray that was placed obsequiously before me. He officiously swept the table of crumbs with a shiny brass handle brush. There was a hasty servility to his movements because other soldiers with their German girls were eager to pay for coffee by the river. I stubbed my cigarette into the ashtray and I tried to leave a fat tip on the table, but Friede commented out loud; "That is just foolish, Harry. That stupid waiter is already rich on Tommy money, better to give him half and we can enjoy the rest somewhere else."

I picked up part of the gratuity and sheepishly thrust it back into my trouser pocket. When I stood up, I noticed Gerda had hastily gathered up spare sugar cubes from the coffee saucers and put them into her pocket.

The three of us walked along the riverbank. The water's surface had a petrol sheen and sluggishly drifted towards the sea. The sterns of scuttled naval ships perched themselves above the waterline like markers leading towards the dockyards. Off in the distance, the harbour was still. It was a testament to the air war against the city. The port was now only broken awnings and collapsed steel cranes resting derelict across docking slips. We strolled on a path along the Alster. It was an exquisite walkway decorated with ancient trees and ornate benches. Above us, the sun's rays fell down, generous and warm, but there was a dusky smell in the air coming from the ravaged city beyond.

We walked with Gerda to a black market where she could barter cigarettes for sausage. The market was in the ruins of the working class district, near the docklands. There were rumours; Gerda said that this place had the best rate of exchange between fags and foodstuffs. While we walked, dust blew up from the bomb craters where buildings had once stood. All around me were gaping holes in the cityscape, as if a giant animal had bitten a chunk of flesh from a carcass. In other places, ziggurats of debris formed, where buildings had caved in on to the street. In some spots, a giant bulldozer had brushed ruined neighbourhoods off to the side as one would rake leaves for burning.

Everywhere, there was a loud, monotonous clicking and scrapping sound originating from old women pecking through the rubble. They were known as the brick Omas. They scavenged around the wrecked streetscapes looking for salvageable masonry to rebuild the sacrificed city. The old women wore rags and torn aprons over their clothing. Brick dust coated their hair and faces, while their hands were blistered and cut from handling bomb debris that they gathered in neat piles and placed along the road way. They worked without complaint, reminding me of the Israelites building Pharaoh's necropolis. Sometimes, scores of old women were killed when they tripped an unexploded bomb trapped in the wreckage.

In the background, amidst the industrious Omas lurked a pack of men in various stages of deformity. A man missing a leg hobbled around on a dubious crutch that barely kept him upright. Beside him stood an armless man whose shirt-sleeves looked like sails empty of wind. In the group, there were several other men whose heads were wrapped in dirty bandages. The war victims huddled around broken concrete as if waiting for the old women to reclaim them like the other refuse in the street. The uncontaminated scent from my crisp RAF uniform stirred them from their crippled indolence.

"Tommy, zigarette fur einen Komarade."

"Tommy, chocolate bitte, fur meine kinde."

"Tommy, Tommy," went the chorus of crippled and maimed men living in the shadows of burnt out buildings.

We quickened our pace and rushed away from these men. I was confused and ashamed by their animal-like state. I couldn't decide whether they were victims or willing participants in their downfall. I didn't know if I could feel any pity for them because I remembered what the SS along with their counterparts in the German army had done in the east. They had pillaged and raped Russia from Belarus to the Caucus Steppes.

We approached the black market where Gerda wished to trade. All around the haphazard, open-air market, thuggish-looking men guarded the perimeter from thieves and the occupational authorities. Generally, the British turned a blind eye to this commerce of survival. However, on occasion, especially if the market was dealing in liquor or medicine, a less than honest occupational bureaucrat, officer, or NCO demanded a kick-back to keep the business permit official, so to speak.

I bid goodbye to Gerda and I uncoordinatedly kissed her cheek. Frieda spoke rapidly and lovingly in German to her. When they finished talking, Gerda called out: "Shuze, Puppe."

"I imagine she'll do alright in there, she's quick-witted and no fool. I like her," I declared.

"If anyone wants to live in Germany, they cannot be a fool. As for Gerda; I trust her with my life and would a hundred times over. She would never betray me, or stab me in the back for money, man, or country. Gerda is not complicated, but she is beautiful in her simplicity. I have other friends, who you shall meet, who are different, but I need them just the same to make me complete."

"What did she just say to you?"

"Oh that," Friede said laughing, "Gerda said, "See ya, doll." We must really begin to work on your German," she added.

"Doll" I responded, puzzled?

Impatient and perhaps a little peeved that a part of her private life was being opened up to an outsider; she explained that it was a pet name for her. Friede's mother, out of guilt for making her live with foster parents, bought her daughter expensive clothes. It made the other children who lived in the working class district think Friede resembled a princess or a doll, fallen on hard times.

5

The city in the shadow of the Michel

Frieda and I walked back towards the river below the city centre. A wind had picked up and the air smelled of burning rubbish, while soot and ash rained down onto the pavement. The eruption originated from a truck puffing, slowing up the thoroughfare in front of us. Its roof was fitted with a boiler and a steam pipe. The vehicle dragged three carriages behind it like a primitive train.

It moved like a rheumatic centipede. A young boy raced across the top of the truck, feeding the boiler with an odd assortment of fuel ranging from chair legs to telegraph poles sawn down to size. The boy, like Vulcan's apprentice, fed the boiler and shifted the burning timber with iron tongs to increase the inferno. The contraption wheezed ahead of us like a castrated dragon let loose on a desolate industrial waste land, belching smoke, ash, and cinder.

"What is the matter?" Friede asked. "Have you never seen German ingenuity before?"

"It's the strangest thing I have ever encountered."

Friede explained that when the Nazis began to run out of petrol; cars and lorries were converted to run off of coal and scrap wood. Mechanics attached primitive steam engines to Volkswagen motors.

They were slow, smelled horrible, and were as dirty as mud. Friede laughed and pointed at the truck painfully meandering up the road and said, "Look, there goes Germany's secret weapon to win the war."

Suddenly, we were near the harbour which flowed out to the Elbe River. Apart from the homeless, few people ventured onto this roadway. Ahead of us was a scattering of refugees who carried the weight of their lives on their backs, or pushed it on baby prams with warped squeaking wheels. I saw a family dragging an enormous clock in their cart, its weights and pulleys clanking and screeching over the bumpy road.

Friede looked at the slim traffic of people and explained, "The DPs always seem to take the most ridiculous objects with them on their journey. I don't understand it. Why would you haul around a time-piece? It can only remind you that your day is done."

"What would you take into exile?" I asked.

Friede thought for a moment and replied, "My friends, my family, books, a phonograph, and if you are good to me, maybe even you, liebchen. What about you, Tommy, what would you take?"

I smiled and quoted Omar Kyam, "A *jug of wine, a loaf of bread and thou, beside me.* I'd also bundle onto my wagon as much luck as it could hold."

"You are a brave soul if that is all you need to make you happy in banishment."

I didn't know where Friede was taking me and I grew concerned about this descent into the dead flesh of Hamburg. We were approaching the epicenter of the catastrophic 1943 Allied bombing mission code-named Operation Gomorrah.

"Are you sure it's safe to be here?" I asked.

"Yes, come on; let's get through this street quickly. Besides you have a gun in case we get into trouble."

I had almost forgotten about my weapon; it was a required accoutrement while outside of camp. It was a Bren gun, which I believed put me in more danger from involuntary discharge than any threat from disgruntled former Nazis.

On either side of the road, windowless, lifeless, disintegrating buildings stood ready to crumble into unrecognizable cement. It was like walking through an excavated Pompeii long after Vesuvius had destroyed its citizens. The neighbourhood was bombed into non-existence because of its proximity to the harbour. Only a handful survived the firebombing; most were condemned to death by flames, suffocation, or drowning. A conflagration was created by the incendiary bombs. It produced hurricane-strength fire winds that melted people, animals, and inanimate objects, as it bellowed across the city consuming anything and everything that was combustible.

The road abruptly opened up onto a boulevard. Against the destroyed cityscape, a resolute statue of Charlemagne stood. The effigy looked bemused. Its sculptured arm pointed rigidly towards the destruction. Behind him, something else had survived, more or less unharmed through those nights of relentless bombing. It had dodged the uncountable bomb tonnage dumped onto this city from flying fortresses during the day and Lancasters bombing the city at night. It alone remained poised, and looked perhaps even nonchalant at its survival.

On closer inspection, I could see that parts of the edifice had suffered some bomb damage, especially the nave. However, in comparison to the surrounding wasteland, it appeared unmolested. The edifice stood proud and defiant against the adjacent ramshackle decay stretching in every direction.

Friede pointed and said, "That is the Michael's Kirche. The Michel is Hamburg's most famous church. The cathedral is over 400 years old and a testament to Hamburg's greatness as a maritime city. It witnessed our downfall under the Nazis. But we believe that as long as The Mikel remains, Hamburg will survive and prosper and its people will rebuild their lives. It is beautiful, isn't it?"

"Yes," I agreed reluctantly, "it is very beautiful."

I had a strained relationship with churches and those in charge of delivering God's word to the ignorant. Belief had long ago been beaten out of me by sexless nuns and alcoholic priests. I suspected that the church survived because it was a reliable geographic beacon for the RAF. It helped guide the waves of bombers onwards to their targets. The cathedral was like a trumpet to the walls of Jericho. Her survival wasn't divine intervention, but military practicality.

"Every Christmas Eve," Friede continued, "the Michel's bells rang at midnight. You could hear their chimes from my mother's home in Fuhlsbüttel, ten kilometers away."

Friede picked up some bomb debris from the ground. Perhaps it was part of a roof or the side of a building; now it was just a shred of mortar. She played with it in her hand as if weighing the consequence of war and wickedness. After some thought, Friede dropped the small souvenir of wreckage and said, "I just can't believe in God, at least not God from the bible."

"How could he exist? What creator allows all this cruelty to inhabit the Earth? What type of God allows Germany to go mad and kill the Jews? What God lets Spain and Russia slaughter their innocents in civil and class warfare? Who would make a world and walk away from it as if it were a sandcastle on a beach at high tide?"

Friede wiped dirt from her hand and brushed away some hair that had fallen into her face.

"After all of this waste and destruction what can you believe in, Friede? What can anyone believe in?" I asked.

She looked at me for a moment and after a brief second of reflection, she said, "I think there is something greater than man. It is not human or divine. It is energy. It came when the universe formed from the void of nothingness. It was like the first spark from a flint. The ember gave humanity conscious life. Our awareness is a gift, but it comes with a price; you only get one turn, one spin at the wheel, and then you are thrown back into the cosmic vapours. There are no second chances. As for eternity; it is unconscious without dreams, the dead are like amoebas floating on the ocean's waves."

"So there is no heaven?" I asked.

"No, you just walk to the end of your road."

"What happens then?"

"There is nothing waiting for you at the finish. We just return to particles, lost memories, lost hopes." Friede's arms were at her sides and the hem of her skirt rustled in a wind coming off the river. "Harry, now you look at me like I am crazy," she said quietly.

She stopped and moved away from me. Friede threw her head back and stared upwards to the church tower that climbed a hundred and thirty meters up towards the horizon. She was caught in the rapture of that afternoon.

"If some beauty still exists, life cannot be that bleak. Come on; let's go, before we are late for the train home." Friede dashed off ahead and left me frozen in my thoughts.

I woke and called out, "Wait up." I jogged to catch up to Friede while the Bren gun bounced against my arm. I was out of breath when I finally reached her on Marseille Strasse, near the Damtoor train station.

"Tommy," Friede said, "if you want to keep up with me, you should take better care of yourself. At school, I always won the hundred-yard dash because I liked the freedom of being alone, rather than being in a pack of schoolgirls."

We now walked together towards the Damtoor train station, located across the street from a rollicking armed forces night club called *The Victory*. The train station was the size of London's St Pancras, but lacked its architectural beauty. The Damtoor was equipped for both inner city and regional travel. In the early days after the war, its primary importance was as a terminal for inner city travel. The U-bahn subway was the only efficient method for people to travel through Hamburg and its suburbs, as petrol was only available for British military vehicles.

We pushed our way through a crowd congregating at the front entrance. Inside, Friede hung on to me as we slid past the queue of people resigned to the new order of things in Germany. The platforms teemed with desperate-looking characters, while overhead, pigeons and sparrows swooped and darted through the exposed skylight. Below, civilians were divided into groups of two or three people. Their eyes darted to the ground when they got sight of a British uniform.

Across the platform, the U-bahn riders scurried to their trains. They dragged uncomfortable and unwieldy luggage stuffed with what remained of their pre-war lives. It was now to be traded for food or medicine. On the inner walls of the train station, message boards had been hastily erected. They were crammed with pictures of lost relatives, lovers, or friends. Sad notes read things like: *Hans Schumann, I am now at Opa's, your loving Inga.* Miserable pictures were tacked up and jammed against a dozen other photos. Each snapshot asked to be recognized, remembered, and loved. However, the hot August sun leaked through the station's rafters, blistering the edges of the photos as if to say, "Don't waste your breath looking for me: I am already dead, my body lies with the nameless who died at the side of the autobahn."

Railway employees patrolled the station wearing worn uniforms that looked ready to disintegrate no matter how cleaned or starched they were. Whistles rested threateningly on their lips while passengers diligently looked to follow their orders. Even in defeat, Germans still craved a well-executed command even if it was only to stand ready for an approaching train.

An electrified train entered the station and edged past us. Passengers were pressed up against the windows like guppies in a fishbowl with too little water. When the train screeched to a halt, middle-aged men wearing old homburg hats and soiled overcoats spilled out of the doors. They shuffled out towards the street with their heads bowed downwards as if frightened to look at the ruins around them and the sunlight above them. Behind them, women followed, clutching cloth bags ripe with silverware and wrapped china to be bartered for food.

Small orphaned children darted around the platform searching for discarded cigarette ends. They were bottom feeders who wore rancid trousers and coal-smeared pullovers as if they were waifs from Victorian London. If they were lucky, they found a handful of partially smoked Capstans or Player's on the dirty platform floor, which were sold for few pfennigs to teenage gangsters employed by the German mafia. The mob recycled the cigarette stubs with the labour of homeless children and destitute women into new cigarettes of questionable quality, taste, or hygiene. Eventually, the newly fashioned cigarettes ended up in the mouths of indigent Germans who tried to quell the hunger pangs created by starvation rations thrown to them by the occupation forces.

The rail police blasted their whistles with menace. The order was barked to immediately board the U-bahn train. Friede and I were herded towards the railway cars. The train embarkation resembled a scramble by passengers on a fast sinking ship with too few lifeboats. We were jostled into the first car by the momentum of the people behind us.

Outside, the rail police held back disappointed passengers that were too late to board the subway. Inside, I was hit by an overwhelming stench of cabbage and body odour. There was an exhausted gloom painted on the occupants' faces. I had seen the same defeated look on unemployed miners in West Yorkshire during the Great Depression. It was an expression of pain and surprise from a person who couldn't quite work out how they lost everything at life's roulette table.

It was claustrophobic in the train, but the Germans either seemed unaware of the lack of oxygen or had grown stoical to the means in which they had to travel around town. Friede said, "There is more air at the rear of the train."

We jostled through the crowd of exhausted travelers. A teenage boy, dusty from a day foraging in the wreckage, saluted me. He offered

297

me his seat and an old woman beside him hissed at his gesture.

"Danke," I said, but offered the wooden seat to Friede, who declined and gave it to a pregnant woman standing nearby instead.

The train entered a tunnel and our car was plunged into darkness, while we sped underground below the wrecked city. In lightless obscurity, people coughed nervously, some joked and others whispered as if they were still in a police state. I felt as if I was choking. It was like being trained for chemical attacks by being locked in a cinder block shed that was filled with tear gas.

Friede said to me, "Let's play a game. Come with me." Friede grabbed my hand tightly and led me through the standing heaps of people.

"Where are we going," I asked.

"You'll see. Don't ask too many questions. It spoils the surprise."

Friede forced us to the compartment door by the front of the train and said, "The rules to this game are simple, but you will have to learn them while we play."

"All right," I agreed with some hesitation.

The U-bahn squealed into Haller Strasse station. On a poorly lit subterranean platform, weary passengers waited to board the subway. The door flew open and warm oxygen raced in to fill my lungs. Friede dropped her hand from mine and disappeared out into the station. I froze for a moment. It was difficult to calibrate what had happened. Instinct took over and I jumped out of the carriage. I saw from the corner of my eye that she had run into the next compartment. I took off towards Friede and maneuvered around passengers and objects. I heard screams from the train guards to halt, which I ignored. I thrust myself into the next compartment and found her grinning at the front of the carriage.

"Next time," she called out, "the game gets more difficult. Keep up with me, Tommy, or you are going to lose me."

"Never," I said.

With a surge, the train took off. It rattled below the streets, clanking against railway ties, and on occasion the train's horn screeched. A woman beside us held onto the overhead railing while beads of perspiration trickled down her squat neck. The woman cursed the humidity and someone slid open a widow, which made the compartment as sultry as a rainforest.

While we pulled into the next station, Klosterstern, Friede prepared herself like a runner on a chalk. "Better keep up this time, Tommy."

As soon as the subway door was ajar, Friede darted out and onto the crowded platform. Energetically, I followed and barged my way through train travellers, who stepped aside as if I was pursuing a criminal rather than playing a schoolyard game. I heard the signal man blow his whistle, which meant the train doors were going to close in seconds. I got nervous, I couldn't find her. I looked in all directions, but couldn't see her through the shuffling phalanx of Germans.

Then, as if the smoke had cleared showing me a pathway, I heard Friede call out to me in her soft accent, making my name sound Arabic. "Hari," she cried. There she was frantically waving and jumping, three cars from me.

I cut through the crowd, shouting, "Schnell, Schnell, out of the way." My Bren gun wrapped around my shoulder, jerked and bounced while I sprinted to reach her. The railway guards blew their whistles and the train doors began to close. Just ahead of me, I saw Friede slide into the last compartment. In front of me, an elderly guard blasted the all clear to the engineer. The subway doors were now closed to new passengers. I raced up to him and demanded to be let inside the train. The guard tapped his wrist watch to indicate I was too late and out of luck. I screamed so loud the whistle fell from his lips.

"Look, mate, Hitler's kaput. We are in charge now, so open up this bleeding door."

I saw Friede's head peek up from inside the train and she smiled at my discomfort. Another train conductor strode up to me and the elderly guard. He wondered why the all clear had not been sounded, making the subway seconds late for its next stop. The two train guards proceeded to argue for several minutes. Finally, the older one relented and allowed me onto the train. I noticed the rest of the occupants eyed me with suspicion and contempt, except for Friede. She rushed up to me and grabbed my hand.

"If you want me, Harry, you have to hold on to me tight or else I will slip away from you and neither of us wants that, do we?"

6

Behind the Screen Door

Occupied Germany was much like a boarding house in the seaside town of Bridlington; every farce or tragedy was hidden behind closed doors. In Fuhlsbüttel, the people kept stum and thought it good table manners. Their ability to conceal unpleasant truths was so evolved, a statue of the three wise monkeys wouldn't have been out of place on the main square. The town was adept at ignoring evil, but their true talents lay in doing evil with suburban routine at the local gaol.

Known by locals and the inmates as Koala Fu; it was constructed in 1911 to house drunks, wife-beaters, and swindlers. By the time British Forces liberated it on May third, it had become a way station for Nazi Germany's undesirables. Many of the regions, Jews, gypsies, communists, Jehovah Witnesses, along with Russian slave labourers marked time at Koala Fu before being dispatched to their deaths at Buchenwald and Ravensbruck.

In the last month of the war, Himmler ordered that the memory of the camp and its prisoners were to be erased from Fuhlsbüttel. On April twelfth, the remaining prisoners were marched out of Fuhlsbüttel and north to the port at Kiel. The SS hoped the prisoners of Koala Fu might disappear into the Baltic Sea fog.

It was difficult to comprehend that this quiet, bucolic retreat from Hamburg was a willing accomplice to the holocaust. Barbarity seemed as out of place in Fuhlsbüttel as litter on the streets or untended gardens. Like people who can't remember where they put their keys, Fuhlsbüttel collectively forgot about Koala Fu or the prisoners' death march along Langenhorner Chausee. I did wonder, if on their way to extermination, the prisoners passed Friede's apartment. But much like the first wise monkey, I thought it prudent and heard no evil.

I was now in Friede's company as often as my duties at the airport allowed. We found it difficult to find any privacy for love-making, except on weekday afternoons at her mother's apartment. Intimacy became more complicated for us after the Gellersons, a homeless couple, were allocated a portion of her mother's apartment by the occupational authorities. When Friede's widowed grandfather showed up at their door, the apartment truly became claustrophobic.

"He isn't even my real Opa," Friede said with disdain, "because my mother is also a bastard."

"Then who is he?" I asked.

"A miserable old man who says spiteful things about Mutti and me any chance he gets."

Before one of our afternoon trysts, Friede greeted me on the street with a kiss and said, "I was getting worried that you wouldn't show. Opa and I have had a terrible row."

"Nothing could stop me from seeing you," I told her. "Look, I brought you some fresh supplies. There is enough meat, veg, and wine to last everyone a week."

"Wonderful, but remember I have to make sure my foster parents get some of the provisions because they can't survive on their rations."

"I've only got two hands," I retorted, overwhelmed by her entire family's need for extra food.

"I know it is hard for you to keep pinching stuff from the base, but

302

it is keeping us from becoming beggars on the street. Look, you can see for yourself what good you have done me. The sores on my legs are healing because of the vitamins you got for me."

When we entered the apartment, a sullen old man greeted me. It was the cuckolded grandfather. He snarled at me in unintelligible German. "What's up with him," I asked.

"Oh, he is in one of his moods today. Isn't that right, Opa?" she asked sarcastically.

Friede turned to me and explained, "He has been on his hobby horse all day: About how everyone is stealing from him. How he never gets enough to eat. Stealing what, I ask? He hasn't had a pfennig to his name since 1913. Before you arrived, he screamed that Mutti and I showed him no respect. We were just illegitimate guttersnipes. I gave the ingrate an earful. I told him he was lucky Mutti let him stay here, considering he chucked her out at twelve years old.

"That is when he got nasty. Isn't that right, Opa? You went on about how the Nazis knew how to do things and wouldn't allow an old man to be treated like rubbish by the daughter of a whore."

The unshaven old man sat on a wooden stool. He wore thick, uncomfortable woolen trousers held up by bulky suspenders. He looked as thin and as fragile as a tall blade of grass in the dry season. The old man muttered, "Thunder and lightning."

"Harry, please give him a cigarette or else we will get no peace."

I pulled out my cigarette case and offered him a Player's. With shaking hands, he pulled one to his mouth. For a moment, our eyes met; his were filled with watery hatred for everything around him.

"Come," Friede said. "Let's get out of the kitchen. I don't know how long we've got until the Gellersons come back. Bring a bottle of wine with you. We'll take it to my room," she said playfully.

It really wasn't a room, but an alcove that housed a woodstove and a chaise lounge. The walls were thin and covered with heavy floral wallpaper. Along the wall, Friede had pinned up small photos of her girlfriends and glamour shots of German movie stars cut from defunct magazines published during the war.

We put some pillows behind our back and propped ourselves up on the day bed. We drank warm Rhine wine out of a shared coffee cup and ate slices of bread slathered thick with butter. "Did you hear," Friede said excitedly, "the British have started up Radio Hamburg again. So we can finally listen to jazz and dance music banned by the Nazis."

I laughed and sipped back my wine. I thought these moments with her were the closest to paradise I had ever got in my short and squalid life. Lying beside Friede was like a wish come true from Aladdin's lamp. To me, she was as mysterious as the sphinx and as sensual as nightfall in an exotic garden. I clung tightly to the hope that my desire for her was more than physical want, and that her interest in me went beyond food parcels. Perhaps that was all we could demand from each other after a long war. Maybe the best we both could hope from each other was the shared warmth from our curled up bodies and to forget the incinerated city waiting outside.

We finished half a bottle of wine and I sang silly songs. I made extravagant compliments to her eyes, her hair, her body, and her soul. After a while, we undressed each other. We made love on the chaise lounge, which was just large enough for us to hold each other tightly, in a selfish and generous longing. For a long time, we remained in Friede's small lair, while outside the thin shuttered door, the old man raged against the occupation, his life, and his new lodgings. The din slowly dissipated and faded into the background like a smudge on the wallpaper.

I must have dosed off because I woke to the nakedness of her back and the curve of her spine. I traced my fingers against her skin and noticed that just below Friede's left shoulder; she carried a horrible discoloured scar. "What are you doing back there?" she asked in a sleepy voice.

"Nothing," I replied nervously as if I had been caught eavesdropping.

304

"You are staring at my war wound, aren't you?" she asked, turning over to kiss me on my forehead.

"Come on then, give us a cigarette," Friede demanded, hungry for nicotine. She drew her knees up underneath the blanket and blew a smoke ring from her lit cigarette. "If you are wondering about the mark on my back, I was in a fire."

"Did it happen in an air raid?" I asked.

"Nothing so dramatic," she replied in a matter-of-fact tone. Friede explained that the Nazis were very big on women being perfect cake and baby makers for the Fatherland. At fourteen, Friede was sent by the Hitler Youth organization to live as a domestic servant with a rich family in Coburg. She was to be taught to be a proper wife, for a proper national socialist, in a new world where Germany controlled the globe.

Friede giggled as she explained, "It was a crazy fantasy world created by Himmler and Goebbels. Every girl in Germany was supposed to be like a Rhineland maiden who cooked and cleaned and fucked like a rabbit to make blue-eyed, blonde-haired Aryans babies for the Reich."

Friede laughed and continued her story. She was sent to live with a horrible family who were fanatically pro-Hitler. "If I didn't clean the silver correctly, the mother scolded me with: "If the Fuehrer was watching you now; he would be very disappointed in you, Friede." I think they treated their dog better than me."

One morning while Friede was making breakfast for the family's youngest son, her back was to the gas stove. She stood too close to the flame and her thick woolen house coat caught fire. The little boy waiting for his meal noticed the smoke rising from Friede's back and screamed, "Fredle, you are on fire."

"I was so stupid," Friede said. "I panicked and fled, running down the hallway."

The last thing Friede remembered before blacking out was running down the hallway towards a giant mirror. There, she stopped and watched, horrified, as her burning body reflected back into her eyes.

Friede awoke in the hospital with third degree burns on her back. It was difficult for her to endure the pain because there was no morphine to ease her suffering. The hospital was overwhelmed with victims from a bombing raid that had caused many casualties in Coburg.

Friede said what was worse than the pain were the cries from the near-dead and dying all around her.

"It was horrible. People were calling for God's help, crying, "Jesus save me. God help me, someone please help me." I was so afraid I was going to die in that hospital and the authorities in Hamburg wouldn't give permission for my family to visit me."

"What about the family you lived with as a domestic?" I asked attentively.

"That stupid family, they came once, maybe twice," she said harshly. "The mother wanted to make sure the doctors understood that my injuries were from my own foolishness. You see, they were a good National Socialist family who always took the correct safety precautions. They didn't want any problems from the police because of my accident."

"It must have been very lonely."

"It was," she said with her eyes closed and her back resting on a pillow. "But there was a nice little boy in the bed beside mine. He called me Edelweiss. His legs were crushed after a building collapsed on him in the bombing. He was very sick, but he was always optimistic and happy and then one day, he said "Edelweiss, I can't feel my legs." It was gangrene and he was dead the next day," she finished sadly. "I don't think he was more than eight."

"Well, now you know how I got my mark. Later, I will tell you about the time I was evacuated to a farm near Coburg. I really enjoyed living with that family, but it had its negative side. Their grandfather was a deviant and tried to molest the girl evacuees when they used the outdoor privy." Friede crushed her cigarette into a saucer and hastily jumped out of bed. I watched her quickly throw on some clothes."

306

"You better go," she said. "Mutti will be back soon. I don't want her to meet you like this, stark naked with a glass of wine in your hands."

"When will I get to meet your mother?" I asked.

Friede was frantically brushing her shiny hair in front of a tiny mirror hanging from the wall. "You will meet Mutti on my birthday, which is less than a month away. I can guarantee you on October 20th; we will be on our best behaviour and not at each other's throats, like we will be today. Especially if she sees you now, looking like some afternoon Casanova. Come on then, I can hear the Gellersons coming through the door, get up."

I stood up from the makeshift bed. I picked my uniform off the floor, while Friede straightened up her room.

Just before she opened the door and breached the safety of her bedroom, Friede said, "Before you go, give Opa a few cigarettes, he will be less mean to me when you are gone."

I followed her out and noticed the old man had not stirred from the kitchen. Suddenly, the front door opened and the Gellersons entered. It looked like they had been foraging for supplies because they were carrying potatoes and firewood for the oven. They greeted Friede warmly and ignored both me and the old man.

Before, I left, I handed the old man a half packet of cigarettes. He grumbled, "Dankeschön." It could have been fuck you, judging by the tone of his voice. I gave Friede a perfunctory peck on the cheek and departed for the base.

It was dusk, but there was still a steady stream of refugees making their way through town. On the way back to camp, I whistled the tune from the *teddy bears picnic* and ignored the dispossessed and homeless spawning down the road.

Not far from our camp gates, I stumbled onto a family stalled on the road. Their cadaverous horse refused to drag the family's rickety cart an inch further. It looked like the beast had probably dragged this family and their weighty, useless possessions along the eastern corridor only paces ahead of the Russian army for the past three months. Not only was the cart packed high and wide with furniture; it also had the added burden of transporting a couple of toddlers and a young teenage girl. The children looked anemic, stricken by both terror and extreme hunger, while at the front of the trap, the parents looked equally desolate.

The father cursed the horse as it stood stooped in the middle of an intersection. He jumped off his wagon and lashed the animal with threats of God's damnation. Froth dripped from the horse's mouth and puddles of foam formed on the cobblestone street below. The man drew a flashing leather whip from his wagon and began to beat the horse. The horse's thin hide was pierced by each lash, while his eyes bulged out of their sockets from pain and hunger.

The blows quickly became too much for the horse; a groan erupted from his mouth. It sounded sad and resigned and it said no more. The horse's bulging eyes turned upwards and watery turds fell exhausted from his backside. His head twisted up and towards me like a ship before its stern drags the bow to the ocean's depths. The horse's agony was over in seconds. He dropped dead to the ground still shackled to his shuck. Even though the horse weighed nothing, he still brought the cart down on its side. The mother in the front of the wagon and the children at the rear crashed down onto the pavement. The contents of their lives aimlessly spilled from the broken wagon and onto the road.

Crumpled on the side of the road, the mother wailed in indecipherable German. The peasant woman made the sign of the cross, but I thought God had left some time ago for home and no one had taken over his shift.

The father stood over the animal. He looked as perplexed as a motorist looking under a car bonnet billowing with steam. It was the expression of *"how could this have happened, I had this car serviced only a month ago."* He dropped the whip and unshackled the horse to right the cart. He loaded the cargo that had fallen across the road back onto to the trap. The children climbed onto the back of cart, the mother sat in the front and continued to gesticulate to Jesus, while the father took the dead horse's place. The man slowly pulled the cart, with his family and the jetsam of their life, away from the intersection.

The dead horse looked like a pile of old clothes dropped on the cobbled streets. His lifeless eye stared up into the setting horizon. Before flies had time to settle on the dead beast, an old woman came out of her house and began cutting into the horse's belly. She yanked out chunks of flesh and threw them into a leather bag.

Others gathered around the old crone and followed her example. They hovered over the horse's corpse with pocket knives or hatchets. They roughly butchered the warm body of the dead animal.

I walked around the famished mob hacking and sawing away at the equine and jogged back to camp. The guard on duty at the gate recognized me and said, "You always come back to camp looking a stone lighter than when you left."

"One of the many benefits of walking," I replied.

"As long as you stick to walking and no monkey business, you be all right, Harry."

"Too right," I agreed and passed through the gates. Inside, my mind was calculating how to keep Friede and her family alive through the fall, let alone the winter, on stolen rations.

7

The Bargain between a Mother and an Uncle

During the last months of 1945, civilian mortality dramatically increased throughout occupied Germany. By October 1945, Hamburg was as desolate as Carthage after Rome laid it to waste. Incessant food shortages, poor sanitation, and disease were now as deadly as aerial bombardment to the inhabitants of Hamburg. As if life couldn't get any more miserable for the metropolis, it also suffered from electrical blackouts, water shortages, and a decreasing amount of food rations for her inhabitants.

German society disintegrated into pre-industrial communities ruled by the victorious armies of the West and the East. The occupiers appeared ill-equipped to manage the responsibilities of peace. During the first year of occupation, Germany plunged to the bottom like an elevator with its cables cut. Hamburg existed in the sub-basement of civilization. Many of its residents lived in hovels dug from the ruins of bombed buildings. It was a miserable time with starvation and hopelessness driving multitudes of women onto the streets to barter their bodies for cigarettes to battle-numb soldiers.

Hamburg was a city where sexual commerce transpired on every boulevard and beneath every burnt-out street light. When it came to distinguishing between a girl on the game and a girl down on her luck, soldiers were myopic.

The week before her birthday, Friede wanted to introduce me to her foster parents, who lived in the Altona district. We agreed to meet each other in the afternoon at Dammtor train station. Unfortunately, I was late for my train and when I arrived, I had forgotten where we were supposed to meet. I walked outside where the glare from the sun temporarily blinded me and left me disoriented in a crowd of strangers. It took me several minutes to adjust to the afternoon brightness, but I finally recognized Friede standing at the entrance to the Victory dance club on the opposite side of the intersection.

Friede was beside an airman in a Canadian uniform. It appeared as if he was arguing with her because several times, he threw his hands up, frustrated.

I crossed the street and yelled out, "Is everything all right?"

Friede looked relieved by my arrival, but the Canadian appeared less so and inquired, "Who the hell are you? Can't you see I'm talking to this Fraulein? I want to ask her out on a date."

Friede spoke hastily to me in German, "This very rude man cornered me and won't let me walk away. He is drunk and stinks of beer."

I said to the Canadian, "I think you are a little confused, mate, she's with me."

"With you?" he asked suspiciously.

I explained to him that we were on our way to meet friends.

"Fuck off," was his response. "Give 'em a bit of chocolate or some cigarettes and these Germans will go with you like a stray dog in Cabbage town. They're all fucking tarts."

"Mind your manners," I told him. "If I were you, I'd get on your bike and move on."

"What ya going to do about it?" he demanded threateningly.

The Canadian swayed drunkenly from one foot to the next and gave me a stare filled with violence and hatred. "You better hop it or I'm going to bust your head open like a tin of kippers," I suggested to him.

The Canadian was about to take a swing at me, but in the distance I saw an MP. I told the drunken airman that the MP was my mate. "He'll throw you into the glass house for disorderly conduct, without looking sideways at you. So best be off home."

I called out to the MP, "Oi, George, over here for a second."

Scared by my bluff, the Canadian tried to run off, but I grabbed his shirt cuff and said, "Before you go, apologize to the lady."

"Sorry, miss," he said in a shallow voice and disappeared into the crowd.

When the MP arrived, he asked what all the commotion was about.

"Nothing, I thought you were my mate's brother. Sorry for the trouble."

"No bother," he said, "this is no place to loiter." He looked suspiciously over at Friede.

"Is this woman with you?" he asked.

"Yes."

"Well then, I suggest you both get a move on."

We walked on and Friede laughed at my deviousness. She gently grabbed hold of my arm and asked, "When are we going dancing in that club."

"I'll take you there in a week, when you turn eighteen," I told her with forced enthusiasm. "How do we get to your foster parents apartment, from here?"

"Today, we will go through Platen un Blomen. We can take the U-bahn from there. It is no more than ten minutes," she said definitively.

Hand in hand, we strolled across the city's botanical park Platen un Blomen. Even in the fall, it was a beautiful green space that included an artificial lake populated by graceful swans. Some of the flowerbeds had been turned into potato and cabbage patches, but it was still more picturesque than London's Hyde Park.

It was a quick walk to the U-bahn station. When we were inside the subway car, Friede gossiped about her girlfriends and how much everyone's lives had changed since the German surrender.

"Gerda for instance is all for having foreign boyfriends. But Ursula wouldn't be caught dead with a Tommy."

"I don't think we've met," I said.

"You probably won't. I love her to bits, but she believes shaking hands with a Tommy is something close to treason.

"What do you think?" I asked jokingly.

Friede paused to collect her thoughts. "My world has changed forever. Nobody knows what is going to happen tomorrow or five years from now. Both the war and now this peace have taught me that I am going to experience my adventures today, because nobody can be sure what tomorrow is going to be like."

When our train passed the Reeperbahn station, Friede spoke in a serious tone of voice. "I've heard rumours that the British are going to cut our food and wood rations by a third. Do you think that will happen because I don't know how Mama and Papa are going to be able to survive if their food allotment is reduced? Papa hasn't been able to work since the end of the war."

I replied, "Don't worry. I will find a way to take care of them through the winter."

"That would be fantastic," she answered in a happy voice.

It would be incredible, I thought, if all my brazen promises to Friede were kept. I calculated that if half of my pledges materialized, everyone would have enough food and fuel to live until the spring thaw. I was terrified that I'd fail and her family's desperate bid to survive was going to end in tragedy. There was only so much I could barter from the mess sergeant or steal from the cook house before someone noticed. If I was discovered, my borrowed philanthropy would end with me on charges and Friede out in the cold.

After emerging from the Altona U-bahn terminal, we went south along the Alle, which had received a lot of bomb damage. The buildings on the street were in a bad state, most were burnt fragments where hungry feral cats and dogs now took shelter. Remarkably, along the way, there were also some apartments and shops that had remained unmolested by the bombing.

"It looks like a lot of people were bombed out here," I remarked.

"Thousands," Friede commented in a faraway voice. "Mama and Papa were lucky. Our building never suffered a direct hit. But I spent a lot of nights in the bomb shelter because we are so close to the harbour. The RAF never seemed to tire from dropping bombs on us."

Friede asked me if I had ever been in an air raid. When I told her no, she sarcastically responded, "Of course not, you are in the RAF. Your job was to drop the bombs."

"Not me," I said, "you know I was on the ground in the mobile communications unit."

"I do," she responded in a softer tone of voice. "That is why you are my boyfriend. I would never have a lover who dropped bombs on Germany."

Ambivalently, I nodded, but I wasn't about to condemn my RAF for the brutality of the air war. I knew there were two sides to this conflict and the skippers and crew of Bomber Command suffered appalling casualties. Those men waged a war they didn't create, but were compelled to win for civilization's sake.

I also understood it was just too difficult for Friede or anyone else that had endured the firebombing to be reminded of General Sheridan's aphorism that war is hell.

When we approached her foster parent's apartment on Klaus Strasse, Friede pointed toward a five-story apartment building on the corner. For a working class apartment block, it seemed stunning and elegant to me. The windows facing down onto the street were immense and although the paint was faded and chipped in places from the masonry, it was an impressive building for the common man.

"This was my home when I was a little girl," she noted with some ambivalence.

"What about your mother's apartment?" I questioned.

"That was my weekend home, but only if Uncle Henry said it was ok to go and visit. That is why I always feel like I am just a temporary lodger at Mutti's. At Mama and Papa's, I was happy." She paused and quantified her statement. "Well, I felt happiest here, when Mama was nice to Papa and didn't call him all manner of names. Do you see the window beside the balcony on the fourth floor?"

I looked up at the apartment window where Friede had been sent to live in the summer of 1932. The day Friede was sent to live with the Bornholts, her mother had treated it as a normal outing. "Mutti packed my suitcase and said, "Hold onto your doll, kid, hold onto your doll.""

Friede wasn't aware that when she left her mother's apartment on Wieden Alle, it was for the last time. On the way to her new home in the taxi, Maria Edelmann prepared her daughter for their separation. Maria told her daughter that she would be in the care of the Bornholts for only a short while. It was to let her mother get back on her feet financially. Friede's mother said there was nothing to worry about because the Bornholts were the kindest of folk and everything was going to work out just fine.

When mother and daughter arrived at the Bornholts' apartment, Marie Edelmann rang the doorbell and kissed Friede on the forehead. Maria Edelmann said to her daughter, "Remember to be a good girl for your mutti and always obey the Bornholts."

The door opened and Max Bornholt and his wife walked out to greet Friede. Maria Edelmann refused to display any sorrow or any guilt she carried for relinquishing her daughter and turned emotionally to ice. Friede's mother let go of her hand and bid Friede a perfunctory adieu. Maria Edelmann didn't look back and she didn't cry out her daughter's name when she rushed downstairs to her taxi, which was waiting to take her to her lover's home in the suburbs.

Friede said. "After Mutti left, Frau Bornholt grabbed me and scooped me inside the apartment. I cried for a week and thought I must have done something very bad to Mutti to be left with the Bornholts."

"That sounds horrible," I said.

"That was life in Germany during the depression. What can you do but survive?" Friede said in a matter-of-fact voice.

Friede explained that the trauma of being separated from her mother quickly passed. "Soon after Mutti left me with the Bornholts the whole neighbourhood was turned into a battleground between Hitler's Brown Shirts and the communists.

It was called the Bloody Sunday massacre of 1932. In that year, the Nazis were a strong political force, but not a supreme power in German politics. The communist party was one of their major rivals and it had a strong following in working class districts of Hamburg. The radical Brown Shirt wing of the Nazis was entrusted with eradicating their red rivals once and for all, in the Altona district where Friede's foster parents lived.

So on a seemingly quiet and normal Sunday in July, a street war erupted between well-armed SA, storm-troopers and the out-gunned but enthusiastic adherents to socialism and communism. The SA hunted down their red enemies from apartment block to apartment block and roof top to roof top. From her bedroom window, Friede witnessed Brown Shirts battle red shirts with pistols and machine guns.

"So after all that bloodshed," Friede said, "I adapted to living with the Bornholts and Mutti visited me on most weekends."

I was still confused and asked why the Bornholts were chosen to take care of her.

Friede explained to me there was no other possible solution for her mother but to have Friede live with the Bornholts because her father Fritz was out of work and out of luck. "He didn't even live with us," she said. "He was like a sailor that rolled in and out of our lives to escape a storm."

Friede's mother loved Fritz, but she knew their affair was doomed. Ever since he was traumatized by his experiences in the German army in the First World War, Fritz had problems keeping a job. After Germany plunged further into economic and political chaos after the Wall Street Crash, life only became more difficult for Fritz. He wasn't any help to himself and he was certainly no real help to Maria Edelman. So Fritz moved on and out of Hamburg with a promise to make things right for his daughter and Maria.

Maria Edelmann didn't put much stock in the words of men, especially sentimental ones damaged in the war. She knew Fritz wasn't going to save anyone. The only thing that was going to keep Maria Edelmann above water was her sex appeal to certain men of influence and wealth.

"My mother wasn't going to let me starve. In those days, she was very beautiful and was a gifted singer and dancer. She did what was necessary; Mutti took a rich, fat, old man as her lover. His name was Hinrich Karp, or as he used to say: "Friede, think of me as Uncle Henry." Uncle Henry liked me, but he liked me best from a distance. He didn't want me in their Fuhlsbüttel love nest because he was a business man and some big shot in business and politics. So I was sent to live here with the Bornholts."

"So your mother chose Hinrich over you?"

"No, it wasn't like that at all," she said, irritated. "Back then, Germany was economically destroyed, just like it is today. How could we have survived if Mutti had not become Henry's lover? Do you know?"

"I'm sorry, I don't know."

"It would have been the orphanage for me and the street for Mutti."

"But why were you sent to live with these people rather than another family I asked "Surely, if your mother couldn't provide for you, the government would have sent you to a foster home?"

Friede laughed and explained to me that Hinrich Karp was a man of some influence and authority. Karp also knew that Maria Edelmann wasn't prepared to forsake, her daughter for him and the safety he provided. It was imperative that Friede be given a good upbringing and that she was never allowed to forget her real mother or the sacrifices she made for her daughter.

Placing Friede in the care of Max Bornholt and his wife was the best solution for Henry because Karp knew Max Bornholt through his import and export business. Bornholt worked for the state railway company in the customs department. He always ensured that Henry got his goods on time with little trouble or government interference. Naturally, for his ability to make Karp's customs problems disappear, Max was rewarded with gifts of cash.

"What did Henry import?" I asked.

"Tobacco, cigars, smoking accessories from lighters to hookahs; he manufactured them or imported them with his partner, Jons Rodmann. Their company *Rodmann und Karp* were known all across northern Germany for good cigars, excellent carved pipes, and elegant silver lighters. How Henry got his goods I was never told, but I am sure there was some dirty business in it. Anyway, you are letting me get away from how I ended up as the Bornholt's foster child."

Friede continued and related to me that Max and his wife Anna weren't happily married. They already had two children, Alvin and Herma, but they were pretty well grown. After their daughter Herma was born, Anna couldn't have any more children. She developed an early menopause, which she blamed on Max's wandering eye for the ladies. Both her and Max thought they might be able to find peace with each other if they could have another child.

So, fortune in the guise of corpulent Hinrich Karp walked into their lives and left Max with an exciting proposal. One typical business day, Karp showed up to Max's office at the railway company to enquire about some tobacco orders held in customs. However, Karp wasn't his usual jovial self and was in a sour mood. So out of sorts was Karp that he began to complain to Max about his mistress' kid Elfriede.

Henry said, "The little so and so is getting in the way and being a real chatterbox."

Max, half-serious, said that he would love to make this problem go away for Henry. He even offered to raise the girl like she was his own. Naturally, whether it was his own or someone else's, there were costs involved with raising a little girl.

"Naturally," said Henry, "and how many Reich marks will this cost me?"

"That many Reich marks," Max suggested, and both men agreed upon a sum to ensure the health and well being of Elfriede.

The crisis of where to put Friede was solved like it was a problem about what to do with a pet dog that was too noisy. After Friede had related to me how she ended up in the care of the Bornholts, she added with no apparent bitterness, "Somehow it is funny to me that to think how I was traded from one household to the next and everyone said they loved me the more for it."

"How is that funny" I asked?

"Well, everyone ended up happy, just like a fairytale. Mama and Papa got a little child to love and some extra money, while Henry got my mother all to himself."

"And what did you get from it?" I asked.

She smiled enigmatically. "I got to survive and was loved. That is more than most people ended up with in this war."

8

Altona Gypsies Hide their Secrets

We stood outside her foster parents' apartment building on Klaus Strasse and I asked, "Shouldn't we go in?"

"No, not yet," said Friede. She then grabbed my hand and dragged me across the street and into an alleyway.

"We still have time to see something else," she said and kissed me.

"I like this part of the tour," I replied.

"Harry, if you just listen to me for a moment longer; you will know more about me than any other boy I have dated."

I grew quiet and allowed Friede to lead me further into her world. Friede said as a very small girl, she played in the abandoned wood lot located behind the alleyway. Being seven, she thought it was a magical place, populated with trolls, wizards, and wonderful secrets. To her, it was like the world found in *Through the looking glass*.

The day I saw it, the spell had definitely worn off because it was now a wasteland and a dumping ground for bomb refuse. It was a much different place during Friede's childhood. Back then, it was a wood lot where gypsies set up camp and lived in their painted caravans. Friede became friends with a gypsy family and played with their two children. However, when her foster mother found out about her new friendships, she was forbidden to play in the woodlot or associate with the gypsies. Friede ignored her foster mother's demand and continued to play with the children from the wood lot.

"What happened?" I asked.

"Nothing happened to me. But later on, the Gestapo rounded them up and sent them to a concentration camp. Naturally, Mama lied to me and said, "Gypsies are like that, they are never in one place for a long time because they are nomads." It was best to forget about them and have friendships with good German boys and girls."

It was some time after the gypsies had been taken, a neighbourhood boy found Friede playing in the abandoned woodlot. He asked her what she was doing there. Friede said she was looking to see if her gypsy friends had returned from their trip. The boy laughed and told her the Gestapo had arrested them.

"How could he have witnessed that?" I asked.

Friede answered, "He said he hid in the bushes and watched them being rounded up, but he was a strange and sinister boy. He warned me about playing alone here and said, *Make sure they don't mistake you for a gypsy, or they will take you next. It will be like you never existed because everyone knows you have no mother or father.*"

Friede pulled me away from the disintegrated woodlot. We went back up through the alleyway and she remarked that a lot of people she knew disappeared while she was growing up. "One day they were here, the next day gone and no one said a word."

"Up the street, there was a candy store. It was my favourite shop. It was popular with all of the neighbourhood kids because the lady who owned it was very nice and always gave out free sweets. One day, we were told not to shop there."

"Why?"

"They were Jews and Mama said the police would give us trouble if we shopped there again." Even my doctor disappeared into the night; he used to let me ride on the side board of his car as he drove to visit patients. He was really a wonderful, kind man," Friede said, her voice breaking.

"As a child, it was hard for me to understand that people simply vanish from the landscape and disappear into the night. It is impossible to comprehend, especially if every adult refuses to tell you where they have all gone to."

Friede stood on the street corner, as distant to me as a ship out at sea caught in a tempest. I went to touch her shoulder, but she shrugged off my ignorant empathy. "Well, well," she said. "I am seventeen, alive, and German. I feel guilty sometimes for feeling happiness. I can't bear to think what happened to my gypsy friends. I don't think things ended well for them or for my doctor or for millions of other people. Let's go; Mama and Papa will be wondering where I got to. Don't tell her I was playing in the memory of the gypsies," she warned.

There was no lift in the apartment so we had to climb four steep flights of stairs. Waiting for us at the top of the landing were Max and Anna Bornholt. Friede's foster father gingerly approached and enthusiastically shook my hand. The foster mother was more reticent and more rotund then Max. She emanated a cold suspicion for me. It didn't appear to be motherly concern for her foster child, but more a condition of her personality that distrusted happiness or good fortune.

After kissing me on both cheeks, Friede's foster mother indelicately thrust me into their large apartment, which was spartanly furnished. At the entrance, their daughter Herma stood beside her young son Uwe. I was barely acknowledged, but her greeting to Friede was frozen in disdain. Herma was eight years older than Friede. Many considered her intensely beautiful, but I didn't see it. To me, Herma wore her good looks like it was a crown of thorns. Her dress and comportment was as animated as a cloistered nun who had taken a vow of silence and self-abnegation. Whatever outward beauty she possessed was poisoned by her vile and vengeful temperament. She didn't hide her jealousy towards Friede, nor conceal her contempt towards her father, Max.

She despised him for adding another daughter to their household. Herma disinterestedly shook my hand and exhaled an atmosphere of black gloom all around the living room.

"Take my chair," said Max.

His wife interrupted, "I am sorry, my husband is slow when it comes to good manners, he should have offered you a seat immediately."

Friede tried to calm down her foster mother and Herma. "Mama, let's go into the kitchen so I can show you all the wonderful supplies Harry has brought you."

It didn't last long and the women began to argue about something I had failed to bring. Max smiled and said, "Women; they are always the happiest when they have something to complain about."

I reluctantly agreed and tried to converse with him.

"It's a warm autumn."

"I have experienced warmer."

"I hope the winter will be mild."

"It will never be as cold as Siberia," responded Max. He tapped a deep scar at the top of his left forehead with his index finger and added, "From the last war. I fought in Russia with the Kaiser's army. A Russian sniper shot me in Galicia. My mates left me for dead, but I was saved by a Russian surgeon who patched up my noggin. I think the doctor fixed me up as good as new. Except in the evenings, I get some fearsome headaches, but that could be from my wife yelling at me."

Max was bald and wore a suit that was much like him; it had seen better days. He was a relic from another time like my father or my grandparents. I looked at my watch and wondered what was keeping Friede in the kitchen.

He suddenly leaned close to me. "You speak quite good German."

"Friede helps me a lot with my pronunciation," I explained.

"But I don't think you understand Germans," he added mysteriously.

I offered him a cigarette.

"Normally I don't, but this time, like an old soldier, I will smoke

323

with you."

He lit his cigarette with a gold lighter.

He saw me admire it and said, "A gift from Hinrich Karp, Maria Edelmann's lover."

He handed me the lighter and I played with it while he spoke.

"You know I have been to many places in the world, first as a soldier, and then as a Reichbahn employee. It is great fun to travel. When I was young, I had love affairs and girlfriends in many different cities across Germany. What wonderful, carefree days they were for me with so many happy memories, for me now. I hope you have had similar experiences in your travels. However, I trust you don't think Friedle is just a bit of fun in a foreign port. I would hate to see her used or hurt by anyone."

"I would never hurt her," I told him.

"Good," Max remarked, inhaling his cigarette.

Max resembled a tired old alley cat sitting on the sofa, who still had enough life in him to pounce at the first sight of a mouse. He looked over to the open window and resumed speaking.

"Friede's had a complicated life, which has been far from ordinary or normal. I love her more than my real daughter. I think I love her more than any person in this world because she was so fragile when she came to live with us. I have tried to make her feel safe and loved. But I don't know if she understands. I am afraid Friede doesn't know where she belongs: with me, with her real mother, or with her real father. Her life is a tangled ball of wool because all the adults in her life have had their own problems and ignored hers."

"Like what?" I asked.

"Her real father Fritz Adelt was a bit of a dreamer whose spirit was damaged in the Great War. Fritz high-tailed it out of Hamburg after Friede was born. It was hard for him to make a living and with the responsibility of fatherhood, he felt like a man on a ledge. So whether he jumped or was pushed, Fritz deserted Friede and her mother. He left them high and dry. Maybe he had another family, I don't know. What I do know is he didn't have any real contact with his daughter, until it was too late. When your father abandons you for whatever reason, it will haunt the child throughout their whole life. I hope I was a good substitute, but I probably wasn't."

"Friede has told me that you are the only man she loves as a father."

Max smiled and said, "Well, at least I was a better father to her than fat Henry. He couldn't abide Friede when she was small. However, when she grew into a beautiful teenager, Hinrich thought she was just swell. I shouldn't speak ill about Hinrich; he had his moments. At least Hinrich paid me on time, for keeping Friede. Not that there is anything now to show for it. Hinrich was good to Friede's mother when times were good: he always kept her in style. But he was too much of a Nazi opportunist for my liking, but I am not a political man."

"What do you mean Nazi opportunist?" I asked.

"Hinrich Karp was a big shot, or pretended to be because it was good for business. If there was money in communism, he'd have quoted Marx instead of Goebbels. But how much he believed in National Socialism is anyone's guess. Nazi lackey or not, Hinrich used his influence sometimes for good and sometimes for bad. For instance, before the war, some meddling Nazi began snooping around questioning Friede's lineage. The party had their doubts about Friede."

"Doubts, what are you talking about?" I asked.

Max leaned forward and using his fingers to count as he replied, "One, Frieda's mother is a bastard, two, Frieda is a bastard. Three, there were rumours about Jews and communists being in on her father's side of the family. Myself, I don't think there was anything to them, but there was some sort of investigation in 1938. I think Henry pulled some strings and people stopped asking questions."

"Is Friede Jewish?" I asked dumbfounded.

"Who knows," he said, raising his hands up towards the ceiling. "In Germany, only a fool goes digging for the truth. It is best to live in the present. The past is dead and buried. Let it rest in peace. Whatever the truth is; Friede's vagabond life has made her emotionally fragile. She may pretend on the outside that she is strong and hard."

"However, on the inside, she is frightened. Elfriede doesn't know who she is as a person, as a German, as a human being because of her family. She needs a fresh start to make herself into the woman she deserves to be. So, I beg you, please treat her gently, she doesn't deserve any more hurt. God knows I have loved her like a daughter, but that is not enough when you don't know who you are and where you came from."

9

Life Observed from Binoculars

By the end of October, our Indian summer retreated against a cold wind blowing down from the Baltic. As the days drew shorter and the afternoon sky dimmed, the bread lines remained pregnant with refugees and German nationals. In the parks, there was the clandestine sound of handsaws as Germans felled trees and cut them into logs to burn in their wood stoves. There were others like Maria Edelmann who kept their apartments warm with stray coal scrounged from alongside the railway tracks that crossed the city.

Inside the confines of our air force base, it was warm and snug. We were well fed and the airport was often somnolent. Scuttled Luftwaffe fighter planes sprouted around the edges of the landing zone with their noses dug into the ground like discarded cigarettes. My mates and I posed for photos beside their rusting fuselages as if we were big game hunters standing near the corpse of an elephant.

Behind the landing zone, a concrete observation tower had been erected by the German aviation league in the 1930s. The five-story monolith housed the airport's telephone exchange system, RAF regional headquarters, and at the top of the building the air traffic control bridge.

My primary responsibility for the RAF was as a telephone switchboard operator. However, on Saturdays, I was seconded to air traffic control and worked from the observation nest. The shift was six hours long and unless I brought a book, it was about as exciting as listening to a leaking faucet.

On the weekend of Friede's birthday, I scanned the autumn clouds like Gordon of Khartoum looking for relief to arrive. On my watch, it was rare for the drone of approaching aircraft to break the monotony of exposed grey sky. That day proved to be lucky for me and my headsets crackled with static and a voice, from above.

In the distance, I saw a Lancaster approach the aerodrome. I responded to the call in a bored and lazy fashion. My landing instructions were simple; if the strip was empty of lorries, pedestrians, or errant cows, use it.

I observed the airmen dismount from their aircraft. They looked bored as a group of bus conductors because they were now pilots on a milk run. There was no excitement or thrill or threats of death except through thrombosis. They walked over to the operations room and surrendered their cargo, which appeared to be condensed milk, mail, and spanners. It occurred to me that the air ministry might have requisitioned the wrenches to reassemble Hamburg as if were a broken meccano toy.

From the air traffic control tower, I was able to see the entire town of Fuhlsbüttel and nothing ever looked out of place. The houses, their gardens, and their parks always looked neat, orderly, and ordinary. It was as if the Second World War had omitted this location from its list of places to destroy. The image of Fuhlsbüttel as an oasis would have been complete except for the steady march of refugees on its streets. For the most part, the forsaken didn't stay long in Fuhlsbüttel; it was just a road that led them north or south towards food. Yet some broke ranks and put down roots at a sprawling squatter's camp two hundred meters from my observation post.

Since 1943, the camp was a familiar landmark to the residents of Fuhlsbüttel. It had been established after Hamburg was fire-bombed. The city's homeless were encouraged by municipal government functionaries to immigrate to the empty, long fallow fields, near the airport and set up shanties. As Hamburg became more desolate and uninhabitable, the tent city grew and became a more permanent settlement. From the wreckage of their former homes, the inhabitants constructed wood huts that were an imperfect incarnation of their past lives. Eventually, shops and little industries sprung up in the squatter's camp to serve the needs of its citizens and the town's people of Fuhlsbüttel. When the war concluded, the squatter camp expanded to accommodate new refugees, from the eastern edges of Germania. "Go to Fuhlsbüttel," they were told, "you will get better rations being shoulder to shoulder with the RAF."

It was rumoured that within its canvas and scrap wood confines, some of the best tradesmen in northern Europe now resided. Friede told me, "If you are brave, you should go into the camp because they have wonderful dressmakers and unique jewellery for sale, from cash-strapped Prussian Junkers."

Her suggestion wasn't subtle, it wasn't nuanced; it was a reminder to me that she considered her eighteenth birthday an important milestone that should be celebrated with an appropriate gift. At the time, bargains were as common as a hay penny, but my salary was only £2.10 a week. The squatter's camp was my best option to locate an object I could afford for her birthday.

When my shift ended, I left the tower and slipped on a pair of aviator sunglasses. At the base of the observation tower, a group of clerks huddled together by the side of the telephone exchange entrance, smoking cigarettes. I knew them from my regular, weekday occupation.

"Fancy a beer, Harry?"

"No thanks, maybe later. I've got to get my girlfriend a present for her birthday."

"Yer German bird?" one of them questioned."

"Girlfriend," I responded. "Bird is for pubs and bowling on a Tuesday night. She's my girl."

"Sure she is," the airman responded caustically. "Those Frauleins are all out for one thing, a good time, until the brass runs out. Then, they'll bugger off to get a new mate to luv 'em."

I ignored his comment. There was no time to waste because I had to go to the armoury before I left camp. RAF regulations required that all personal carry a firearm while off the base. It was a precaution in case there were civil disturbances by disgruntled Germans.

The airman in charge of weapons opened up the lock up and handed me a weapon, along with a warning. "Try not to shoot yourself with it, last night two of our boys were wounded from glass shrapnel after they opened a clip into a lorry of empty bottles."

"I'll keep that in mind."

I don't know what I would have done if I had been faced with a situation requiring the use of my gun. I would have turned and fled or used the gun as a blunt instrument rather than discharge it. My only experience with a firearm was in England, during my numerous RAF training exercises. It only proved to me and my drill instructor that I was no rifle man. My targets, like the milk bottles at a carnival, were safe from harm with my wild aim.

I quickly left the armoury. My Bren gun was strung around my shoulder as if I were a gangster. At the entrance to the airbase, the guard called out, "Up to some of yer monkey business, Harry?"

"Not today, Tom, I am just out for a parson's stroll."

I moved along the perimeter of the airfield towards the haphazard city of the dispossessed. The wind picked up and scattered dead leaves, dirt, and an army of young boys hunting for cigarette ends around me.

"Cigaretten?"

"You're too young to be smoking," I muttered and tossed them

330

some loose candy from my trouser pocket.

The young boys scattered like the blowing leaves and the dirt around us. In between the gusts of wind, I heard them jibber thanks and curse me in German. As the children moved away, the refugee camp quickly came into my full focus. It looked even more jumbled from the ground than from my lofty air traffic control tower. The encampment stretched from the end of one desolate field to the next. It was a community strung together with canvass wood and fastened unhappily by the glue of desperation.

There wasn't an official entrance to the shanty town. There was no sign announcing *"you are now entering the refugee camp,"* there was no bridge to cross, and no toll to pay. I just walked between some huts and sauntered into the shambles.

Inside the squatter's camp, it was as claustrophobic as if it was an ancient slum. Everything was built tightly together, with one building using another structure as support. Rope, nails, and luck seemed to be the only things holding the flimsy buildings upright. Most were ready to collapse into dust when the next strong storm burst into the camp.

It was an awful place and within these thin walls made from bomb debris, people lived like the forsaken with little time for laughter or love. Coming from every tent or wood structure, I smelt the seeping stink of an over-ripe tip. Between the dense smell of decay, there was an odour of soups, heavy on cabbage being boiled to oblivion that drifted through the air like a virus.

Around me, old women with brooms made from coarse tree branches swept the dirt and dust into organized piles. They looked me over strangely, as if I were a tourist from an ocean liner come to port for a one-day stopover.

At first, the residents seemed distrustful towards me, until like a pack of dogs, their noses sniffed and determined I was harmless. The first to approach was a shoemaker who jumped out from a tiny wooden stall. The skinny cobbler wore a leather apron and a patch over his right eye. A leather workman's cap rested on his head as if it had been placed there at his birth. "Meine Herren," he yelled out and introduced himself. "Gut to meet." The cobbler thrust out his hand to me, which was caked in dirt.

I refused to embrace it with a quick shake of my head. Nervously, he plunged it back to his side, where he began wiping it down across his apron.

"I habst for you, excellent shoes, best price, no shit, only excellent leather, Meine Herrin. I give only the best for you, being such a fine officer."

"I'm not an officer, mate."I said and tried to step around him and make my way down the lane.

"No, please, shoes are good," he said, blocking my exit.

"Don't need shoes. The RAF provides me with proper boots."

"Maybe you need a belt?"

I looked down at my frayed, aging belt and agreed with him.

He pulled off his cap and scratched a bald head as if thinking how he might fleece me. He began to grin at me with a jack-o'-lantern mouth containing three black teeth. "Forty cigarettes and I sell you one."

"You're off your bicycle," I replied. "I must have made the wrong turn and ended up on the High Street in Manchester."

"Wass?" he asked.

"Never mind," I replied.

"Twenty cigarettes," he said with similar enthusiasm.

"Four cigarettes," I responded with the voice of a seasoned barterer, which I wasn't.

Down cast, the shoemaker was about to return to his tiny stall when he cried out, "For you, a friend, I can do it for five cigarettes."

"Done," I replied in a matter-of-fact tone.

"Tommy, give me the cigarettes now."

"No, I think, I will wait and see what you have to offer first."

The shoemaker measured my waist with a greasy piece of string and then returned to his cubby hole. In it were strands of leather with different dimensions and belt buckles. I wondered if his entire inventory was purloined from the morgue, but thought it best not to question the provenance of his goods. He fished out a belt for my approval, which had a giant metallic buckle.

"Too flashy," I said.

The cobbler scrounged around for a while longer at the back of his stall. Triumphantly, he thrust a belt into the air as if he had pulled a trout from a river and called out, "Is this besser?"

"That will do just fine," I told him.

"Wunderbar, my good Sergeant Tommy," he said, handing me the belt.

"Hey, Fritz, I'm not a sergeant. Look at the badge. I'm just a bloody wireless operator. I'm like the girl at the Altona hotel, I just transfer calls to the penthouse suite."

"You should be a sergeant."

"Sure," I said, "and you should have a proper shop but the world had other plans for us."

There was some truth in the shoemaker's words. I could have been a sergeant, but declined the invitation because my mates said it was a bad idea. "Like being bloody foreman down at mill," said one. "Once you start wearing stripes, you'll be having your pints alone."

So in a foolish spirit of comradeship, I declined the promotion as I wished to remain with my fellow LACs. However, there was one in my group who was shrewder than me. He wisely calculated that the raise in pay, stature, and grander possibilities outweighed drinking alone and volunteered to wear the patch on his sleeve in my place.

"Ok, Tommy. See, Mein Herr, I am the best. No disappointments with my work."

I handed him the agreed five cigarettes, which he grabbed anxiously.

"You come back again, Tommy," he said. "I am good business."

As I was about to move on, I asked him, "Hey, Fritz, I'm looking for some nice jewellery, a brooch or a necklace."

He thought for a while and said, "Go up ten stalls. There is a widow, some officer's wife from Prussia. All fancy and fine; she has got things for sale. But don't let her cheat you; she is a crafty old crow."

I walked away from his stall and moved further into the village of refugees. Children with dirty faces and torn clothing ran past me, reminding me of my own miserable youth. It was easy to find the Prussian widow's quarters because it was near a communal bog. She looked to be in her late fifties. Her hair was streaked with grey and she wore a smart dress and flat shoes, flaked with mud. At first, she didn't look at me when I spoke to her. Her wilted eyes were fixed on the children playing near the bog.

After a while, the widow responded. "You want jewellery," she said to me in perfect English. "I have many interesting pieces that were given to me over the years. As you can see from my present circumstances, I have no use for ornaments. Please come inside," she requested. The woman drew back a tent flap revealing a tiny living space with a camp bed and a broken dining chair.

Pointing to the chair, she said, "Sit down if you like, but I am afraid it is not very comfortable." By her bed, there was a picture of a man in a Wehrmacht uniform looking too proud for his own good. The woman noticed my gaze and said, "My husband, in happier times. "What are you looking for?" she inquired.

I really didn't know. I had never bought jewellery for a woman before then, unless it was some cheap, shiny clasp from Woolworths.

"You are looking for something for your girlfriend?" inquired the widow.

"Yes, it is her birthday today."

"What colour is her hair... and her eyes?"

I told her. The woman smiled and said, "She sounds very beautiful." She added ruefully, "It is a sad time to grow into German womanhood.

I think I have something for you."

The widow fetched a biscuit tin from underneath her bed. She lifted the lid and sorted through the stray bits and baubles from a bygone time. Eventually, she pulled out a sterling silver necklace pendant with a tiny sliver of fossilized amber mounted into the delicate metal work. Its beauty was simple. It wasn't ostentatious, but quietly elegant and sensual. The widow saw my appreciation for the jewellery.

"It was my daughter's," she said in an empty voice.

"How much is it?" I asked.

"A carton of cigarettes," said the widow, as she handed me the jewellery so I could feel the workmanship. "It's real silver, "she asserted.

I didn't haggle and handed over the required sum.

As I left, the widow said, "I hope it brings more happy memories to your girlfriend than it has to me."

10

The Birthday Party

I stumbled through my love affair with Friede in ignorance and youthful lust. I had neither a map to chart my affair nor a lexicon to define its development. In truth, I didn't even have a compass to show me the true direction where love might be found. My past was certainly not a reliable guide; it only harboured betrayal, hunger, and familial misdeeds. As for my previous love affairs, they were few, brief, and about as satisfying as eating soggy chips in a November rain. So, it was only natural for me to believe that my developing attachment to Friede was beyond my learning experiences.

Even a birthday party was an exotic occurrence for me. Friede's eighteenth birthday was the first coming of age celebration I had ever attended. For my own eighteenth birthday, I prepared for induction to the RAF; where I was to be taught to kill or be killed by Germans. Now my only apprehension about Germans was whether Friede's mother was going to find me an acceptable match for her daughter.

Friede had described her mother from so many different angles; I began to think of her as a cubist canvas of vice and virtue, coloured by sacrifice and sensuality. To Friede, her mother was impossible, glamorous, selfish, and loving. In sentimental moments, Friede showed me pictures of her mother and said, "Wasn't she beautiful?" The studio portraits revealed an attractive woman, but I also noticed steel in her beauty, flashing from her eyes.

On my way to the birthday party, I fretted that her mother was going to dismiss me as unworthy because I lacked their continental outlook. I dreaded a cold rebuff similar to my treatment by Friede's foster mother, Frau Bornholt. She had accepted me as a sort of English delivery boy who was welcome to stand at the apartment entrance while she took my gifts from the RAF storehouse.

When I arrived, Friede was waiting for me at the front entrance to the apartment. She rushed over to greet me. I kissed her and whispered into her ear, "Happy birthday."

"Thank God you are here."

"Why?" I asked.

"Mutti and Grandfather have been fighting for the last hour because the old man keeps stealing the cigarettes you gave me. The old Nazi cuckold says he has a right to everything because we are all horrible, immoral women. What a crazy man he is. I think Oma must have died to get away from him. Let me take those flowers from you. Mutti is dying to meet you and has been practicing the English expressions I taught her. I am afraid she has not had much luck in pronouncing them correctly."

I hope it's not bugger off, I thought.

Friede's mother stood at the top of the landing by her opened apartment door. Maria Edelmann emitted a rehearsed warmth and welcome for my arrival; whether it was sincere or false was anyone's guess. She took my hand affectionately kissed me on both cheeks and spluttered out some fractured English, "Velcom, you to mein haus, Gut," and escorted me into their fashionably furnished apartment. Bucolic paintings of carefree vagabonds and laughing children adorned her hallway walls. The apartment's hardwood floors were covered with a series of worn Caucasian tribal carpets. In the background, the other guests chattered and laughed in staccato German.

Since the dining room was now occupied by the homeless Gellersons, Maria Edelmann ushered me to the kitchen. Inside, the Gellersons and Gerda huddled around a small table whose top was cluttered with cut up smoked sausages, schnapps glasses, and a crystal ashtray. A fresh breeze blew in from open French doors leading onto a balcony. The kitchen overlooked a hilly field and, in the far distance, a railway spur.

"Sit, sit," her mother instructed me in the voice of an accomplished hostess. For the moment, I felt well looked after. Although it seemed Maria Edelmann was treating me more like livestock that must be cuddled before being sent to the butcher's block.

"Mutti, don't fret over him. He is not made of glass," Friede said with some irritation.

"It's all right," I said, trying to defuse the tension.

"How was your day?" she asked.

I was about to respond when her mother interrupted to thank me for the supplies I had sent to prepare the birthday meal.

"It was nothing," I responded. "Frau Edelmann, it is always a pleasure to help you and your daughter."

"Please call me Maria," she said, with the precision of a coquette.

"Mutti," Friede chortled at her mother. "What about the stew?"

Her mother apologized and went over to the wood stove, while the Gellersons and Gerda approvingly sniffed the aroma coming from the cooking pot.

Friede took my arm and said, "Let's go on to the balcony and have a cigarette."

Outside, Friede said with a laugh, "I thought I'd never be rid of her." She whispered, "We have been fighting all day like the dog and the cat."

"Over what" I enquired?

"The dinner, of course," she said. "My mother is such a perfectionist when it comes to making a meal. I think that is how she trapped Uncle

Henry. Of course, while Mutti prepared dinner Opa was a giant bore. He complained that nobody cared and said terrible things to Mutti. My mother retaliated by telling him she'd turn him out on his ear if he didn't smarten up." Friede paused and then asked "Do you have a cigarette? I am dying for one. My mother doesn't like me smoking. She says it is just too modern for her. I don't know why it bothers her so much, considering Uncle Henry's business was in tobacco. It certainly kept her in fantastic dresses for years."

"Friedle," her mother called out from the kitchen, "I have ears, so mind what you say out there." This made everyone else in the kitchen laugh.

Friede sighed over her mother's comments and then asked, "What do you think about girls smoking?"

"I like it," I said. "It makes them look like movie stars."

"Me too," she said, blowing blue smoke over the balcony and across into the open field. At that moment, she looked both distant and alluring, like a movie star on a billboard poster. Friede was wearing a yellow summer dress that was too thin for the cool weather outside and she began to shiver.

I offered her my tunic, but she refused and explained, "It's old, I know. I bought it a long time ago, in the war. I really need new clothes, but there is so much else we need before fashion. I better see what Mutti is doing. Don't go anywhere," she said playfully and stubbed her cigarette out.

"Even if the balcony catches on fire, I will remain until your return," I replied in a lustful and longing voice and whistled as she turned around to leave.

Friede laughed and remarked, "See, my legs are now almost as good as Greta Garbo's because the medicine you gave me really worked. Look, how those horrible wounds have turned into just blemishes. It's a pity my legs were not like that in the summer."

Friede left me alone for five minutes or so and then popped her

339

head out from the small kitchen and asked, "Harry, can you be a dear and fetch Opa. I imagine he is in the wood cellar, sulking. Give him one of your cigarettes; that will put him in the right mood."

I said, "What about opening the present I got you?"

"It will have to wait until after you get Opa. I want him to see me open my gifts. Maybe then, he will understand what my true friends think of me. It might even change his opinion about the Edelmann women," she said with a laugh.

Maria Edelmann interrupted and said, "Only when hell freezes over will that old man have a kind word for you or me."

The warm smell of dinner trailed behind me as I left the apartment and walked down to the basement. In the cellar, there was a supply of neatly stacked wood, along with a collection of hutches holding rabbits for eating.

The cellar had a tiny window that allowed small particles of light to filter down into the dusky basement. I called out for Opa. There was no response. I crept around a wood pile, still calling his name. There was no reply except a thumping noise coming from the rabbit cages.

"Opa, I have an American cigarette for you," I called, thinking that I could bribe him to come out from his hiding space. Again there was no answer. I thought we must have missed each other and the old bugger was already at the table slurping his soup.

"You are giving me a lot of trouble, Grandfather." I put a cigarette to my lips and struck my Zippo lighter. Its flame illuminated a silhouette that was obscured by some boxes over to the right of me. I drew closer to investigate and soon realized the shadow was Opa and he was dead. The old man had committed suicide. His body was hanging from an old rope wrapped around a wooden beam running across the ceiling. A stain ran down his trouser legs. He had pissed himself when he had kicked the box over and began to die from strangulation.

His lifeless body reminded me of the executed German deserters I had seen while we drove into Germany just before the end of the war. He must have killed himself right after he stormed out of his step-daughter's apartment. "Well," I said to the corpse, "that will show them, hey, Opa."

I righted the box and stood upon it to cut him down with my pocket knife, which was normally used to quarter apples. Now it sliced through the strands of rope inches above his skinny, blue neck. When I was half-way through cutting the noose, his body's weight snapped the last strands from the beam. The old man's corpse crashed to the dirt floor like a bushel of vegetables.

"Crickey," I said in apology for Opa's undignified descent. On the ground, I pulled his crumpled body as straight as possible and regretted there was no blanket or tarp handy to cover him.

Nothing that made him human remained. Everything was gone, even the hectoring; the jaded and jilted moaning had vanished from his old face. He just looked dead. His eyes were vacant and stared towards nothingness. I closed them shut and folded his hands over his chest. I stood beside his body and told him, "Well, you were a right bastard, but now you can harm no one. So, wherever you are going, have a safe journey."

When I got back to the apartment, everyone was seated around the kitchen table. They were waiting for me to return with Opa to begin the birthday dinner. In between drinking from their wine classes, they conversed in a lively and carefree fashion.

"What took you so long?" Friede asked. "Where is Opa?"

Everyone's eyes were on me and I stammered for a bit. Finally, I blurted out, "I'm sorry, Opa is dead."

Friede asked in disbelief, "Dead?"

Her mother took a sip of wine and laconically remarked, "Tot."

Her tone suggested to me that Maria didn't question his lack of existence, but wondered why it took so long. Everyone else was silent and embarrassed and looked as if a fart had been ejected into the atmosphere. I placed an opened cigarette pack on the table and watched hand after hand reach for the Player's.

Friede's mother spoke in a restrained tone, "So the old so and so finally topped himself. Well, well, you would think it was my birthday. This is the first time that man has given me anything to be thankful for. Quite a gift he left us, hey, Friede."

I was confused and somewhat offended by their reaction to the old man's departure.

"Gift" I asked?

"Yes, he finally showed some good sense," she said, toying with her glass of wine. "It would have been rude and selfish of him to eat first and then kill himself. At the moment, death is more abundant than food in Hamburg. Still, he could have shown me the kindness of doing himself in at my sister's house. She at least was his natural daughter, while I was just the bastard child."

"Mutti," Friede screamed.

"Hush, Friede. Well, I supposes, it is bad manners to speak ill of the dead." Maria Edelmann sighed quietly and took a sip from her wine.

"Perhaps," Friede suggested, "Harry could go to the police and tell them about Opa. If he reports it, there will be no scandal because he is a Tommy."

"Yes of course," I said. "I will fetch a policeman. I won't be long."

"I will keep your dinner warm," Friede said, but as I left the apartment, I heard her mother doling out spoonfuls of stew to the other guests.

The police station was a quick stroll down the road. When I arrived, a duty sergeant in his twenties was sat behind a desk, typing with one finger. In his immaculate police uniform, the copper looked as Prussian as Bismarck. After several seconds, the policeman noticed me. Even though he outranked me, the German stood to attention and saluted. I returned the salute and explained Opa's death. The policeman took out a note book and asked for my name and the address where the incident occurred.

"You don't happen to have a spare cigarette on you?" he asked. I handed him a near-empty pack. "Keep it, I have plenty more."

"I don't see this as a problem," said the policeman. "It sounds like a pure and simple suicide."

"Good," I replied, "the family has gone through enough as it is."

"Yes," he remarked, disinterested. "Suicide is not an uncommon occurrence in Germany today. A lot of old people do away with themselves because they are a burden and they can't live with the defeat of Germany. Go back to your dinner. I will send a constable to the apartment to confirm the death. It is just a formality. I will telephone the morgue to expect the body. As a small piece of advice, it will probably be easier if you arrange for a truck to collect the suicide victim. There is no telling when I could get a vehicle to gather the body. It might be quite some time."

"Time, how long is this going to take?"

"It could be a couple of days before I could get someone to fetch the body and by then the neighbours will complain of the stench coming from a decomposing body."

The policeman let me use his telephone and I called the motor pool at the airfield. I arranged for a truck to take the body to the morgue. It cost me a week's wages, but it ended any threat of scandal or inconvenience over the hanging to either Friede or her mother.

When I returned to the apartment, the Gellersons had already decamped to their room. Friede and her mother were in an argument over the corpse in the basement, while Gerda cleaned up the dishes. I explained what I had done and Friede jumped from the table and hugged me affectionately.

"I don't know what we would have done without you," she told me.

Maria remained seated, sipping her wine, as she complained, "Even those who I disliked have deserted me. I have no one left to help me."

"Oh Mutti," Friede groaned. "Stop your melodramatics."

"What is she on about?" I asked.

343

"Nothing," Friede said. "It is the German affliction, sturm und drang."

"Nothing," Maria said. "I have no one to rely upon since your Uncle Henry died."

"Oh Mutti, stop calling him Uncle Henry; he was your boyfriend. I am not a little girl anymore. I know all about Henry; you were his kept woman."

"Don't talk that way to me, child, not tonight, not ever. Maybe you will understand me better when you are grown up and not such a foolish teenager."

I heard the RAF truck pull up outside. I asked Friede and her mother if they would like to go down to the morgue and say goodbye to the old man.

"No, I see no purpose in that," said Maria. "But I am now going downstairs to check his pockets. If he left any pfennigs, they are ours, not some orderlies."

She thanked me for coming over for dinner and disappeared from the room. Friede looked at me apologetically. "Now do you see why I don't want any drama in our relationship? I promise next time we will have a proper meal, but I think you should go now."

"What about opening my gift?" I asked.

She kissed me on the lips and said afterwards, "I am sorry, Harry. With all these theatrics going on, I don't feel like opening any presents. I promise I will open it soon with you."

When I walked out of the door, she called out to me. "Harry, I can't thank you enough for your help. I think maybe you are the one person who may come to understand me."

Outside, the RAF driver had Opa's body draped over his shoulder like it was an overcoat.

"Do you need a hand?" I inquired.

"Nah, this bloke is as light as a baby," he said, dropping him into the back of the truck like broken goods going off to the tip.

Maria Edelmann came outside and kissed me farewell. She acted as if suicide and body disposal was a normal occurrence at a German birthday party.

When I got into the truck, the driver looked at me and said, "Sometimes, it's probably best to stay at the NAFFI with feet on stool, near the fire."

The truck started up with a bang and we pulled out towards the morgue several blocks away. When we drove away, I looked in the side view mirror and caught sight of Friede standing with her mother and Gerda. They waved goodbye to me and good riddance to Opa, who was rolling around in the back of the lorry like an unsecured empty drum.

11

Advent for the Desolate

Hamburg's Indian summer struggled against November like a sputtering flame from a votive candle in a desolate church. Cold temperatures from the Scandinavian Peninsula stomped into town and extinguished any optimism that the ice and sleet season would give us a miss at the end of 1945. Most days, the horizon was charcoal grey as the distant sun hid behind low clouds. In winter's chilly four o'clock light, the city's bombed out sections looked even more forsaken than during spring and summer. In the eleventh month, a frost covered the destroyed city like a cocoon.

When St Andrews's day arrived, snow storms raged up and down the northern tip of Germany. The brick Omas came out and swept the streets clean of snow with the same industriousness they used in June to clear the streets of war debris. As the mercury dropped, it became more difficult to provide supplies for malnourished Germans because roadways across Europe were closed due to the ferocious weather. The old, the sick, the young, and the dispossessed died from exposure and incremental starvation. Decimation wasn't an official policy for Germany's collective sins; it was the product of inept bureaucratic planning. The government failed to make accurate projections. Their ledger books didn't have sufficient columns to calculate the effect of mass refugee migration to the western zones, nor could slide rulers estimate starvation rates produced by the total collapse of agriculture and industrial output.

Yet as Germany slipped into hypothermia, famine, and death, I was warm and well fed within our airbase enclosure. Outside the fence, chaos and bedlam reigned supreme, but inside everything was routine and orderly. Transport planes arrived with fresh supplies and departed with demobbed men who had worn the King's uniform for long enough and were now allowed to return to Civy Street. I was beginning to feel like the odd man out as no one was left from my square bashing days at Padgate at the war's beginning. Pretty well everyone I knew was gone, even the men from my training days at St. Athan or even from my pissed up antics at Chigwell had packed up and buggered off home.

I was now surrounded by National Service virgins. They were five years my junior and when the sergeant major counted them in the mornings for king and country, these lads shouted out too eagerly their attendance and readiness for the RAF. I didn't share their neophyte enthusiasm. I acknowledged my presences with a familiarity of a cat being called to tea. An NCO once cried back, "Almost time for your gold watch and farewell party, LAC Smith."

At twenty-two, I was an antique in the ranks of the stripe-less RAF men of Fuhlsbüttel. Only two blokes remained from my first days in Germany: Sid Ward and Dave Needles. We chummed around and got drunk on the nights I wasn't busy with Friede. Sid stayed on in Germany because there wasn't much prospects for him back in the Midlands. "When I go back," he said, "it is either as a man in pit or as a pony in pit. Not much difference, except the pony gets straw for his bed." As for Dave, he stayed on for the adventure, but said he'd be heading home some time sooner rather than later because he missed his family in Nottingham.

I smiled and said, "Sure, I know what you mean," even though I couldn't comprehend Dave's hunger to return to his family. I couldn't get far enough away from mine or their grubby lives in Halifax. It didn't matter how much I wanted to renounce my kin, they weren't going to renounce me or my responsibilities to them. I received my mother's annual plaintive yuletide letter, which as always was as succinct as cuneiform.

"Help out your poor old Mam. We're tight from all the rationing. Yer brothers need feeding and I am not getting any younger and my man Bill isn't pulling the wages he did before the war. Remember, son, it is soon Christmas time and we must all look out for t'other."

I hastily sent my mother a letter which read: *"Mam: enclosed is £10; it should help you through Christmas. What I see in Germany today makes me weep and remember our own days ruined by starvation. I am sure the pounds I've sent will keep your chin up, at least until New Year's Day. Your loving son, Harry."*

My six-month extension with the RAF was almost up. It didn't take the toss of a coin for me to know that I wanted to remain in Germany: Friede was here and unhappy memories of England were across the sea. There was no opposition from the RAF to my request and I was granted an extension of service. They were happy to oblige as I was a trusted and experienced old man on base, who could be relied upon to do my duties at both air traffic control and switch board operations. At least the air ministry believed it had got its money's worth by training me and not killing me during the conflict.

During my almost five years in the RAF, I developed a good rapport with my superiors. In Fuhlsbüttel, the NCOs and officers knew me to be a capable individual not prone to tattle after school. I was granted extraordinary privileges because of my reputation for competence and discretion.

I even requested a change in my sleeping quarters.

"You what?" asked a sergeant. "You want to move from barracks to your own room. It's a bit early in the morning to be asking me for a 'ouse, Why don't you try for something smaller first, like a bleeding blanket or an extra towel," he retorted.

"I'm not asking for a 'ouse, Sergeant. It's nothing that grand. It's no bigger than a cubby hole; it's just an unused room on base that would do nicely for my sleeping quarters."

"Where is this hidey-hole?" he asked suspiciously.

"It's on the second floor in the air traffic control tower. I'd never be late for a shift if I kipped there," I responded encouragingly.

The NCO looked around as if he had been asked to sneak a woman onto our military enclosure. The sergeant contemplated my suggestion and after a while, he shrugged his shoulders. "Smith, as long as you don't turn it into a pub, pawn shop, or apothecary, be all right with me. I'll square it with the muckedy mucks and then it's yours. Mind you, if you fuck this up, Smith, your next 'ouse, will be the dog 'ouse."

My new quarters were the best digs I'd ever lived in, asides from my brief stay in a Dutch villa on our way to Hamburg. To make my lodgings complete, I commandeered a giant double bed from storage, which had once given gentle sleep to a Luftwaffe officer. Now, it cradled me like a baby. It was far better than the straw-filled mattresses I normally slept on. I was even able to trade some coffee to a dodgy motor pool mechanic and get a portable wireless radio. Tuned to Armed Forces Radio, it entertained me between my work shifts, with crooners singing about unhappy love affairs or comedians gently pulling the leg of military life.

My quarters even had a writing desk where I arranged my slim collection of books: Wordsworth's Sonnets, St Exuperey, and some novels by Dickens.

The desk stood at the back of the room beneath a large window that opened up onto an expansive view of the neighbourhood. When I was off duty, I'd smoke cigarettes while perched up on its cold ledge. In between blowing smoke rings, I tried to make out which snow-covered rooftop was Friede's apartment, while dreaming of our next encounter.

Having my own quarters in the communications tower was a definite advantage to my love affair with Friede. The building worked on a twenty-four cycle, meaning no one took any notice of my presence or my absence from the building. Living there allowed me to ignore curfew because no one was checking up on me. It was easy for me to sneak out of the camp; I just hopped over the barbed wire enclosure behind the tower. It was my preferred exit because the guards at the main gate began to conduct random searches for stolen RAF food supplies and medicine. The looting of RAF stores was becoming too common and too enormous for the brass to ignore. So the officers tried to stop a flood of racketeering by dropping a sandbag against a river. It might have blocked the small-time entrepreneur, but the bigger operators were never searched because they never walked out of camp, they drove.

My capacity to disappear over the wire increased as we came closer to the holiday season. I preferred to spend my time in Friede's company rather than the enforced jovialness produced at the camp canteen. During that December, there was little cheer on the streets of Hamburg. The Germans were somber and subdued, burying their feelings about Christmas under the heavy coats they wore while trading away their history on the black markets. Their grim looks were understandable because many were still mourning their war dead to follow the rituals of celebrations. Even in Friede's apartment, the inhabitants were sullen. They all wore an aggrieved look as they ground their teeth in angst over the question: what happens next?

Maria Edelmann and the elderly Gellersons were exceptionally gloomy because they remembered the anarchy that fell upon Hamburg after the Great War.

"Back then, it was civil war," said Herr Gellerson, while his wife nodded in agreement.

Maria Edelmann retorted, "If the Tommies don't sort out the food crisis, it will be war again. The Germans will only take so much and rise up against them."

"Hush, Mutti," Friede, said. "Don't talk your nonsense in front of Harry."

After six months of occupation, life was getting worse not better for them. Their only supply of fresh food above their calorie allotment came from me. Maria Edelmann was no romantic and understood that my love for her daughter was a precarious rope to hang on to for salvation. Their pessimism lingered around the apartment like incense. Only a week away from Christmas and there was no tree, candles, or any sign of the approaching holiday in their lodgings.

One evening, before I left Friede to sneak back into camp, I asked in a rather cold-hearted fashion whether Germans celebrated Christmas. Friede responded sarcastically, "We did until the British reduced our fat and milk rations and said Happy Christmas."

It was a cold, goodnight kiss for me. Before I could offer an apology, she slammed the door shut and I left with my tail between my legs.

I walked back to camp through dark and quiet streets, while overhead a clear sky was punctured by distant cold stars. I wasn't a sentimentalist and my memories of Christmas were as pleasant as an abscessed tooth. As a lad, they were bleak and unhappy occasions spent with my sister at a Catholic Church charity. The alms house was short on toys, but long on sermons about the grace of poverty. The Christmases of my past taught me it is best to expect little from others, except that too much gin produced a sad cheer on my mother who had run out of hope.

I don't know what made me double back that night to Friede's apartment, except maybe guilt over my Christmas cynicism. When I reached the building, I snuck into the basement, where I found an axe they used to cut firewood. I grabbed it and walked towards the field opposite the back of their dwelling. The snow was fresh and it felt like walking into the shallow edges of a lake. In the middle of the pasture, just below the hill leading to the railway spur, I found some blue spruces that were around two meters in length. I took the axe to one of them and chopped through the base of the tree. I dragged it back through the snow to Friede's mother's place.

When I placed it to the side of Friede's apartment door, the tree smelt of resin and the cold winter's night. I banged loudly and ran back out into the street. As I walked back down Langenhorner Chausee, I heard the main apartment door swing open. Friede called out "Dankeschön, Meine Harry, danke."

I turned around and saw her standing in her nightgown. She waved to me and I returned her gesture with a silent bow.

In the last mail before Christmas, parcels and letters arrived from my mother and my sister . I took the packages to my room and put them on my desk. I retrieved a bottle of brandy in my writing desk and poured a shot of 'eau de vie' into a tin mug. I opened my sister's parcel first. There wasn't much to it: a photo of her with her son, a note about people I didn't know, from a world I was trying to forget. She had enclosed a scarf and a post script that read: *"To keep yourself warm and snug, think of it like my hugs, when we were wee and you were as frozen as an icicle because there was no coal in the grate."* She thanked me for my gift of money; she said it would buy a nice pair of shoes for her boy Derek. She ended the missive with: *"I'd luv to see ya home, but I think you haven't yet found a place for your heart to kip."*

In my mother's small parcel were Christmas greetings from her, her lover Bill the cowman, and my two half-brothers. She thanked me for the money I'd sent and also enclosed a wristwatch. Its value was ten shillings or less. The watch was light and flimsy to my touch. I wasn't offended by the cheapness of the timepiece; it was the paucity of time my mother employed to consider my gift. My mam probably bought it in a rush, while storming past a second-rate shop window on her way to or from a pub. I handled the watch with a mixture of curiosity and disdain; I wondered about her commitment to me. Was she at least as loyal as a mother bird to its young? *"Now you can fly, bugger off, because Mam's got another kid on her tit."*

My musings were interrupted by a knock at my door. I hid the watch underneath some papers, but left my sister's scarf exposed. It was Sid.

"Do you fancy going out for a beer?"

I said sure.

"What are you doing for Christmas Eve?" Sid asked.

"I'm with Friede and her family."

"Lucky bugger, you should hook me up with Gerda, your girl's best friend, so I can get some kisses for New Year's."

"I'll see what I can do. Give me a minute," I said, "and I'll meet you downstairs."

Sid left and closed the door behind him. I picked up the watch and looked at its cheap face. I wondered about the past and the time spent with my mother during our days of starvation. That night, I couldn't decide whether she was either the sin, the sinner, or the one sinned upon, or whether it even mattered. I buried my mother's present deep into the drawer of my desk; for all I cared, it could lay there until time stopped. I picked up my sister's scarf and wrapped it around my neck, turned out the lights, left my room, and proceeded outside to meet up with Sid.

12

Stille Nacht

It snowed on Christmas Eve day. It fell like icing sugar and dusted the city as if it were a stale and crumbling Christmas cake. The peddlers, black marketers, and cigarette hustlers scrambled to finish their commerce before the church bells pealed to celebrate the birth of Christ. Along the St. Pauli district, steam-powered trucks delivered beer and wine to the whorehouses, who expected exceptional business from nostalgic servicemen. Across the Reeperbahn, the lights burned bright, while in the refugee camps, the homeless huddled down against the cold, warming themselves with watery soup and kind words provided by visiting Lutherans priests.

The airport was somnolent; the service men charged with keeping it operational were as sluggish as a cat curled up on a pillow before a fire. Outside the communications tower, LACs took long cigarette breaks, draped in their great coats. In between puffs and guffaws, they swapped lewd jokes or tales about their sexual exploits with German women.

The air traffic control nest was unmanned for the next few days. The radio transmitters hummed emotionlessly because the ether above was empty and the clouds ripe for snow. Nothing was expected to arrive or depart until Boxing Day. On the ground, the roadways around the airport were quiet because the fleet of RAF vehicles was stabled at the motor pool for the duration of the holiday. Everywhere, it was still, except on the runway where a platoon of new recruits cleared snow from the landing area.

At the telephone exchange, the switchboard was staffed by a bored skeleton crew who waited for their shift to end. The normal frenetic noise and activity from hundreds of calls being patched and dispatched through the camp to the military world in Germany and Britain was hushed as there were few people left to either place or receive a call. Some communication operators hovered around mute teletype machines, which awoke every hour and furiously printed out wind speed, temperature, and ceiling levels, "For bloody Saint Nick," someone remarked.

This was a unique Christmas because for the first time since 1938, the entire world was at peace. So anyone who was able took leave and abandoned our aerodrome for a ten-day furlough. For those of us who remained, a Christmas committee was formed to organize festivities. The Yule spirit around camp mirrored row house Britain. It was constructed out of cut-price lager and crate paper decorations with the unspoken motto: "cheap but cheerful cheer in Fuhlsbüttel." In the mess hall, a giant Christmas tree was erected dangerously close to a wood stove by the Xmas team. They had festooned it with glittering ornaments and placed faux presents underneath its boughs. Sleighs and Father Christmas figures cut from heavy paper were pinned to the walls as festive decorations. Mistletoe dangled from light fixtures and gave our dining hall the appearance of a holiday party at a carpet mill in Halifax.

On the morning before Christmas, I negotiated with the head cook for extra rations for Friede and her family to allow them a holiday meal. The cook was an obliging Londoner whose mastery of culinary arts began and ended with the breakfast fry up. Never one to saying no to

355

sweetening his own pot, the cook amicably took my bribe of tailored shirts in exchange for food. He let me fill my kit bag to bursting with tinned meat, savouries, and sweets.

"Give the Hun a bit of a treat tonight," he said. "Take the pork pie along with a bit of plum pudding."

"What about some cheeses?"

"Sure, I've got plenty, could be a bleeding monger at market with all the gouda and edam," the cook said. No cheddar though; it's for the toffs with shiny clogs."

From a cheese wheel, he cut a week's portion of gouda and wrapped it in wax paper for me.

"Hold on a moment," he said, walking to a cabinet that contained wine, spirits, and beer. The cook removed some champagne and bottled ale for my parcel. He cautioned, "Mind you don't get caught with this. Give my best to the missus. Pity I can't give you a trifle, but it would spoil on the way." As I departed, he called out, "Happy Christmas. Remember, mum's the word."

"Are we still on for next week?" I asked.

"If you bring shirts as soft as this one, I am always open for business to you," he said, stroking my bribe as if it were a dog. "Now, off with ya. Can't you see I have lunch to prepare for you useless and thankless lot."

"Don't burn the water and have a Happy Christmas," I replied and left the cook house.

It was late in the afternoon before I had a drink with Sid, Dave, and some other mates at the canteen. We played several games of skittles where I displayed my poor gamesmanship. I lost a few shillings, but redeemed myself with a good showing in darts. Through each drag on my cigarette, I nervously wondered when it was expedient to sneak out of camp to go to Friede's with my bag of food and Christmas gifts.

The minute hand on the wall clock walked slowly through another hour of conversation about football clubs and Christmas back in

Britain, "They were magic."

So, everyone agreed including me that the holidays' at home were magic and we drank more beer to celebrate those "bloody magic days of youth." To myself, I thought Christmas was more witchcraft than magical in the dirty thirties, but I wasn't going to spoil this celebration by denying their beliefs in happy childhood memories. I just wanted to depart and have a "bloody magic moment," on Christmas Eve 1945. The minute hand moved reluctantly forward like a prisoner on his way to the gallows. It was time to go and I swallowed down my beer, in one mouthful.

I patted Sid on the back and said, "Don't wait up for me."

"Tara," he responded with a half pint of bitter in his glass and foam racing around his lips.

"Are you going over the top or charging through the gate tonight?"

"Straight ahead, the bloke on duty will look the other way with a pack of Christmas fags."

On my way to Friede's, the streets were cold, desolate, and empty of pedestrians. Anyone with a place to stay was already safely tucked warmly inside. When I arrived at the steps of Friede's apartment, it was just after eight. I hesitated at the front door and nervously adjusted my hair. From inside the apartment, I heard Christmas carols float out from the wireless. Self-conscious and unskilled at family situations, I hoped I wasn't going to make an ass of myself or reveal my poor upbringing. Just as I was about to ring the bell, Friede swung the door open. She looked confident, happy, and flushed from drink. In the background, I heard her mother talking to Frau Gellerson.

"Hello, Happy Christmas," I said in a voice that sounded as if I was unsure of the correct greeting.

"Merry Christmas, Harry, come in. You must be cold. Let me take your coat." Friede slipped it off my shoulders and placed it onto the standing rack. After I slid off my boots, she took my hand and said, "Let's go and say hi to everyone."

"In moment," I said. "I want to stay here for a while longer and have you all to myself. You look so wonderful." She blushed at the compliment and her eyes sparkled with the sensuality of youth.

Friede was wearing a delicate black, wool sweater with a slender skirt and dark nylon stockings that ran seductively up her legs. Around her delicate long neck dangled the necklace I had bought for her birthday. Her lips were crushed with a faint rouge colour, while her raven hair was combed back and had a light perfumed scent of spring flowers.

"You look so beautiful," I stammered.

Friede blushed and whispered, "I did this for you."

I was about to respond, when her mother shouted out. "For heaven's sake, bring him inside, he is not a tradesman come to fix the plumbing."

Friede ushered me into the kitchen, where her mother was preparing a fish soup for the evening meal. The Christmas tree stood at the right-hand side of the entrance. On its branches, lit candles burned from their holders and cast warm shadows across the room.

"Harry," Maria Edelmann said with a note of accomplishment in her voice, "I actually found carp in a market today."

"Mutti, you didn't find the whole fish, just the heads," Friede interjected.

"It was still a miracle, considering that the British with their private restaurants and clubs are gobbling up all the best Christmas foods." She wiped her hands on an apron that protected a very becoming evening dress. Maria Edelmann walked over to me and greeted me with a kiss and said, "Instead of carp for dinner, we will have bouillabaisse, which will be just fine."

"I've brought some things that should help with the festivities." I opened up my satchel and produced the wine, the meat pies, cheeses, and cakes. The women cooed in appreciation at the additions while Herr Gellerson looked at the wine and approved the vintage.

"Harry, choose a wine quickly," Friede exclaimed, "because I am slowly dying from this homemade schnapps."

Herr Gellerson interjected and said, "I could sell it on the black market as petrol and we would all be rich."

I easily opened the cork to the French sparkling wine, but, I recklessly over-filled our glasses and spilled much of it onto the table. After a hasty toast, the Gellersons retreated to their room and Friede's mother resumed dinner preparations. I disappeared with Friede into her tiny sleeping alcove where we talked and kissed.

"I should give you your present now," I said, excited like a schoolboy looking for approval.

"No," she said putting her finger to my lips. "We will eat first. Just before midnight, we open up our gifts. It is custom. It is silly that you do not know this. What on Earth did you do in England for Christmas?"

I smiled and said, "Things are different there. We opened presents in the morning." To myself I thought, if you were lucky to get one.

Friede changed the subject and started to smoke a cigarette.

"There is a lot of gossip going around these days about Germans being forced into work details around the city."

"This is news to me," I responded.

"I think it is true," she said with a note of seriousness in her voice. "I have heard the British and the new German civilian authorities are going to send German women to work."

"Work where?"

"In any factories that are still functional. There is also talk of German entrepreneurs returning from abroad. They made deals with the British to build their manufacturing empires on cheap labour as punishment to the Germans who stayed with Hitler. Like we had a choice," Friede added sarcastically.

"What type of deal?"

"Don't be a dumkoff, the oldest agreement in the world: I scratch your back, you scratch mine; it is bribes, liebchen, old-fashioned cash bribes."

"But why are they going to force the women to work in these places?"

"There is no one left in Germany, but women and babies. All of our German men are either dead or in concentration camps in Russia. Anyway, if this happens, we will be treated like the foreign workers were under the Nazis. I don't think I could survive under those conditions."

"I've never heard anything about this," I said, "but I am sure it will have nothing to do with you."

"I hope not," she said, unconvinced. She curled up a leg behind her and became child-like. "I want this holiday, this New Year to be special. During the war, Christmas was very sad with so many causalities at the front and so much destruction around at home. I never felt safe and it never felt particularly joyful."

"I will try to make this Christmas a happy time for us," I said, convinced I could alter history.

Friede didn't sound persuaded and asked, "What is going to become of us next year?" "We get poorer by the day. Mutti is getting older. Look, even her hair has turned grey because she is all alone with no one to look after her. I don't think she will find another man like Henry to take care of her and protect her at her age."

"What about your real father?" I asked.

Friede sighed. "Poor Fritz, he never got to know me. I wonder what he would have thought about me. You know, through my childhood, he did write to me and sometimes he sent me birthday cards. The last letter I got from him was in January. He was working in Berlin at an army truck factory. He said he was an engine fitter."

"Want else did he say?" I asked.

"Oh, you know, the same old Fritz. "Let's get to know each other better, you are my only daughter." I wrote him back to say that after ignoring his only daughter for all of those years. I was just doing fine without him."

"Did he write back?"

"No, he was probably killed defending Berlin from the Russians like most of the other old men and boys who were press-ganged into the Volksturm. Anyway, I haven't heard anything from him since his last letter to me. But who knows with Fritz, maybe he will show up one day with a fantastic story to tell."

"I'm sorry about your father," I said.

"It doesn't matter," she responded. "I never knew him. Papa was the only man who was like a real father to me. Poor Papa, he is out of work and too old to help me with anything. So you see, Harry, I have no one to protect me. I am just a German girl amongst millions with no money or influence." She sighed and continued, "I will never be able to finish my education and I am useless at anything practical. The world had enough dreamers. So what am I going to do?"

"Don't worry," I said. "I will always help and things do get better."

"How?" she asked sarcastically. "Germans and Tommies aren't supposed to fraternize. Sure, you can have a German girlfriend, but a German wife is verboten by Britain. They don't want us to have a future together. So don't make promises you can't keep, Harry."

I was about to dispute her claim, but decided it was pointless to get into an argument over occupational policy. She was correct; the authorities in charge didn't want us to develop deep or lasting relations with Germans. The unwritten code promoted by the British military government was: trade with them, steal from them, fuck them, but for God's sake, don't fall in love with them. The last thing England needed was a bunch of half-breeds in lederhosen sapping reserves off council boards.

When dinner was called, the Gellersons brought out a gramophone and set it up in the kitchen. Over dinner, we listened to ancient pre-war 78 RPM discs where German carols were performed or nostalgic songs about Hamburg were sung by soloists. During the meal, there was an element of make believe to our conversation and in the expression and gestures of the diners. Between mouthfuls of soup and warm bread, my hosts remembered and relived old Christmases when there was no war and their life was not dictated by occupation. Maria Edelmann, the Gellersons, and Friede laughed at old worn jokes. They spoke about people now missing from their lives, but at one time had passed over their hearts and left a shadow.

Friede turned to me and smiled as if to say, "All these old people and their memories; I will make a thousand better ones." Watching them, I understood that I was an outsider looking into their world. It was a universe of memories from a collapsed galaxy. It was odd that even though their lives had been so horribly altered by the war and their present filled with hunger and pessimism, they were still thankful for being alive.

Their stories about better days grew as thin as the candles burning on the tree and a melancholy fell across the room as the night dwindled down towards midnight. Friede and her mother looked as soft and sad as English rain. Their hearts ached for a finished era, dead family, friends and lovers.

"Harry, fill up everyone's wine glass," Friede instructed and stood to toast Christmas Eve. "To life, to being alive, and to all us being fed, healthy, and happy," Friede proclaimed.

Everyone clapped and drank from their glass. I noticed Maria Edelmann drained the entire contents of her glass and quickly refilled her glass with a trembling hand.

Maria than asked me, "So does your own mother make such a feast on Christmas Eve?"

I lied and said, "On Christmas Day, my mam puts out a roast goose with all the trimmings," where upon everyone enviously applauded my fictitious family festivities.

"Look at the time," Herr Gellerson said, observing his pocket watch. "It is almost midnight; we should exchange gifts."

Another bottle of wine was opened while Friede handed out presents which were under the tree. From Maria Edelmann I received a small book of Shilller's poetry and the Gellerson's presented me with a pair of socks. When Friede opened up my gift, her eyes became as effervescent as champagne bubbles.

"What is it?" her mother asked.

"It is so wonderful," Friede said. "Everyone come here and have a look at it."

She held up into the air an exquisite silver bracelet where each link in the chain was a tiny silver elephant. Friede clapped her hands and said, "This is fantastic," as she placed it on her wrist for everyone to admire. Friede then handed me an envelope and said nervously, "I hope this is all right, I hope you understand."

Inside the envelope was a large photo of Friede. The portrait showed her wearing the necklace I bought for her birthday. My hands shook as I absorbed the photo and everyone around me faded away from consciousness.

Friede smiled invitingly from the photo and I swam in the depth of her eyes. They shone out from the picture and radiated a singular love for me. On the back of the photograph was inscribed: *Fur Meine Harry, Ich Leibe Dich.*

"Do you like it?" she asked nervously.

I was silent and she repeated the question and woke me from my dreams. "Yes," I responded quietly.

"It was very difficult for me to find a photographer let alone someone with developing fluid and paper to make the portrait. There is literally nothing left in Hamburg to make photos."

I leaned over to kiss her and said thank you a thousand times. I was overwhelmed and excused myself and went to get some air on the balcony. In the cold quarter to midnight air, I lit a cigarette and felt the wind dry my face stained with tears.

Friede came out onto the balcony and asked if I was ok. "Yes," I responded. "Your present was beautiful," I told her in a breaking voice.

"What is it, then? Why are you so sad?" she said.

"Not sad, it's just, before this, no one ever gave me a gift like yours. It's hard to explain but I don't even think anyone has ever said they love me like you did in the photo."

"No one?" she asked in disbelief.

"Not a one," I said, "neither my father nor mother ever really said they loved me. There was only my sister Mary who said she loved me before you. She'd say it when we went to bed as children, hungry and dirty from scrounging coal to try to keep our house warm."

Friede, with wide open and caring eyes, kissed my hand and said, "Well, I love you. Our past lives are history. Let's just try to love each other and hope it will survive the winter and the occupation."

Maria Edelmann and the Gellersons came out onto the balcony. They held lit candles to confront winter's darkness. With one arm around Friede and my other hand holding onto a burning taper, I heard the bells across the city strike midnight. As the bells rang, people from neighbouring apartments stepped onto their balconies holding lit candles. Eventually, the clamour from the bells drifted away and all that remained was an expectant emptiness in the air. A male voice stirred from four apartments away. He began in a low, strong tone, singing the words to *Silent Night*. His voice was joined by other singers until the melody reached our balcony and we also sang Braham's lullaby to mankind. The tune travelled deep into the blackened city and dissipated into the Elbe River, where it drifted out to the cold, dark, Baltic Sea.

13

Winter 1946

Around Epiphany, the colour of the sky over Hamburg changed from a watery, drab white to the grey pallor of death. The heavens dropped low over the city like a sheet spread out over a corpse. Fat crows perched on hibernating trees and cawed with menace from their lookouts. The mercury dropped and standing water turned to ice. Rivers and lakes hardened to a frozen slush. Winds born in Siberia lashed the exposed skin of the homeless or those who searched for food at Hamburg's ever-expanding black markets. Heating fuel was hard to beg, borrow, or steal because coal shipments from the Ruhr were always late. When the trains finally arrived with fresh supplies of coal, it didn't help matters much because most of the cargo had been plundered before the coal cars reached Hamburg. Some said the only heat being generated in Hamburg were in the bordellos along the Reeperbahn.

Water pipes froze and windows iced over from Lubeck to the working class district of Altona. Apartment dwellers burned books in their kitchen stoves and sipped questionable moonshine purchased near mortuaries to stave off winter's chill. During the months known as the Hunger Winter, few thought or cared about culture; if you couldn't eat it or burn it; it was worthless. So it wasn't surprising that most of the city's frozen and desolate inhabitants were neither informed nor invited to the Hamburg Opera Company's performance of the *Marriage of Figaro* held in a makeshift auditorium during the second week of January.

British occupational authorities sanctioned the concert as a gesture of goodwill to downcast highbrow Germans, who felt abandoned by civilization. However, for most citizens, Mozart's return to Hamburg was treated with cynicism. Maria Edelmann scoffed at the news.

"The British won't feed us, but they'll stuff our souls with culture. How many calories are in an aria, I wonder?"

Friede believed that the opera gala's attendees were just Nazis dressed up as democrats. "I imagine," she said with disgust, "that Germany's new entrepreneurs, the black marketer, sat beside reformed Nazis and unrepentant communists. I bet each of them made a deal and sold out the German people during the performance. It doesn't matter whether it is a politician, egg-head, or spiv; they are all painted from the same corrupt brush. They think Hamburg is their personal trough to stick their snout in and eat every last morsel."

Not many days after the after the newly de-Nazified orchestra conductor was cheered by the well-heeled opera audience; a decree was issued by municipal authorities: the city's youth were to be put to work in factories owned by democratic capitalists.

The order was brief and to the point. Hamburg was rebuilding and all hands were needed to create a prosperous and democratic city. To that end, each young person not in school was required to register at the labour exchange located near the Rathaus, Hamburg's seat of municipal government. Failure to register the order stated would result in forfeiture of one's ration book. Letters were sent out to Hamburg's youth to reassure them that their future work assignments were to be based on skill and ability.

"What does this mean?" I asked, staring at the letter. It looked more like it had been written in the days of Hitler than in the year of liberation.

"It means it is over," Friede responded angrily. "I will be sent onto a work detail and they will destroy me there."

"When do you have to report?"

"I have one week before I must appear at the labour exchange. So we better enjoy it, my love, because after that I will be property of the new Reich and the spivs that control the country."

"Maybe, it will be all right," I said ignorantly.

"Sometimes you are so blind," she screamed at me.

"Why? It just looks like they want to get everybody working again. What harm can there be in that?" I reasoned.

Friede walked to other side of the kitchen and stared out from the French doors and onto the snow-covered hills. She spoke more to herself than me. "The bloody war interrupted my schooling. I have no skills for a proper job; I can't type, take shorthand, or even bake a cake. You know in this modern world it doesn't matter if I can recite Goethe by heart, it doesn't matter that I write and speak German like a university educated person. My papers say I am uneducated. I will be assigned the lowest and most brutal work duties, where my only chance for advancement is to let the manager pinch my backside."

"I won't let that happen," I said emphatically.

Friede laughed and said, "Harry, you work wonders down at the air base kitchen, but you are a tiny, tiny fish in a big ocean of sharks. You can't help me from this; no one can stop this from happening."

The week before she was to report to the labour exchange, Friede and I spent our time together doing the usual: we made love, drank wine, and ignored the world outside.

Even though she was against it, I accompanied her to the labour exchange. On the U-bahn into the city, we ate a breakfast of cold bacon sandwiches while famished commuters looked on in envy. From the Banhof, we walked south in the direction towards the Rathaus and the labour exchange building located nearby.

It was a cold day and the temperature hovered at minus ten Celsius. Our breath stuck to our faces and Friede snuggled up close beside me to stay warm. Even though her body was near; she was emotionally distant. Friede had to battle her own demons and fears about her coming work assignment alone.

When we arrived, Friede sternly said, "Whatever happens, promise me that you won't interfere with the outcome."Reluctantly, I agreed.

Inside the giant labour, we waited in a long queue with hundreds of other anxious young women each awaiting their uncertain assignment. Finally, our turn came and a man with thick spectacles at an information desk directed us to an office down the hall. There we were greeted by a plump and miserable woman, who told Friede, "You must wait until your name is called for your interview. I can answer none of your questions, so don't bother asking me anything."

There were no vacant seats so Friede and I stood close together and I observed her frustration and despair grow as we waited. After awhile, Friede whispered angrily at me, "See, I should have forbidden you to come with me. I am the only girl here with a Brit; I look like a complete traitor."

I let her rant and fret knowing that nothing I could say was going to change her mood.

After two hours of waiting, a woman with a pie-shaped face and drab wide slacks called out for Friede. I attempted to tag along to the interview room, but Friede stopped and scolded me.

"You're not going anywhere. I want you to stay here," she said in a tone familiar to any dog that was told to wait outside a shop by his master. The dour woman led Friede behind a glass partition.

Feeling out of place, I went outside and stood on the steps of the building smoking a cigarette. Frozen, I watched young girls wrapped in great coats shuffle through the labour exchange doors where dubious new professions awaited them created by occupation grants and dubious industrialists. I didn't stay out in the cold for very long before I returned to the office to wait for Friede. Around me there was a continuous sound of telephones, typewriters, and stamps being crushed against paperwork. It was another hour and half before Friede emerged from behind the partition. She held in her hand a sheaf of papers and said to me, "Let's get out of here. I need to get a coffee."

We found a cafe near the government building. We took a table close to a cast iron oven that had a few embers of coal burning in it to heat the entire restaurant. Friede barked out her order to the waiter for coffee and brandy. She fell silent and looked off in to the distance until our drinks arrived. Friede quickly drank her brandy and requested another. She asked me for a cigarette, which I lit and handed to her.

"So what happened?" I asked.

Friede blew smoke from her mouth and began sipping on her second brandy.

"It was as I expected; nothing but rubbish. These new employment directives are just a sop to the occupiers. It is going to make the industrialists rich on slave labour, just like under Hitler."

I took a sip from my drink and asked tentatively, "What job were you assigned?"

Friede continued as if she didn't hear my question. "This is just shit. It is only to prevent us from going out and protesting in the streets. It is to stop us from rising up against the occupation. These new work orders are to keep us cowed and happy with our starvation rations. This is our punishment for the war." Friede looked directly into my eyes with a dismissive and disdainful gaze. "The labour exchange has put me to work in a factory."

"What sort of factory?" I asked reluctantly.

"The best kind," she said, "one that makes lampshades to sell to a city that has no electricity." She laughed bitterly and repeated the word lampshade to herself. "It's over," she said.

"What's over?" I asked.

"Sometimes, you don't want to listen or understand me, do you?"

"Look," I said, growing frustrated, "I'm sorry they have forced you to work in this factory, but we can change that."

"No, you can't, Harry. Anyway, it is wrong to wriggle out of this new hell. In the past, I was saved too many times from my real fate. This is my retribution for being German; I can't escape it while everyone else is being punished." Friede reached out to hold my hand and while stroking it, she said, "I once asked you to promise me the moon. Now I am going to ask you to guarantee me something else."

"Anything," I said. "I'll do anything."

She let go of my hand and said without inflection, "We must stop seeing each other. There is no future for us, only a miserable present because we can never marry."

I was about to interrupt her when Friede dismissed my protest. "Harry, we can't marry; that is the law. Those are the regulations of your country. How long is the RAF going to allow you to remain in Germany? It is wrong for either of us to hang on to a hope that is false, a lie. "We can't go on like this, drinking wine, kissing, and forgetting the past or that we have no future together. You are nice; you are a kind man, Harry; go home to England and find a girl back in Yorkshire who isn't as complicated as me. You have to make a life for yourself and so do I. It is just pointless to continue as friends. There is nothing we can look forward to but drinks in a cafe. Thank you for everything that you have done for me." Her voice was as icy as the wind outside. She stood up, put on her gloves, and wrapped a scarf tightly around her neck.

Standing beside the table Friede said, "I must ask you to stay away from me forever."

With those final words, Friede walked firmly out of the cafe and onto the frozen street. I lit another cigarette and stared at the brandy glass that had smudges of her lipstick around the rim.

14

Spring

When spring came to Hamburg in 1946, it was a hard thaw. Bitter rain fell and made the city miserable, damp, and dirty. If there was any enthusiasm over winter's passing, widespread hunger erased it. Daily rations allotments were still horrendous and the calorie intake was insufficient to sustain the average person. Only black market entrepreneurs looked healthy and wealthy compared to their grey-faced compatriots. It was little wonder that few Germans paid little attention to the war crime trials underway in Nuremburg. Naturally, many just wanted these prosecutions to be over and done with, rather like pulling a diseased tooth.

"Sure, Goring, Ribbentrop, and Hess are guilty. Send them to the gallows," the people said. "But leave us ordinary Germans alone, we were just following orders."

Gradually, the weather warmed and the days lengthened, but it did nothing to brighten my spirits. Instead, it depressed me because it reminded me too much of the year before, when hope and happiness lay at my feet, like garlands cast to victorious soldiers on parade. I was still raw from January when Friede broke off our affair. Weeks after Friede had fled the cafe, I looked for her like a dog run wild in the woods, but she wasn't going to let me find her.

It didn't matter where I searched because Friede had left no trail for me to follow. Most of her friends ignored me or reluctantly said that they had not spoken with her for some time. I went back to the restaurants we used to frequent and retraced my life with Friede. It was a futile hope that maybe I'd run into her. It never happened. I never caught sight of her. Even the waiters who remembered us shook their heads and politely said, "Sorry, the Fraulein has not been in for weeks, maybe you would like to meet my cousin. She is just as pretty."

I purposely walked down Langenhorner Chausee hoping to confront Friede about our break up, but I never saw her. One time, I even got up the courage and banged on Maria Edelmann's apartment door and asked the whereabouts of her daughter. Her mother said, "Friede is not here, she is at work."

I wanted to say, "Tell her that I stopped by," but her mother interrupted me and told me, "She doesn't want to see you anymore, so it is best to respect her wishes." I tried to leave some food rations for her, but Maria Edelmann declined and said, "Please don't call again; it is embarrassing for everyone." So I gave up and went back to the air base. I let my wounds fester for weeks.

Finally, my mate Sid grew tired of moaning and told me, "Cheer up, there's plenty of fish in the sea, especially in Hamburg. Let's get pissed." So we did. Through that winter, I drank and went to parties and got stinking drunk as many times as it snowed, trying to forget my misery of the heart.

As I was hung-over most days, I attended to my duties at the airport telephone exchange reluctantly. The work was unimpressive and dreary, as I was imprisoned in the air traffic control tower in a large stark room with windowless charm. My responsibilities were uncomplicated; I connected incoming or outgoing telephone calls to our airport from the hundreds of other military bases across Europe and the UK. It was a simple job made easier because we used captured push-button

German technology, which was superior to our primitive British patch cord system employed at RAF bases in Britain.

It may have been more efficient, but it didn't change the fact that it was numbingly dull. There was always an incessant back ground hum from whirring teletype machines or the thump of keyboards being heavily struck by one-fingered type-writing impresarios. All around me, there was the constant chatter of male telephone operators connecting calls from one trunk to the next, with the politeness of a lift operator.

On duty, my vocabulary was limited to: "Fuhlsbüttel BAFU, how may I direct your call?"

My fingers pushed buttons that connected one officer with his wife in Surrey and another digit patched another captain through to his mistress in Elmsbuttel.

With Friede out of my life, I seriously considered packing it in and begging to be demobbed back to Halifax. By this point, I was so jaded and heartbroken, I thought I may as well go and live in a glum flat and work as a serf in a wool mill on a pound a week wages as recompense. When I griped to my mates, Sid and Dave, they argued against my foolishness. "Steady on, lad, bide your time, things change and life isn't pleasant for the serious-minded. We've got the day off and the sun is shining, so let's get a couple of drinks at the *Malcolm Club*." I agreed and the three of us made our way from our airport base to the nearby club.

The social club was founded by the parents of Wing Commander Hugh Malcolm to honour their son who died in combat over the enemy skies. Anywhere the RAF was stationed, a *Malcolm* was close by to provide refuge, relaxation, and tankards of beer or cider at a generous price.

Our *Malcolm* was located a short walk from base in a requisitioned restaurant that stood on the banks of a large artificial pond. We took advantage of the warm sunny day and drank our pints outside on benches overlooking the water. Out on the lake, there was a flotilla of canoes each being paddled by a soldier with a girl sitting at the bow. I ruefully said, "I did that last year with Friede."

"Shut it, Harry," said Sid. "We agreed no talk about girls. Pay the penalty, stand the next round."

When I returned with the beer, Dave asked, "Do you remember the chap from base that went mad last year?"

Sid shook his head, but I remembered. "Wasn't he a mechanic or something?"

"That's right," remarked Dave. "He paddled a canoe out into the middle of the lake and scuttled it with a pocket knife."

"He was unaware," I added, "that the reservoir was only waist-deep."

Dave finished the story. "The mad bugger was put on charges for not paying for the ruined canoe. All he wanted to do was end his life and he got clapped into irons for it."

That afternoon, we got seriously drunk and by tea time we had spent all our money. Leaving the *Malcolm*, we sang RAF ditties and stumbled back towards camp, but lost our way. Instead of winding up at the gates of the aerodrome, we came upon an urban stable.

Dave suggested, "Let's have a peek inside."

"All right," Sid and I both reluctantly agreed.

"We might be able to purloin some horses."

"Steady on, Dave," I said.

"What? You don't fancy a ride back to base? The women will go wild seeing you on a stallion. You'll look quite gallant."

"I'll look a right tosser, you mean, I responded."

It took the three of us to open the stable door because we were pissed and uncoordinated. Light filtered into the barn and suddenly, I heard the sound of horses snorting and hooves clawing at their stalls. The stable was in immaculate condition. The floor was swept clean of debris. Dung was heaped in orderly piles ready to be collected and used as fertilizer.

"It's bloody marvellous," I said to my mates. "The Jerries are so fucking clean. Look at this place. It's neater than a lot of flops I've kipped in back home. Even the horse shit looks like it has been polished."

Sid agreed and added, "They're a sanitary lot, but dirty buggers when it comes to war. Remember how they left Holland? They didn't even bother to switch off the lights or close the door behind them."

While Sid and I talked, Dave walked up to a brown quarter horse and began to stroke his mane. "Now there's a good lad."

"Where did you learn that?" I asked.

"My Granddad had a patch of land where he kept an old horse. I think he fancied himself a gentleman farmer with that old nag. Be a sport, Harry, and play waiter," Dave said, while stroking the horse's flanks. "They all look in need of a good tuck in."

"What bout uz?" asked Sid. "We haven't eaten since lunch."

I fetched three buckets of oats for the horses. I handed them out to my friends. I brought mine over to a white mare that seemed anxious and famished. The horse stuck her mouth into the bucket and chomped on the fodder.

"Pity there's no bridle around," said Dave.

Idiotically, I pointed to the wall where bridle and bits were hanging. Below the riding gear there should have been a written warning: *"A horse, especially a German horse may not appreciate a foreign occupier as its master."*

Dave grabbed the equipment from the wall and expertly prepared the horses and calmed them by speaking gently as if they were his children. He led two of them by their reins out of the stable and told me to do the same with the other horse.

I protested, "Look, Dave, I am not Nanette, the bareback rider of *Barnum and Bailey* fame. How am I supposed to get up on that beast without stirrups?"

Sid agreed, "We're just playing silly buggers, let's get back to camp for tea."

"I've never ridden a horse," I screamed. "We were so bloody poor as kids, Mam couldn't even afford to have me dragged on a pony down the beach at some derelict English seaside town."

"Steady on, old chums," Dave said. "It will be no problem getting you lads up and down. Follow me and mind the fresh turds."

We tagged behind and I muttered, "Dave, since you are so good with horses, perhaps you can get Hans to stop farting. He's got more wind than the base padre."

Dave tethered off his horse and took mine and Sid's to a firm pile of bricks stacked neatly in the courtyard. "Climb up onto that load of bricks. You can mount your horse from there. It will be like getting into bed."

"What about when we are done?" Sid asked.

"For Christ's sake," said Dave. "Can't you lads be a bit more sporting? When we are done, we'll go back to the bricks and you can jump off from there. It's simple, now hop on."

Reluctantly, I obeyed and Sid followed my lead. I slipped onto the horse like Tarrus Bulba's half-wit brother. The horse held her footing while I nervously climbed on top. Off to the side, I noticed Dave effortlessly leap onto his bareback horse. My horse and Sid's stirred slowly away from the bricks.

"This is not too bad," I said, and Sid nodded his head in agreement.

I was just getting comfortable in my role as horseman when suddenly the horse pricked her ears up. Her head reared up as if she had heard the bugle for the Cheltenham Derby. The horse charged out of the courtyard while I bounced on top of her like an unsecure pogo stick. I looked back and saw Sid's horse charging in my wake. Dave's horse cantered at an even pace behind us.

Dave screamed out to us, "Dig your knees into the horse's flank and pull back on the reins."

"For Christ's sake," I screamed at Dave, "it took me three days to master driving a bloody Leyland lorry and it had a flipping clutch.

Right now, I'm just going to hang on for fucking life."

The three horses raced from the courtyard and out onto a side street. Their hoofs made a heavy thundering noise on the cobblestones. We charged into the town's main square. We skirted parked military vehicles. We dodged slower moving carts propelled by temperate horses, whose passengers looked disoriented by our reckless speed. I was out of breath from screaming at Dave to stop this ride, before the horses bolted towards the heather-strewn fields in the countryside.

The horses circled the town square twice, as if the second time were a victory lap. The horses opened up at full throttle and bolted down a long open street. My stomach churned as if I was on a rough ferry crossing to Zee Bruck. Ahead of me, I heard Dave and Sid crying out with excitement. When I glanced up, they looked as happy as children riding on a merry-go-round in England.

Evidently, the horses knew these streets well and maneuvered them with practiced precision, while I clamoured for Dave to stop this carnival ride gone berserk. Perhaps the animal didn't understand English.

So I screamed at the horse, "Halt, du veruct tier. Stop, you crazy beast."

This mare was indifferent to any language. She only listened to her own internal voice that called on her to charge and gallop faster through the laidback streets of Fuhlsbüttel.

An MP on the roadside blew his whistle at us. He cried out as we rode past him at breakneck speed. "What do you fat heads think you are up to? Stop this business at once!"

If I had any means to reason with Bucephalus, I gladly would have complied, but this horse was its own master. Finally, the horses charged down Langenhorner Chausee and out onto the common near the U-bahn terminal. We sped across the open field and newly dug vegetable patches. In the distance, I even saw Friede standing with her mother on the apartment balcony. I hoped she didn't recognize me, but I was still overjoyed to catch sight of her for a brief and galloping second.

After twenty minutes, the horses tired and slowed their pace. With a snort, they returned to a dull, languid trot and headed back towards the stables. We retraced our meandering way through the back streets of Fuhlsbüttel. Dave, Sid, and I looked like inept conquistadors ill-equipped to even tilt at windmills. Bystanders, who only minutes ago clung to the sidewalks or hid fearfully behind shop doors, now derisively applauded and called out to us while standing on the roadside. "Tommy, bravo Tommy."

"Not exactly Christ's ride into Jerusalem," I called out to the other two.

"Watch out, they may start throwing flowers at our triumphant arrival," Sid responded.

At the entrance to the stable, we were met by the irate stable master. He was a man so cylindrical in shape; he could have doubled as a postal box. Evidently, the stable owner was very comfortable with losing his temper. He upbraided us and called us all manner of curses in German. He gesticulated with his arms. Finally, in utter frustration, he took his cap off and threw it to the ground in disgust at our actions.

Exhausted, I called out to him, "Oi, Fritz, shut your cakehole. Your bloody horses could have killed us with their bleeding antics. So mind yourself, I've got your four-legged friends' number."

Dave said to him, "It was a delight to take your horses for a ride. As a show of good measure for your troubles, take a packet of cigarettes, compliments of the Royal Air Force."

Dave reached into his pocket and produced a packet of Capstans. The German greedily grabbed the cigarette pack. He seemed appeased, so much so in fact, he tried to strike a bargain with Dave that would have given him unlimited horseback rides as long as he could supply a good number of cigarettes to the fat German.

My horse led me back to the pile of bricks, where I weakly

dismounted from the creature. Sid and his horse returned to their own brick pile.

Dave dismounted from his horse as graceful as a ballet dancer and his face looked refreshed and invigorated. Sid and I, however, looked green and bilious.

We swore never to go drinking with Dave again. "It hurts too much," I grumbled.

My testicles felt as if they had been twisted, bent, and crushed beyond repair. My balls had the same sensation as if someone put walnuts into a brown paper bag and bashed them with a hammer. I limped back to camp, cursing my friend and all horses in general. I made a solemn pledge that I would never in my life mount a horse or even a bike again.

15

The Sad-eyed Girl at the Victory

As it does in April, it rained. The rain came down in sheets and at other times like mist, but it was steady and felt like it would never end. At night alone in my quarters, I chain-smoked and watched the rain splatter against my windowpane.

In my sister's monthly letter, she wrote: "*Life in Britain was shite, shite for work, shite for marriages and shite for relations between mothers and daughters.*" She asked how my love affair with Friede was progressing. I replied with a lie and wrote that everything was smashing and my life had never been better.

Friends dropped by my room and asked, "All right?"

I replied, "Aces."

Drinking and carousing deadened my feelings for Friede, dulled my wits, and blunted my nerves, but it was only a temporary relief to the ache. When off duty, I escaped into a world of unfulfilled expectations at the *Victory Dance Club*. Why not, I reasoned, may as well have a bit of fun and get what you give. I thought hanging out in dance halls was a bit like carbolic soap, a strong astringent to scrub love off from my hands like it was muck. Unfortunately, it achieved the opposite and I felt grimier each time I returned from the club. The more I tried to drown my loitering funk with drink, loud music, and conversations with nameless girls, the more my unhappiness stuck to me.

There was a predictable pattern to each of my nights at the *Victory*. Before I headed out, I vigorously shined my boots and boasted to anyone in earshot that the tips reflected the moon's gleam. I kneaded generous amounts of Brylcream into my scalp so that no hair shifted from its brushed position. My pressed uniform snapped to my body and I was ready to join the queue in front of the *Victory*.

No matter the time spent in preening or practicing suave pick up lines, I had little success with the opposite sex at the *Victory*. Not being able to dance and afraid to try, I wasn't able to keep a girl's attention for long. So any woman who joined my table didn't linger for longer than a moment. The Frauleins tapped their feet to the rhythm of the drummer on stage. They fidgeted with the contents of their purse and pretended to hear my wooing words over musicians performing Benny Goodman covers with counterfeit enthusiasm. Normally, the young woman politely finished her drink and said, "Are you sure you don't want to dance?" And I'd respond "Sorry, game leg, from the war, you know."

Embarrassed, she'd smile and promise, "I'll be back shortly."

Within minutes of her departure, I'd see her jitterbugging with an American or another airman from camp. Loneliness and self-pity twitched over my body as I watched them dance. Whisky and water or strong lager quickly numbed my solitude.

Most nights at the *Victory Club* were like that for me: lots of whisky and lots of German girls, who blew me off once they realized I didn't dance and wouldn't buy them a champagne cocktail. It didn't take long for the varnish to thin on my expectations of love or sex at the *Victory Club*. I decided it was a waste of my money and my time to prowl for birds in a club that tried every night to re-create the joy and relief we had found on the day the war ended in Europe.

It was on my last visit to the club, where sobriety was a sin, and prudence a crime, that I met a woman who looked as sad as me. She approached my table and said, "I don't want to dance. I just want to rest my feet. Do you mind?"

Her name was Sonya and she was very beautiful. She claimed she was thirty, but I think she was probably older. I began to date her because it seemed the easiest way to clear Friede out of my head for good. In a strange way I liked Sonya because she was totally disinterested in me, except for my money and the rations I provided her. The woman also had rules for our relationship. It was made clear to me if I wanted to remain her boyfriend; I was to obey her strange whims.

"Whatever, you want, darling; if I can only see you on Tuesdays and Thursday', that is fine by me," I said with much enthusiasm.

Sonya lived in the tony part of Hamburg near the Alster. So I found her requests for generous supplies of cigarettes and tinned coffee unusual, even suspicious. I presumed this well-to-do neighbourhood was insulated from the troubles of total war and rationing.

Outside of kissing and some uncomfortable hand-holding, we were never physical with each other. Sonya didn't want to pursue sex and I didn't push the matter. I tried to get her to come out with me to restaurants or the park, but she refused.

"We can only meet at my home," she said, while taking a packet of coffee from my duffle bag and disappearing with it into another room. "I prefer to spend our time alone," she explained.

It looked like she also favoured to spend her time alone with my Maxwell House coffee because she never offered me anything from her larder, but tepid cups of camomile tea.

While in my company, Sonya generally sat morosely in a wingback chair and stared aimlessly at anything but me. After much silence, she'd asked me to pour her some wine. She didn't even have a gramophone to drown out her heavy sighs.

After a month of visits, I was overcome by curiosity and asked, "What do you do with all the cigarettes and coffee I bring you? You're not trading it for food because you look as thin as a sheet."

"Must you always ask so many questions?" She tried to evade answering my enquiry with another sigh, but I smelled a strong scent of cigarettes coming from her bedroom.

"Why is it that your house always smells of cigarettes even when we're not smoking?"

"I don't know what you mean," she said defensively.

"Do you live alone?" I asked.

"Of course," Sonya replied.

"So there isn't someone in your bedroom taking a fag break?" I asked suspiciously.

She got up from her chair and moved towards the bedroom door as she claimed, "There is no one in there."

"Do you have a cat then who has taken to smoking Kensington's because I distinctly smell a burning cigarette?"

Almost hysterical, Sonya screamed, "You are such a fool and I think it is time you go."

She grabbed my coat and pushed me out the door and asked, "Are we still on for Thursday?"

I yelled back at her, "You're barmy."

"Remember to bring more cigarettes and coffee when you come again," she responded.

I went back to my quarters in Fuhlsbüttel swearing under my breath that I wasn't going to see Sonya anymore. She could go hang. Thursday, however, intervened and I had nothing planned. So I returned to her house and Sonya wasn't surprised by my arrival, despite my harsh words at our last encounter.

"Did you bring the cigarettes and coffee?" she asked anxiously.

"Yes," I said irritably. "Is that all I am to you, a corner shop?"

Sonya responded with little eagerness and purred, "You can sleep with me if you want, I don't mind at all." She began unbuttoning her blouse.

"I don't think you understand me," I said naively. "Sure, I'd like to sleep with you, but not because I gave you cigarettes. We'd have to at least like each other a little or this is just all wrong."

"Have it your way," Sonya said. "If you want to complicate things, go ahead and complicate them. See, now I won't sleep with you; are you happy? But I still need the cigarettes and coffee," she said, while doing back up the buttons on her blouse.

"Hold on," I said, "this is just nuts. What are you saying? Why do you need so many cartons of cigarettes and tins of coffee? I should think you are doing just fine. Look where you live? You obviously come from money and you are exceptionally beautiful, so I don't understand your desperation for black market trading goods? You must still have good connections around town."

Before I was able to finish my sentence, the bedroom door opened. Out came a man wearing a suit two sizes too big for him. He was unshaven and I guessed he was a little younger than Sonya.

"What the hell?" I interjected, standing up and thinking I was about to be robbed.

"Sonya, you better tell him," the man told her. The woman started to cry quietly. The man put his arm around Sonya and comforted her as he spoke to me. "May I call you Harry?" he asked. "I feel as if I already know you."

"Have you been in that room every time I've been here?" I asked.

"I am afraid so."

"What the hell were you doing in there?"

"I am the reason she needs the cigarettes and coffee from you."

"Oh Christ," I said in an irritated voice. I lit a cigarette and blurted out, "You're on the lam and hiding from us."

"Let's just say I have no papers and leave it at that," he said.

Sonya stopped crying and interjected. "Hans is my boyfriend and

384

I love him, but I can't get him a ration book without an ID card. The cigarettes and coffee along with the jewellery I sold were going to help us get out of Hamburg and start a new life somewhere else."

"So you go around to the dance clubs looking for soldiers who will give you extra rations? That is your plan? Fleece soldiers so your boyfriend can eat and live underground, undetected by our military?" I demanded cruelly. "How many boyfriends does it take to keep Hans fed?"

"Several," she replied tearfully.

"Blimey, both of you are real pieces of work. I don't know who is dirtier in this whole sorry business. Hans, you are a real gent letting your woman do all the dirty work so you can stay out of trouble. My advice to you is to turn yourself into the authorities." He was about to answer when I told him, "Forget it, mate, don't tell me. I don't want to know. From this point onwards, I don't want to know anything."

I made my way to the door and Sonya said, "Are you going?"

"Yes."

"Are you ever coming back?"

"Not bloody likely," I responded.

"Please don't tell anyone about us."

I never shopped Sonya and Hans out. I was too ashamed that I had been taken in by sad eyes and a hard-luck story in the most expensive part of Hamburg when I came from the lowest end of Halifax. My discomfort at being Sonya's dupe soon dissipated. I didn't much care for her and I thought I was well enough rid of her and her sad eyes pleading for coffee and fags. I kept the story to myself because I knew if Sid or Dave or anyone else got wind of my stupidity, I would have been base fool for the year.

In May, Sid asked, "What happened to Sonya?"

"She wasn't my type and like you said, there are plenty of fish in the sea," I responded.

"Too right, too right," said Sid. "Fancy a beer?"

385

"No, I am going to Platen un Blomen to see if I can clear my head of bloody women."

I never got to the park. I never got to clear my head of bloody women. Right after, I left the U-bahn station in the downtown core, I saw Friede on the other side of the street.

17

The Girl from the Lampshade Factory

It had been four months since I had last seen Friede. At first, I wasn't sure if it was Friede or my imagination just winding me up. But then a surge like a static electric shock sparked through my body and told me the person across the way was Friede. She walked towards the Dammtor Banhof and one thing was definite: her looks had drastically changed since we last met.

Her hair was tied up at the back in the manner of a factory girl. She was thinner and looked as frail as straw. Friede walked timidly as if she was going into a pool of water with an uncertain current. Everything about her was different, even her clothing. Instead of a fashionable dress, she now wore grubby, worker's overalls covered in dark paint. Friede looked like every other German in the city: beaten, preoccupied, and disillusioned by hunger and a questionable future.

I darted across the road to get to her side of the street and almost collided into a jeep. Until we got to the Dammtor Banhof, I followed at a discreet distance. Inside, Friede struggled towards the U-bahn's platform. As usual, it was hot inside the terminal and packed with factory workers and rubble clearers waiting for their connection to go home. Friede's head was bowed, fixed on the cement as if in contemplation, empty prayer, or just because she was too tired to look at another commuter.

Loudspeakers declared the arrival of another subway train. Above me, the cast iron ceiling vault was still exposed, naked to the elements because glass enclosures were a luxury for a city on its knees. I turned my eyes downwards and away from the pigeons darting through the uncovered steel ribs of the Banhof. I looked towards Friede imprisoned in the crowd and didn't know whether to follow her or let her be and let us be.

I watched her slip anonymously onto a subway car. Impetuously, I thought, *to hell with it, better jump right back into the muck.* At the very last moment, while a train guard whistled the all-clear, I hopped onto her train car.

Friede stood at the far end of the compartment from me. She held onto a vertical metal bar in front of a wooden seat occupied by a thin ragged woman whose mouth was ajar as if rigour mortis had already set in. Friede swayed with the motion of the train, like cargo not completely secured down. By the time we were half-way to Fuhlsbüttel, I had edged my way from one end of the car to the other and now stood right behind her.

There was a strong chemical odour boiling off her clothes. It smelled something like turpentine and copper. Sweat and dirt glistened in her hair and ran down the nape of her neck. I wondered if she turned around, how I was going to explain my reasons for travelling on this train.

Oh hello, fancy meeting you, on the U-bahn, after all this time. I'm brilliant. How about you?

A series of phrases I'd learned from B movies, each one more of a cliché than the last, swirled in my head. I knew if she turned around and asked me to explain myself, quoting Trevor Howard in *Brief Encounter* wasn't going to work on Friede. I worried that she'd be cross with me for following her. *Christ,* I thought, *now I've done it, she will hate me or start a scene. People will stare at me and I will look the proper ass.*

For a moment, I wanted to sneak off the train, disappear into a crowd, and hope she never knew that I'd been running after her. I suppose my thoughts leaked out of me like an ice cube melting on a counter top, because Friede twitched to my presence. She cleared her throat and adjusted her purse. She kept her back to me but spoke. "Harry?"

"Yes."

"I see you still like staring at my back," she said in a whisper.

"No, no," I said in apology, "nothing like that at all. I was just..."

Friede interrupted my insincere apologies. "I think this time, you might beat me in the game we once played."

"What game was that?" I asked, confused.

"Don't you remember? We'd run between train cars and see who got left behind at the station." The lights overhead flickered as our subway ducked into a tunnel.

I said, "Well, I'm not much good at sports. So why don't we call it a draw?"

As we travelled underground, I saw our faces reflected in the window. I smiled, but I think it was more a grimace and hoped she wouldn't notice the difference.

"How've you been?" I asked tentatively in formal German, reserved for strangers and superiors.

"I can tell you one thing for sure; my feet have known happier times because right now, they ache beyond description. As for the rest of me, it wouldn't say no to a decent cup of coffee and a good night's sleep." Friede shifted her feet and brushed her hand against her hair and fell silent.

Was this all that was going to be spoken between us, I wondered.

389

When our train emerged from the tunnel and into daylight, with her back still facing me, she asked,

"And how have you been?"

"Me, I've been all right, busy you know, with work at the base and being out with the mates," I said, lying brazenly and badly. "Mind you, I've missed you some," I added, trying to dismiss my false bravado.

At Olhsdorf, the last stop before Fuhlsbüttel, the train pulled out from the station with a sudden surge. Friede slipped backwards onto me. For the first time in a long while, our bodies touched each other. Quickly, she righted herself and broke away from me like a balloon let out of a child's hand.

Over the clack of rail ties, she said, "I missed you too, Harry, but what's a girl to do?"

We arrived at the Fuhlsbüttel terminal and the door beside her opened up. She said, without looking back, "I will see you later, Harry."

She stepped off the train and into the sunlight and I trailed behind her.

"Can you just stop for a second?" I begged.

"I don't want you to see me like this."

"I don't care."

"Well, I do mind you seeing me like this. If you want to talk to me, come by the little cafe near my mother's apartment, around seven tonight. We can talk then." Friede skirted away and disappeared down a set of stairs that took her to street level.

I rushed back to camp and cleaned myself up for our rendezvous. During my preparations, I don't know whether I hoped for an explanation for her leaving me or a resumption of our love affair. Either way, I felt awkward and raw from our time apart.

I arrived at the cafe early. Friede was late and didn't show until almost half past seven. Although she still looked tired, any traces of her afternoon proletarian demeanour had vanished. She wore a breezy summer dress that was a size too large for her. The necklace I had

390

given to her for her birthday dangled around her neck. Her hair was no longer tied up, but fell luxuriant to her shoulders. I also noticed that her leg ulcers had returned from lack of vitamins. I stood to greet her and said, "You look fantastic."

She touched my cheek lightly and whispered, "Hello."

She smelled of rose water and fresh air, unlike the afternoon when she was covered in industrial grime.

When the waiter arrived, she ordered cake, coffee, and brandy. Friede ate it ravenously and excused herself. "I am sorry. I haven't eaten since lunch at the factory."

"Would you like some more cake?" I asked.

"No, but perhaps I could have some more coffee with a touch of brandy. May I have one of your good cigarettes?"

I lit it for her. "I missed your good manners," she noted and swept some stray strands of hair that had fallen across her face. "No one at the factory or anyone around me has the time for good manners. It is all about getting rations, or getting out of the manager's roving eye."

The brandy came and she said, "You are going to get me drunk."

I smiled and replied, "As long as I can get drunk with you."

Friede sighed. "If only that were possible but five o'clock comes early and it is brutal work. I think it would kill me if I had to do a shift hung-over."

I thought this was almost like old times. Yet when I looked into her eyes, I understood a lot had changed between us. We were now separated by the culture of victory and defeat. No one was spared, except those with connections to officials who could offer employment deferrals.

Friede noticed my meditation and said, "Go on then." "You want to know about my new life and how horrible it is, so please, ask me."

I hesitated for a second and said, "I don't know if I want to find out what you've been up to."

"Come on," she urged me. "You were always so curious about my

391

life during the war. You may as well know what my life is like in post-war Hamburg, post-Harry."

So over the next hour and a bit, she told me about her new life as a factory worker for a questionable industrialist.

"It is ironic," she said, "but my factory is near the docklands. It is not too far from Uncle Henry's old office; where he used to do all of his big tobacco deals during the war."

The factory where Friede worked wasn't as grand as Uncle Henry's office block. It was a single-story building that had somehow survived the bombing and was used as it had been under the Nazis, for light industrial assembly and storage.

"I will never understand," she said contemptuously, "how the British dropped so many bombs on this city and missed blowing up this factory. It isn't even a real factory; after all, we only assemble ugly lampshades, not Volkswagens."

Her factory, Friede explained, was licensed by the German civilian authorities to assemble lampshades for commercial sale.

"I don't even know if some other part of this company makes the actual lamps for the shades. Anyway, the owner doesn't give a damn because he is well taken care of by the British."

I sipped on my drink and said, "I don't see how the Brits are interested in some small-time company."

"Harry," she said without malice, "you are sometimes such an innocent. The British think that businessmen like him keep young Germans occupied and out of trouble with mindless tasks. Hard work for rotten wages, they believe, will keep us from grumbling about our pitiful rations and living conditions. No one can riot in the streets if they are forced by law to work in factories run by corrupt capitalists. I am also sure that some of the Brits are even getting large gifts from these industrialists as a thank you for all of the start up money wasted on murky businessmen."

According to Friede, the owner of her factory was given sacks of cash by the occupational government to form his company. Apparently, money was always available no matter how stupid or unprofitable the businesses as long as the owners were on sufficient good terms with the British.

Stabbing at her cake with a fork, Fried continued. "To get money from the British, the spivs make sure their shoes don't smell of Nazism. The owner," Friede added sarcastically, "Herr I-am-a-big-shot-now, once came out onto our factory floor. He gave us girls a speech about how his company was rebuilding Hamburg." The factory owner said he had lost his old business under the Nazis. "It was some sob story or another about how his loss was our gain because we are now part of this great enterprise to make lampshades." She laughed and continued. "I am sorry he lost his business under Hitler, but does that make it right that our weekly wages barely pay for a loaf of bread?"

Friede admitted she didn't know or care much about her employer's life or his problems with the Nazis. It was black and white for her because she was certain that her boss was out to line his own pockets. In Friede's description, the factory owner believed that cronyism and democracy were identical and that his stealing from the purse of Britain and dead victims of Hitler wasn't only justified, it was progress. Friede thought the industrialist was going to grift his way to a nice house in Switzerland.

"Harry, this I can promise you; he is not going to thank Britain or Germany for his good fortune."

"I am sure some of these new businesses are on the up and up," I said, with not much conviction.

"Of course there are honest men in Hamburg," Friede responded, "but they are hard to find even in daylight."

These new German capitalists, according to her, were all in on the deal to profit from the chaos around them. "They are all hacks and friends of the civilian government," she said, lighting another cigarette. Friede got a little drunk and started to giggle after her third brandy.

"Where I work, I call it a sweat shop rather than a factory."

Friede described her working day, which did sound pretty horrible and pointless. Wire frames were sheathed with a canvass covering. Paint was applied and then Friede had to coat the fabric with asbestos as a fire retardant.

"The dust gets in my eyes and in my mouth and I cough up horrible things after a day at work. Do you see now, Harry, what it is like in Germany without connections? Our great Hamburg labour council could care less about me; I am just a worker for a corrupt factory owner that manufactures lampshades. Our city doesn't need more light to see they are hungry. It's crazy, we can't even make lampshades in different colours. All of ours are the same bloody colour: hideous green," she said in despair. "In five years, everyone in Hamburg is going to have an ugly green lampshade. Maybe in Bremen they are making red lampshades and in Frankfurt yellow," she said sarcastically.

She finished speaking and played with the remnants of her cake. Friede looked away from me and told me, "I always feel so tired and useless now."

The hurt, anger, and self-pity I'd endured when Friede left me simmered away like margarine on a skillet. I knew I hadn't stopped loving her, but I also felt helpless holding onto that love.

Her experiences over the last several months left me hollow because they led me back to the hopelessness of my childhood. It was something I knew since I was weaned off my mother's breast: whether the love is strong or weak, it cannot survive hunger, it cannot endure the immutable harshness that life showers upon individuals too poor to have connections or luck. For the destitute, death is the only intervention that ends despair.

At twenty-three, I finally understood that this was how my father must have suffered when he couldn't feed his children in the Great Depression and faded out of our lives. I wasn't sure what I could do for Friede. What was I going to offer her, words? I didn't want to abandon her to handling dangerous chemicals for pennies a week. But I was just a radio operator, a cavalier switchboard receptionist. I was just a young man who knew right from wrong. But I was no match against black marketers and dodgy industrialists. Naively, that night, I offered her hope. It was a life line that was sure to snap when faced with the morning's cold reality.

"Give me the address of this factory. Tomorrow I will meet you there for lunch and get you discharged from that miserable place."

Friede laughed and said, "It will never happen. This is beyond you."

"If I do this, can we see each other again?" I asked.

She touched my hand. "I don't think you can do anything for me, Harry. But you can try. Don't worry if you fail because I still have many feelings for you."

"I love you," I said impetuously. "It hurts, God damn it, when you're not around me, when you left me."

"Harry, I never stopped loving you, but I learned from my mother that you can't live off love. Now I must go," she said and on a piece of paper she wrote down the factory's address for me.

"If you really want to try and help me, meet me at the front of the building at 12:30. It is when we take our lunch break."

"Who should I talk to at the factory?"

"It won't be the owner because he is out spending his money. His toady is a man named Papp. He is a pig who is always trying to touch the girls' bottoms." Friede let go of my hand and added, "I'll see you tomorrow." She walked out of the cafe without looking back.

I settled the bill and returned to camp. That evening, I worked out a plan to free Friede from her dangerous factory job.

17

The Rathaus; Where Dreams are painted the Colour of Money

The following morning, I asked my mates Sid and Dave to come with me to the plant. I needed them to help set Friede free from her hazardous job at the lampshade Fabriken Haus.

"Who do you think we are the three bleeding musketeers?" asked Sid.

"More like the Marx Brothers," responded Dave.

"Right," said Sid in a conspiratorial voice. "Since there's nothing more exciting to do today than break a few laws and probably a few heads, I'm all for busting your bird out from the evil German's factory. So we may as well get on with it," he concluded. "I've got one question, before we go. If we do liberate Friede, you owe me big. Can you can get her friend Gerda to go out with me."

"I'll see what I can do."

Dave said, "Don't bother to get me a German lass, you can just get me a pint and we're square."

"What about getting us a jeep from the motor pool?" I asked.

"That will be two pints," he replied.

We set out for the factory just before noon. Dave drove, I rode shotgun, and Sid lounged in the back like a pasha out for a trip around his domain. When we pulled out of the camp gates, Dave asked, "So what's your plan?"

"I've got none except for you guys to look tough and I'll try to bribe her manager."

"It'll never bloody work," they both said.

"Say, Harry," Dave started, "once you bust Friede out of the lampshade factory, what are you going to do then? You still can't marry her. The law says you can't bring any Frauleins home to England. Anything you take from Germany has got to fit in yer kit bag."

"I know, I know," I said. "It's a real bugger. But I've heard the labour government is thinking of changing the law."

"At least Prime Minister Atlee is not a shit like Churchill," said Sid.

"What do ya mean?" Dave responded sarcastically. "Winston got me this plum job."

"That's what I'm talking about," said Sid. "Winnie thought we was all right when we fought them on the beaches. It was when we wanted to make love to them by Brighton Rock his gang said no bloody way."

I agreed. "With the Tories, it's right, lads, tea break's over; you've done yer part and beat Hitler. Shut yer gob. Get back to Britain and get back to work at end of bloody shovel."

"Go on," Dave said skeptically, "where did you hear this news about his nibs letting us marry foreigners."

"I got it from one of the officers on base. I was on shift at the telephone exchange when I placed his call to some other muck in Lubeck. I left the line open by mistake and got to hear an earful. He told his mate that parliament is going to change the law prohibiting soldiers marrying foreign nationals."

"I guess too many blokes were putting girls up the spout or falling in love with exotic beauties from Belgium and France," Sid added.

"Don't know and it doesn't matter," I responded. "They can be up the Khyber, but it's not the trump card for getting the marriage approved. The couple has to demonstrate a mutual affection for each other and the proposed Missus can't be a security risk to the nation."

"If those conditions were applied to couples wanting to get hitched in Nottingham, no one would be married," said Dave. "Starting a month before marriage, everyone begins to hate each other."

"Till death do them part," replied Sid.

"Anyways," I continued, "the officers weren't too happy about it. The new law includes all serving personnel, not just NCOs and officers, but enlisted men as well."

"Makes 'em think they got rights or something," Sid screamed from the back seat of the jeep.

"That's all right for you then, Harry," Dave said, after blasting his horn as we passed a slow moving horse-drawn carriage.

"Maybe," I responded. "These officers were really browned off and said that *"Blighty already had enough wogs but to add Germans into the mix was going to turn the island into a mongrel's paradise."*

When we arrived at Friede's workplace, Dave parked the jeep by its front entrance. The factory was sandwiched between two destroyed buildings. Out front, I saw Friede and her co-workers dressed in smocks looking dusty and grey.

Sid said, "Jesus wept, Harry, they look a sad lot. Maybe after tea we can bust some waifs out of a match factory."

"It's the orphans next, Sid," I answered. "Remember to get your priorities straight." I jumped out of the jeep and my two friends followed suit.

I walked up to Friede, but she gave me a cold look as if to tell me not to be too familiar with her while there were other workers around.

Hastily, she said, "Our break is almost over. I was afraid that last night was just a dream and you were not coming. I have to go back inside now. Wait outside until all the girls have gone back to work and then you can talk to Papp, my manager." I nodded my head in agreement.

Friede said, "I don't think anything good will happen, but I will cross my fingers for luck anyway." Friede slunk back into the factory with her fellow workers.

"What's the story?" asked Dave.

"Give them a couple of minutes," I responded.

"Then what?" asked Sid.

"We charge in and see if her manager will take my bribe and let her go."

"He'd be a block-head not to take the coffee," said Sid.

"As long as we don't end up in the glass house, Harry," Dave warned. "Do what you must, but try to keep us out of lock up."

A sign was posted on the factory's front door that read in German: *Unauthorized personnel are forbidden to enter.* "What does it say?" Dave asked.

"It says welcome." I pushed open the heavy fire door and we walked inside to discover a nineteenth century work shop. This netherworld was miserly lit from distant sunlight that shone through several broken windows located near the ceiling. A fog of dust and paint drifted like a chemical apparition around the structure. Some of it clung to my uniform while the rest sunk to the cement floor. I noticed that my polished black boots were prematurely greyed from particles scattered on the ground. There was a strong chemical odour that burned my nostrils and made my eyes water. "Fuck," I said to no one in particular.

"Oi," Sid said, "look around. It's only birds working in this factory."

He was right. There were about thirty females labouring in the building. Their work area was divided up into various stations of assembly. On one long table, eight women stretched fabric across flimsy wire frames. At another table, women painted the lamp shades a green hue that resembled algae growth on a dead pond.

It was at the final and must dangerous work station where Friede and several other girls earned their meager wages. With thin paint brushes, they applied a noxious asbestos fire retardant resin to the one-size-fits-all lampshades. Inside the building, the air was so polluted that the women hacked and spat bits of paint and the chemical residue onto the floor. This wasn't a factory; it was a workhouse run with the cruel inefficiency of Oliver's Twist's orphanage. It was a business enterprise with one motivation: to profit through exploitation and substandard working conditions. There was nothing here that redeemed either the owner or the workers; it was pure and simple slavery.

At the far end of the factory floor, I saw Friede. She was dragging a heavy sack over to her work table. The bag was ripped and its contents sprayed into the air like feathers and landed in her hair and across her face. "This is a fucking nightmare," I hollered.

My two friends agreed and said, "Go get the bastard, Harry."

Friede looked towards me and pointed to an office door; it was her manager Papp's lair.

With Sid and Dave in tow, I marched over to her overseer's room and barged into the office without knocking. Inside, Herr Papp sat behind a desk, smoking a cigarette and reading a newspaper. He was about forty with cauliflower ears, a close-cropped haircut and small colourless eyes. His face was lost in the eclipse of a five o'clock shadow. His grubby features aptly reflected his inner grime.

"Papp," I hollered. He wasn't startled when he looked up at us crowded into his room. He seemed to expect this treatment by others who were in power.

"What?" he grumbled.

"I need you to release one of your workers from her contract with this company."

He laughed and demanded, "Under whose authority?"

"Mine," I said.

He laughed even louder. "Who the fuck are you?" he asked with incredulity.

Dave screamed, "Please, let me hit him Harry."

"No, you can't," I said and then yelled out to the manager, "Herr,

Papp, your company is unfairly treating its workers. I demand that this cease immediately. I also request that one of your workers is released from their contract with this company."

Papp got up from his desk and moved towards me, his cigarette hanging from his lip like a birth mark. He stood in front of me, smoke pouring from his homemade fag.

"What is this to you?" he asked, and then angrily demanded, "Where are your orders?"

"I've got none," I said.

"Then you are wasting my time. No papers, no worker, fuck off."

"I have coffee," I said.

Papp pulled the wet, yellow cigarette stump from his mouth and began to contemplate the offer. "How much coffee do you have?"

"Two kilos; that can buy you a lot of stuff on the black market," I told him.

"That is a great deal of coffee," he noted greedily as if considering the trade.

With more friendliness in my voice, I said, "Come on, one worker for two kilos of coffee. That is a fair trade and it's not going to harm your operation. You would never miss one girl, would you?"

Papp laughed like a man who has just seen a child stumble from their bike. "Me, I wouldn't miss any of these bitches if they fell off the edge of the world. "But," he added, "the big man who owns this Fabriken Haus might have something to say about it. Especially since those cows out on the floor make him money. The boss likes money and he counts his gelt every day. My chief knows what he is worth down to the last pfennig and he's not going to be cheated out of anything that is his."

Papp walked past us and opened up his door. He pointed towards the factory floor outside. He said, "Take a look around; the government pays my boss to make those bitches work. He's paid handsomely for the shit those girls make in this factory. One less girl is one less lampshade being produced, which is like stealing a mark from the boss's wallet. Verstehen?"

"Who's your fucking boss, the Cyclops in *Ulysses*?" I asked.

"Go away," said Papp, returning to his desk.

"I'm not going anywhere," I said with irritation.

"Look, English man, you are nobody. So fuck off and get out of my office before I call the military police."

I would have lunged at him, but Sid jumped in my way and told me, "Time to leave, we'll cook this square head's goose another day and wipe the smile off his flipping mug."

My two friends dragged me out of the office while I screamed, "I'll be back, you bastard."

As we left the factory, Friede stuck her head up from her work bench and gave me a sad and resigned look.

When we returned to the jeep, Dave said, "Well, that's it then. We may as well head back to camp. Sorry, Harry, better luck next time."

On our way back to camp, I sat in the front seat of the jeep sullen and angry. I felt I caused Friede more harm by returning back into her life than if I had just left her alone. Dave drove through Hamburg's downtown core.

"Why are you going this way?" I groaned.

"Just trying to cheer you up, it's a longer way home, but maybe we can think of a way of getting your Friede out of that hellhole."

"Let's just get back to base," I said forlornly.

My mind was drowned in anger and self-pity. My thoughts didn't clear until we drove by Hamburg's Rathaus, their seat of civic government.

"Hold on," I said, "I have an idea." I would plead my case to the city's Burgermeister to release Friede from her indentured employment. My friends weren't too pleased with this new scheme.

"Harry, we're all going to be on charges," Dave said.

"Why are you going to involve the bleeding mayor?" Sid asked.

"The mayor helped enact this new work regulation with the occupation authorities. Maybe he can change it for one of his citizens if I plead with him. I'll keep you two out of it. Don't worry," I told them.

Dave let me out of the jeep at the front of the municipal building. Before they drove off, I added, "I'll catch up with you later. If anybody asks me about today, I'll say I was alone. So no worries, mates, I'll keep stum. If it's my head, it's my head, but you two aren't going to end up in stir."

The jeep drove off. I walked nervously towards the Rathaus. It was built in a neo-renaissance style to reflect the power, wealth, and the influence of the town burgers, the shipping magnates, and the community's rich bankers and brokers. It was an impressive edifice and any Venetian Doge would have gladly taken it as his palace.

When I walked through the portico, I was overcome by the building's opulence in contrast to the factory's squalor. Inside these walls, bureaucrats and patricians played out games of power, influence, and double dealing, on a Herculean scale. It was here and at British HQ that the lives of millions of Germans were settled over a handshake or a cigarette and sometimes just a wink and a nod.

I grew unsettled as I walked across the immense Italian marble floors and felt dwarfed by destiny. Papp was right. I was nobody. Unnerved, I was still determined not to show it. I marched towards a reception desk like I was an air commodore. I approached the counter where a pretty blonde secretary looked up and smiled at me. She asked the nature of my business, in English.

Without hesitating, I replied, "I am here to see the Burgermeister: my name is Harry Smith."

She looked down at an appointment book and replied in a friendly tone of voice, "Burgermeister Peterson is expecting you."

"Expecting me?" I said with some hesitation.

"Yes, you are on the list of approved visitors," she replied, reading from the appointment book. "Here it is: H.Smith, from Flensburg. You are a bit early but that is all right, the Burgermeister can see you now."

Considering that there was another Smith on his way to see the mayor, I thought it was best to get to him as quickly as possible and get out of this government building before being arrested. The secretary asked if I knew my way around the building and I replied that I didn't.

She left her desk and said, "Follow me."

I was led up an elegant marble staircase to the second floor, which housed the offices for the civilian government functionaries. The corridor to the mayor's office was long and paneled in heavy oak. The floors echoed from the sound of my boots and the secretary's shoes clapping against their polished surface. Carved busts of former senators and statesmen stuck on pedestals glared at me in stony silence. The secretary looked at me and asked, "Is this your first time here?"

"Yes."

"Did you know that the Rathaus is bigger than your Buckingham Palace?"

"No," I replied, "and I can assure you that it is definitely not my palace."

The secretary laughed and said, "We have arrived." She knocked on an ornate double door and escorted me inside. Behind a mahogany desk sat Rudolph Peterson, former shipping magnate, exile from Hitler's Germany, and now the British-appointed civilian leader of Hamburg.

At the moment the secretary announced me, Peterson got up from his leather chair and crossed over to greet me with a handshake. He dismissed the secretary and said, "I think Trudy has confused you with someone else I was expecting."

"Yes. I am sorry for the mix up."

"Do you have business with me?" he asked kindly.

"I believe I do."

404

"Well then, please have a seat. My office is always open to the RAF."

The mayor first began by asking me where I was stationed and where I came from in Britain.

When I told him I was from Yorkshire, his eyes lit up like a birthday candle.

"I know the moors very well and spent many a happy time there. You are very lucky to have been born in such a beautiful spot," he said.

"Yes, it is beautiful," I agreed. It was a lie, but this wasn't the time to disagree and say that for the poor, the moors and the mill towns were a miserable place to be born and die.

"Well, what brings you to see me?" he enquired.

I told Peterson about my relationship with Friede and how we had been dating since 1945. I explained to him that his mandatory work edict had landed her in an unspeakably horrible factory.

He interrupted my story and asked for the name of the company and its address, which he wrote down in a notebook on his desk. Peterson told me, "The work program has been very successful, it has helped businesses rebuild and assisted Hamburg in getting back on her feet. You have seen the suffering in the city, there is no other way to rebuild our country and transform our nation into a democratic state, but through sacrifice and hard work."

"This is not in dispute," I said, "and it is not my business to find fault with your government. I am asking that you release my girlfriend from a dodgy operation that is only benefiting a corrupt factory owner."

"So, what will she do to eat if she is released from this work order?"

Confidently, I said, "I'm going to marry her."

Peterson retorted, "You know that is not possible at the moment."

Smiling, I told him, "You are probably more aware than me, but that law is being changed."

The mayor nodded and I continued, "I give you my word as an Englishman that I will provide for this woman and her family from this time forward. For this city to arise from the ashes; it needs not only capital and brawn, it needs hope. It needs people to trust each other again. I love this woman and she loves me. The burden is mine and mine alone," I concluded, without understanding the gravity of my pledge.

Peterson tapped his finger on his desk for several moments. He asked me to stand outside his office while he concluded some business.

I excused myself and went outside to stand in the company of statues that glorified an extinct city and nation smothered in the corruption of Nazism and post-war politics. After twenty minutes, the Burgermeister opened his door and asked me to step inside and return to my seat.

"Herr Smith, I think you are a good man if somewhat idealistic. What you have said to me might be true, but most would ask the question: what is the cost for love and devotion in this new world? I don't know if you will be able to afford the price of your dedication to this romanticism. I hope you can and I will throw a penny into your hat to aid your cause. I have ordered your girlfriend to be released today from her work at that factory. She will face no penalties. However," he said sternly, "she is now your responsibility. I trust I have made the right decision."

"Yes you have," I said, thanking him profoundly. When I left, I turned to the mayor and asked him about the factory and the other women working there.

Peterson interrupted me. "That is a different matter all together. I make no promises, but I will see if they can be helped. Good day and good luck, Herr Smith."

18

Closing the Ring

On July 31, 1946, The House of Lords struck down the marriage ban between British servicemen and ex-enemy nationals. I don't know if it was by design or omission, but the government didn't go out of its way to trumpet the right of servicemen to marry nationals from former belligerent countries. In fact, the news didn't reach me until mid-August, when I read an old copy of the *Daily Mail*. The announcement, momentous to me, was buried in its back pages between advertisements for hair tonic and football scores. The newspaper report made it official; I was free to marry Friede. Perhaps my life was to end on a happier note than predicted in dismal West Yorkshire.

I didn't rush out to buy Friede an engagement ring or confess to her this wonderful change of events. I was mindful that my enthusiasm was easily crushed by Friede's pragmatism. It was better to wait for a moment when we were alone and thoughtful. It was several days after I had read the news that I suggested we go to the *Malcolm Club*.

There we sat and drank wine on their outdoor deck into the late afternoon. It was a humid and lazy day and the sun danced through the leaves of the trees surrounding the club. Swans and ducks floated leisurely on the artificial lake adjacent to the *Malcolm*. So that we could be alone, I invited her to go out on to the water in a canoe with me.

There was no better place, I thought, to bring her the news that we were free to marry than on these calm and cool, flat waters, during a hot summer's afternoon. I dug my oar into the sluggish reservoir and navigated us from the shore that rippled with laughter from couples enjoying a drink on the club's patio. Friede reclined at the bow, and her right hand skimmed the top of the water. She was has half-asleep from the wine we drank earlier on.

"Luv," I asked, "where are you?"

Friede smiled and said, "Here, as always, with you in a canoe. I will always be with you in this canoe at three o'clock in the summer time and the wine shall always be crisp and cool to my mouth."

"We can be together like this forever," I told her.

She giggled and responded, "Your arms would get tired if you had to paddle for an eternity." Friede's head was tilted towards the water. "Forever for us must be the stray bits of time we are allowed to spend with each other. It can be nothing more than that."

"No, I mean it," I said. "I have wonderful news; the government has lifted its ban on marriage to Germans. We can get married."

Friede raised her hand from the water and dropped it back into the lake. She scooped water with the cup of her hand and splashed me, until liquid beads ran down my shirt.

"Really?" she asked incredulously. "So are you proposing?"

I laughed and said, "Naturally, as I have wanted to since the day we met. Will you marry me, Elfriede Gisela Edelmann, and be my wife until we set like the sun?"

She scrambled over to my side of the canoe and almost tipped us into the lake. At first, she didn't say yes or no. Instead, Friede kissed me and replied, "We have much to discuss."

What was there to discuss, I wondered. Marriage for my kind

was simple, a trip to the registry office, a lunch at the pub, and the following morning back to the pits or to the mills to punch the clock until retirement.

"You need to find out what we must do to get married. It may not be as simple as you think," she said suspiciously.

"But you will marry me?" I asked.

Friede touched my face with her hand and answered, "First, let's find out if it can be done. After that, you can take me in your canoe until the sun sets on our lives."

So I did as Friede requested and spoke with my wing commander to make sure we weren't tumbling into an ocean of regret.

My dealings with Group Captain Cox before my request for marriage were few, but he was agreeable to me marrying a German. "You'll be the first under my command who has taken the plunge," he said. "However, it is a not as simple as a marriage back in your home county."

He told me it was going to take as long as a year to get the necessary permission to marry from the RAF and the British government. The wing commander asked me to return in a week so he could gather the paperwork required to proceed with my request.

I wasn't put off by the seemingly endless time it would take to arrange my marriage to Friede. Actually, I welcomed it and hoped it was going to give me enough opportunity to get used to my new responsibilities. I had no happy examples from my life in Britain on how one succeeded in marriage. My only navigational guides were books, the cinema, and my instincts to not repeat the sins of my parents to surrender to poverty and hopelessness. The following week, I returned to the wing commander's office; he handed me a series of forms and requisitions.

Looking serious, he said, "The onus is on your fiancée to be like Cesar's wife, above reproach."

It was explained to me that Friede had to first undergo some very intimate medical tests to determine if she was pregnant, suffering from any venereal diseases, or just medically unsound for Britain. If she passed the medical exams, the police were to examine her for political or criminal activity that would invalidate her for marriage to a British subject.

Cox took out a cigarette, lit it, and told me. "As this is the first foreign national marriage under my command, don't cock it up for me or the squadron. Any sign of trouble, please abort your mission because all prying eyes from HQ are watching you, me, and this airbase."

After I was dismissed, I went straight to cook in charge of the officer's mess hall. I wanted to get an extravagant wine, usually reserved for the officer's club to celebrate my new status.

He wiped his hands on his greasy apron and declared, "I got just thing for two love birds who want to celebrate." He went to the locked wine cabinet and produced two bottles of Bollinger's 1938 champagne.

"How much is it?" I asked.

"It's a fiver for you because I've got a soft heart for love."

I thanked him and tucked them away in my haversack. I left the camp and went to meet Friede on Hamburg's High Street Jungfern Steig. It was several blocks north of the train station. The expansive boulevard overlooked a small reservoir flowing in from the Alster River. The lake was filled with tiny sail boats navigating around a Baroque water fountain positioned in the middle of the reservoir.

The war had not destroyed the street; its shops and restaurants were still intact. They did a bustling business with the families of old wealth and the nouveau riche. Jungfern Steig was inoculated against ration-book sadness and the despair of rootless refugees because the shoppers on this street knew their happiness was assured and as predictable as the fresh cream on their sacher tort. They were the ones whose wealth and cynicism protected them while under fascism and now under occupation.

Friede and I had arranged to meet on the street on a bench by the

410

water. There, I explained my meeting with the group captain and the paper journey we would have to take to get married.

Friede shrugged her shoulders and calmly said, "So be it. Now don't you think it is time you bought me an engagement ring?"

"I couldn't agree more," I replied.

"I want something nice and simple, nothing extravagant," she said as we left the bench to walk to a jewellery store.

I wondered why we couldn't get the ring on the black market. Friede, however, was adamant that buying an engagement ring from the black market would invite bad luck to our upcoming marriage.

"We can't profit on the misery of others and hope to live happily ever after. Simple is better," she said "especially when it doesn't come wrapped around with someone else's sorrow."

When we were in the jewellery store, Friede allowed me to act as if I knew what I was doing. I looked through the glass counter that held all types of diamond rings. I scanned my finger down the case, like a boy trying to choose a treat from a sweet shop.

Finally, she cleared her throat and said, "What do you think about that one?"

She pointed to a ring tucked away to the side. The sales woman let me hold it. I looked at it with the keen eye of twenty-three–year-old unaccustomed to jewellery, to rings, and to testaments of everlasting love. Simplicity was its virtue. It was a simple band of gold, with five diamond chips studded around it. It didn't trumpet wealth, glamour, or bad manners; it made a simple statement: beauty need only be devotion and trust in good or bad times.

Hesitantly, I asked, "Is that what you would like?"

Friede nodded approvingly. She hastily left the store so I could purchase the ring.

Outside, she grabbed my arm and said, "Take me to the Botanical Park. You can put the ring on my finger there."

So beneath a bow of beech trees, I knelt and asked her to marry me. When she said yes, I slipped the engagement ring on her finger. She kissed me and said excitedly, "Now let's go tell Mutti."

It was late when we arrived at her mother's apartment and Maria Edelmann was cleaning up the dishes from her evening meal. "Tardy once more for dinner," she noted in a half-hearted tone of disapproval. "You didn't miss much," she added with a sigh. "It was potato soup again."

When Friede waved her hand under her mother's nose and displayed the ring, her mother's stern manner disappeared. Maria Edelmann embraced her daughter and kissed her affectionately.

"So you are to be married. This is a wonderful and happy end after we have suffered so much through the war and through the peace," she exclaimed.

I produced the Bollinger's and Friede's mother looked over the bottle of pre-war French champagne. "At least in this life there is the pleasure of good champagne, a beautiful daughter, and a new son-in-law to take away all of its hurt and anguish."

"Open it quickly," Friede instructed me while Maria Edelmann fetched the Gellersons. I popped the cork and poured the bottle's contents into some champagne flutes. We stood in the kitchen and were toasted by her mother. "To your new life, may it be long, happy, and filled with riches and adventure."

After a while, the Gellersons brought out their phonograph and everyone danced a circumscribed waltz with Friede. When it came to my turn, Friede led and my feet somehow moved with dignity and élan. Outside the apartment, the light dimmed as the late summer's darkness slowly crept over the town.

19

The RAF's Prenuptial Poke and Prod

When September came, the summer retreated behind dark, corpulent skies. Most days were overcast or foggy with pockets of rain. On many nights, water spattered against my bedroom window and thunder barked from low-hanging clouds. Across town during those evenings, Friede kept her mother awake until the early morning hours. Every aspect, detail, and outcome of our wedding ceremony and reception was plotted by Friede and her mother.

Friede believed our union was going to put an end to any questions about her and her mother's illegitimate start in this world. Friede wanted our marriage to extinguish the stigma of being a bastard. Finally, all the shame and humiliation Friede had endured as a child and teenager would vanish by the marriage registrar's signature.

Maria Edelmann cautioned her daughter that the walk to the altar was a long road. It was best to be mindful of the dangers that lay ahead. Friede's mother was a keen observer and victim of life's cruelties, punishments, and trials of patience. Maria knew that unhappiness was often a visitor who called on those who demanded a different destiny than they were allotted at birth.

Friede dismissed her mother's prescience's to me as widow's envy.

"Mutti is just nervous for me because men were happy to share her bed but never her life."

It was mid September when the wing commander's adjutant, Flight Lieutenant Locke, informed me that Friede's medical examination was to take place at Wandsbeg Hospital in Hamburg.

I asked her if she would be all right going alone. Friede laughed and asked, "What can they possibly do to me? German doctors have examined me before without any problems."

Unfortunately, Friede had never experienced the cold hands of a disgruntled British army doctor. From the moment she entered the hospital; Friede was treated like live stock, with possible hoof and mouth infection. Her reception wasn't surprising considering the hospital wing was designated for British personnel; a German who was neither a cleaner nor a cook in that section of hospital was regarded as something close to a contagion.

The admitting nurse, fearing that her comprehension of English was insufficient, yelled instructions at Friede. It was hard to find fault with the nurse because she followed a simple rule that our island had employed for centuries: English was best digested by foreigners in a blustering tone. Friede was rewarded with less dignity and more intrusion than a new recruit would receive during an RAF medical inspection.

They took Friede to a cold room in the hospital's basement. She was interrogated by an obese GP from Putney. He noted on Friede's medical files her age, her hair and eye colour, that she had all her teeth. In between chain-smoking cigarettes, the doctor asked about her family's medical history. Were there any idiots or enfeebled relatives, any genetic defects from madness to mental retardation in her background?

Friede answered his questions with a polite yes or a no. She wanted no dubious shade of doubt to colour his assessment. The doctor continued his questions and discovered that Friede was illegitimate.

He told her that it was his opinion that Germany was a country loose in morals.

After the oral interview was complete, the fat GP from Putney ordered Friede to disrobe. A matron who must have learned her nursing skills in Broadmoor prison assisted him in the examination. Friede was probed like she was the elephant man.

She was palpated, weighed and measured while the doctor coughed phlegmatically. Blood samples were taken, followed by urine and stool samples. Friede was x-rayed and inspected for TB. Her day ended with a painful and humiliating rough inspection of her sexual organs. During the gynaecological examination, the overweight doctor quizzed Friede about her sexual encounters. He asked Friede when she became sexually active. He asked her how many sexual partners she had in her life. Mortified, she told the doctor that it was irrelevant as it was evident that she was healthy and free of any disease.

The GP insisted on the necessity of compliance. It was impossible otherwise for him to complete the examination or for her to be allowed to marry. Defeated, she answered each question in a monotone voice and her responses were written down by the assisting matron.

When the ordeal was over, Friede related to me that she didn't know what the doctor disliked most: women, sex, or just Germans.

Friede told me that when the medical inquisition ended, the physician bestowed upon her one last insult. He bid her goodbye while he lit a cigarette from the dying embers of his last one and said, "Not for me to say, but I think it is just bloody wrong for you to be allowed to marry one of our kind. Your lot are nothing but bloody Nazis, good day, madam."

Friede left the hospital and returned home where she cried in her mother's arms, declaring "It was just horrible, unspeakable, and barbaric."

The results from her medical examination were sent to RAF HQ Germany where they remained for weeks. Finally, a clerk dispatched them by sea to a non-descript office in London. There, an unknown cipher would decide whether Friede was chaste and healthy enough to marry the son of a coal miner.

While we waited nervously for the results of Friede's medical examination, the first stage of the Nuremberg War Crime Trials concluded. The outcome wasn't surprising considering the overwhelming evidence against the accused. The Nazi architects who orchestrated the war, the holocaust and the systematic looting of the occupied countries were found guilty. Out of the twenty-one defendants in history's first trial for crimes against humanity; eleven of them were condemned to death.

Hang them quickly, I thought, *it's time to get on with it and be done with this evil past*. Around camp, there was little talk about a former foreign minister and some field marshals who sat uncomfortably in their cells awaiting the hangman's call. It was beyond our rank or our comprehension of evil to offer any opinion other than, "'angings too good fer 'em. Drop those dirty Nazi bastards into the sea from a Lanc and let 'em sink."

As for me, I spent no great energy reflecting on their guilt or specious claims that they were just following orders. I was more apprehensive about Friede's medical reports. I wanted the results as quickly as possible so we might proceed with our wedding plans. As the condemned in Nuremberg no doubt wished to slow down time, Friede and I wanted it to fly furiously towards our future together. Time, however, passed as it should, one second after the other, one hour after the other, until each man or woman's fate was revealed.

I thought perhaps we might have some positive news before Friede's birthday, but nothing arrived from London. It was probably foolish to believe that her medical report was going to be processed during that week. It was too soon and we were mere granules of sand in the Royal Air Force's order of commitments.

The military might have been sluggish in analyzing Friede's medical examination, however, on setting an execution date for Nuremberg's eleven condemned men, they were expeditious. The men were to swing on October sixteenth. Herman Goring, former head of the Luftwaffe and morphine addict, cheated justice the day before his scheduled appointment with God. A sympathetic guard smuggled in a cyanide capsule, which Goring used to commit suicide. In Hamburg, the general consensus was good riddance, considering that Goring's incompetence had assisted the Allies in leveling their city.

We celebrated Friede's nineteenth birthday without any word back from London.

"Next year," I said, "you will be a married woman and we will never have to depend on the government again."

Friede laughed and replied, "We must wait and see about next year. Your government hasn't even said yet whether I am medically fit to marry an Englishman."

With all this waiting, my patience began to fray and wear like a jacket worn for too many years through good and bad seasons. My daily visits to the adjutant officer's duty room were a disappointment.

"Sorry, perhaps tomorrow, you know the wheels of government. They turn as slow as a mill stone."

Guys Fawkes Day rushed upon us and I saw the days shorten and the nights lengthen. November lumbered onwards, the cold winds from the Baltic returned, and snow and sleet fell onto the streets of Hamburg. Winter was upon us and I grew downhearted. The wait for Friede's medical clearance was endless and malicious for me. I was about to resign myself to another month of grinding anticipation when the adjunct officer informed me one morning at breakfast that Friede was healthy enough to marry a Brit.

"Now we will need a thorough police and background check to see if her soul is as clean as her lungs," he told me with a laugh. He wished me good luck and added, "Life would be a damn sight easier if we didn't have to contend with these fools in government, drowning us in paperwork."

The following day, Friede went with me to the police station located on her mother's street. She requested they complete a criminal and political background check on her for the British government. We were lucky that it was the same duty sergeant who had investigated her grandfather's suicide.

He remembered me and said, "It was in unhappier circumstances the last time we met."

I handed him a few packs of cigarettes to show my appreciation. He said he would try his best to have the information back to the RAF within a month. The sergeant realistically pointed out to us the problems in obtaining any documents from before or during the war. "It is difficult, you know, because most of the records in Hamburg were destroyed in the bombing."

So during that December month, someone from what remained of Hamburg's civil service climbed through stacks of documents to collect Friede's political and security history.

It was time, I decided, to let my sister and my mother know that I was going to marry Friede in 1947. I wrote my sister a Christmas card: "*I am happy. Wish me luck and let's hope I don't bugger it up.*" I also enclosed some money and a snap of Friede and me.

I was more apprehensive about informing my mother Lillian. I would have preferred to not tell her until the last moment, fearing her biter tongue. In her return letter, my mother didn't acknowledge my announcement, but did ask for money: "*For keeping body and soul alive,*" as she put it.

My sister wrote back to congratulate me: "*Mam being Mam called you a daft bugger when she learned about your upcoming marriage. She be a right cow until the holy ghost takes her kicking and screaming out of this world. It's smashing news,*" Mary wrote. "*I can't wait to see you back home where you were born and bred with your woman beside you.*"

I loved my sister and knew that her devotion to me was absolute.

Yet her words about my birthplace, my so-called homeland Halifax, Bradford, and West Yorkshire made me cringe and squirm like a ferret in cage. It was a reprehensible location, as odious and cruel for me as the cracked cement floor where butchers let the blood of pigs drip clean. I planned to stay in Germany in the RAF for as long as possible because I was sure that Friede couldn't survive the harshness of life in Halifax.

20

Bizonia as Usual

In December 1946, a prehistoric deep freeze smothered Europe and like a glacier, the cold stretched deep into the New Year. Eighteen months after the surrender, life in the occupied city was still nasty, brutish, and short. During that winter, Hamburg was the literal spot where hell froze over for anyone down on his luck. Resentment towards the British occupational forces grew amongst the inhabitants as the thermometer plummeted to inhospitable temperatures. People grumbled vigorously about every indignity and shortage they endured, from inadequate food rations to insignificant coal allotment to heat their stoves.

The population was impatient. They wanted their standard of existence to change from this porridge bowl reality they believed was foisted on them as retribution for the war. Germans pointed their fingers towards their over lords; the British and the Americans. They were to blame, they whispered, for their hunger, their cold, and their destitution. The occupation leaders realized that the docile and suppliant German population was going to turn into an angry and dangerous mob if not placated.

A consensus developed amongst the Western occupational

governments that, outside of biblical revenge, governing Germany as a series of medieval states served no purpose. Punitively denying the German people anything but a pre-twentieth century existence wasn't only costly, if the strategy were to continue, it would breed a hostile population with a tepid allegiance to both Britain and America. However, returning occupied Germany to its natural industrialized, no-nonsense capitalistic society was a difficult, if not impossible, undertaking for the Allies. The Western sectors were subdivided into occupation zones controlled by Britain, the USA, and, to a much lesser degree, France. Each country ran their segment as judiciously as possible, but to the benefit of their mother country. Growth was stifled through tariffs, trade barriers, and a prohibition on the free flow of labour between occupational zones.

America and Britain begrudgingly accepted that reducing Germany to an agrarian society benefited no one, except perhaps Russia. However, by 1946, The Soviet Union was considered a dodgy ally at best and a possible belligerent at worst. Many political operatives began to accept that Russia was perhaps as dangerous and as aggressive as Nazi Germany was in the 1930s.

London and Washington gradually sobered to the fact that the Soviets had not liberated Eastern Europe at the cost of twenty million soldiers to germinate democracy. It was to create an empire as diabolical and cruel as Hitler's Liebenstrum.

The United States and Great Britain agreed that their occupational sectors were to be gradually transformed from a defeated vassal state into a new German nation. The new country could act as a buffer against any future Russian aggression. The genesis of this new state was an economic union between the British and American spheres of influences. This new trade zone was to be called Bizonia. It was a name assured to set no German heart a flutter with nationalistic pride, unless of course he was an accountant, businessman or enterprising spiv.

For the worker picking through the rubble in British-controlled

Hamburg, American-controlled Frankfurt or the hundred or so other gutted Stadts and Pladts, this new economic union did little to improve their day-to-day existence. However, for the businessman or the black marketer attempting to turn an honest or dishonest dollar into an immense profit; it was a new and bright beginning.

While economist and bankers hailed the creation of Bizonia as a giant leap towards Europe's future, I was more interested in getting my own house in order. I was almost twenty-four and impatient to marry Friede. I was finding the paperwork and the multi-layered sets of approvals we needed for our wedding becoming more insurmountable by the day. It was only natural that my love life and my own future occupied my imagination more than resuscitating the German wolf to keep Russia on guard in her new and enlarged lair. The men with briefcases and dark sunglasses were free to do their deals with old Nazi industrialists. It was none of my business as long as I was left alone to get on with my business with the least amount of interference. Yet while every questionable Nazi industrialist lined up to rebuild their commercial empires without impediments, Friede's own politics were scrutinized.

At the same moment Bizonia was born at the end of January, I was called into a meeting with the adjutant officer about Friede's security clearance. When I arrived at his office, Flight Lieutenant Locke looked as apprehensive as a bank manager upon review of a shaky business overdraft.

"There were issues of concern," the commander announced.

"What concerns?" I asked incredulously.

He cleared his throat. "You know Elfriede Edelmann's mother was a Nazi."

Not this again, I thought.

Politely, I tried to explained Maria Edelmann's reasons. "Yes, she joined the Nazi party, but she was hardly friends with the Bormanns," I replied sarcastically. "My understanding is that Maria Edelmann's involvement with the Nazi party was limited to paying its yearly dues. Marie Edelmann joined the party late in the war. That hardly indicates a dyed-in-the-wool Nazi. Look," I continued, "this woman was pressured to join the party."

"How so?" asked the officer.

"She was engaged in a love affair with a married man who was a former politician and a notable businessman named Karp. He gave no truck to the Nazis, but he did trade with them. I think you should also know that Maria Edelmann was under considerable pressure to join the party because Friede, my wife-to-be, is illegitimate. Moreover, her father was a socialist and communist sympathizer."

"I wasn't aware of this," said the adjutant. "And what are your fiancée's current politics?" I replied, "The same as mine. We want to live in a society where we are free; we can work for a fair wage and live in a decent home. We don't go much in for politics, except to know you can't trust them after they've got your vote."

He thought for a while and announced, "This is really absurd; I will write to HQ and explain that there is nothing to this news about her mother. While we are awaiting their response, I'd advise you to get a letter from the civilian authorities that will attest to her good character. When are you planning to marry?" he asked.

"We were thinking about the late summer."

"We should be able to give you the go ahead to marry well before then."

"I hope so," I said and left his office.

When Friede asked about the security check, I lied and said, "No problems, it's been approved. We better start working on getting you that letter attesting to your good character."

"That will not be a problem," she responded. "Mutti has already arranged a letter from one of Uncle Henry's associates who knows the new mayor."

"So, your mother is still in contact with her dead lover's

connections?" I asked.

"Of course," she replied, "and, why not? Mutti was like a wife to Henry. No one from his business thinks ill of her." Friede then grabbed me by the arm and sat me down at the kitchen table. She told me, "What we really must talk about is our wedding day."

It was something I hadn't given much thought to up until that moment. The same couldn't be said of Friede, who had given much consideration to the details surrounding her wedding day. The notion of marriage, legitimacy, and a union recognized by society had occupied her daydreams from the time she was a lonely child.

It was a simple motif that kept her strong as a little girl. It was the belief that her mother and she were going to be rescued by a prince. As a forlorn and lost child, this fantasy gave Friede great comfort. It was a source of consolation and an emotional retreat from the two worlds Friede straddled: the weekday plebeian life in the care of her foster parents and the bohemian existence she experienced with her mother on weekends.

At around the age of seven, Friede dreamed that her real father Fritz would return from Berlin and marry her mother in a fairytale wedding. It was a make-believe world drawn by an imaginative child who wanted to be envied by the other schoolgirls rather than be the object of their teasing. As Friede grew older, the daydream matured and she realized that Fritz wasn't coming back to marry her mother and legitimize his daughter. So, as a teenager it was her hope that Henry Karp, her mother's lover, would make an honest woman of her mother. It became a teenage obsession that Henry would marry her mother and adopt her as his daughter. When Henry died of a heart attack in 1944, Friede accepted that her mother was condemned by society to be the fallen woman. Friede, however, was never going to concede to the same fate.

To Friede, marriage was more than just a contract of love between two young adults. Our ceremony was to be the instrument that corrected the mistakes of her family's history and her illegitimacy. It was necessary that our wedding day captured and replicated the intricate map she had drawn and redrawn since childhood. Our wedding was to bring to fruition her dream of stability, respectability, and honour.

Over a few glasses of wine, Friede unfolded her vision of our wedding. Friede insisted that the wedding was to be intimate, neither too big nor too small. It must be a great celebration for everybody who attended it.

"It will be something," she said, "our friends and family will remember for a lifetime. Will your family come from Britain?" she asked.

I replied without a hint of sarcasm. "I don't think they will be coming. They have never left the north and I don't think my wedding or funeral would budge them. They would only go if it was in Blackpool and we paid for the dodge 'em ride afterwards."

Friede was intrigued to know what weddings were like back in Britain. I explained to her the only time I witnessed a wedding was as a delivery boy bringing the victuals for the feast. In my class, I told her most weddings were civil ceremonies with a ploughman's lunch reception to follow.

"What about your parents' wedding?"

I laughed. "It would be safe to say that no one in my dad's family and no one in my mom's family were happy that day. If there were any tears shed, they were of regret."

Friede looked cross with me. I tried to placate her by telling her that our wedding was going to come as close to her dreams as humanly possible.

Friede's wedding plans weren't ostentatious or pretentious, but they were comprehensive. It was imperative that our wedding service be conducted in a church. The announcement took me by surprise and made me almost cough out the drink I had just swallowed. Up until her declaration, I really hadn't considered the church of my youth, her church, or anyone else's church as ever again being involved in my life. A miserable childhood spent in the guilt-ridden and brutal hands of semi-sober nuns and priests had left me distrustful of any institution that promised salvation while beating my backside blue.

I couldn't remember the last time I had been in a church, let alone been to confession and taken communion. It certainly didn't appeal to me, returning to church and having a priest absolve me of my crimes against God. I wasn't even sure if Friede understood the gravity of what she requested from me. So I tried to gently persuade her against a religious ceremony.

"You know I am a Roman Catholic," I told her, with about as much pleasure as if I were admitting to membership in the Nazi party. "It's not that I hold much love for Rome," I continued, "but I think it might be a problem to marry in another faith because who knows how long conversion takes?"

"Of course, I know. I don't mind becoming a Catholic," she responded. "I think they might be better Christians than the Lutherans, who are all so mortified by guilt. Remember what I told you at the Michel church so long ago; it is not necessarily God that I believe in, but some spirit of creation, some energy that is beyond our comprehension."

I kept quiet and tried to respect Friede's spiritual acceptance of things I believed to be rot. God, I believed, and his acolytes had caused a lot of bother and destruction in my life and the lives of millions of other poor supplicants. However, at this moment I wasn't going to let him get in the way of my happiness with Friede.

So I postponed any more talk about Catholicism. "Let's work on the conversion at a later time," I told her.

I changed the subject to what I considered an easier problem to solve. "What about your wedding dress?"

Little did I realize that to obtain a wedding dress in 1947 Germany was as arduous as going on a crusade for the Holy Grail in the eleventh century.

426

Friede looked at me and responded seriously. "A wedding dress cannot be bought; it must be unique and one of a kind. It must be created from a beautiful fabric by an expert dressmaker."

Talking about her wedding dress made me realize I was swimming in the deep end without a life preserver. So I stopped speaking, smiled, and waited to see if Friede had a solution to her wedding gown. It didn't take her long to assure me that she knew the right people to deal with this delicate situation.

"We have no problems; I already have a dressmaker. Frau Schroeder, she is an old friend of my mother's. Before the British came, she was the number one dressmaker for an excellent shop in Hamburg. We can go see her tomorrow. Frau Schroeder will sort everything out for us," Friede explained with a satisfied voice.

I exhaled and told her, "Well, that's a relief. It seems you have most things covered."

"Yes, she has already measured me."

It felt odd to have all of this secret activity occurring under my nose. At one moment, I was relieved that many matters relating to this wedding were being handled by others. At other moments, it was as if my intention to be married was being hijacked by someone else's convention. I began to worry about the cost of the wedding and whether I was leaving myself and Friede open for disappointment. I kept quiet about my doubts because it was impossible to derail Friede's excitement over her wedding. I didn't want to dampen her belief that this ceremony would transform her from a disjointed, passionate, nineteen-year-old girl into a serious-minded woman.

Our nuptials were like an ancient rite of passage to her. I didn't know what they were to me except a means to keep my love from flying away and an attempt to put down roots that my own parents were denied by bad luck.

I realized that if I thought too much about the mechanics of the actual wedding day, I'd go into a funk and begin to doubt the worth of it. I resolved to accept her wishes passively and hoped that the day and our future weren't going to be a disappointment for either of us.

"Tomorrow, Frau Schroeder is going to show me her preliminary designs. You must bring her some coffee so she knows we can pay for her services."

On the following afternoon, we travelled to Frau Schroeder's house. The woman lived alone with her husband in a comfortable bungalow located near the Alster. Her husband greeted us at the door. He was military thin and had a shock of white hair running down his forehead. He looked arrogant and baronial to me, but he greeted Friede warmly. I received a stiff handshake and an aloof hello. No one ever told me what he did in the war and I never asked, but I was sure whatever it was, he was a devotee of Hitler.

Frau Schroeder was a thin, prim, and exacting woman who was several years older than Friede's mother. She appreciated my gesture of a half kilo of coffee and thanked me graciously. Her words were amiable, but across her face there was an implied expression: I was a fool if I thought the dress she was making was an inconsequential undertaking.

At the start of our meeting, Friede and I sat with the elderly couple in their parlour, which was furnished in oppressive heavy furniture. After a few minutes, Frau Schroeder left the room and returned with a sketch book.

She looked at me caustically and announced, "It would be bad luck for you to see the dress before your wedding day. Please talk with Herr Schroeder while I show Friede these drawings."

I got up from the heavy sofa and moved to sit near her husband, who didn't look pleased at my arrival. He exchanged a curt and dismissive smile and tried to ignore me.

Across the parlour, Friede and Frau Schroeder flipped through her sketchbook. The dressmaker made notes while Friede whispered ideas in her ear. One might have thought the conspiratorial way the two women viewed the sketches of the wedding dress, they were approving the blueprints for the Bismarck. After a while, the two women finished their deliberations and the sketch book was closed shut with satisfaction.

Coffee and cake were served. Frau Schroeder presented an elegant cake, triple-layered in what appeared to be butter cream. As I tried to enjoy my cake and coffee, Frau Schroeder spoke to me about the dress.

"You know this is a one of a kind dress."

I smiled ignorantly and said, "But of course."

The old dressmaker looked at me impatiently. Friede interrupted her and explained, "What Frau Schroeder means is my dress will be made from satin and silk is impossible to come by in Hamburg. It is also very expensive."

My heart dropped a beat. "Can we make the dress from another fabric?"

"Of course not," shouted Frau Schroder.

"What are we to do then?"

"It has been taken care of," Friede said. "We have the material, but it is unfortunately in Brussels. It is a wedding gift from Uncle Henry's partner, Herr Rodmann. However, he cannot get a travel permit to go there, so perhaps you can go to Brussels to pick up the material."

"That is very considerate of Uncle Henry's partner," I responded.

Friede, smiled and added, "He was pleased to do something for us. It was the least he could do considering how Henry helped conceal his communist past to the Nazis."

Frau Schroeder interrupted to insist that I make the trip as soon as possible, so that she could get to work on the dress. "I don't want any problems," she said "with the material."

I told the women I would get a pass to travel to Belgium as soon as possible. When I walked Friede back home from the Schroeder's, her footsteps were light and she beamed with happiness. I told Friede, "You better give me all of the instructions to get the dress materials."

Friede stopped and spoke with some hesitation. "There is one other thing, it is nothing, but Uncle Henry's partner has asked that you take a letter with you to Belgium. He wants you to give the letter to the person who has our silk for the dress."

"What is the letter about?" I asked suspiciously.

"It is nothing for us to be concerned with. He just wants to resume contact with old business partners. You know what everyone is saying now; it is business as usual."

21

Grand Place Brussels

A month after Frau Schroeder commanded me to go to Belgium, I was granted leave to travel to Brussels. It was fortuitous that my travel warrant was delayed because I needed to save extra money for the trip. The moment Friede's mother learned about my upcoming journey, she suggested it was wise to also purchase lace for Friede's veil.

"If you are going to travel that far for her dress material, it would be foolish not to buy Belgian lace as it is the world's finest," she told me knowledgably. "Perhaps," Friede added, "While you are there, you can look for some wedding shoes for me."

Dutifully, I nodded my head and said that was an excellent idea. The growing extravagance for our nuptials worried me. My RAF wireless pay wasn't much and I was living life like an officer with an annuity. I wasn't in debt, but I was running a tight line between solvency and destitution. Were it not for the perks of living overseas in a country where everyone was on the fiddle; my romantic life would have been more circumspect and certainly less eventful. Anxious as I was about covering the outlay, I still desired to create a perfect wedding day for

Friede and for myself.

I dreaded that my wish to please and be pleased in return was setting both Friede and myself up for future disappointments. Nobody I was acquainted with had had a white wedding, with a church service and an afternoon reception along with numerous pre-marriage parties. I was frightened my life was going pear-shaped and it was going to be witnessed by everyone I knew as if it were up on the cinema screen.

I even complained to Sid about my misgivings. Fortunately, he was wise enough to know that it was better to have a go rather than sit the dance out.

"How many times are you going to get married, mate? Sure, it's over the top if you were back at home, but you're not. Live it up because there won't be much when you're back in Britain with the missus except fond memories to go with your mushy peas and chips."

"Right you are," I said.

No matter the price and damn the consequences, I was going to marry Friede in style. I'd pay the piper and go to Brussels to get Friede's material for her wedding dress.

My travel warrant to Belgium was only valid for twenty-four hours, so I booked passage on a locomotive that left the Banhof at six in the morning. To keep me warm and fed on the way, the camp cook packed me a lunch with a thermos generously filled with whisky and coffee. Dave drove me to the station. He promised to return at midnight when my train was due to arrive back in the city.

I found a window seat on the train and watched Hamburg disappear into a whirl of steam and snow. I felt at peace with myself because this wrecked maritime metropolis had beguiled and seduced me. Hamburg's independent come-as-you-are attitude made me feel like I belonged with its diverse citizens. I closed my eyes and listened to the rhythm of the train as it sped along the track and I travelled further away from the city.

For the first time in my life, I was sure that regardless the distance covered that day, there was someone who loved me and was waiting for me in Hamburg.

My train companions were mostly British soldiers being shunted to other occupational areas. On board, there were also a few British civilian government workers. They were easy to recognize by their wool overcoats, thin lips, and cynical expressions. During the long trip, they were as supercilious as public school boys who thought they were destined for better things than riding an uncomfortable train through the wreckage of Germany's heartland.

It was still well below freezing that day and, at times, the scenery disappeared into a blinding snow storm. In spite of the nasty weather, labourers were outside in the cold rebuilding ruined structures or driving horse-drawn carts filled with rubble, coal, or firewood. At each train stop, the engine snorted like a beast recovering from a gallop. Sometimes, I wiped the window clean of condensation with the palm of my hand and peered onto the soot-stained railway station's platform. Standing on it, there was a familiar cast of characters: hustlers, lost refugees, and orphaned children harvesting cigarette butts. Nobody else in my compartment seemed to notice or care about these flash photographs of desperate folk. Some of the soldiers played cards while the civilians in suits talked in clipped accents about upcoming summer vacations in France.

After I spent many hours staring out of the joyless window, we finally reached Cologne, which meant we were near the border. It also indicated that we had crossed over into the American sector. GIs began to swagger on board. Their cocky self-assuredness turned the civil servants' faces sour with envy and disgust, but I welcomed their independent optimism over our self-defeated aloofness.

As the train drew closer to its final destination, I grew excited about seeing Belgium. Just before the end of the war, my unit was briefly stationed at an abandoned Luftwaffe airfield on the outskirts of Antwerp. The few short weeks I spent there were my first experience in a different country with a diverse culture. I enjoyed Belgium in the winter of 1945, despite battles raging only a hundred kilometers away from me. I wondered how the country had changed from those final days of conflict, when it was used as a marshalling yard, pushing troops up into Holland or across the Siegfried Line.

The border control at the frontier was minimal. A jolly, rotund Belgian custom's guard made a cursory check of my travel papers. Looking outside, Belgium appeared well recovered from the war. Across the lowland countryside, the villages and hamlets appeared undamaged and prosperous. I saw giant cauldrons of smoke blazing from chimney pots on top of Flemish cottages. In the fields, fat milk cows exercised in pastures covered in a thin blanket of snow. Even the roadways were overweight with private and commercial vehicles belching black petrol fumes in the open skyline.

When the locomotive steamed through Brussels towards the station, it was a marvel to see a vibrant city, clean and free of bombing debris. The train arrived just after lunch hour at the city's Nord terminal. There were no wastrels and waifs blocking my exit on the train platform. Instead, it was filled with young Belgian women wearing the newest hairstyles. They were wrapped smartly in furs. Dazed, I bumped against them and excused myself. Their laughter along with the smell of expensive perfume and carefree days trailed after me. Those females at the stations wore a prettiness that most German girls in Hamburg couldn't afford. Here, the girls had the luxury of being attractive without being hungry. It was revealing and wonderful to look at them enjoying being youthful, without a cynical and harsh world demanding that they pawn themselves for survival.

I walked from the station hall into a large thoroughfare. From my great coat pocket, I pulled out my instructions from Friede. Her note told me to proceed to the Grand Place, which was Brussels' main square. When I arrived at Grand Place, I was astounded by its sheer beauty and that it was completely intact. There was no destruction,

434

no gutted palaces, no burial pyres of bricks and mortars. It was a wonderful and revealing cityscape. Looking around at this unmolested capital, I realized for the first time that the war was over.

The parts of Brussels I walked through looked confidently towards their future. Living for so long in occupied Germany, I had grown use to the atmosphere of defeat and horrendous daily suffering. It made one think that the world was at the razor's edge, ready to be bled in sacrifice to a pagan god. Brussels was like fresh air in a room stifled by stale cigar smoke.

I regretted not having the time to explore more of Brussels, but my instructions were exact. It wasn't difficult to find the shop where I was supposed to exchange the letter from Uncle Henry's partner for the silk for Friede's wedding dress. It was a luxurious tobacco store located on a side street near a palace the RAF occupied and used as a hotel for military personnel on leave.

When I entered the store, the shop was empty of customers. There was a man about my age arranging a pipe display. I walked over to him and smiled. I told him I had come from Hamburg with a letter for the owner. The clerk excused himself and walked into an office located at the rear of the store.

After several minutes, the owner, a woman, appeared. She carried in her arms a package wrapped in brown paper. She asked my name. When I told her, she said, "With my compliments," and we exchanged our holdings.

Our swap took less than five minutes. Afterwards, the owner disappeared to the rear of the store and I exited. For the briefest of times, I wondered what might be in the letter, but was more than satisfied with what I had received in return.

I carefully stored the silk for the dress in my haversack and looked for a shoe shop. At the other end of the Grand Place, I located a stylish store. There I provided a cut out of Friede's feet and explained the purpose for the shoes. The saleswoman brought me an assortment of shoes each more expensive than a year's wages for me. I explained in pigeon French that I was on a budget.

Displeased, the sales clerk found a beautiful pair of white shoes, but said, "Sadly this is last year's style."

"It will have to do," I told her, "because this year's money doesn't buy much in Brussels."

After purchasing them, I asked the clerk if she could direct me to a lace shop to purchase material for the veil.

The sales girl responded in a snotty accent, "You will not be so lucky to find last year's style with lace; it hasn't changed in a hundred years."

I was in Brussels for a little under five hours but I spent three months wages. Walking back to the station, I felt satisfied that I had done well with my money. At the lace market, I was even able to buy my sister a delicately knitted handkerchief. By the time I got back to the train station, I desperately wanted a beer or something to eat but the coins in my pocket rattled forlornly.

I walked around the train station looking for a cafe. Instead, I spotted a fruit-mongers stall where bunches of ripe yellow bananas hung like exotic jewellery. Until that moment, the closest I had come to a banana was viewing them at the cinema on Carmen Miranda's head. It was as rare to me as pearls from the South China Sea.

I wondered what they tasted like and I wasn't even sure if you ate the peel. I hurried over to the fruit stand and marveled that the seller had more bananas hanging in his tiny stall than I thought the whole of the tropics could produce. I pulled the change out of my pockets and pointed at a ripe bunch. The monger took pity on me. He counted the money out of my hand and let me take twenty bananas.

On the journey home to Hamburg, there were no seats and I was forced to stand in the train's aisle way. My bag filled with the silk and lace for Friede's dress was kept safe and guarded behind my legs. For the length of the trip, I held on to the banana bunch and only ate two of them. I was determined that the rest were to be a treat for Friede's family. The taste from the banana lingered with me from Liege until we arrived at the Banhof.

When Dave picked me up and noticed my fruit cargo, he asked, "Where have you been now, the bloody Congo?"

22

The Booth Town Road Prodigal

In 1947, after the snow, the prehistoric low temperatures, the ice, and the sleet, Europe was subjected to biblical winter rains. Torrential flooding occurred in Britain, Germany, and many other parts of the continent. Hamburg's gutters turned into rivers and its bomb craters into lakes filled with black polluted water. It was rumoured that the sun had gone into exile from our hemisphere. We kept warm fires raging in our mess hut, but it still took a long time to burn the chill out of my bones. For the rest of Germany, they burned what they found: coal dust, wood chips, and books to keep hypothermia away. Back in Friede's apartment, her mother fed damp kindling into their wood stoves. It sparked, sizzled, and fumed, releasing a foggy heat throughout their rooms.

It was miserable inside Germany and the situation wasn't much better for a lot of other countries. Along with the rain, sleet, and howling bitter winds, hunger, corruption, and violence lingered and poisoned much of Western Europe. Greece succumbed to civil war. Italy teetered between anarchy and total decay. Great Britain was sinking in nature's downpour along with an insurmountable war debt. Across the Home Counties, housing was in short supply or inadequate for working families. Even with a socialist government, decent paying employment was hard to find. The empire that every schoolchild knew was Britain's right by God was dying. India, the jewel in the crown, battled for independence from us while the rest of our colonies waited restlessly for the end of their subjection.

On the continent, Western Europe asked what path we must follow: the capitalism of America or the collectivisation of Russia. No one really knew the answer or the outcome to that reply except that they wanted a decent life for themselves and their children. As the weather grew more and more inhospitable, voices from German citizens grumbled and demanded to know when their yoke of occupation would end.

It was underneath those wet, black, and unfriendly skies that the British government finally approved Friede's security clearance. We were free to marry. Some man in a damp suit with a name like Tastscome or Longnarrow placed his initials on her file and stamped it harmless to British interests. The gatekeepers gleamed that Friede was nineteen and only endangered conformity. When it was agreed her political background was risk-free, I was granted home leave. It was the last requirement before permission was granted to marry a former enemy national. The return home was supposed to be a cold splash of water for the serviceman intent on marrying a German girl. It was the government's logic that a trip home might remind the lad that there were pretty lasses down at his local who fancied him. The government's other motive was the hope the serviceman's mother would knock some sense into him with a clout behind the ear.

My sense of hearth and home wasn't revived when I returned to Halifax and my mother's house. Riding the bus from the train station to Boothtown Road was like being electrocuted with a cattle prod. As I sat smoking on the bus's upper deck, all of the negative emotions from my youth in this blighted northern county regurgitated into the back of my throat. Everything in Halifax, from the people to the buildings, looked in need of a good scrub. There was two centuries of industrial muck on every brick facade and on the blanched almond faces of my fellow bus riders. I laughed to myself and thought in Halifax the rains were always plentiful, but they never washed the grime away from this town.

The last time I had taken leave to see my family was in 1941. Nothing had changed on this street or any other road in Halifax. Each one looked sad and neglected; the city was a cul-de-sac to trap unhappiness.

When I walked up to the front stoop of my mother's cramped tenement on Boothtown Road, there was no welcoming committee to greet me. The milk man, I thought as I rattled the front door, would have received a warmer welcome than me. The moment the door opened and my mam welcomed me home, I knew that she, like the town, the road, the houses, and thankless lives most led in Halifax, was no different than when I had left it. Like everything else in Halifax, my mam had just become stouter.

My mother's looks had once been her source of pride and comfort. In her youth and well into her middle age, my mother's shapely body had turned the heads of miners, mill workers, and itinerant labourers. Years of drinking generous portions of lager had turned her into a fleshy tank of a woman. The extra weight didn't make her look fat, it made her seem like she was wearing, body armour underneath her clothing.

Even though I had given sufficient forewarning of my arrival, the first words out of her mouth to me were, "You'll have to make do with a cold spam butty. We got naught extra because of the rationing."

Time may wear down the rocks on Brighton Beach, but it seemed to sharpen my mam's anger at the world and the resentment she carried to her own brood. "Never you mind, Mam," I said. "I ate well this morning and I'm in town only for a day and a night."

"That's a pity," my mother said with the some doubt in her voice.

"Well, give us a kiss anyways."

Afterwards, I followed her into the kitchen where I found Bill Moxon hovering near a steaming kettle. He was her lover, drinking companion, and sparring partner. Moxon had replaced my father in my mother's bed some twenty years earlier. I always had the suspicion that he regretted that fateful leg-over more than if he had killed a man and spent the succeeding years in jail.

Age or my mother's over-powering personality had mellowed him, I thought.

He shook my hand. "Look all right Harry. War done someone some good then," he added to me as a sidewise compliment.

He then opened his mouth to smile and it revealed that he still refused to purchase dentures. "Bloody useless to get fitted up with teeth when me gums can cut into an apple like an axe," he had once remarked.

That day, however, he had no wisdom to impart to me, except, "It's time for a bit a quiet." Bill Moxon then disappeared off to the outdoor privy with a newspaper.

With Moxon gone to the thunder box, my two younger brothers presumed it was safe to come into the kitchen and greet me. They looked as uncomfortable as I felt. We eyed each other up down as dogs do from different litters. Since each of us had a different father, we recognized each other more by our differences than by any shared similarities.

Matt, the eldest of my younger brothers, had grown. He was now seventeen, tall and lanky with jet black hair and a raven's face. He looked a lot like his father, the Irish transient who was the first of many to cuckold my real father. Matt had developed into a cocky teen. He wasn't the small boy I remembered. He wasn't the wee one my sister and I used to keep a watchful eye over anymore when our mam was on the piss.

Matt showered a grin on me that said more about what he lacked in experience than what he gained by learning about life on Booth Town Road. With piss and vinegar on his words, he shook my hands and said, "How ya doing, Harry. Did you kill any Germans?"

"Sorry, mate, I killed no Germans."

News that my war exploits lacked bloodshed and daring seemed to disappoint him. He looked downcast, but cheered up enough to ask me, "What did you bring me back from the war?"

"I brought you Hitler's moustache," I told him.

"Stop pulling his leg," my mother reprimanded. "He wants his war booty, like all of uz do."

"Right," I said. "You were supposed to get this after tea, but here it is."

I pulled from my kit bag a silver German wrist-watch. It had intricate Roman numerals on its face and a new leather strap around it. Matt looked at with wide-eyed wonder. His amazement at the timepiece convinced me the only time he knew was when it was best to bugger off from our mother. His appreciation was laconic. "That's all right then," he said.

Happily and awkwardly, he put the watch onto his wrist and admired its look.

"Show me the bloody watch," my mother belted out.

Matt walked over and our mother grabbed hold of his wrist. She eyed the watch as if she was sizing it up for a future trip to the pawn shop.

My other half-brother, Billy, stood awkwardly in the background. He was twelve and the product of too much cider and gin between Moxon and my mam. Billy and I didn't know each other because we were a generation apart in age, experience, and sentiment. Before the war, I thought he was a nuisance and an embarrassment. For me, he was more evidence of my mother's philandering irresponsibility. In our confused family hierarchy, I considered Billy to be no more significant than my pet mouse, which my mother killed by crushing it

442

with her rocking chair leg. I don't think Billy thought any better of me and openly referred to me as, "He's not Moxon. He's a bleeding Smith problem."

"What did ya git for junior?" Mam screamed out to me, even though we were within arm's reach.

I pulled out my wallet and handed Billy a pound note and said, "There's your gift. That pound was given to me by Goring as war reparations. Now it's yours to spend on Mackintosh sweets."

"Ta," he said, fingering the note as if he were checking to see if it were counterfeit.

The excitement of my return quickly wore off on my two brothers. They hastily said their good-byes to me and quickly left our mother's dingy house. Outside I heard them cursing all the way up the street.

With my brothers gone, my mother informed me that my sister was expected to arrive shortly.

Silently, I looked around the house while my mother sat at the kitchen table and slurped a cup of tea as viscous as treacle. It looked as if the interior of this house hadn't seen a fresh coat of paint since Queen Victoria died. My mother and the cowman couldn't afford the paint and probably reasoned why cover up what is plain for anyone to see: we live in shite. I thought compared to Europe, Britain had the worst type of poverty. England's poor were a filthy lot kept like dogs in a shit-filled kennel by masters who should have been jailed for their cruelty and greed.

"Those two boys are a handful," my mother lamented to me about my departed brothers. "Shame that there's no one to ever give me a hand."

While my mother's words ground onwards like the lamentation of Job, I lit a cigarette. I counted in my head the time left before I had to catch my train and return to Manchester and fly back to Germany.

At around seven, Mary arrived. She hugged me deeply, numerously, and transferred an endless amount of love back to me. It was what I most admired about my sister, her boundless loyalty to those she loved.

"Let's have a look at you", she said. "God, you've gotten big and strong on RAF food. You're not that bag of bones who said tara to me six years ago."

"You look good too," I replied deceptively. Mary appeared to me thin as a tubercular patient and had developed a strong smoker's cough.

"Bloody liar," she retorted. "Go on now," she said encouragingly, "show us a picture of this true love of yours."

I pulled out a small snapshot of Friede whereupon Mary cooed, "She's right lovely, isn't she, Mam?"

My mother looked at it and snorted. "I've seen worse. It's beyond me, lad, why you want to go and marry a bloody Nazi. You're just like thy dad, head in the clouds, a bloody dreamer."

"Go on now, Mam," Mary said defensively. "Harry's got a right to dream and be in love. There's no crime in wanting what your heart fancies."

"Bollocks," my mother retorted. "The both of you I can see are from the same Da. Dreaming did him no bloody good and uz no bloody good. In this life, keep yer feet firmly planted on the bloody ground, even if you are knee-deep in shite. No dreams, no looking with milk cream eyes to sky is gonna save thee and pull thee from the muck."

"Wasn't his fault, Mam," Mary said in our dead father's defense. "In those days, our only friends were bad luck and cold porridge and it weren't Dad's mistake for our fall into misery. Anyways, Mam, if our dad was a dreamer, at least you wuz the schemer. So, no harm done, Mam, cause you landed us in the right tip when we wuz wee young."

As the two argued and bickered, I shrunk into the background. It felt like I was a ten-year-old boy again caught between their conflicting feelings of love and hate for each other. After a while, the fires in each of them dimmed and we sat around the kitchen table. I listened to them gossip to me about my uncles and aunts and their own strange

444

lives during the war. Before Mary left, I took out the lace handkerchief I bought for her in Brussels. She cooed over it as she once did when we were small and I treated her to a chocolate bar.

It was time to give my mother her gift. Friede had bought her a green blown glass fruit bowl, which looked too beautiful for this house or any fruit that might mistakenly end up in my mother's larder.

My mother opened her gift, which was wrapped in plain brown paper. Her eyes lit up as she looked at the delicate blown glass. "Now that's real Nazi booty," she declared.

"Crickey, Mam," I interrupted. "Friede bought that for you. It's not loot."

"Wait until I show your aunties this. It's actual German war booty. They'll be gob-smacked. Bloody marvellous, it's bloody marvellous, son," she said.

Mary whispered to me, "Don't let the old girl down; let her believe that it's from Hitler's bunker if she wants. She's a daft old cow, but she is our mum."

My sister reached over and took a cigarette from my pack. She told me, "I think, your Friede is beautiful."

"She's still a bleeding German," my mother interjected. "Wot's she going to do in Halifax? I don't see many jobs going for Nazis down at mills or in shops. Bet she can't even speak bloody English," my mother said with an undereducated self-satisfaction.

"Mam, shut it," Mary said. "It's beautiful that Harry is going to marry a German girl. She did nothing to harm uz and you better remember that, Mam, before you go and open up yer cake-hole and say something cruel to her when you meet her. " She turned to me. "When are you coming home with her?"

"Not for a long while I hope," I replied thankfully.

Before my leave ended, my mother in her own emotionally amputated way tried to mend the loose and torn threads of our relationship.

"I'm right proud of ya, Harry, for bringin yer mam back sum war booty, right proud of you. As a peace offering," she added, "if you've got to go and marry a German and live your life in the clouds, try not to scrape yer knees when you tumble. There's nobody in this world that's going to catch you or me when we fall," she said ruefully. It's bloody tough but there you are. It's a bloody hard life, but it's a damn sight better than resting in the dirt like yer dad."

23

A Pawn Takes a Bishop

By 1947, I had lived through several springs in Germany and experienced two of their most brutal winters. Hamburg was still pursued by three furies: chaos, corruption, and destruction that held onto the city like a pack of crazed Alsatians. There was little difference in any other part of Germany because reconstruction moved at a meandering and tepid evolutionary pace. On many occasions, German economic and spiritual renewal regressed back into the sea as it struggled through the avenues of incompetence, myopia, and avarice. Human nature being what it is, it didn't surprise me that the new Germany was built on the foundations of their old evils and temptations. In each individual, community, success, and growth depended on the kinship benevolence shares with malevolence or greed with charity. Even the economic union Bizonia launched in the winter months between the American and British sectors was slow going.

Commerce between the two zones was blighted by power black outs, capital shortages, and theft. It was profoundly worrisome that the rest of Western Europe was infected by this same financial and spiritual malaise. It was clear to anyone that the continent was broken from Lublin to Lombardy. The continent's infrastructure, from bridges to ports, factories, and warehouses was either destroyed or in such disrepair, the owners had abandoned them to be reclaimed by nature. The inhabitants weren't much better off and most populations struggled with incessant food shortages.

Two years after the Second World War ended, Europe's attrition became a grave concern to the United States. Their worry was echoed by journalists, academics, and writers, who feared the whole European continent was tumbling into the Soviet sphere of influence through neglect and poor planning. George Marshall, the American Secretary of State, proposed a radical solution in June 1947. The United States was going to rebuild and feed Europe on low interest, long-term American loans. He believed bank-rolling Europe wasn't charity but good commerce. A financially sound continent was more likely to be democratic, pro-capitalist, and eager to buy American manufactured goods. Cash and commonsense were his only weapons against the Soviet allure of equality amongst men and the collectivization of wealth.

I wasn't sure if Europe had its chips, but I was getting scared that my day was done if the RAF didn't give me permission to marry. My greatest fear was being demobbed back home before the event; because I was on my last permissible six-month extension and it was due to expire in the fall.

Through most of June, I fretted and sweated over my predicament. Flight Lieutenant Locke had no answers for me. I was advised to, "Keep a stiff upper lip, Smith." He intimated that I must accept the karma of military life with, "It will come when it will come."

By the end of the month and a year since I began my journey to marry Friede, word was sent to me to meet with my commanding officer. His adjutant, Flight Lieutenant Locke, was also in attendance at the meeting. I didn't know how the conference was going to unfold, but I did feel self-assured because both Cox and Locke were fair and decent men. Cox flipped through a file on his desk. It was my dossier that possessed every document pertaining to my service with the RAF and my year-long quest to marry a German girl.

Cox looked up from the papers and said with sincerity, "I must congratulate you LAC Smith. You have confounded and defeated the RAF with your diligence to paperwork. It gives me great pleasure to inform you that as far as the Air Ministry is concerned, you are free to marry your fiancée, Elfriede Giselle Edelmann." Cox looked as relieved as me that everything had apparently worked out for the best.

"At the beginning of this odyssey," the wing commander said, "I mentioned to you that you were the first under my command to request marriage to a German woman. I am pleased that you succeeded where many others would have given up on this mighty challenge. It demonstrates that you are of good character."

"Thank you, sir."

Locke interjected, "Good show, Smith."

I thought I was about to be dismissed when Cox coughed and added, "There is one more issue we must discuss; your status in the RAF. I have been informed that you are scheduled to be demobbed in the upcoming months. So I must caution you to get this wedding over with, on the double. You don't want to get shipped home without your wife-to-be."

The wing commander was correct; efficiency dictated that my marriage ceremony be a quick affair. However, I had concocted a plan to keep me in Germany and in the pay of the RAF for a long while. I was simply going to re-enlist into the RAF for their standard three-year tour. I decided not to tell the wing commander until after my wedding. I feared the wing commander would cashier me out of the services if he knew I wanted to stay in Hamburg with a German national for a wife.

I replied to Cox that I intended to get married in August.

"That is cutting it a bit short," interjected the adjutant.

"I know, sir, but we want a church wedding and I am RC."

449

"Oh," he noted, as if I had confessed to necromancy.

"I thought most everyone nowadays has a civil ceremony," he commented.

"My fiancée wants a religious wedding service," I explained.

"I think you should talk to the padre about that," said the wing commander. "It really isn't my speciality. I am sure he can round up a man with a Catholic dog collar."

"Perhaps to expedite matters, sir," the adjutant interjected, "we could ask the vicar. He might be able to arrange a meeting for LAC Smith with someone in authority at the Roman Catholic Church in Hamburg." The wing commander thought this a very good idea.

Before I was dismissed, Cox noted that the RAF was doing everything for my wedding, but throwing me a night out with the lads.

I thanked both officers for their support and left the office elated. Once I had finished my duties in the communications tower, I rushed straight to Friede's apartment. When I told Friede our good news, she kissed me passionately.

"Finally," she said, "we are to be married. I won't believe it until we are truly wed in a church." Friede added, "I won't tell anyone but Mutti until we have spoken to a priest and arranged the day."

"It is coming soon," I reassured her. Silently, I dreaded what the reception was going to cost and what would happen if I was demobbed prematurely.

One week later, I was called in to see our base padre, Chaplain Walker. He was a youngish man, with a kind face. He seemed generally concerned for his flock. Walker greeted me in a warm and friendly voice. "I've had a spot of good luck and was able to arrange a meeting for you and your fiancée with the Catholic Bishop who governs this parish."

He flipped through some notes on a pad of paper and added, "Oh yes, here it is: the bishop is Wilhelm Berning von Osnabrück. Try saying that three times," Walker remarked good-naturedly.

"The bishop doesn't live in Hamburg but told me he is prepared to meet you in the city at Pastor Wintermann's residence. He is a monsignor with the church. The bishop wants to discuss with you your intent to marry this German woman," the padre added with a note of dismay.

"What is there to discuss?" I asked suspiciously.

Walker nervously laughed and explained, "I think perhaps you know the Germans better than me. Your bishop has some bee in his bonnet, but he wasn't about to reveal any secrets to me." The padre wrote the address and appointment time on a scrap of paper and handed it to me.

When I was about to leave, the padre wished me luck and warned me. "Smith, I know you are RC."

Not by much, I thought.

"But I must advise you that having spoken with this bishop; he is a bit of a character."

"What do you mean?" I asked.

"Well, for starters, he is one of the most disagreeable persons I have ever encountered in Germany. I've asked around and the man wasn't a Nazi per se, but he certainly doesn't believe in a democratic modern society. My impression was that he still has a bone to pick with Luther for the Reformation."

"I see," I said.

"One last thing," Walker added. "My final impression of the bishop is a man who doesn't accept dissent. I think he still believes in pitchforks, devils, and the fiery bowels of hell. Remember, fools rush in where angels fear to tread. Be careful what you say and do while in the company of the bishop. Let me know how it turns out for you. I am always here to help if something goes amiss."

Several days later, Friede and I went to meet the bishop. Friede dressed as reverentially as possible and wore a plain long cotton dress with dowdy shoes. I wore my best uniform.

Pastor Wintermann's residence was located in a prosperous neighbourhood in the northern part of the city. We came to his door and I rang the bell with trepidation. To my surprise, the monsignor answered his own door. He let us in to a large hallway, whose walls were covered in small pictures of saints and church leaders. Wintermann informed me that the bishop was upstairs in his office. We were led to the second floor by Wintermann. Our footsteps on the staircase were cushioned by an ancient Persian carpet runner. The interior of the house was cast in gloomy dark colours. It was as quiet as a funeral parlour, except for the annoying heavy sounds coming from the mechanical parts of old clocks in desperate need of lubrication.

Wintermann knocked and announced us. I walked into the room holding Friede's hand. The drapes were drawn as if sunlight were a sin and an impediment to ecclesiastical work. The monsignor was like a mute assistant to a medieval inquisition. He gestured and pointed for us to sit in two chairs positioned before a large desk. Behind it sat the bishop, who ignored our entrance and continued working strenuously on some composition. He was dressed as a simple priest and was around sixty with thinning white hair.

Friede and I sat close together holding each other's hands. After some time, the bishop looked up from his writings and took off his reading glasses. "And you are?" he asked with prosecutorial skill.

The bishop was perfectly aware of our identities and purpose, but I indulged his charade and told him our names and our reason for being before him. At the start of our interview, he spoke exclusively to Friede. His tone was supercilious, but seemed harmless. He concerned himself with knowing more about where she was born and baptised, the schools she went to, and where she now lived. The bishop spoke to her for no more than five minutes and then dismissed her.

"Child, please wait outside. I must discuss some matters with your fiancé."

I wanted to protest, but sheepishly let the bishop remove Friede

452

from the room. Once the heavy door was safely closed, the bishop clasped his hands together and remained in a trance of contemplation or contempt for my presence. "Your Excellency," I asked, "does the church have an issue with my wish to be married?"

"There is no issue for you, my son," the bishop said. "You are Catholic. Perhaps you are not particularly pious, but you are a Catholic. Where the problem lies is with that woman, your fiancée. She is not Catholic and I know she is certainly not pious."

In his condescending tone, the bishop outlined his reservations for my marriage to Friede. The Catholic Church in Germany, he explained, was under attack by modern forces that had undermined its moral authority. From the moment the Kaiser abdicated in 1918, Germany, according to the bishop, had begun to decay and rot inside, from every venial and mortal sin. It was his duty to God, to his church, and to his country to stop this decay before it permanently ruined the German people.

"I cannot bless this marriage union between you and that German girl," he said.

If he were to sanction my marriage, the bishop reasoned, he was inviting sin to flourish in Germany. To marry this woman was an affront to the Catholic Church and its beliefs. I sat with my back ramrod against an uncomfortable wooden seat. I listened to his homily and held my tongue until he reached the apogee of his argument.

"You must be strong, my son, and accept my wisdom and decision. I shall not sanction your marriage to that woman now or ever."

"Why?" I asked indignantly.

"I have read about Elfriede Edelmann's background. She is illegitimate. Her mother is illegitimate, and compounded her sin by living for many years with a man out of wedlock. This profane life is not acceptable to the church. These people," he continued, as if they were less than animals, "are unfit to be called Germans let alone be allowed into the Catholic faith."

453

"Your Excellency," I started, my hands crushed tightly against the armrest of my chair in an attempt to hold the anger growing within me. "This is impossible. My fiancée is not immoral."

The bishop unfolded his hands and replied, "You are young and naive. I say this with a heavy heart, but Nazism and Hitler turned German women into licentious wanton women."

He pointed past the shut drapes and said in a measured tone, "Hamburg is a city of prostitutes and I am afraid you have been duped because the only German girl who wants to marry an occupying soldier is a prostitute."

If I had the courage, I would have struck him down and bashed in his smug head. Instead, I fell into a contemptuous laughter for this man and the ridiculous church he served. "Your Excellency, I will marry her."

"It is impossible, the church forbids it."

"You forbid it," I retorted.

"Rome shall forbid it. Do you wish me to seek their guidance?" he asked as if wagering me.

"I am afraid I don't have years to waste on silly ecclesiastical squabbles. So I shall marry her and I don't care what the church thinks."

The bishop rose from his seat as if he were a mountain lion waiting to leap onto his prey. "If you marry her without the church's blessing, you are on the path towards excommunication and eternal damnation from Jesus Christ, our lord and saviour."

It was my turn to stand and I addressed the bishop. "Your Excellency, if the church believes this woman to be evil and a threat to it, I gladly accept excommunication. I am not afraid of eternal damnation because before I met Friede, I was in hell. She is my salvation. So sod you and sod your bleeding church."

I left the room and met Friede downstairs and we walked hurriedly out and the fresh air of the street. "What happened?" she asked with worry in her voice. "Is everything ok? Did I do something wrong in there?"

"You, my love, did nothing wrong in there. Unfortunately, I was the problem. The esteemed bishop believes I'm not a good Catholic and not a good match for you. He won't condone a marriage between an immoral British soldier and a good German girl. So I'm afraid I made a bit of a mess of it."

We stopped walking and stood close together on the pavement. I looked into Friede's eyes and spoke. "So I ask you again, will you marry me, even if the Catholic Church thinks I am a bad and fallen man?"

Friede gripped my hand and replied, "I am yours forever. What a silly church to think you are a bad man."

"It's a stupid church, isn't it," I agreed.

"But who will marry us then?" Friede asked perplexed.

I laughed and told her, "I have it on good authority that God runs a couple of other churches that might be willing to accept me as a member."

24

The witch before the wedding

The summer dragged on from one humid day to the next like a morbidly obese man at the sea shore. When July melted into August, Hamburg was as comfortable as a blast furnace. The sky above us was an endless pastel blue that was only broken by the jet stream from RAF transport planes. No one escaped the heat wave beating down on the city from sunrise to sunset. Even the street hustlers, prostitutes, and black marketers looked for relief from the high temperatures and decamped to cooler surroundings.

During those uncomfortable dog days of summer, cafes along the Alster advertised chilled beer, ice cream, and umbrellas to shield their patrons from the persistent and heavy sun. The water on the artificial lake behind the *Malcolm Club* grew tepid and stagnant. The depth of the reservoir shrunk as it evaporated into the atmosphere. Punters beached themselves in the middle of the basin as if they were near shore.

Night time was just as unbearable as the day because there was no breeze and the air was thick and heavy as lard. The act of breathing was as uncomfortable as inhaling the hot atmosphere found behind a closed oven door. Many evenings, Friede and her mother took to the balcony for respite from the inferno inside the apartment and cooled themselves with colourful Chinese fans and drank white wine until the early morning hours. Now that all formalities and official requests had been met, the two women finalized plans for the wedding set for the sixteenth of August.

The base padre made good on his word and proved that he was always a friend for those in need. When he found out about the Catholic bishop's displeasure for my marriage, he said, "Those Germans sometimes make a lot of bother over nothing. I have a simple solution to your dilemma; it would be my pleasure to officiate at your wedding and conduct a Church of England service."

I said it was no trouble for me and thought he could have married us in a voodoo ceremony if it got the job done.

Wisely, he suggested that we use a Lutheran church called St Luke's for our wedding ceremony because it was only blocks away from Friede's mother's apartment. Considering that our reception was scheduled to be held at Maria Edelmann's residence, it was a perfect solution. The chaplain recommended that we pay a call on the pastor to thank him for lending us St Luke's for our wedding.

A week before our marriage, Friede and I paid him a call. As a token of our appreciation, I gave the minister some coffee to be used for trade on the black market. He thanked me and to my surprise greeted Friede as one of his flock. It was a revelation for me to discover that while I slept late on Sunday mornings, Friede frequented the church to listen to the parson's sermons.

The Lutheran was delighted at being able to volunteer his church for our marriage. The old pastor displayed a great deal of affection for Friede and presented her with a copy of The New Testament. Inside the book, the pastor wrote an inscription to remind her of her faith and her fatherland. Friede handed it to me and I smiled politely and flipped through the pages with as much interest as if it were Sanskrit or excerpts from the Egyptian Book of the Dead. I returned the testament back to her without a word. I knew that my keepsake was Friede because she was my love, my faith, and my homeland.

My understanding of marriage rituals was slim and Friede had to remind me that I required a best man. At the last moment, I asked Sid if he would fulfill the function. "S'all right by me," he said.

The only other person I invited from base to the wedding was Dave. All of the other invited guests were Friede's family and friends. On the night before the wedding; I attended a Polteraben with Friede. The Polteraben was a Germanic pre-wedding celebration. The custom dated back to a dark, primal time when Germany was covered in forest and its inhabitants were savage tribes who waged war and made love in pagan excess.

The ritual combined large amounts of drinking, witchcraft, dancing, singing, and smashed crockery. When I arrived at her mother's apartment, it was standing room only. It seemed everyone on the street had shown up to wish us well. I walked from one room to the next squeezing between people as if I were an animal penned for the butcher. Hands slapped my back while others tried to shake my hand. Women kissed my cheek and men tried to top up my wine glass. The temperature inside the apartment was tropical and the male guests poured shots of snaps and begged me to join them. In the hallway, outside the apartment, women danced to music coming from a gramophone.

"Come drink with us," they beckoned, but I shook my head and politely declined.

When darkness fell, a neighbour dressed as a medieval witch came to the party, complete with broom in hand. In a great barking voice, she evacuated the apartment and pushed the drunken revelers to the outside of the building. She commanded the gods of the forest and the gods of the mountains to help us achieve a life rich in promise, security, and love. One by one, the guests took an old plate, bowl, or cup they had brought with them from home and smashed it against the threshold of the apartment's entrance. They dropped them heavily on to the ground and made ribald jokes as the crockery broke into a myriad of pieces.

Everyone laughed when someone shouted out that more crockery was broken that night than in all of the British air raids during the war. One after the other, friend, family, or neighbour went to the entrance and dropped their plate, shattering it on the cement. The ground was littered with shards of tableware. The witch urged more destruction and demanded that a chamber pot be crushed to give a lifetime of happiness and good luck to us.

Friede and I were in the crowd standing together arm- in- arm, when the hag approached and drank from each of our wine glasses. "I have now blessed your life in the tradition of the woodland gods," the witch said, slurring her words. "Prosit," she called out to everyone, who returned her toast.

I was told that with each glass of wine drunk that night, it was a good wish upon our marriage. It was an irreverent consecration by her family and friends and I welcomed it as sincere. It was something I wasn't accustomed to seeing back in Britain, where we concealed our joy as much as our pain.

Later on, the retired sea captain who lived on the top floor apartment brought out his accordion and serenaded us with waltzes and polkas. Near the end of the festivities, I was commanded by the witch to sweep the stoop clean of the shards of broken dishes.

"You must know who is in charge," cackled the witch. "Friedle is now your master. Treat her well through this life and you will be rewarded with the riches of a hundred kings," she announced, before downing her last glass of wine and stumbling homewards.

The party lasted many hours and near its end, the guests lingered and drank the last dregs of wine and beer. They shared shag cigarettes and memories of their own Polteraben.

Just before midnight, I kissed Friede goodnight. I was slightly drunk and very happy. "The next time I see you," I said, "we'll be at the church. I can hardly believe I'm to be a married man, to you, the most wonderful, beautiful person on this planet."

"Hush," she said and put a finger close to my lips. "It is only you who I love or will ever love. You are now my life and my love, but go because tomorrow we shall be wed."

Chapter Twenty-Five:
August 16 1947

On the way back to camp, I quietly sang to myself the song: *I'm the man who broke the bank of Monte Carlo.* When I returned to my quarters, I was surprised to find that Sid and Dave had broken in and were waiting for me with a bottle of whisky.

Dave said, "I'd been saving this for a special occasion and since nothing came around, I thought why not drink it tonight."

So my two friends and I drank whisky and toasted our old lives together. Sid told me, "You did all right, Harry. Didn't get much loot out of Germany, but you did steal the prettiest girl."

"That I did," I responded.

"What happens now to you and Friede?" Dave asked.

I told them that the RAF regulations required servicemen who married a foreign national were provided accommodation off base. "I'll be chuffed," said Sid.

"It's a brilliant set up." I explained that Friede and I were allotted rooms in a beautiful house, ten minutes from the base. The rent and all our living supplies would be paid by the RAF.

"I wouldn't let that get out," Dave warned me, "or everyone in the RAF is going to marry a German girl, just for the housing."

"Harry, you and Friede deserve it. Best of luck," Sid toasted me. "Now we better be off or else you'll be over-sleeping on your wedding day."

That night I didn't sleep much due to the wine, the heat, and the anticipation of the wedding. Until the sun rose, I endured restless and disquieting dreams. I was relieved to be awake and away from my subconscious, which was like a cemetery where too many corpses were buried in shallow graves. In my dreams, I saw my dad's sad face. I wasn't sure if the dream was wishing me well or warning me of rough times ahead.

Whether the dreams were omens or glad tidings, I realized that I still had to prepare for my wedding and ensure that all the food and drink were available for the reception. For a hefty bribe, I had made arrangements with the camp cook to provide all the food for the feast from cakes to exquisite sandwiches. The three-tier wedding cake was made by a pastry chef attached to the NAFFI in Hamburg. Everything for the wedding reception was transported in on an RAF truck and delivered for ten a.m. I had press-ganged some other servicemen with promises of beer on a later date to help unload and set up the banquet tables, chairs, food, and flowers, for the reception. Everything was assembled in Maria Edelmann's oversized bedroom as it was the only suitable space to fit twenty-five guests.

While we got to work putting the room together, Friede argued with her mother, who was arranging her hair and assisting with her make up in the Gellersons' room.

Frau Ghellerson said to me, "You must be quick and go; it is bad luck to see the bride in the morning before your wedding."

I left as quickly as I could. On my way out, I saw the men from the *Malcolm Club* deliver a giant keg of beer, which they struggled to take down to the cellar where it could be kept cool during the sweltering August afternoon.

With haste, I returned back to camp to get cleaned up for the ceremony. As I dressed, I started to shake and had to sit down and have a cigarette. I was overcome by my good fortune and the fear it was going to run out. How is it possible, I asked myself, that I fell into this joy, this great promise of better days? I didn't know the reason except blind luck. There were so many others who missed out on life and were cut down before their time because of the Great Depression or the war. Yet I had somehow survived. I was granted by fortune or endurance or whimsy the chance to love and be loved in return. I had arrived at the entrance to a life worth living. "Don't bugger it up," I said while brushing my hair tightly back.

When Stan and I rode up to the church in a jeep, I saw there was a growing crowd of inquisitive onlookers loitering around the entrance. Stan and I quickly rushed through the church doors and passed the assembled guests as we moved towards the altar. While I waited for Friede, Stan cracked jokes to me and the vicar.

It was hot inside the church and the air was stagnant. The padre was sweating and the organist looked uncomfortable on his stool. I mopped my brow with a handkerchief, while Stan said, "Hope none of the neighbours nick the beer while we are at church."

After several more perspiring moments, I heard the doors open at the back of St Luke's. The guests shuffled in their seats and then made an appreciative collective sigh. Friede had arrived with her foster father, Max. The music was struck and Friede walked slowly towards me. I knew that she was drinking in this moment. I knew that every step Friede took, she believed was a final and absolute negation of her stigma. Walking up that aisle, she wasn't just coming towards me; she was walking away from her childhood sorrows, pains, and humiliations. I wanted to turn around, but dared not. Stan glanced backwards and whispered to me, "Blimey, she's beautiful."

Finally, Friede and Max were beside us. The organ notes faded away like a feather caught in a breeze. Max ceremoniously relinquished Friede to my care. He whispered in my ear, "Be well and remember to be tender to my Friedle."

Friede and I sheepishly smiled at each other. She whispered the words, "Ich liebe dich." The satin bridal gown magnified her loveliness and made her beauty appear timeless, untouchable, and seductive. Her beauty, her history, and her fragility humbled me as I stood in my RAF blue dress uniform. Friede held a bouquet of wild flowers, whose scent perfumed the air around us. It was a wonderful fresh aroma that made me think of our time walking in the botanical gardens.

Our wedding service wasn't long but it was charged with emotion, laughter, and human kindness. The chaplain joined us as man and wife, but said this was also a marriage unique for this town and for our garrison. It was the first post-war marriage between a Brit and a German. It was a signal, he said. It was a harbinger of peaceful days to come because if love could germinate between two young people from different cultures; the world was healing its wounds from the war. Finally, the vicar pronounced us man and wife. He blessed the union and we were wed.

Friede and I walked slow and steady to the church's exit and on our way out, we received the adulation from the pews. I whispered a "thank-you" to Friede. She smiled and had tears in her eyes. For a brief second, I felt afraid of my new responsibility and I hoped I wouldn't disappoint her. I didn't want to muddle up destiny's kindness towards me.

On the steps of the church, a wedding photographer took our picture. Once the pictures were taken, the guests were ferried to the reception in a fleet of Volkswagen taxis I had commandeered earlier on in the day for a hefty black market bribe..

The feast, the feelings of good will, and the emotional atmosphere were never better at Maria Edelmann's apartment than on the day of our reception. Everyone was content; no one brought any disgruntled and disjointed emotions to the party. There were toasts from Friede mother. There were speeches from Sid and Dave. Congratulatory telegrams arrived from my mother and sister. Friede translated them into German and read them out to the guests, who applauded my English family for their warm-hearted support.

We drank wine and beer, and ate cakes and delicate sandwiches. Cigarettes were shared and hands held. I felt proud that I had orchestrated this feast of love for Friede, her family, and her friends. Halfway through the reception, Friede slipped out of the room. She quickly returned and sat beside her mother. They talked in low voices and then hugged each other warmly. Friede walked over to a painting hanging on the wall and placed a small wallet-sized photo of her father Fritz along the edges of the frame. She raised her glass and announced,

"To my mother who loved me in dangerous times; to my foster mother for caring for me; to my foster father who loved me as his own." The wedding table broke into applause at the dedications. When the clapping stopped, Friede continued, "I raise my glass to Harry, who will love me until the ends of days, and I shall love him whether the sea is in storm or the waters calm."

26

The End of the Party

For the first few days following my wedding, the skies above Hamburg remained clear, blue, and peaceful. The summer held us in her grip and it was sunny and humid; time stood to catch its breath. I quickly grew accustomed to life as a married man with a bit of status and wealth, compliments of the RAF. I was having too much of a good time to notice the ominous threats all around me. Sometimes in the afternoons, I heard the rumble of thunder far off in the distance, but Hamburg remained sweltering and dry. *It will never reach us,* I thought. *The summer will continue well into October,* I reasoned. *Even when the winter comes,* I dreamed, *life will be grand in this new house. We will sit by a roaring fire while a roast chicken cooks in the oven.*

I believed I had a long life coming to me, which was to be spent in Hamburg. I had it all planned and measured out. We would live in this requisitioned house for a couple of years. Friede and I were going to loaf from one lazy summer day to the next down at the *Malcolm Club* getting drunk on lager and youthful desires. We were going to enjoy life and after my time with the RAF was over; I was going to find a trade that would make us comfortable and secure.

Those days we spent in our new house on Berg Koppel Weg

gave me a sense of serenity and comfort I had never experienced in my entire life. It was a suburban, almost posh address and it was a home designed for someone well-placed in the middle class. We shared the house with the owner, a widow, and her daughter, who occupied the upstairs rooms. Friede and I lived very comfortably on the lower floor, where our bedroom overlooked a well-tended back garden. The basement was reserved for the owner's dachshund and her litter of puppies. The mother and her pubs scampered through the house as if they were the true owners who graciously allowed us to stay with them.

In between my work at the base, we threw dinner parties and drank wine in the garden until late in the evening. At nights when Friede and I were alone, we shared cigarettes and watched the sun sink behind the linden trees and disappear into the horizon. I was unconscious to the danger of change. My new marriage and carte blanche life lulled me into a euphoric state as dreamlike as a body injected with morphine.

One night as I undressed and folded my clothes, placing them in the giant wardrobe, in our bedroom, I was stung by an insect.

"What is it?" Friede asked in a sleepy voice from the bed.

"Nothing," I responded, "just a bloody midge."

At first, the bite wasn't anything to be concerned about; it was red, itchy, and a nuisance.

However, by the following morning, Friede said, "You should have it looked at."

I said, "Nonsense, it's just a scratch. Let's enjoy our breakfast out on the front porch before I leave for the base."

Days passed, friends dropped by and every night was a party at our new dwelling. However, the small bite on my arm grew sceptic and I fell into a fever. A fortnight after my wedding and a week after the mosquito had supped on my blood, I was rushed to hospital chattering and delirious. I almost went mad from the insect's venomous bite. For two nights, I lay in a parallel state in that country bordering life and death. Doctors pumped my body full of newly invented antibiotics.

466

Friede remained at my side, but in my fever, I didn't recognize her and screamed and babbled like a man taken by senility or drink.

While I was hospitalized, Friede was frightened that her days as a bride were numbered. She asked her mother "Is this what happens to all the Edelmann women, must we always end up alone and abandoned?"

Eventually, the medicine took hold; the sweating, the fever, the delusions, and the terror were purged from my body. Yet when I was discharged from the infirmary, I felt that my recent brush with mortality was a sign that my run of good luck was rapidly coming to its end.

I returned to work at the airport's telecommunication's tower during the second week of September and a sergeant reminded me, "You'll be demobbed next month, Smith. I hope you've got a fancy house back in England, for your new missus."

The snide comment was like an electric cattle prod to remind me that not everyone wished me well or thought my situation was proper. The following day, I went to the adjutant officer's secretary to see if I could make an appointment with Flight Lieutenant Locke. The adjutant officer had recently replaced his secretary. The new gatekeeper was an offensive prim boy who wanted to make himself a name in the RAF through slander, innuendo, and trading in false rumours.

When I arrived, the secretary berated me as if he were an officer. "Can't be always coming and going to see the adjutant," he said to me. "Really, you see the man more than his wife does. It's just not proper."

"Why don't you just stick to making the tea and bringing the biscuits," I told him sarcastically.

"What is the nature of your meeting?"

"I wish to join the peace-time RAF."

"Aren't you the patriot?" he said, making notes.

Fuck off, I thought and replied, "Oi, chop to it and put me in for an appointment with the adjutant."

"Well, I'll try to slot you in before you are demobbed, but the

Flight Lieutenant is a busy man, you know."

A week later, I got my meeting with the adjutant, who had a stern and displeased look on his face. "Are you sure you want to sign on for three years, LAC Smith. It's a long tour. You have been an excellent member of the RAF during war time and during this occupation. However, I'm not sure you're made for a long career in the Royal Air Force."

"Sir, I believe I am just the type of man suited for the RAF."

"This has nothing to do with your recent marriage?" he asked cynically.

"No," I said in denial.

Locke looked at me as if I was a fool and recanted. "I will approve it with reluctance. Remember, you're signing away your life for three years and you are ours to do as we wish."

"I know." I wasn't going to tell the adjutant, but I had read the contract beforehand. In the fine print, there was a buyout clause that could be initiated within the first six months of the contract. For £20, if things got unbearable with RAF, I could walk away and learn to be a civilian again.

When Sid found out, he screamed at me, "You big bloody fool. They are going to give you a bollocking like you have never imagined."

"Perhaps," I said, "but I had no other recourse to stay on in Germany."

I went back home to Friede that night and told her what I had done. She was relieved, but still had as many misgivings as Sid. "Let's hope it works out for us, she said, "and if not, then we hold on until the bad weather has passed."

Later on that night, I found her crying and she confessed that she didn't want to leave Germany and her family.

When the contract took effect, I was now no longer a draftee, but a regular. I had moved from amateur to professional with the stroke of a pen. At first, nothing changed for me in either my work duties or how

I was treated. I began to believe I'd dodged another bullet. I started to think that I had out-foxed the air ministry and was going to remain in Fuhlsbüttel for another ten years. I was a fool to be so optimistic. The moment I signed on for three more years in the RAF, plans from above were in motion to remove me from Fuhlsbüttel.

In late September, I was called in to see the adjutant officer. It was a brief and succinct meeting. It lasted no more than three minutes and Flight Lieutenant Locke's eyes never met mine. "You have been transferred to Lubeck. You are to report there tomorrow morning. So you must take the train tonight."

It was like being punched in the stomach and not being allowed to cry out. "Might I ask why I am being transferred?" I asked as if the reason mattered.

"Because the RAF wants you there," Locke replied in a fed-up tone.

"What about my wife?"

Locke said succinctly, "That is your problem, not ours. Naturally, for the time being she can remain at the lodgings provided her, but that may change at any moment."

I left the office and went to tell Sid about my transfer. "I told you, they are never going to let an enlisted man stay in Germany with a wife and a home. It sets a bad example that every punter can get a chance for happiness. Buy yourself out, Harry, and get back to England. Jump man, jump back into the real world, shite as it is, before it is too late."

When I told Friede, she took the news well enough. "It is not so bad; we can see each other on weekends and if you are there long enough, we can find a house in Lubeck."

I didn't have the courage to tell her that I feared the move was just the first in a series. I knew the RAF was just toying with me until I jumped back into the civilian world and the unemployment line in Britain.

When I arrived in Lubeck, I found there was very little for me to do, but try to be scarce. It was a humiliation for me. I was returned to my earlier days in the RAF when I had no privileges. I bunked with new recruits in a Nissen hut. I ate my meals alone in the mess house and found the days friendless and long. On weekends, I was allowed to return to Hamburg and visit Friede and stay in our house.

By my second week in Lubeck, I understood that my number was up. Sergeants yelled at me for imaginary infractions. "You might do that in Fuhlsbüttel, but here in Lubeck we follow the King's regulations."

The berating and belittling continued for almost two months. Finally, I was called before the commanding officer for Lubeck. He looked me up and down like I was an orphaned pit pony. "The RAF doesn't require your services anymore in Germany," he said definitively. "You've been transferred to Manchester. It's effective immediately."

"But, sir, I am married."

"You'll be glad to see the wife when you're back in Britain, then."

"No, sir, my wife is in Hamburg."

"Oh," he noted, "that's right. You were the one who went off half-cocked and married a German. Take seventy-two hours to make good on your transfer to Manchester," he told me.

I was given three days to say goodbye to Friede and start a life in England without her. There wasn't even time to say goodbye to my mates or most of her family as I made the dash back to Hamburg for the final time.

27

Manchester 1947

It was dawn in late November when I left Hamburg. On the horizon, strands of smoky, grey clouds jostled against the dark sky. Winter had begun to creep through the city and a light frost covered the ground. I slipped away from our home on cat paws, while Friede was asleep, looking lost in a pleasant dream. For the last time, I walked dejectedly on the path to the airport. The guard at the gate lazily waved me into the still half-asleep air force base. I didn't look left or right or back through the camps gates; I just made my way to embarkation. There I stood in a pencil-thin line waiting to board a Dakota, back to Britain.

"Oi, it looks like it's going to snow," said the teenage RAF recruit standing behind me.

I grunted, yes or no or maybe. I didn't care because it was colder, wetter, and more inhospitable where I was going than right now on this tarmac. The queue moved slowly towards the aircraft. When it was my turn, I put my hand on the stepladder and climbed through the fuselage's hatchway.

The DC 3 was already loaded with men. They sat hunched on wooden benches that skirted both sides of the plane's interior. The centre of the plane was stacked with sacks of mail, documents, and loot. I slung my kitbag underneath my legs. It didn't contain much: pictures of Friede, my spare uniforms, and some cartons of cigarettes.

A sergeant came on board to do a head count. When he was satisfied, he called out, "Strap yourself in, lads, the pilots tell me it's going to be a rough flight. So, say cheerio to Germany because you lucky sods are going home."

The prop engines awoke to life like a coal miner in the morning, with a wheeze and a phlegmatic sputtering cough. While we taxied across the runway, gathering speed for takeoff, I turned my head around and stared out the porthole window. Violently, the pilot thrust the plane's throttle forward and we jerked into the air, gulping altitude like it was oxygen to an asthmatic.

In no time, the airport disappeared from view. For a brief moment, the plane dipped over my house on the deserted Berg Koppel Weg. I put my hand against the porthole as if I could reach out and touch my old life. Then it was gone from sight as we banked and swept over the city of Hamburg. From above, the metropolis resembled an ancient city, abandoned to the elements and to the mob. Cooking fires from the refugee camps smoldered below while the gutted docklands and working class districts slowly began to awaken from their uncomfortable slumber. A U-bahn train departed the Banhof station and cut across the shattered city, moving eastward towards Berlin, another broken city.

As we climbed into the clouds pregnant with snow, the landscape escaped my grasp. I turned away from the window and pulled out a flask of tea and whiskey. I sipped on it to warm my body, while my hands shook in unison to the engine's vibration. For a few brief seconds, the cockpit door swung open and slammed shut in the turbulence. Soon, we were over the cold North Sea. I closed my eyes and let the monotonous hum of the engines lull me into an unhappy sleep.

When I arrived at Gatwick, an NCO scanned my transfer orders and said, "You better get a move on if you want to kip in Manchester tonight."

"Why?"

"Problems on the rails," he explained, "because of snow, sleet, and shite. Everything's buggered and you're not travelling on the Flying Scotsman."

I looked up at the grey light streaking from the damp, heavy sky and knew he was right.

I saluted him and disappeared into the main terminal building to find a urinal. Standing beside me in the WC was a fellow Yorkshire man.

"Nivva mine t'bus, I've getten to drive van in ter tawn."

He took me to Piccadilly. While darting through traffic and dodging a stalled double decker bus, the driver said I was lucky to be heading to the midlands.

"At least ya can smell 'ome from there."

I lied to him with a smile.

I grabbed my bag and hopped out of the van, disappearing into the train station. It was choked with disgruntled commuters. I stood in front of a departure and arrival board. It clattered like old women shuffling their chairs at a boarding house. I inhaled London's desperation. It was a heavy collective breath of poverty and confusion as our empire crumbled like a lime stone cliff into the sea. All around me were men wearing dirty mackintosh coats and bloodless ashen faces. They slithered between women with cheeks beaten red from the wind or Woolworth's cosmetics. Everyone in the station had a defeated look of life lived on a ration book existence.

At the Manchester train platform, a locomotive rested like a tired beast panting soot and sweating filthy water down the sides of its engine carriage. A conductor read my travel warrant card and pointed me to the second-to-last car. Inside, it was standing room only. I followed the flow of heads covered with grimy hats and scarves to the middle of the train where I leaned against a dirty window.

My train dragged itself out of London like a hung-over drunk. While, we churned slowly northward, snow hit the window behind me. Immediately, it turned into grimy black tears that streaked down the glass and obscured the world beyond the locomotive. I was crushed up beside a middle-aged man. His face was obscured behind the pages of the *Daily Mail*. Its creased and ruffled front cover announced the partition of Palestine. The broadsheet warned that the weather was to get colder, uglier, and more inhospitable as the days moved towards Christmas. I turned away from the man wedged into his newspaper and felt nauseous from hunger and sad, unpleasant memories.

When we arrived in Manchester, I was knackered. I clambered out of the train with the other passengers like sweating livestock. Trying to make my way anonymously out of the station, a portly woman with thick glasses and bow legs accosted me.

"Cuse me, luv, got a light." With a sigh, she rested her handbags beside me. She pulled a fag end of a cigarette out of her purse. I lit it with my Zippo.

"Flash lighter," she noted and fell into a coughing fit.

I walk to the bus stop and asked a conductor, "Which bus takes me to Ringwell RAF base?"

With blackened teeth and a wry grin, he told me it would take several buses and a lot of tolerance to reach my destination.

At RAF Ringwell, a guard patrolled the front entrance. He marched back and forth with the intelligence of a metronome. The guard stood six feet and towered over my featherweight frame. He scrutinized my papers with the diligence of a building society manager with a mortgage application.

"Fuck off," I said impatiently. "I don't have all day and I want to get some grub."

"All right, all right, can't be too careful these days with who we are going to let in, ya know."

474

The guard stood down and let me pass. I swaggered past him and in a parting gesture thrust my two right fingers upwards. Past the gate, Ringwell expanded into an encampment many times larger than Fuhlsbüttel. Trucks barreled past and churned up snow and gravel that splashed against my greatcoat. The further I walked into the camp, the louder the racket became. Coming from the parade ground, I heard sergeants barking at teenage boys who were being squad-bashed into submission.

I presented my transfer papers to a lieutenant. He had light coloured hair, effeminate hands, and looked like he got his commission before he was given permission to shave. His young face had a disdainful countenance. It appeared as if he found his Manchester billet an unappetizing location, a barbarous place compared to Kent or Sussex. In an Oxbridge accent, he told me, "You'll find we do things differently here. This is not Germany. I expect discipline and order and no funny business with the natives if you get my meaning."

"Natives" I asked? I thought perhaps this camp in Manchester was surrounded by Picts and Saxons from the dark ages.

"You know full well what I mean. I've heard what you enlisted men got up to in Germany with the black market and the girls."

Inside, I grimaced and grew rigid. "Terrible business that was, sir, the lower ranks were like the dish that made off with the spoon."

The newly commissioned officer grumbled. "Yes, well none of that here."

"Sir, will I be permanently stationed here?" I asked.

"Nothing is permanent; there are problems all over the empire, who knows where you shall end up. We've got you for another three years. So I imagine you're going to see quite a bit of the world before your time is done with us."

That was the last thing I wanted to hear. "Excuse me, sir, but the reason for my asking is because I'm married and my wife is still in Germany."

"Married a Hun, hey, well that's your problem. The RAF takes care of our own. Wives are a different matter. She can follow you here, but if you are going into a combat zone, she's out of luck."

The officer turned silent as if he had forgotten his script from the officer's training course he had taken at Oxford.

"Sir" I asked?

"Oh, the sergeant outside will see to your kip and your duties."

I saluted, stamped my feet, and turned smartly out of his office.

"Lucky days for you, Smith," the sergeant in the foyer told me. "We've got the best assignment for a man of your brainy character."

"I am sure," I said. "Go on, let's have it."

"We've put you in charge of a squad of lads who are as thick as treacle. We've got brave and dangerous work for you and your boys."

"Come again?"

"There are about 100,000, nah, maybe ten times more than that; who knows the numbers..."

"A hundred thousand what" I asked puzzled?

"Radio receivers and transmitters, lad, and we need them all smashed to kingdom come. "

"Why?"

"Cos the government bought 'em off the Yanks during the war and the toffs probably spent twenty million pounds on them. So, now it's time to destroy them. Surely, you can get it through your noggin that the stuffed shirts don't want them in the hands of Mrs. Jones on Kettle Way. It might upset the radio manufacturers or it might lead to mutiny if they got into the hands of the colonies."

"I was transferred from Germany for this?"

"Sure, from your service records, it says you are a good wireless operator. So you are going to be a brilliant radio basher. Any questions?" the sergeant asked.

"Just one: how do I get out of this mad house?"

My feeling of gloom didn't get any better when night arrived. I went to my sleeping quarters, which was a banged up old Nissen hut filled with fresh and unblemished raw recruits. *Children*, I thought when I got a look at them. They had experienced the war and its aftermath by a coal fire, while their mothers fetched them tea. I must have looked like a pensioner to them.

As much as I wanted to fall asleep, I couldn't. There was just too much alteration to my life in one day. It was like being thrown back to the first days of my induction at the start of the war. I tried dreaming of the curve of Friede's back, the smell of her hair, or the smile from her lips. It didn't work. It made things worse. The images of my wife evaporated like advertisement billboards at the side of a road. Thinking of her just made the longing worse. I closed my eyes again and wanted just blackness to curtain my heart and my head. I rolled over and the boy in the bed beside me intruded into my skull as he snored and farted through the night. To the other side of me was a habitual sleep-talker. His somnolent conversations appeared to be as dull as his waking intercourse with others. Throughout the twilight hours, I clutched my pillow as if it were the neck of the air ministry. I silently repeated as it if were the catechism, I *am in the shit now. How am I to get out of this mess?*

Morning came abruptly and ugly. An NCO introduced us back to consciousness with the familiar scream of, "Wakey, wakey, sunshine."

It was both cold and dark and no one had thought to light the stove. I scrambled out for a cigarette. The American fag sparked me to life as the nicotine burrowed into my blood. I decided it was time to collect my duty roster.

After breakfast, I made my way to the parade ground. A sergeant ordered me to assemble the twenty-eight recruits, who were listed in my work detail manifest. I was ordered to march them to a work shed located at the far end of the camp.

"It's a mile down road way to the smashing and bashing shop," said a sergeant. "You'll find enough work there to keep you and yer lads busy till kingdom bloody come. We've got more radios than dogs on this island."

I assembled my twenty-eight men on the parade ground, while behind us the Union Jack flapped furiously against an angry winter wind.

Before we left, I ordered the men to gather sledge hammers from a storehouse to assist in their Luddite occupation.

I quick-stepped them towards the work shed with a clipboard resting underneath my armpit like a major's riding crop.

The men moved with too much excitement and too much racket from the parade square. "Shut it," I screamed. I was irritated by their enthusiasm because it was an eagerness that only an eighteen-year-old can muster who marches with a sledge hammer resting on his shoulder and the thought of a day's pay for a day's destruction.

My work detail proceeded with inane determination to the warehouse where the surplus receivers awaited their execution. Upon arrival, I was greeted by another LAC who told me, "I hope you brought a book because the last man who was in charge of this project went stark raving mad from the bleeding boredom."

He took me inside and showed me around the building. The warehouse was divided into two rooms; one was stacked with disused radios, while the other had a series of tables and chairs.

"At end of day," said the LAC, "a truck will pull up to the back of the building where your men are to load the busted pieces into the wagon."

He handed me a cigarette and asked, "Any questions?" I shook my head and thanked him. As he left, the LAC shouted back to me, "Remember, it doesn't matter how fast or slow you do this job because it's going to be yours, for the rest of your life."

My men worked in teams and opened up the back of the receivers to remove the radio tubes, which were to be stored in wooden boxes. The castrated transmitters and receivers were placed onto the concrete floor and a team of men with sledge hammers crushed them beyond recognition.

For the first few days, I walked around the demolition site like a foreman inspecting the labour of skilled journeymen. With a keen look, I observed my men while they smashed thousands of pounds worth of radio equipment. I congratulated brawny men for their hammer swinging acumen that obliterated radio after radio. Receivers that had intercepted the surrender of Singapore or acknowledged clandestine tapings of our spies in the darkness of Nazi occupied Europe were pulverized. I had one command and one order to follow to turn these radios into scrap to be hauled away by the bin man.

"Put some passion behind it, man," I told one new recruit as he lazily swung his hammer.

Each day walked into the next day with the same banging routine. For eight hours a day, I sat behind a desk. I took my scheduled tea break and returned diligently to supervise the wrecking of communications equipment that was considered too expensive to keep, but too cheap to sell. I wondered how much we borrowed during the war from the Americans to buy these receivers only to destroy them in peacetime. Whatever the price, I knew the debt was still outstanding. We were still paying for lend lease. We were still paying for Churchill's exhortation to Britain to defend our island, *"Whatever the cost may be."* The arrears were enormous and our nation still suffered from rationing. We were rich in war and poor in peace.

Day in day out, I marched the men to our work place and ordered them to do their duty. I observed them hammer, bang, and crush radio receivers to dust. My ears rang and I drowned in the noise created by our obligation to the state. With every hour that I endured this destruction, I reasoned, I had gained another sixty minutes to scheme and locate a solution to end my sufferance, my sodding contract to the RAF.

Each day, I wrote letters to Friede in Germany. I tried to lower

479

her expectations of what life was to be like in Britain. I wrote that it was very different from Hamburg, but I promised that our life in Yorkshire was still going to be pleasant. It would still be filled with excitement. Each night, I went to bed knowing that I was lying to her and fooling myself if I believed life would be as good as Germany. Each morning, I woke to wondering how peace had become a battle for me and my nation. This peace, this hard-fought peace was as dark and as terrible as the days in the Great Depression. I was like a fish on a hook, wriggling and squirming trying to get the metal barb out of my throat and instead it plunged deeper into my flesh.

No matter how hard I fought to escape my present, no matter how much I planned for my future, the hammers came down and the dust flew up from splintered and crushed electronic corpses of the radio receivers. My ears stung from the deafening pounding and my spirit almost broke from the pointlessness of my task. At break time, I sipped weak tea in a chipped mug and dreamed of that beautiful spring at the end of the war in 1945. I dreamed of the spring to come, when I could buy my way out of the RAF and be reunited with Friede.

The only problem was, even in my dreams, I was afraid and I was alone. There was no one to confess my terror and dread that my luck had run out. I recoiled in despair knowing that I was plunging back into my old life in the festering mill town of my youth. Except this time, I was returning with a foreign bride who was not prepared for Yorkshire in all its post-war gloom. I asked myself, how was it possible that after surviving the war and seven years service in the RAF, I was starting out where I began, except this time, I had something to lose. I was petrified of what was to become of me after I got out of Ringwell. All I wanted was a future that was better than my past and the honest chance to find work, to feed myself, and my family.

Made in the USA
Charleston, SC
19 January 2012